BEST ROAD TRIPS
SPAIN &
PORTUGAL

-------→

ESCAPES ON THE OPEN ROAD

Regis St Louis, Gregor Clark,
Duncan Garwood, Anthony Ham, John Noble

SYMBOLS IN THIS BOOK

 Top Tips   History & Culture   Essential Photo

🛇 Link Your Trips   🚶 Family   🏃 Walking Tour

💬 Tips from Locals   🍷 Food & Drink   ✕ Eating

↩ Trip Detour   🌳 Outdoors   🛏 Sleeping

📞 Telephone Number   @ Internet Access   📖 English-Language Menu

⊙ Opening Hours   📶 Wi-Fi Access   👪 Family-Friendly

Ⓟ Parking   🌱 Vegetarian Selection   🐾 Pet-Friendly

⊖ Nonsmoking   🏊 Swimming Pool

❄ Air-Conditioning

MAP LEGEND

Routes
▬▬▬ Trip Route
▬ ▬ Trip Detour
▬▬ Linked Trip
▬▬ Walk Route
▬▬ Tollway
▬▬ Freeway
Primary
Secondary
Tertiary
Lane
Unsealed Road
Plaza/Mall
Steps
)= = Tunnel
Pedestrian Overpass
Walk Track/Path

Boundaries
― ― ― International
‐‐‐‐‐ State/Province
⊥⊥⊥⊥ Cliff

Hydrography
River/Creek
Intermittent River
Swamp/Mangrove
Canal
Water
Dry/Salt/ Intermittent Lake
Glacier

Highway Markers
[A20] Highway marker

Trips
1 Trip Numbers
9 Trip Stop
🚶 Walking tour
↩ Trip Detour

Population
✪ Capital (National)
◉ Capital (State/Province)
● City/Large Town
○ Town/Village

Areas
Beach
Cemetery (Christian)
Cemetery (Other)
Park
Forest
Reservation
Urban Area
Sportsground

Transport
✈ Airport
Cable Car/ Funicular
Ⓜ Metro station
Ⓟ Parking
Train/Railway
Tram

Note: Not all symbols displayed above appear on the maps in this book

---

CONTENTS

Northern Spain & the Basque Country
p103

Barcelona & Eastern Spain
p181

Portugal
p315

Madrid & Central Spain
p37

Andalucía & Southen Spain
p241

Contents

COVID-19

We have re-checked every business in this book before publication to ensure that it is still open after the COVID-19 outbreak. However, the economic and social impacts of COVID-19 will continue to be felt long after the outbreak has been contained, and many businesses, services and events referenced in this guide may experience ongoing restrictions. Some businesses may be temporarily closed, have changed their opening hours and services, or require bookings; some will unfortunately have closed their doors permanently. We suggest you check with venues before visiting for the latest information.

Azulejo (hand-painted tiles), Capela das Almas, Porto (p390)
ADRIENNE PITTS/LONELY PLANET ©

WELCOME TO
SPAIN & PORTUGAL

Spectacular beaches, mountaintop castles, medieval villages, stunning architecture – and some of the most celebrated restaurants on the planet: Iberia has an allure that few destinations can match.

There's much to see and do amid the enchanting landscapes that inspired Picasso, Velázquez and the great epic poets of Spain and Portugal. You can spend your days feasting on seafood in coastal Galician towns, feel the heartbeat of Andalucía at soul-stirring flamenco shows, hike across the flower-strewn meadows of the Pyrenees, or chart a winding route through the spectacular vineyards of the Douro Valley. The 32 trips in this book offer something for everyone: beach lovers, outdoor adventurers, family travellers, music fiends, foodies and those simply wanting to delve into Iberia's rich art and history.

And if you only have time for a single journey, make it one of our nine Classic Trips, which take you to the very best of Spain and Portugal. Turn the page for more.

Carvoeiro beach (p346), Portugal
PAWEL KAZMIERCZAK/SHUTTERSTOCK ©

SPAIN & PORTUGAL HIGHLIGHTS

A Coruña
San Cosme
Avilés Gijón
Santiago de Compostela
Lugo
Oviedo
Parque N de lo de
Sarria
Pontevedra
Ourense
Monforte de Lemos
Ponferrada
Le
Vigo
Astorga
Sahag
Río Miño
Parque Natural de Montesinho
Benavente
Viana do Castelo
Braga
Chaves
Bragança
Valla
Villa do Conde
Vila Real
Miranda do Douro
Zamora
Porto
Río Douro
Peso da Régua
Vila Nova de Foz Côa
Salam
Tord
Aveiro
Viseu
Guarda
Ciudad Rodrigo
Á
Coimbra
Parque Natural da Serra da Estrela
Béjar
Pombal
Fundão
Plasencia
Navaln de la M
Leiria
Fátima
PORTUGAL
Castelo Branco
SPAIN
Caldas da Rainha
Río Tejo
Peniche
Abrantes
Cáceres
Trujillo
La Nava de Ricomalillo
Torres Vedras
Portalegre
Santarem
LISBON
Vendas Novas
Estremoz
Elvas
Mérida
Don Benito
Cascais
Setúbal
Évora
Badajoz
Almadén
Alcácer do Sal
Zafra
Peñarr Pueblo
Sines
Moura
Monesterio
Beja
Vila Nova de Milfontes
Parque Natural Sierra Norte de Sevilla
Cór
Bollullos Par del Condado
Écija M
Silves
Huelva
Seville
Osuna
Sagres
Lagos
Tavira
El Rocío
Arahal
Albufeira
Faro
Parque Natural de Doñana
Arcos de la Frontera
Ante
Chipiona
Málа
Cádiz
Parque Natural del Estrecho
Ma
Barbate
Gibral
Tarifa
Tangier
Ceuta (Spain)
MOROCCO

ATLANTIC OCEAN

Roving La Rioja Wine Region Discover the wealth of the grape on this peaceful countryside drive. **2–3 DAYS**

Historic Castilla y León Madrid to Soria via some of inland Spain's captivating towns and villages. **7 DAYS**

Artistic Inspiration on the Costa Brava Enjoy beachside seafood then visit the world of Dalí. **2–4 DAYS**

Mediterranean Meander Over 1000km of coastline celebrating the ever-changing Mediterranean. **7 DAYS**

Costa del Sol Beyond the Beaches More than touristy resorts on the misunderstood southern coast. **3–4 DAYS**

Spain & Portugal's best sights and experiences, and the road trips that will take you there.

SPAIN & PORTUGAL HIGHLIGHTS

Barcelona

Home to cutting-edge architecture, world-class dining and vertiginous nightlife, Barcelona has long been one of Europe's most enticing destinations. Days are spent wandering the cobblestone lanes of the Gothic quarter while nights are spent taking in gilded music halls and first-rate tapas bars. The great city of Gaudí is all the more memorable when spied on a grand road trip across Spain, such as on **Trip 20: Mediterranean Meander**.

Trips 18 19 20

Barcelona La Pedrera (p257)

Algarve Beaches Praia da Falésia (p346)

La Rioja Wine Country

La Rioja is the sort of place where you could spend weeks meandering along quiet roads in search of the finest drop, with bodegas offering wine tastings and picturesque villages sheltering excellent wine museums. You'll also find plenty of surprises, such as a Frank Gehry–designed masterpiece in a tiny village on **Trip 8: Roving La Rioja Wine Region**.

Trip 8

Algarve Beaches

Beach-lovers have much to celebrate on a drive along Portugal's sundrenched southern coast. Breezy islands, dramatic cliffs and seemingly endless stretches of coastline set the stage for rewarding exploring on **Trip 28: Alentejo & Algarve Beaches**. After a day of surfing or basking, roll up to a beautifully sited restaurant for a seafood feast overlooking the crashing waves.

Trip 28

Lisbon

With mazelike lanes and hilltop panoramas overlooking the Rio Tejo, Lisbon is marvellous for wanderers. Its neighbourhoods delight the senses: you'll pass breadbox-sized grocers, brilliantly tiled buildings and candlelit taverns, as the mournful rhythms of fado drift on the breeze. The hardest part of visiting will be tearing yourself away on **Trip 29: Medieval Jewels in the Southern Interior**.

Trip 29

Spanish Summits Teleférico de Fuente Dé (p140)

BEST ROADS FOR DRIVING

The coastal road to São Vicente A clifftop stunner en route to Europe's southwestern-most tip. **Trip** 28

The road to Pinhão Terraced vineyards at perilous heights above the meandering Rio Douro. **Trip** 27

Valle del Roncal Tower above the clouds on this ascent through the Pyrenees. **Trip** 18

The road to Sant Feliu de Guíxols Spectacular cliffs and crashing waves along the Costa Brava. **Trip** 15

Central Picos Mountain magnificence and the gateway to adventure. **Trip** 9

Spanish Summits

Prepare to be dazzled on a jaw-dropping journey through some of the most spectacular mountain scenery in Spain. Set back from the ever-changing coastline of Cantabria and Asturias, the dramatic limestone massifs you'll see on **Trip 9: Lofty Roads: the Picos de Europa** are unique in Spain but geologically similar to the Alps and jammed with inspiring trails.

Trip 9

13

Alto Duoro Vineyards Terraced vineyards (p330)

Alto Douro Vineyards

The oldest demarcated wine region on earth has steeply terraced hills, stitched together with craggy vines that have produced luscious wine for centuries. On **Trip 27: Douro Valley Vineyard Trails**, you'll travel impossibly scenic back roads with countless vintners offering tours and tastings. Some spots have heritage accommodation – mighty handy when you want more than just a sip.

Trip **27**

BEST PLACES FOR FOODIES

Valencia Birthplace of paella and home to superb eateries.
Trips **19** **20**

- -

Galicia Seafood feasting in beautiful coastal settings.
Trips **7** **13**

- -

Sagres Top spot for traditional Portuguese specialties like cataplana (seafood stew).
Trip **28**

- -

The Basque Country Home to some of the best restaurants in Spain.
Trips **8** **12** **18**

- -

Segovia Famed for its roast suckling pig and other meaty dishes.
Trip **1**

HIGHLIGHTS ★

Madrid Museo del Prado (p43)

Sierra Nevada Hiking towards Mulhacén (p283)

Madrid

Madrid has a dizzying array of attractions, not least of which is its astounding collection of fine art. You can spend the day gazing at works by Goya, Velázquez and El Greco, then head out into the night for artfully prepared tapas and roaring nightlife. The wall-to-wall bars, small clubs, live-music venues and cocktail bars make a fine finale to **Trip 4: Spain's Interior Heartland**.

Trips 2 4

Sierra Nevada

Spectacular mountain vistas are only one attractive feature of **Trip 23: The Great Outdoors**. Spain's highest peaks are also the setting for outdoor adventure aplenty: walking, horse riding, climbing and mountain biking, with skiing and snowboarding in winter. There's also wildlife, including ibex. You could spend days exploring Spain's biggest national park and barely scratch the surface.

Trip 23

Asturian Coast

Wild and unspoilt, the secluded sandy stretches and mysterious coves lining the Asturian coast hide some of Spain's most beautiful beaches. On **Trip 12: North Coast Beaches & Culture** you'll want to pull over frequently to admire the green hills and rocky headlands. You'll also eat well at the pretty villages along the way – the food here is famous throughout Spain.

Trip 12

Porto

It would be hard to dream up a more romantic city than Portugal's second largest. Laced with narrow laneways, it's blessed with countless baroque churches, epic theatres and sprawling plazas. Its Ribeira district – a Unesco World Heritage site – is a fascinating place to explore. As scenic as it is, it's just a prelude to the gorgeous landscapes you'll encounter on **Trip 27: Douro Valley Vineyard Trails**.

Trip 27

Seville

A city of capricious moods and soulful secrets, Seville has played a pivotal role in the evolution of many peculiarly Spanish passions, including baroque art and Mudéjar architecture. It's also blessed with year-round sunshine, fuelled by ebullient festivals, and the epicentre of flamenco, Spain's evocative soundtrack – hear it in abundance on **Trip 22: Golden Triangle**.

Trip 22

ROSSHELEN/GETTY IMAGES ©

Left: **Porto** Ribeira district (p331)

Below: **Seville** Flamenco dancers (p274)

PATFAX/BUDGET TRAVEL ©

Pintxos in San Sebastián

Chefs here have made bar snacks an art form. Sometimes called 'high cuisine in miniature', *pintxos* (Basque tapas) are piles of flavour often mounted on a slice of baguette. The choice lined up on the counter in any bar in central San Sebastián will leave first-time visitors gasping. **Trip 12: North Coast Beaches & Culture** takes you to Spain's most celebrated eating scene.

Trips

BEST SCENIC VILLAGES

Sos del Rey Católico Gorgeous medieval village in the Pyrenees. **Trip** 18

Albarracín A stunner in rocky Aragón, on the meandering Guadalaviar. **Trip** 19

Tamariu A beautiful seaside settlement backed by pine-covered hills. **Trip** 15

Capileira White-washed village that overlooks the lofty Sierra Nevada. **Trip** 23

Monsanto Surrounds an age-old castle, with great walks nearby. **Trip** 32

19

IF YOU LIKE

Granada The Alhambra's Moorish architecture (p276)

Beaches

Spain and Portugal have some magnificent stretches of sand, from people-packed beaches to remote windswept shores. Despite Iberia's summertime popularity, you can find unspoiled beaches if you know where to look.

15 Artistic Inspiration on the Costa Brava
Rugged coast with pine-dappled cliffs, pristine coves and wide beaches.

20 Mediterranean Meander A showcase of coastal charm, with beach-loving favourites such as Cabo de Gata and Sitges.

21 Costa del Sol Beyond the Beaches Spain's most famous coastline, with draws like classy Marbella and beautifully set Nerja.

28 Alentejo & Algarve Beaches Portugal's south coast is a stunner with cliff-backed beaches, seaside villages and great surf.

Wine

In Iberia, wine is king, and the fruits of its picturesque vineyards are famous throughout the world. Rioja and port are well known, but there's more to discover in this great winery region.

8 Roving La Rioja Wine Region Bodegas, wine museums and vineyards to the horizon – this is Spanish wine's heartland.

27 Douro Valley Vineyard Trails Head to northern Portugal for breathtaking views over terraced slopes and luscious red wines.

16 Central Catalonia's Wineries & Monasteries The Penedès plains are the capital of cava country, with cellar tours and vast vineyards.

31 Tasting the Dão Surrounded by mountains, this is the go-to spot for some of Portugal's best drops.

Art

Spain's artistic tradition is one of Europe's richest, from local masters to the continent's finest, who flourished under Spanish royal patronage. The result? Art galleries of astonishing depth.

2 Back Roads Beyond Madrid Countless galleries and three world-class museums – Madrid looms large in the global art scene.

15 Artistic Inspiration on the Costa Brava Delve deeply into the world of Salvador Dalí, one of Spain's greatest artists.

20 Mediterranean Meander See artwork by Spanish greats, from Picasso in Malaga to Catalan giants in Barcelona.

32 Highlands & History in the Central Interior A Portugal ramble that showcases Roman collections, Renaissance art and eclectic global works.

Briones Vivanco Wine Museum (p127)

Architecture

The great building designs across Iberia span centuries, from Roman-era aqueducts and Islamic-era palaces to fantastical 19th-century Modernisme and the cutting-edge works of today.

12 North Coast Beaches & Culture Take in jaw-dropping designs by legendary architects in Bilbao and Santander.

19 Barcelona to Valencia Visit Barcelona's great Modernista masterpieces followed by stunning 21st-century works in Valencia.

26 Atlantic Coast Surf Trip Iconic works range from 15th-century monasteries to postmodern music halls.

22 Golden Triangle Peer back in time while studying exquisite masterpieces built by the Moors.

Outdoor Activities

Adventure comes in many forms in Spain and Portugal, with seaside activities (kayaking, surfing and swimming), cycling, white-water rafting and great walks in nearly every region.

23 The Great Outdoors With surfing, mountain climbs and wildlife watching, the south of Spain has it all.

17 Peaks & Valleys in Northwest Catalonia Get off the beaten path for white-water rafting and hikes through a stunning national park.

9 Lofty Roads: the Picos de Europa Dramatic peaks set the scene for magnificent walks and kayaking along the Río Sella.

28 Alentejo & Algarve Beaches Sun-drenched days of surfing, sea kayaking and dolphin watching.

Great Scenery

With soaring peaks and flower-filled valleys, Spain and Portugal have glorious landscapes, which make a fine backdrop to country walks – or for simply taking in the view from the open road.

13 Coast of Galicia Bask in the untamed beauty of Galicia's wild beaches, jagged cliffs and tiny coves.

18 The Pyrenees Stunning scenery lurks around every curve on this soaring drive across northwest Spain.

30 The Minho's Lyrical Landscapes Head to northern Portugal for meandering rivers and granite-strewn peaks.

3 The Forgotten West Enter a world of fertile mountain-backed landscapes and dramatic river valleys.

NEED TO KNOW

Climate

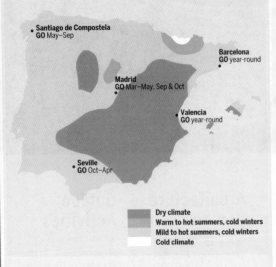

- Santiago de Compostela
  GO May–Sep
- Barcelona
  GO year-round
- Madrid
  GO Mar–May, Sep & Oct
- Valencia
  GO year-round
- Seville
  GO Oct–Apr

Dry climate
Warm to hot summers, cold winters
Mild to hot summers, cold winters
Cold climate

When to Go

High Season (Jun–Aug, public holidays)
» Accommodation books out and prices increase by up to 50%. Low season in parts of inland Spain. Expect warm, dry and sunny weather; more humid in coastal areas.

Shoulder (Mar–May, Sep & Oct)
» A good time to travel with mild, clear weather and fewer crowds. In Spain, local festivals can send prices soaring.

Low Season (Nov–Feb)
» Cold in central Spain and Portugal's interior; shorter, rainier days in both countries. Mild temperatures in Andalucía, the Mediterranean coast and the Algarve. This is high season in Spanish ski resorts. Many hotels are closed in beach areas but elsewhere prices plummet.

Your Daily Budget

SPAIN

Budget: Less than €75

» Dorm bed: €18–40

» Double room in a budget hotel: €50–65 (more in Madrid and Barcelona)

» Tapas: €2.50–4.50

Midrange: €75–175

» Double room in midrange hotel: €65–140

» Lunch and/or dinner in local restaurant: €20–40

» Flamenco show: €18–40

Top end: More than €175

» Double room in top-end hotel: €140 and up (€200 in Madrid and Barcelona)

» Fine dining for lunch and dinner: €150–250

» Regularly stay in Spanish *paradores* (luxury state-owned hotels): €150–280

PORTUGAL

Budget: Less than €60

» Dorm bed: €15–25

» Lunch special at a family-run restaurant: €8–12

» Basic hotel room for two: from €45

Midrange: €60–120

» Double room in a midrange hotel: €60–100

» Lunch and dinner in a midrange restaurant: €24–40

» Admission to museums €3–8

Top end: More than €120

» Boutique hotel room: from €120

» Dinner for two in a top restaurant: from €80

» Three-day surf course: €150

Eating

Tapas bar Tapas and drinks; open longer hours than restaurants.

Taberna Rustic place in Spain serving tapas and *raciones* (large tapas).

Panadería/Pasteleria Bakery (Spanish/Portuguese); good for pastries and coffee.

Vinoteca Wine bar where you order by the glass.

Cervecería/Cervejaria (Spanish/Portuguese) Beer hall; the place for snacks and draft beer (*cerveza/cerveja*).

Marisquería/Marisqueira Eatery specialising in seafood.

SPAIN & PORTUGAL

Price categories indicate the cost of a main course:

€	less than €12
€€	€10–20
€€€	more than €20

Sleeping

Casas rurales/Casa no campo (Spanish/Portuguese) Comfy village rooms, houses or farmhouses for rent in the countryside.

Hostales Simple guesthouses in Spain with en-suite rooms.

Paradores/Pousadas (Spanish/Portuguese) State-funded accommodation, often in castles, converted monasteries and old mansions.

Pensión/Pensão (Spanish/Portuguese) Inexpensive, extremely basic guesthouses, often with shared bathrooms.

SPAIN

Price categories indicate the cost of a double room with private bathroom in high season:

	BARCELONA & MADRID	REST OF COUNTRY
€	less than €75	less than €65
€€	€75–200	€65–140
€€€	more than €200	more than €140

PORTUGAL

Price categories refer to a double room with bathroom in high season. Unless otherwise stated, breakfast is included in the price.

€	less than €60
€€	€60–120
€€€	more than €120

SABINO PARENTE/500PX ©

Above: **Lisbon** Pastel de nata (custard tarts)

Right: **Barcelona** Plaça Reial (p231)

JACK/GETTY IMAGES ©

Arriving in Spain

Barajas Airport (Madrid)

Rental cars Major car-rental agencies have desks in the airport at arrival terminals.

Metro and buses Cost around €5 and run every five to 10 minutes from 6.05am to 1.30am (24 hours for buses); it's 30 to 40 minutes to the centre.

Taxis Cost €30 and reach the centre in 20 minutes.

El Prat Airport (Barcelona)

Rental cars Major car-rental agencies have concessions at arrival terminals.

Buses Cost €5.90 and run every five to 10 minutes from 6.10am to 1.05am; it's 30 to 40 minutes to the centre.

Trains Cost €4.20 and run every 30 minutes from 5.42am to 11.38pm; it takes 25 to 30 minutes to reach the centre.

Taxis €25 to €35; you'll reach the centre in 30 minutes.

Seville Airport

Rental cars You'll find all the normal firms at airport arrivals.

Buses Cost €4 and run to the city centre every 15 to 30 minutes between 5.20am and 1am.

Taxis €23 to €32; it takes 15 to 25 minutes to reach the centre.

Arriving in Portugal

Aeroporto de Lisboa (Lisbon)

Rental cars There is a wide choice of car-hire companies at the airport.

Metro €2 (including €0.50 Viva Viagem card); red line from Aeroporto station; transfer at Alameda for green line to Rossio and Baixa-Chiado. It's 20 minutes to the centre; frequent departures from 6.30am to 1am.

AeroBus €4; every 20 minutes from 8am to 9pm.

Taxis €15–€20; around 20 minutes to the centre.

Aeroporto de Faro (Faro)

Rental cars Car-rental agencies have desks in the airport.

Buses €2.50; every 30 minutes weekdays, every two hours weekends.

Taxis €15–€20; around 20 minutes to the centre.

Internet Access

Wi-fi is available in most lodgings and cafes (and is usually free). Internet cafes are rare.

Mobile Phones

Local SIM cards are widely available and can be used in many international mobile phones.

Money

ATMs are widely available throughout both Spain and Portugal. Credit cards are accepted in most hotels, restaurants and shops.

Tipping

Menu prices indicate a service charge. Most people leave small change if satisfied: 5% is fine; 10% is considered generous.

Useful Websites

Lonely Planet (www.lonely planet.com) Travel tips, accommodation, recommendations and more.

Turespaña (www.spain.info) Spanish tourism authority with interactive maps featuring key attractions in every region.

Turismo de Portugal (www. visitportugal.com) Portugal's useful and official tourism authority.

RAC (www.rac.co.uk/driving -abroad) Info for British drivers on driving in Spain and Portugal.

Opening Hours

Banks 8.30am to 2pm or 3pm Monday to Friday.

Shops 10am to 2pm and 5pm to 8pm Monday to Friday, 10am to 2pm Saturday in Spain; 10am to noon and 2pm to 7pm Monday to Friday, 10am to 2pm Saturday in Portugal.

Restaurants 1pm to 3.30pm and 8pm to 11pm in Spain; noon to 3pm and 7pm to 10pm in Portugal.

Bars 6pm to 2am.

Clubs 11pm to 6am Thursday to Saturday.

For more, see Road Trip Essentials (p392)

CITY GUIDE

BARCELONA

From Gothic to Gaudí, Barcelona bursts with art and architecture. It's also home to celebrated Catalan restaurants, fascinating neighbourhoods and simmering nightlife. Cap it off with pretty beaches, hilltop viewpoints and historical relics dating back to the Romans, and it's no wonder Barcelona continues to be one of Europe's best-loved destinations.

Mercat de la Boqueria (p239)

Getting Around

Heavy traffic and narrow, one-way streets can exasperate even diehard city drivers. Luckily Barcelona has an excellent metro system with stops all across town. One-way fares cost €2.40; a day pass is €8.60.

Parking

On-street parking can be difficult to find. You're better off using a car park (like those located near Plaça de les Glòries or Estació del Nord). Parking costs around €3 per hour or €20 to €30 for 24 hours.

Where to Eat

For fresh seafood, visit the family-run eateries in La Barceloneta near the seaside. Poble Sec and Sant Antoni have some great local favourites, particularly for tapas.

Where to Stay

Base yourself in El Born for access to great restaurants and cocktail lounges. Bohemian spirits are drawn to El Raval, with its eclectic eateries and live-music-charged nightlife. L'Eixample lacks historic charm but has great architecture and the city's top restaurants.

Useful Websites

Barcelona Turisme (www.barcelonaturisme. com) City's official tourism website.

Lonely Planet (www.lonelyplanet.com/ barcelona) Travel tips, accommodation, articles and more.

Miniguide (www.miniguide.co) Insight into Barcelona's food, culture, nightlife and fashion.

Trips Through Barcelona

For more, check out our city and country guides, www.lonelyplanet.com

TOP EXPERIENCES

➡ **Strolling La Rambla**
Few pedestrian thoroughfares can rival La Rambla as it cuts a swathe through old Barcelona and down to the shores of the Mediterranean. It's a canvas, catwalk and stage all in one.

➡ **Historic treasures at La Catedral**
Barcelona's cathedral spans the centuries like a sombre and silent witness to the city's history. Don't miss the leafy cloister inhabited by geese.

➡ **Panoramic views in Park Güell**
The playfulness of Gaudí's imagination runs wild in this hilltop park, an equal combination of verdant garden and Modernista sculptural fantasy.

➡ **Tapas at Mercat de la Boqueria**
One of Europe's great produce markets, this is also the centrepiece of Barcelona's culinary culture. Browse enticing fruits, seafood and baked goods, then head to the back for a tapas feast.

➡ **Gaudí's genius in La Pedrera**
One of Gaudí's great gifts to the city, this apartment block is extraordinary outside and in, and only gets better the higher you climb.

➡ **Bar-hopping in El Born**
Join locals on an evening of bar-hopping and tapas nibbling in one of Barcelona's best-loved neighbourhoods, El Born, whose tangle of streets surround the Basílica de Santa Maria del Mar.

MADRID

Madrid has transformed itself into one of Spain's premier style centres and its calling cards are many: astonishing art galleries, relentless nightlife, an exceptional live-music scene, a feast of fine restaurants and tapas bars, and a population that's mastered the art of the good life.

Getting Around

It's easy to get lost in this sprawling metropolis. Luckily you can take advantage of Madrid's extensive metro system (Europe's second-largest network). A single ticket costs €1.50. A 10-ride ticket is €12.20.

Parking

Do yourself a favour and leave your vehicle in a car park (they cost around €3 per hour and €20 per day).

GILLES GAONACH/SHUTTERSTOCK ©

TOP EXPERIENCES

➡ **Grand masterpieces
at Museo del Prado**
One of the world's great art galleries, this
must-see showcases Spanish paintings
including works by Goya and Velázquez.

➡ **Idyllic walks in
Parque del Buen Retiro**
Join locals on a scenic stroll through
beautifully landscaped gardens, laid out
in the 17th century by Felipe IV.

➡ **Captivating artworks in
Centro de Arte Reina Sofía**
A spectacular gallery that stages
outstanding contemporary shows. It's
impossible not to be moved while gazing
upon Picasso's heart-wrenching *Guernica*.

➡ **Royal decadence at
the Palacio Real**
This lavish palace is a fine place to lose
yourself among Italianate baroque
decadence.

Parque del Buen Retiro (p43)

Where to Eat
Splendid tapas bars abound everywhere,
but La Latina is the undoubted queen.
Restaurants in Malasaña, Chueca
and Huertas range from glorious old
tavernas to boutique eateries across all
price ranges.

Where to Stay
Base yourself in Madrid's Salamanca
district if you're seeking somewhere quiet
and upmarket – plus it's perfect for serial
shoppers. Staying in Plaza Mayor or Real
Madrid will put you in the heart of the
busy downtown area. If it's nightlife you
seek, book a place in Huertas or Lavapiés.

Useful Websites
Es Madrid (www.esmadrid.com) Nicely designed
town hall website with info on upcoming events.

Le Cool (https://madrid.lecool.com) Upcoming
events with an emphasis on the alternative and
avant-garde.

Madrid Diferente (www.madriddiferente.
com) Restaurants, shops and upcoming events
with a refreshingly offbeat style.

Trips Through Madrid 1 2 4

CITY GUIDE

LISBON

Spread across steep hillsides that overlook the Rio Tejo, Lisbon has captivated visitors for centuries. Windswept vistas at breathtaking heights reveal the city in all its beauty: Roman and Moorish ruins, white-domed cathedrals and grand plazas lined with sun-drenched cafes. But the real delight of discovery is delving into the narrow cobblestone lanes.

Getting Around

Driving around Lisbon is challenging, particularly in the narrow, winding lanes in the old centre. The city has a good metro system, and tram lines (particularly number 28) are an atmospheric way of getting around town.

Parking

Car park rates can be expensive in the centre, and street parking spaces are often scarce. Good free places to park are Campo de Santa Clara near the Alfama (good daily except Tuesday and Saturday when the market is on) and along Av 24 de Julio, west of Cais do Sodré.

GRZEJNIK/SHUTTERSTOCK ©

Lisbon's famous yellow trams

TOP EXPERIENCES

➡ **Atmospheric lanes of the Alfama**
Plan to get lost in Lisbon's medina-like district of tangled alleys and terracotta-roofed houses that tumble down to the river.

➡ **Architectural wizardry in Mosteiro dos Jerónimos**
This 16th-century monastery is pure eye candy, with a magnificent facade, columns like tree trunks and an elaborate cloister.

➡ **Magnificent views from Castelo de São Jorge**
On a windswept hilltop, this centuries-old fortification offers a window into Lisbon's Visigoth, Moorish and Christian past. The views are jaw-dropping.

➡ **Hearing fado in Mesa de Frades**
Hear the raw power of fado at this traditional, tile-lined dining and concert space in the Alfama. (www.mesadefrades.com)

Where to Eat

Follow the scent of chargrilled sardines and the sound of fado (traditional Portuguese melancholic song) to lively outdoor restaurants in the Alfama. Foodies should head to the Chiado, which has some excellent restaurants. Though better known for its nightlife, nearby Bairro Alto also has some gems.

Where to Stay

Base yourself in the Chiado for elegant boutique hotels with great restaurants and bars close by. The web-like lanes of the Alfama have great charm but getting to other parts of the city is

challenging. Leafy Príncipe Real has some good options and feels less touristy than other areas.

Useful Websites

Go Lisbon (www.golisbon.com) Curated info on sights, restaurants, bars and shops.

Lisbon Lux (www.lisbonlux.com) Trendy city guide.

Visit Lisboa (www.visitlisboa.com) Culture, food, city highlights.

Trip Through Lisbon 29

SPAIN & PORTUGAL BY REGION

Sparkling beaches, towering peaks, medieval villages and world-class dining: there's much to discover on an Iberian road trip. Here's your guide to what each region has to offer and the best drives to experience.

Madrid & Central Spain (p37)

With celebrated restaurants, vertiginous nightlife and hallowed museums, Madrid is a great place to start the journey. Beyond the capital, you can roll across ancient Roman bridges in Extremadura, explore the many treasures of Toledo and chase the ghosts of La Mancha on the Don Quixote Trail.

Tilt your wheel toward windmills on Trip 5

Portugal (p315)

You can explore lovely Lisbon with its heart-wrenching fado, hilltop views and atmospheric neighbourhoods, then head south for the coastal allure of the Algarve. Up north lies the jawdropping scenery (and luscious wines) of the Douro Valley, while the interior is awash with age-old villages and looming castles.

Follow the scent of char-grilled fish on Trip 26

Northern Spain & the Basque Country (p103)

Ruggedly beautiful, northern Spain is a land of towering cliffs and windswept coast – not to mention stellar seafood. Dining is particularly outstanding in Basque Country, home to some of Spain's best restaurants. Add to this the great wines along the Rioja trail and hiking adventures in Picos de Europa.

Discover unspoiled seascapes on Trip

Barcelona & Eastern Spain (p181)

Barcelona enchants visitors with its mad-cap architecture, Gothic quarter and brilliant restaurants. Beyond lies the picturesque beaches and seaside villages of the Costa Brava, the soaring peaks of the Pyrenees and much more to discover in the hinterland (medieval towns, mountain monasteries, vineyards).

Breathe in the crisp mountain air on Trip 18

Andalucía & Southern Spain (p241)

The cradle of flamenco, Andalucía is a soulful, traditional place of blindingly white castle-topped towns, bustling beaches and elaborate palace-fortresses of unrivaled magnificence. There's much to see and do here, from frolicking off sun-kissed beaches to marvelling at the grandeur of the Alhambra in Granada.

Gaze out to Africa from the 'Rock' on Trip 21

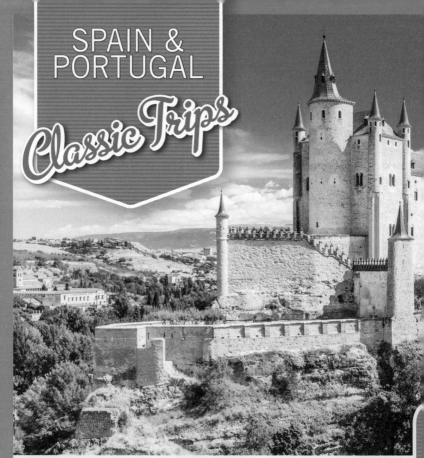

SPAIN & PORTUGAL
Classic Trips

EMPERORCOSAR/SHUTTERSTOCK ©

1

What Is a Classic Trip?

All the trips in this book show you the best of Spain & Portugal, but we've chosen nine as our all-time favourites. These are our Classic Trips – the ones that lead you to the best of the iconic sights, the top activities and unique Iberian experiences. Turn the page to see a map of these Classic Trips and look out for them throughout the book.

Above: **Segovia** Alcázar (p43)
Left: **Seville** La Lonja (p254)

Madrid &
Central
Spain

WELCOME TO THE SPANISH HEARTLAND, TO THIS MOST SPANISH OF SPAIN'S REGIONS where history is writ large and magnificently on seemingly every corner. On your journeys across the *meseta*, Spain's high plateau that surrounds Madrid, you'll encounter some of Spain's most spectacular cities – from Cáceres to Cuenca, Segovia to Salamanca – as well as cathedral towns par excellence (Toledo, León and Burgos). Savour castles and Roman relics, tilt at windmills in the finest tradition of Don Quixote, and tread lightly through some of the most beautiful villages (Covarrubias, Atienza, Chinchón) and medieval towns (Trujillo, Sigüenza, Cuenca) in Europe. Above all, you'll get a taste for Old Spain and the stirring relics it left behind.

Madrid Plaza Mayor (p60)
MAYLAT/SHUTTERSTOCK ©

Madrid & Central Spain

ATLANTIC OCEAN

Bay of Biscay

N
0 — 10
0 — 50 mile

Santander
Ribadesella
Torrelavega
Parque
Nacional de
los Picos de
Europa
Torre
Cerredo
(2648m)
Riaño
Reinosa
Bilbao
San Sebastián
Miranda de Ebro
Vitoria-Gasteiz
Est
(Li
A1
Logroñ
AP66
León
Aguilar de
Campóo
A67
Najera
Calahorra
N111
Ponferrada
A6
Sahagún
Burgos
Astorga
Osorno
Salas de
los Infantes
Puebla de
Sanabria
Becilla de
Valderaduey
Palencia
A1
1
A52
Aranda de
Duero
Benavente
Soria
Chaves
Parque
Natural de
Montesinho
Valladolid
Peñafiel
4
Mirandela
Miranda do
Douro
Zamora
Calatañazor
Parque Natural do
Douro Internacional
Rio Duero
Tordesillas
N110
PORTUGAL
Rio
Medina del
Campo
Puerto de
Somosierra
Atienza
Vila Nova de
Foz Côa
Lumbrales
A62
A6
A1
2
4
Salamanca
1
Segovia
A2
Molina de
Aragón
Guarda
Ciudad
Rodrigo
Ávila
N110
Collado
Villalba
Guadalajara
Peña de
Francia
(1732m)
Béjar
Pico de
Almanzor
(2592m)
MADRID
Alcalá de Henares
Torrejón de Ardoz
Granadilla
Plasencia
3
Valverde de
la Vera
Parla
N401
A3
N400
2
Cu
**Navalmoral
de la Mata**
A5
Aranjuez
Tarancón
A66
Cáceres
Rio Tajo
**Talavera de
la Reina**
Toledo
Alcántara
Rio Tejo
Arroyo de
la Luz
Trujillo
N502
Villacañas
Belmonte
5
A4
A31
Mérida
Miajadas
SPAIN
Consuegra
Socuéllamos
A5
Alcázar de San Juan
Badajoz
A66
Don
Benito
N430
Daimiel
Tomelloso
Almendralejo
Almadén
Ciudad Real
Manzanares
Albacete
Almagro
Valdepeñas
N502
Puertollano
Villanueva de
los Infantes
6
Zafra
Peñarroya-
Pueblonuevo
Pozoblanco
A4
La Capitana
(959m)
Parque Natural Sier
La Carolina
El Yelmo
(1808m)
Parque Natur
Sierras de Ca
Segura y las
**Fregenal de
la Sierra**
Monesterio
Montoro
Bailén
Beas de
Segura
Castaño
(960m)
Aracena
Parque Natural
Sierra Norte
de Sevilla
Córdoba
Andújar
Linares
Empanadas
(2107m)
Revol
(2001
Parque Natural Sierra de
Aracena y Picos de Aroche
Palma del Río
Rio Guadalquivir
Úbeda
Huéscar
Valverde del
Camino
Torredonjimeno
Jaén
Cazorla
María
(2045m)
A66
Écija
El Almadén
(2032m)
Baza
Puert
Huelva
A4
Lucena
Bermejo
(1476m)
Seville
Puente
Genil
Parque Natural
Sierras Subbéticas
Parque Natural
Sierra de Baza
Lumbrera

El Toboso Don Quixote sculpture (p88)

DON'T MISS

Covarrubias

Stunning – and little known – riverside village. Step behind its walls and into another world on Trip **1**

Café de la Iberia, Chinchón

Chinchón hides between motorways that whisk travellers elsewhere. Eat where Goya ate, overlooking a special square on Trip **2**

San Martín del Castañar

Lost in the wilds of Spain's west, this village ranks in the country's top five for at least one Lonely Planet writer. Find it on Trip **3**

El Toboso

Other towns have windmills, but if you really want to understand the cult of Don Quixote, visit El Toboso on Trip **5**

Museo del Jamón, Monesterio

Extremadura's most celebrated *jamón*-producing town has a museum worthy of this peculiarly Spanish obsession. Get a taste on Trip **6**

Classic Trip

Historic Castilla y León

This journey through Spain's Castilian heartlands takes in some of the country's most engaging historic cities and larger towns, with many time-worn pueblos (villages) en route.

1

TRIP HIGHLIGHTS

611 km

Burgos
Arguably Spain's foremost Gothic cathedral

653 km

Covarrubias
One of Spain's most beautiful villages

9

10

FINISH
● Soria

Valladolid ●

Aranda
de Duero

92 km

Segovia
Disney castle, Roman aqueduct and lively streets

4

2

☆ MADRID
START

Salamanca
Golden sandstone architecture without peer

254 km

---

7 DAYS
764KM / 475 MILES

GREAT FOR...

📖

BEST TIME TO GO

March to May, and September and October to avoid extremes of heat and cold.

ESSENTIAL PHOTO

Plaza Mayor, Salamanca, floodlit at night.

BEST FOR CULTURE

Irresistible Salamanca street life against a glorious architectural backdrop.

Classic Trip

1 Historic Castilla y León

From Segovia to Soria, the towns of Castilla y León rank among Spain's most appealing historic centres. Architecture may be central to their attraction, but these are no museum pieces. Instead, the relentless energy of life lived Spanish-style courses through the streets, all set against a backdrop of grand cathedrals and animated stately squares. Out in the countryside, postcard-perfect villages complement the clamour of city life.

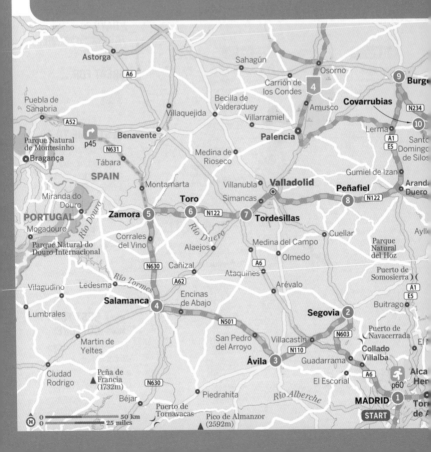

① Madrid

Madrid is the most Spanish of all of Spain's cities. Its food culture, drawn from the best the country has to offer, makes it one of Europe's more underrated culinary capitals, while its nightlife and irresistible *alegría* (joy) exist like some Spanish stereotype given form. But there is more to Madrid than just nonstop colour and movement. This is one of the premier art cities on the continent, with three world-class galleries – the

Museo del Prado (www.museodelprado.es; Paseo del Prado; adult/concession/child €15/7.50/free, 6-8pm Mon-Sat & 5-7pm Sun free, audio guide €3.50, admission plus official guidebook €24; ⏰10am-8pm Mon-Sat, to 7pm Sun; Ⓜ Banco de España), **Museo Thyssen-Bornemisza** (☎902 760511; www.museothyssen.org; Paseo del Prado 8; adult/child €13/free, Mon free; ⏰10am-7pm Tue-Sun, noon-4pm Mon; Ⓜ Banco de España) and **Centro de Arte Reina Sofía** (☎91 774 10 00; www.museoreinasofia.es; Calle de Santa Isabel 52; adult/concession €10/free, 1.30-7pm Sun, 7-9pm Mon & Wed-Sat free; ⏰10am-9pm Mon & Wed-Sat, to 7pm Sun; Ⓜ Estación del Arte) – all clustered close to one of the city's main boulevards and a short walk from the Parque del Buen Retiro, one of the loveliest and most expansive monumental parks in Europe. In short, this is a city that rewards those who linger and long to immerse themselves in all things Spanish.

The Drive » Getting out of Madrid can be a challenge, with a complicated system of numbered motorways radiating out from the city. Drive north along the Paseo de la Castellana, turn west along the M50 ring road, then take the A6, direction A Coruña. Of the two main roads to Segovia from the A6, the N603 is the prettier (92km).

TRIP HIGHLIGHT

② Segovia

Unesco World Heritage–listed Segovia is a stunning confluence of everything that's good about the beautiful towns of Castilla. There are historic landmarks in abundance, among them the Roman **Acueducto**, the fairy-tale **Alcázar** (☎921 46 07 59; www.alcazardesegovia.com; Plaza de la Reina Victoria Eugenia; adult/concession/under 6yr €5.50/3.50/free, tower €2.50, audio guide €3; ⏰10am-8pm Apr-Oct, to 6pm Nov-Mar;), which is said to have inspired Walt Disney, and Romanesque gems such as the **catedral** (☎921 46 22 05;

LINK YOUR TRIP

2 Back Roads Beyond Madrid

Also starting in Madrid, this loop south and east of the capital takes in the historic towns and villages of Madrid's hinterland.

4 Spain's Interior Heartland

From Santander's ferry port, we take you through Roman ruins, buzzing towns and soaring cathedrals on your way to Madrid.

Classic Trip

www.turismodesegovia.com; Plaza Mayor; adult/child €3/ free, Sun morning free, tower tour €4; ☺9am-9.30pm Apr-Oct, 9.30am-6.30pm Nov-Mar, tower tours 10.30pm, noon, 1.30pm & 4pm year-round, plus 6pm & 7.30pm Apr-Oct) or the **Iglesia de San Martín** (Plaza de San Martín; ☺10am-6pm Mon-Sat).

This is also one of the most dynamic towns in the country, a winning mix of students and international visitors filling the city's bars and public spaces with an agreeable crescendo of noise. To cap it all, the setting is simply superb – a city strung out along a ridge, its warm terracotta and sandstone hues arrayed against a backdrop of Castilla's rolling hills and the often snow-capped Sierra de Guadarrama.

There are many vantage points to take in the full effect, but our favourite can be found anywhere in the gardens near the entrance to the Alcázar.

✕ ⊨ p50

The Drive » It's 66km from Segovia to Ávila along the N110. The road runs southwest, parallel to the Sierra de Guadarrama, with some pretty views en route. Around halfway, you'll cross the A6 motorway.

❸ Ávila

Ávila's old city, surrounded by 12th-century *murallas* (walls) with eight monumental gates, 88 watchtowers and over 2500 turrets, is one of the best-preserved walled cities in Spain. Two sections of the **Murallas** (☎920 35 00 00; www.muralladeavila.com; incl multilingual audio guide adult/ under 12yr €5/3.50, 2-4pm Tue free; ☺10am-8pm Apr-Jun & Sep-Oct, to 9pm Jul & Aug, to 6pm Tue-Sun Nov-Mar; ⬆) can be climbed – a 300m stretch accessed from just inside the Puerta del Alcázar, and a longer 1300m stretch that runs along the old city's northern perimeter. The best views are those at night from **Los Cuatro Postes** (Calle de los Cuatro Postes, off N110), a short distance northwest of the city. Ávila is also the home city of Santa Teresa, with the **Convento de Santa Teresa** (☎920 21 10 30; www.teresadejesus.com; Plaza de la Santa; church & relic room free, museum €2; ☺10am-2pm & 4-7pm Tue-Sun) as its centrepiece and plenty of other important religious buildings nearby.

✕ ⊨ p50

The Drive » The N501 runs northwest of Ávila to Salamanca, in the process traversing the pancake-flat high *meseta* (plateau) of central Spain and covering 109km en route.

LOCAL KNOWLEDGE: FROG-SPOTTING IN SALAMANCA

A compulsory task facing all visitors to Salamanca is to search out the frog sculpted into the facade of the **Universidad Civil** (☎923 29 44 00, ext 1150; www.salamanca.es; Calle de los Libreros; adult/concession €10/5, audio guide €2; ☺10am-7pm Mon-Sat, to 2pm Sun mid-Sep–Mar, 10am-8pm Mon-Sat, to 2pm Sun Apr–mid-Sep). Once pointed out, it's easily enough seen, but the uninitiated can spend considerable time searching. Why bother? Well, they say that those who detect it without help can be assured of good luck and even marriage within a year. Some hopeful students see a guaranteed examination's victory in it. If you believe all this, stop reading now. If you need help, look at the busts of Fernando and Isabel. From there, turn your gaze to the largest column on the extreme right of the front. Slightly above the level of the busts is a series of skulls, atop the leftmost of which sits our little amphibious friend (or what's left of his eroded self).

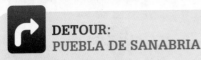

DETOUR:
PUEBLA DE SANABRIA

Start: ⑤ Zamora

Northwest of Zamora, close to the Portuguese border, this captivating village is a tangle of medieval alleyways that unfold around a 15th-century castle and trickle down the hill. This is one of Spain's loveliest hamlets and it's well worth the detour, or even stopping overnight: the quiet cobblestone lanes make it feel like you've stepped back centuries. Wandering the village is alone worth the trip here but a few attractions are worth tracking down. Crowning the village's high point and dominating its skyline for kilometres around, the **Castillo** (adult/child under 12yr €3/free; ☉11am-2pm & 4-8pm; 🅿🚻) has some interesting displays on local history, flora and fauna and superb views from the ramparts. Also at the top of the village, the striking **Plaza Mayor** is surrounded by some fine historical buildings. The 17th-century *ayuntamiento* (town hall) has a lovely arched facade and faces across the square to **Iglesia de Nuestra Señora del Azogue** (Plaza Mayor; ☉noon-2pm & 4-6pm Fri, 11am-2pm & 4-7pm Sat & Sun), a pretty village church which was first built in the 12th century. If you're staying the night, the **Posada Real La Cartería** (📞980 62 03 12; www.lacarteria.com; Calle de Rúa 16; r from €90-150; ❄@🛜) captures the essence of Puebla de Sanabria's medieval appeal with both rooms and a restaurant.

TRIP HIGHLIGHT

④ Salamanca

Whether floodlit by night or bathed in the sunset, there's something magical about Salamanca. This is a city of rare beauty, awash with golden sandstone overlaid with ochre-tinted Latin inscriptions; an extraordinary virtuosity of plateresque and Renaissance styles. The monumental highlights are many, with the exceptional **Plaza Mayor** (illuminated to stunning effect at night) an unforgettable highlight. Built between 1729 and 1755, it is widely considered to be Spain's most beautiful central plaza. But this is also Castilla's liveliest city; home to a massive Spanish and international student population that throngs the streets at night and provides the city with so much youth and vitality.

🍴 🛏 p50

The Drive ⟫ The N630 runs due north from Salamanca to Zamora (67km), a relatively quiet road by Spanish standards and one that follows the contours of the rolling hill country of Castilla y León's west.

⑤ Zamora

If you're arriving by road, first appearances can be deceiving and, as in so many Spanish towns, your introduction to provincial Zamora is likely to be nondescript apartment blocks. But persevere as the *casco historico* (old town) is hauntingly beautiful, with sumptuous medieval monuments that have earned Zamora the popular sobriquet 'Romanesque Museum'. Much of the old town is closed to motorised transport and walking is easily the best way to explore this subdued encore to the monumental splendour of Salamanca. Zamora is also one of the best places to be during Semana Santa, with haunting processions of hooded penitents parading through the streets. Whatever time of year you're here, don't miss the **Museo de Semana Santa** (📞980 53 60 72;

WHY THIS IS A CLASSIC TRIP
ANTHONY HAM, AUTHOR

The towns north and west of Madrid are windows on the Spanish soul, each with their own distinctive appeal. Segovia, Ávila, Salamanca, Zamora and Burgos are all Spanish classics, dynamic cities with extraordinary architectural backdrops. Throw in some beautiful villages along the way and you've captured the essence of this remarkable country in just a week.

Top: **Covarrubias** Old Town (p49)
Left: **Burgos** Cartuja de Miraflores (p48)
Right: **Segovia** Roman Acueducto (p43)

www.semanasantadezamora.
com; Plaza de Santa María
La Nueva; adult/child €4/2;
⏱10am-2pm & 5-8pm Tue-Sat,
10am-2pm Sun).

🍴 🛏 p51

The Drive » The A11 tracks
east of Zamora – not far out
along the sweeping plains that
bake in summer, take the turn-
off to Toro. Total distance: 40km.

----

❻ Toro

With a name that
couldn't be more Spanish
and a picaresque history
that overshadows its
present, Toro is your
archetypal Castilian
town. It was here that
Fernando and Isabel
cemented their primacy
in Christian Spain at the
Battle of Toro in 1476.
The town sits on a rise
high above the north
bank of Río Duero and
has a charming historic
centre with half-timbered
houses and Romanesque
churches. The high point,
literally, is the 12th-
century **Colegiata Santa
María La Mayor** (Plaza
de la Colegiata; church free,
sacristy €4; ⏱10.30am-2pm
& 5-7.30pm Tue-Sun Apr-Oct,
10am-2pm & 4.30-6.30pm
Tue-Sun Nov-Mar), **which**
rises above the town and
boasts the magnificent
Romanesque-Gothic
Pórtico de la Majestad.

The Drive » Return to the
east–west N122 road that lies
east of Toro and continue to
Tordesillas (46km).

Classic Trip

❼ Tordesillas

Commanding a rise on the northern flank of Río Duero, this pretty little town has a historical significance that belies its size. Originally a Roman settlement, it later played a major role in world history when, in 1494, Isabel and Fernando, the Catholic Monarchs, sat down with Portugal here to hammer out a treaty determining who got what in Latin America. Portugal got Brazil and much of the rest went to Spain. Explaining it all is the excellent **Museo del Tratado del Tordesillas** (☎983 77 10 67; Calle de Casas del Tratado; ⏰10am-1.30pm & 5-7.30pm Tue-Sat, 10am-2pm Sun Jun-Sep, 10am-1.30pm & 4-6.30pm Tue-Sat, 10am-2pm Sun Oct-May). Not far away, the heart of town is formed by the delightful porticoed and cobbled **Plaza Mayor**, its mustard-yellow paintwork offset by dark-brown woodwork and black grilles.

The Drive » From Tordesillas, E80 sweeps northeast, skirts the southern fringe of Valladolid and then continues east as the N122, through the vineyards of the Ribera del Duero wine region all the way into Peñafiel (83km).

❽ Peñafiel

Peñafiel is the gateway to the Ribera del Duero wine region and it's an appealing small town in its own right. **Plaza del Coso** is one of Spain's most picturesque plazas. This rectangular 15th-century 'square' is considered one of the most important forerunners to the *plazas mayores* across Spain. It's still used for bullfights on ceremonial occasions. But no matter where you are in Peñafiel, your eyes will be drawn to the **Castillo de Peñafiel** (Museo Provincial del Vino; ☎983 88 11 99; Peñafiel; castle adult/child €3.30/free, incl museum €6.60/free; ⏰10.30am-2pm & 4-8pm Tue-Sun Apr-Sep, 10.30am-2pm & 4-6pm Tue-Sun Oct-Mar), one of Spain's longest and narrowest castles. Within the castle's crenulated walls is the state-of-the-art **Museo Provincial del Vino**, the local wine museum.

✕ 🛏 p51

The Drive » The N122 continues east of Peñafiel. At Aranda del Duero, turn north along the E5 and make for Lerma, an ideal place to stop for lunch. Sated, return to the E5 and take it all the way into Burgos (108km).

TRIP HIGHLIGHT

❾ Burgos

Dominated by its Unesco World Heritage–listed cathedral but with plenty more to turn the head, Burgos is one of Castilla y León's most captivating towns. The extraordinary Gothic **catedral** (☎947 20 47 12; www.catedraldeburgos.es; Plaza del Rey Fernando; adult/child under 14yr incl audio guide €7/2, from 4.30pm Tue free; ⏰9.30am-7.30pm mid-Mar–Oct, 10am-7pm Nov–mid-Mar) is one of Spain's glittering jewels of religious architecture and looms large over the city and skyline. Inside is the last resting place of El Cid and there are numerous extravagant chapels, a gilded staircase and a splendid altar. Some of the best cathedral views are from up the hill at the lookout, just below the 9th-century Castillo de Burgos. Elsewhere in town, two monasteries – the **Cartuja de Miraflores** (☎947 25 25 86; www.cartuja.org; ⏰10.15am-3pm & 4-6pm Mon-Sat, 11am-3pm & 4-6pm Sun) and the **Monasterio de las Huelgas** (☎947 20 16 30; www.monasteriodelashuelgas.org; Calle de Alfonso XIII; €6, 4-5.30pm Wed & Thu free; ⏰10am-1pm & 4-5.30pm Tue-Sat, 10.30am-2pm Sun) – are worth seeking out, while the city's eating scene is excellent.

✕ 🛏 p51, p120

The Drive » Take the E5 south of Burgos but almost immediately after leaving the city's southern outskirts, take the N234 turn-off and follow the signs over gently undulating hills and through green valleys to the walled village of Covarrubias (42km from Burgos).

⑩ Covarrubias

Inhabiting a broad valley in eastern Castilla y León and spread out along the shady banks of Río Arlanza with a gorgeous riverside aspect, Covarrubias is only a short step removed from the Middle Ages. Once you pass beneath the formidable stone archways that mark the village's entrances, Covarrubias takes visitors within its intimate embrace with tightly huddled and distinctive, arcaded half-timbered houses opening out onto cobblestone squares. Simply wandering around the village is the main pastime, and don't miss the charming riverside pathways or outdoor tables that spill out onto the squares. Otherwise, the main attraction is the **Colegiata de San Cosme y Damián** (€2.50; ⊙ guided tours 11am, noon, 1pm, 4.30pm & 5.30pm Mon & Wed-Sat, 1pm & 4.30pm Sun), which has the evocative atmosphere of a mini cathedral and Spain's oldest still-functioning church organ; note also the gloriously ostentatious altar, fronted by several Roman stone tombs, plus that of Fernán González, the 10th-century founder of Castilla. Don't miss the graceful cloisters and the sacristy with its vibrant 15th-century paintings by Van Eyck and tryptic *Adoración de los Magos*.

The Drive » The N234 winds southwest of Covarrubias through increasingly contoured country all the way to Soria (111km). En route there are signs to medieval churches and hermitages marking many minor roads leading off into the trees.

⑪ Soria

In the heart of the Castilian countryside, Soria is one of Spain's smaller provincial capitals. It's a great place to escape 'tourist Spain', with an appealing and compact old centre and a sprinkling of stunning monuments across the town and down by the Río Duero. The streets of the old town centre are pretty enough, but by the river is the **Monasterio de San Juan de Duero** (☎975 22 13 97; Camino Monte de las Ánimas; €1, Sat & Sun free; ⊙10am-2pm Sun year round, 10am-2pm & 4-8pm Tue-Sat Jul-Sep, 10am-2pm & 4-7pm Tue-Sat Feb-Jun & Oct, 10am-2pm & 4-6pm Tue-Sat Nov-Jan), Soria's most striking sight, and it's a pretty 2.3km walk to the **Ermita de San Saturio** (☎975 18 07 03; Paseo de San Saturio; ⊙10.30am-2pm & 4.30-8.30pm Tue-Sat, 10.30am-2pm Sun Jul & Aug, shorter hours rest of year); the stroll is especially pretty in autumn.

 p51, p83

DETOUR: SANTO DOMINGO DE SILOS

Start: ⑩ Covarrubias

Nestled in the rolling hills just off the Burgos–Soria (N234) road, this tranquil, pretty village is built around a monastery with an unusual claim to fame: monks from here made the British pop charts in the mid-1990s with recordings of Gregorian chants. Notable for its pleasingly unadorned Romanesque sanctuary dominated by a multidomed ceiling, the **church** (Calle de Santo Domingo; ⊙6am-2pm & 4.30-10pm, vespers 6am, 7.30am, 9am, 1.45pm, 7pm & 9.30pm) is where you can hear the monks chant. The monastery, one of the most famous in central Spain, is known for its stunning **cloister** (☎947 39 00 49; www.abadiadesilos. es; Calle de Santo Domingo 2; adult/child €3.50/free; ⊙10am-1pm & 4.30-6pm Tue-Sat, noon-1pm & 4-6pm Sun), a two-storey treasure chest of some of Spain's most imaginative Romanesque art. Don't miss the unusually twisted column on the cloister's western side. For sweeping views over the town, pass under the Arco de San Juan and climb the grassy hill to the south to the Ermita del Camino y Via Crucis.

Eating & Sleeping

Segovia ❷

✖ Restaurante
El Fogón Sefardí
Jewish €€

(📞921 46 62 50; www.lacasamudejar.com; Calle de Isabel La Católica 8; tapas from €3.75, mains €13-22, set menus €20-35; ⏱1.30-4.30pm & 8.30-11.30pm) Located within the Hospedería La Gran Casa Mudéjar, this is one of the most original places in town. Sephardic Jewish cuisine is served either on the intimate patio or in the splendid dining hall with original 15th-century Mudéjar flourishes. The theme in the bar is equally diverse. Stop here for a taste of the award-winning tapas. Reservations recommended.

🛏 Hotel Palacio
San Facundo
Historic Hotel €€

(📞921 46 30 61; www.hotelpalaciosanfacundo. com; Plaza de San Facundo 4; r incl breakfast from €81; ❄ @ 🖥) Segovia's hotels are adept at fusing stylishly appointed modern rooms with centuries-old architecture. This place is one of the best, with an attractive columned courtyard, a warm colour scheme, chic room decor and a central location. The breakfast buffet is more generous than most.

Ávila ❸

✖ Soul Kitchen
Castilian €€

(📞920 21 34 83; www.soulkitchen.es; Calle de Caballeros 13; mains €9-19; ⏱10am-midnight Mon-Fri, 11am-2am Sat, to midnight Sun) This place has the kind of energy that can seem lacking elsewhere. The eclectic menu changes regularly and ranges from salads with dressings like chestnut and fig to hamburgers with cream of *setas* (oyster mushrooms). Lighter dishes include bruschetta with tasty toppings. Live music, poetry readings (and similar) happen in summer.

🛏 Hotel El Rastro
Historic Hotel €

(📞920 35 22 25; www.elrastroavila.com; Calle Cepedas; s €30-45, d €45-90; ❄ 🖥) This atmospheric hotel occupies a former 16th-century palace with original stone, exposed brickwork and a natural, earth-toned colour scheme exuding a calm, understated elegance. Each room has a different form, but most have high ceilings and plenty of space. Note that the owners also run a marginally cheaper *hostal* (budget hotel) of the same name around the corner.

Salamanca ❹

✖ La Cocina de Toño
Tapas €€

(📞923 26 39 77; www.lacocinadetoño.es; Calle Gran Via 20; tapas from €1.60, mains €11-23, set menus from €17; ⏱11am-4.30pm & 8-11.30pm Tue-Sat, 11am-4.30pm Sun; 🖥) This place owes its loyal following to its creative *pinchos* (tapas) and half-servings of dishes such as escalope of foie gras with roast apple and passionfruit jelly. The restaurant serves more traditional fare as befits the decor, but the bar is one of Salamanca's gastronomic stars. Slightly removed from the old city, it draws a predominantly Spanish crowd.

🛏 Microtel
Placentinos
Boutique Hotel €€

(📞923 28 15 31; www.microtelplacentinos. com; Calle de Placentinos 9; r incl breakfast €38-110; ❄ 🖥) One of Salamanca's most charming boutique hotels, Microtel Placentinos is tucked away on a quiet street and has rooms with exposed stone walls and wooden beams. The service is faultless, and the overall atmosphere is one of intimacy and discretion. All rooms have a hydromassage shower or tub and there's an outside whirlpool spa (summer only).

Zamora ⑤

✕ La Rua　　　　　　　　　Castilian €€
(📞980 53 40 24; Rúa de los Francos 21; mains
€9-21; 🕐1-4pm Sun-Fri, 1-4pm & 8.30-11.30pm
Sat) Devoted to down-home Zamora cooking,
this central place is a good place to try *arroz a la
zamorana* (rice with pork and ham or chorizo),
although you'll usually need two people
ordering for staff to make it. It is sometimes
closed on Tuesdays in winter.

🛏 NH Palacio del Duero　　　Hotel €€
(📞980 50 82 62; www.nh-hotels.com; Plaza de
la Horta 1; r from €80; 🅿 ❄ @ 🛜) In a superb
position next to a lovely Romanesque church,
the seemingly modern building has cleverly
encompassed part of the former convent, as
well as – somewhat bizarrely – a 1940s power
station (the lofty brick chimney remains). As
you'd expect from this excellent chain, the
rooms here are stylishly furnished and the
service is attentive.

Peñafiel ⑧

✕ Asados Alonso　　　　Spanish €€
(📞983 88 08 34; www.facebook.com/
restauranteasadosalonso; Calle de Derecha
al Coso 14; mains €14-23; 🕐1-4.30pm Sun
& Tue-Thu, 1-4.30pm & 8.30-11.30pm Fri &
Sat) Staff keep it simple at this long-standing
asador (restaurant specialising in roasted
meats), with roasted spring lamb cooked in a
wood-fired oven and served with salad – many
a visitor's idea of bliss.

🛏 Hotel Convento
Las Claras　　　　　Historic Hotel €€
(📞983 87 81 68; www.hotelconventolasclaras.
com; Plaza Adolfo Muñoz Alonso; r/ste from
€85/199; 🅿 ❄ 🛜 🏊) This cool, classy hotel
– a former convent – is an unexpected find
in little Peñafiel, with quietly elegant rooms,
as well as a full spa with thermal baths and
treatments. On-site is an excellent restaurant
with, as you'd expect, a carefully chosen
wine list. Lighter meals are available in the
cafeteria.

Burgos ⑨

✕ Cervecería Morito　　　　Tapas €
(📞947 26 75 55; Calle de Diego Porcelos 1;
tapas/raciones from €4/6; 🕐12.30-3.30pm &
7-11.30pm) Cervecería Morito is the undisputed
king of Burgos tapas bars and as such it's
always crowded. A typical order is *alpargata*
(lashings of cured ham with bread, tomato
and olive oil) or the *revueltos Capricho de
Burgos* (scrambled eggs served with potatoes,
blood sausage, red peppers, baby eels and
mushrooms) – the latter is a meal in itself.

🛏 Hotel
Norte y Londres　　　Historic Hotel €
(📞947 26 41 25; www.hotelnorteylondres.com;
Plaza de Alonso Martínez 10; s/d from €40/45;
🅿 @ 🛜) Set in a former 16th-century palace
and decorated with understated period charm,
this fine, family-run hotel has spacious rooms
with antique furnishings and polished wooden
floors. All rooms have pretty balconies and
double-glazed windows; those on the 4th floor are
more modern. The bathrooms are exceptionally
large and the service friendly and efficient.

Soria ⑪

✕ Baluarte　　　　　　　Castilian €€€
(📞975 21 36 58; www.baluarte.info; Calle de los
Caballeros 14; set menus €57-70; 🕐1.30-4pm
& 8.45-10.45pm Tue-Sat, 1.30-4pm Sun) Óscar
García Marina is one of Spain's most exciting
chefs and this Michelin-starred venture in
Soria appropriately showcases his culinary
talents. Dishes are based on classic Castilian
ingredients but treated with just enough foam
and drizzle to ensure that they're both exciting
and satisfying without being too pretentious.
Reservations essential.

🛏 Apolonia　　　　Boutique Hotel €€
(📞975 23 90 56; www.hotelapoloniasoria.com;
Puertas de Pro 5; s/d from €60/68; ❄ @ 🛜)
This smart hotel has a contemporary urban
feel with its charcoal, brown and cream colour
scheme, abundance of glass, abstract artwork
and, in four of the rooms, an interesting, if
revealing, colour-lighting effect between the
main room and the large walk-in shower –
possibly best for romancing couples.

Back Roads Beyond Madrid

2

This trip through the Spanish capital's hinterland is a cracker, taking in some of Spain's most eye-catching old cities and more beautiful villages.

TRIP HIGHLIGHTS

72 km

Toledo
Historic centre with architecture spanning civilisations

522 km

Sigüenza
Historic architecture at every turn

Atienza

6

START
MADRID

Guadalajara

Alcalá de Henares
FINISH

4

2

Tarancón

5

Chinchón
One of Spain's most memorable town squares

Cuenca
Dramatically sited town with remarkable views

141 km

262 km

5–7 DAYS
664KM / 413 MILES

GREAT FOR...

BEST TIME TO GO

April to May or September to October for milder weather.

 ESSENTIAL PHOTO

The *casas colgadas* (hanging houses) of Cuenca.

 BEST FOR HISTORY

Toledo is extraordinarily rich in historical landmarks.

nca *Casas colgadas* (hanging houses; p56)

2 Back Roads Beyond Madrid

Travel south and east of Madrid and you won't have to go too far to encounter some pretty special places, taking in former royal playgrounds (Aranjuez), a storied university town (Alcalá De Henares), lovely villages (Chinchón and Atienza) and some of Spain's most spectacular old cities (Toledo, Cuenca and Sigüenza). Throw in castles, quiet back roads and an astonishing architectural portfolio and this trip is definitely a keeper.

① Madrid

Madrid is the kind of city that gets under your skin the longer you stay. Art-lovers will adore the galleries on offer, especially the Museo del Prado (p43), Museo Thyssen-Bornemisza (p43) and Centro de Arte Reina Sofía (p43). Fabulous food and an irresistible tapas culture is another Madrid speciality, showcasing the best that Spain has to offer in one place.

The Drive » The quickest way to get to Toledo from Madrid by road (72km) is along the dual-carriageway N401 that runs southwest of the capital. And in this case there's no advantage to taking quieter B roads – the flatlands between the two cities are not Spain's prettiest.

TRIP HIGHLIGHT

② Toledo

Perched dramatically on a steep ridge high above the Río Tajo, Toledo looms large in the nation's history and consciousness as a religious centre, bulwark of the Spanish church, and once-flourishing symbol of a multicultural medieval society. The old town today is a treasure chest of churches, museums, synagogues and mosques set in a labyrinth of narrow streets, plazas and inner patios.

✗ 🛏 p59, 92

The Drive » Aranjuez lies just 48 rather dull kilometres northeast of Toledo along the N400.

③ Aranjuez

Just back inside the Comunidad de Madrid, Aranjuez couldn't be more different than Madrid, and therein lies its whole raison d'etre: Aranjuez was founded as a royal pleasure retreat, an escape for Spanish nobility from

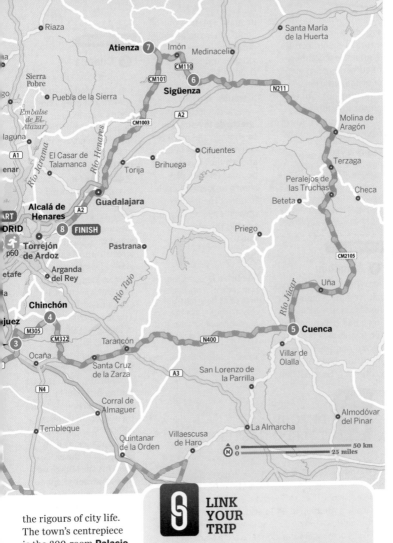

the rigours of city life. The town's centrepiece is the 300-room **Palacio Real** (☎91 891 07 40; www. patrimonionacional.es; palace adult/concession €9/4, guide/ audio guide €4/3, EU citizens & residents last 3hr Wed & Thu free, gardens free; ☺palace 10am-8pm Apr-Sep, to 6pm Oct-Mar, gardens

LINK YOUR TRIP

1 **Historic Castilla y León**

Visit some of Spain's most appealing cities north and west of Madrid.

5 **Route of Don Quixote**

Beginning in Toledo, go in search Spain's errant knight of literary fame.

8am–9.30pm mid-Jun–mid-Aug, shorter hours rest of year), a sprawling, gracefully symmetrical complex filled with a cornucopia of ornamentation. Sweeping out into the palace grounds are stately gardens and royal pavilions.

The Drive » The expansive royal gardens of Aranjuez segue nicely into pretty riverine woodlands lining the M305, which follows the Río Tajo east of town then breaks away northeast to Chinchón, 21km from Aranjuez.

TRIP HIGHLIGHT

④ Chinchón

Arriving in Chinchón, you may wonder what all the fuss is about – a modern town has grown out from the town's old core. But persist and you'll discover that Chinchón's old centre may be small, but its main square is one of Spain's more memorable *plazas mayores*. The village's unique, almost circular **Plaza Mayor** is lined with sagging, tiered balconies and is watched over by the 16th-century **Iglesia de la Asunción**. In summer the plaza is converted into a bullring and it's the stage for a popular Passion play shown at Easter. Lunch in one of the *mesones* (tavern-style restaurants) around the plaza is a must.

✕ p59

The Drive » From Chinchón, take the M311 southeast, then head south along the CM322, crossing the Río Tajo en route. At Villarubia de Santiago, turn left (east) along the N400. After 35km you'll pass through Tarancón. Stay on the N400 for a further 86km to reach Cuenca.

DETOUR: TOLEDO CASTLES

Start: ② Toledo

The area around Toledo is rich with castles in varying states of upkeep. Situated some 20km southeast of Toledo along the CM42 is the dramatic ruined Arab castle of **Almonacid de Toledo**. A few kilometres further down the road is a smaller castle in the village of **Mascaraque**. Continue on to Mora, where the 12th-century **Castillo Peñas Negras**, 3km from town, is on the site of a prehistoric necropolis; follow the sandy track to reach the castle for stunning big-sky views of the surrounding plains. Next, head for the small, pretty town of **Orgaz**, which has a handsome, well-preserved 15th-century **castle**. Around 30km southwest of Toledo, the hulking 12th-century Templar ruin of **Castillo de Montalbán** stands sentinel over the Río Torcón valley.

TRIP HIGHLIGHT

⑤ Cuenca

Coming from the west, Cuenca's modern town sprawls out across the plains with little to inspire, but climbing the hill between the gorges of Ríos Júcar and Huécar to the east is one of Spain's most memorable cities. Its old centre is a Unesco World Heritage stage-set of evocative medieval buildings. Just wandering the narrow streets, tunnels and staircases, stopping every now and again to admire the majestic views, is the chief pleasure of Cuenca. The most striking element of medieval Cuenca, the *casas colgadas* (hanging houses) jut out precariously over the steep defile of Río Huécar. Dating from the 14th century, the houses, with their layers of wooden balconies, seem to emerge from the rock as if an extension of the cliffs; one contains the **Museo de Arte Abstracto Español** (Museum of Abstract Art; 📞969 21 29 83; www.march.es/arte/cuenca; Calle Canónigos; ⏰11am-2pm & 4-6pm Tue-Fri, 11am-2pm & 4-8pm Sat, 11am-2.30pm Sun), another an excellent restaurant. For the best views of the *casas colgadas*, cross the Puente de San Pablo footbridge or walk to the mirador at the northernmost tip of the old town. Also don't miss the **catedral** (📞969

ANGEL L/SHUTTERSTOCK ©

Sigüenza Plaza Mayor

22 46 26, 649 693600; www.
catedralcuenca.es; Plaza Mayor;
€5; ☺10am-7.30pm Jul-Oct,
to 6.30pm Apr-Jun, to 5.30pm
Nov-Mar) or the **Museo de
la Semana Santa** (☏969
22 19 56; www.msscuenca.
org; Calle Andrés de Cabrera
13; adult/child €3/free;
☺11am-2pm & 4.30-7.30pm
Thu-Sat, 11am-2pm Sun, closed
Aug), which celebrates
the city's famous Easter
processions.

✖ 🛏 p59

The Drive » There are faster
ways to get from Cuenca to
Sigüenza but we recommend
taking the narrow CM2105 to
cross the heavily wooded and
decidedly craggy Serranía de
Cuenca. After tracking northeast
across the mountains, continue
north to the A211 and then follow
the signs to Sigüenza. Plan on
at least six hours for this stretch.

TRIP HIGHLIGHT

⑥ Sigüenza

Your prize for a long day
in the saddle from Cuenca
is Sigüenza: sleepy,
historic and filled with
the ghosts of a turbulent
past. The town is built
on a low hill cradled by
Río Henares, and the
beautiful 16th-century
Plaza Mayor is the ideal
place to begin exploring.
Rising up from the heart
of the old town, the
city's centrepiece, the
catedral (☏949 39 10 23;
www.lacatedraldesiguenza.
com; Plaza del Obispo Don
Bernardo; adult/child €6/4.50;

☺10.30am-7pm), was badly
damaged during Spain's
Civil War but was largely
rebuilt. Calle Mayor
heads south up the hill
from the cathedral to
a magnificent-looking
castle, which was
originally built by the
Romans and was, in
turn, a Moorish *alcázar*
(fortress), a royal palace,
an asylum and an army
barracks; it's now a
luxury hotel.

🛏 p59

The Drive » After the long
drive from Cuenca to Sigüenza,
the pretty 31km to Atienza will
feel like you've hardly had time
to get out of third gear. Take the
CM110 northwest, then west,
then northwest again.

Toledo (p54)

7 Atienza

Atienza is one of those charming walled medieval villages, crowned by yet another castle ruin, that seems to appear with anything-but-monotonous regularity in the most out-of-the-way places in inland Spain. The main half-timbered square and former 16th-century marketplace, **Plaza del Trigo**, is overlooked by the Renaissance **Iglesia San Juan Bautista**, which has an impressive organ and lavish gilt *retablo* (alterpiece). There are several more mostly Romanesque churches, three of which hold small museums.

The Drive » Meandering generally south from Atienza, the CM101 twists and turns for 33km to Jadraque, from where the equally quiet CM1003 tracks southwest until just short of the regional capital of Guadalajara. Having rejoined the main motorway, the N2, there's nothing for it but to stick with it all the way into Alcalá De Henares. Total distance 111km.

8 Alcalá de Henares

Alcalá de Henares is first and foremost a university town, replete with historical sandstone buildings seemingly at every turn. Founded in 1486, the **Universidad de Alcalá** (91 883 43 84; www.uah.es; guided tours €5; 9am-9pm) is one of the country's principal seats of learning. A guided tour gives a peek into the Mudéjar chapel and the magnificent Paraninfo auditorium, where the king and queen of Spain give out the prestigious Premio Cervantes literary award every year. But Alcalá has another string to its bow – this is the birthplace of writer Miguel de Cervantes Saavedra, and his birthplace is recreated in the illuminating museum, the **Museo Casa Natal de Miguel de Cervantes** (91 889 96 54; www.museocasanataldecervantes.org; Calle Mayor 48; 10am-6pm Tue-Fri, to 7pm Sat & Sun), which lies along the beautiful, colonnaded Calle Mayor. Throw in some sunny squares and a young student population and it's an ideal place to catch the buzz you'll find in Madrid without the hassles of being back in the big city.

Eating & Sleeping

Toledo ②

🍴 Alfileritos 24
Spanish €€

(📞925 23 96 25; www.alfileritos24.com; Calle de los Alfileritos 24; mains €19-22, bar food €6-12; ⏰1.30-4pm & 8-11.30pm) The 14th-century surroundings of columns, beams and barrel-vault ceilings are cleverly coupled with modern artwork and bright dining rooms in an atrium space spread over four floors. The menu demonstrates an innovative flourish in the kitchen, with dishes such as cannelloni stuffed with Iberian pulled pork, partridge with mushroom marinade, and trout with beets and fennel.

🛏 Hacienda del Cardenal
Historic Hotel €€

(📞925 22 49 00; www.haciendadelcardenal. com; Paseo de Recaredo 24; r incl breakfast €112-183; ❄🛜🅿) This wonderful 18th-century former cardinal's mansion has pale ochre-coloured walls, Moorish-inspired arches and stately columns. Some rooms are grand and others are more simply furnished, but all come with dark furniture, plush fabrics and parquet floors. Several overlook the glorious terraced gardens. Attached is a fabulous restaurant (p92).

Underground parking is available nearby (€15 per day).

Chinchón ④

🍴 Café de la Iberia
Spanish €€

(📞91 894 08 47; www.cafedelaiberia.com; Plaza Mayor 17; mains €13-28; ⏰12.30-4.30pm & 8-10.30pm) This is definitely our favourite of the *mesones* on the Plaza Mayor. It offers wonderful food, including succulent roast lamb, served by attentive staff in an atmospheric dining area set around a light-filled internal courtyard (where Goya is said to have visited) or, if you can get a table, out on the balcony.

Cuenca ⑤

🍴 Figón del Huécar
Spanish €€€

(📞969 24 00 62; www.figondelhuecar.es; Ronda de Julián Romero 6; mains €18-25, set menus €26-36; ⏰1.30-3.30pm & 9-10.30pm Tue-Sat, 1.30-3.30pm Sun; 🛜) With a romantic terrace offering spectacular views, Figón del Huécar is a highlight of old-town eating. Roast suckling pig, lamb stuffed with pine nuts and foie gras, and a host of Castilian specialities are presented and served with panache. The house used to be the home of Spanish singer José Luis Perales.

🛏 Posada de San José
Historic Hotel €€

(📞969 21 13 00; www.posadasanjose.com; Ronda de Julián Romero 4; s/d €65/90, with shared bathroom €37/52, d with view €97-162; ❄@🛜) This 17th-century former choir school retains an extraordinary monastic charm with its labyrinth of rooms, eclectic artwork, uneven floors and original tiles. All rooms are different; cheaper ones are in former priests' cells and share bathrooms, while more costly doubles combine homey comfort with old-world charm. Several have balconies with dramatic views of the gorge.

There's a reputable restaurant on the ground floor.

Sigüenza ⑥

🛏 El Doncel
Hotel €€

(📞949 39 00 01; www.eldoncel.com; Paseo de la Alameda 3; d €60-80; ❄🛜) With earthy colours, exposed stone, spot lighting, fridges (for the *cava*), and marshmallow-soft duvets and pillows, this place is aimed squarely at couples on a romantic weekend away from Madrid. It's comfortable and attractive, and the on-site restaurant is one of the best in town.

STRETCH YOUR LEGS
MADRID

Start/Finish Plaza Mayor

Distance 3.8km

Duration Two to three hours

Madrid's compact and historic centre is ideal for exploring on foot. So much of Madrid life occurs on the streets and in its glorious plazas, and it all takes place against a spectacular backdrop of architecture, stately and grand.

Take this walk on Trips

1 2 4

Plaza Mayor

So many Madrid stories begin in its grand central square. Since it was laid out in 1619, the Plaza Mayor has seen everything from bullfights to the trials of the Spanish Inquisition. These days the grandeur of the plaza owes much to the warm colours of the uniformly ochre apartments, with 237 wrought-iron balconies offset by the exquisite frescoes of the 17th-century **Real Casa de la Panadería** (Royal Bakery).

The Walk ≫ Walk down Calle de Postas off the plaza's northeastern corner, cross busy Plaza de la Puerta del Sol, then continue east along Carrera de San Jerónimo. At elegant Plaza de Canalejas, turn right.

Plaza de Santa Ana

There are few more iconic Madrid squares than Plaza de Santa Ana, a local favourite since Joseph Bonaparte carved it out of this crowded inner-city neighbourhood in 1810. Surrounded by classic Madrid architecture of pastel shades, the plaza presides over the Barrio de las Letras. The outdoor tables are among the city's most sought-after.

The Walk ≫ Walking west, cross Plaza del Ángel, walk along Calle de la Bolsa, cross Calle de Toledo and make for Calle de la Cava Baja, a glorious medieval street lined with tapas bars. Keep Iglesia de San Andrés on your right, and stroll down the hill to Plaza de la Paja.

Plaza de la Paja

Delightful 'Straw Sq' slopes down into the tangle of lanes that once made up Madrid's Muslim quarter. In the 12th and 13th centuries the city's main market occupied the square and it retains a palpable medieval air, and at times can feel like a Castilian village square. **Delic** (☎91 364 54 50; www.delic. es; Costanilla de San Andrés 14; ☺11am-2am Sun & Tue-Thu, to 2.30am Fri & Sat; ⓂLa Latina), with tables on the plaza, is brilliant for a mojito, while **Jardín del Príncipe Anglona** (☺10am-10pm Apr-Oct, to 6.30pm Nov-Mar; ⓂLa Latina), a walled 18th-century garden, is a peaceful oasis in the heart of this most clamorous of cities.

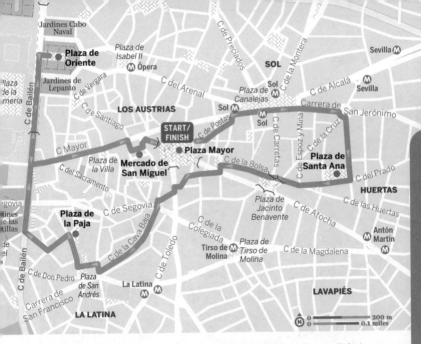

The Walk >> Take any lane heading west through La Morería, the old Muslim quarter, to Calle de Bailén. Turn right, cross the viaduct, pass the cathedral and continue to Plaza de Oriente.

Plaza de Oriente

Cinematic in scope, Plaza de Oriente is grand and graceful. It's watched over by the **Palacio Real** (📞91 454 87 00; www.patrimonionacional.es; Calle de Bailén; adult/concession €10/5, guide/audio guide €4, EU citizens free last 2hr Mon-Thu; ⏱10am-8pm Apr-Sep, to 6pm Oct-Mar; **M**Ópera) and the **Teatro Real** (📞91 516 06 96; www.teatro-real.com; guided tour €8-30, audio guide €7; ⏱ guided visits 10am-1pm, self-guided visits 10.30am-4.30pm Sep-Jul & 10am-6pm Aug; **M**Ópera) – Madrid's opera house – sophisticated cafes, and apartments that cost the equivalent of a royal salary. At the centre of the plaza is an equestrian statue of Felipe IV designed by Velázquez, and nearby are some 20 marble statues, mostly of ancient monarchs. Local legend holds

that these royals get down off their pedestals at night to stretch their legs.

The Walk >> Return south along Calle de Bailén, then turn left (east) up Calle Mayor. After passing the intimate Plaza de la Villa on your right, Mercado de San Miguel appears, also on your right as you climb the hill.

Mercado de San Miguel

One of Madrid's oldest and most beautiful markets, the **Mercado de San Miguel** (📞91 542 49 36; www.mercadodesanmiguel.es; Plaza de San Miguel; tapas from €1; ⏱10am-midnight Sun-Thu, to 1am Fri & Sat; **M**Sol) is now an exciting gastronomic space. Within the early-20th-century glass walls, stalls serve up all manner of tapas, from fishy *pintxos* atop mini toasts to *jamón* or other cured meats from Salamanca, cheeses, pickled goodies and fine wines.

The Walk >> To return to where you started, leave the market, walk down Calle de la Cava de San Miguel, turn left and climb the stairs through the Arco de los Cuchilleros to the Plaza Mayor.

The Forgotten West

3

From medieval Cáceres to Parque Natural Arribes del Duero, this journey takes you along some of the country's quietest roads and to the least visited villages in Spain's west.

TRIP HIGHLIGHTS

464km

Ciudad Rodrigo
Glorious sandstone architecture within medieval walls

Parque Natural Arribes del Duero

FINISH
Lumbrales

405km

San Martín del Castañar
Fabulous village of fine architecture away from well-travelled routes

17

15

Bejar

305km

Granadilla
Haunting abandoned village by the water's edge

12

Valverde de la Vera

7

Cáceres
START

Cuacos de Yuste
Classic La Vera architecture with an unlikely royal monastery

156km

4–6 DAYS
538KM / 335 MILES

GREAT FOR...

BEST TIME TO GO

From March to May and September to November, to avoid summer's searing heat and winter's bitter cold.

ESSENTIAL PHOTO

The half-timbered houses of La Alberca.

BEST FOR FOODIES

Valle del Jerte during the cherry harvest in May.

3 The Forgotten West

This journey begins in Cáceres and ends high above the canyons north of Ciudad Rodrigo. In between, we take you through the forgotten villages and food culture of La Vera and the Sierra de Francia. In Cáceres, Plasencia and Ciudad Rodrigo, you'll experience three of Spain's most underrated cities, but the heart and soul of this journey is the opportunity to soak up village life far from tourist Spain.

❶ Cáceres

The old core of Cáceres can seem like little more than a rumour as you make your way through the modern suburbs that surround it. But no sooner have you set foot in the Plaza Mayor than the city begins to work its magic. The Plaza itself is a glorious variation on the fine Spanish tradition of town squares as the focal point and architectural highpoint of local life. But in Cáceres it's just the beginning. Climb the steps, pass beneath the Arco de la Estrella and you enter another world of cobblestone streets free of traffic, imposing palaces and churches, and the unmistakeable sense of an ancient world, silent and somehow intact five centuries after its heyday.

🛏 p101

The Drive ❯❯ Casar de Cáceres lies around 12km north of Cáceres and is well signposted off the N630 to Plasencia.

❷ Casar de Cáceres

Extremadura may be well known for its *jamón* but one of its cheeses is equally celebrated in Spanish culinary circles. The Torta del Casar is a pungent, creamy cheese that's aged for 40 days and eaten most often as a spread on *tostas* (toasts) or even with a steak. The otherwise nondescript town of Casar de Cáceres, where the whole place can seem deserted on a summer's afternoon, is where the cheese was born and its main street is lined with shops selling the

local product. There's even the small **Museo de Queso** (📞 927 290 081; Calle Barrionuevo Bajo 7; 🕙 10am-2pm & 4-6pm Tue-Sat, 10am-2pm Sun) dedicated to it.

The Drive » It's just 4km from Casar de Cáceres back to the N630, then 11km north to where the EX302 branches off to the west. A further 11km across low, scrubby and strangely appealing hills brings you to Garrovillas.

---

❸ Garrovillas

At first glance (and the sensation can stay with you longer if you lose yourself in the confusing tangle of streets), Garrovillas looks like any rural Extremaduran village, with whitewashed houses, shuttered windows and locals who stop to stare as you drive past. But you'll be rewarded if you persist into the village

---

🔗 LINK YOUR TRIP

1 Historic Castilla y León

To reach Salamanca and join this trip, drive 77km northeast of La Alberca, or 89km northeast of Ciudad Rodrigo.

6 Ancient Extremadura

The trajectories of these two trips intersect at Cáceres before going their separate ways.

centre and to the truly remarkable Plaza Mayor, which is surrounded by arched porticoes. It's one of the prettiest in Extremadura, and that's no small claim.

The Drive >> Return to the N630, turn left (north) and be ready to stop around 7km further on for a fine lookout over the Embalse de Alcantará (Alcantará dam). The road thereafter sweeps northeast and 45km later you arrive in Plasencia.

 Plasencia

Rising above a bend of the Río Jerte, Plasencia, which retains long sections of its defensive walls, is quite a sight. Inside the town, life flows through the lively, arcaded Plaza Mayor, meeting place of 10 streets and scene of a Tuesday farmers market since the 12th century. The best-preserved defensive tower of the old city wall, located at the top of the old town, has been converted into the **Centro de Interpretación de la Ciudad Medieval** (☏927 01 78 42; Plaza de Torre Lucía; ☺10am-2pm & 5-8pm Tue-Sat Jun-Sep, 10am-2pm & 4-7pm Tue-Sat Oct-May, 10am-2pm Sun all year), which tells the history of medieval Plasencia and provides access to a walkable chunk of the wall. Romanesque churches are something of a Plasencia speciality. Part of the **catedral** (☏927 42 44 06; www.catedralde plasencia.org; Plaza de la Catedral; adult/child €4/free; ☺11am-2pm & 5-8pm Apr-Sep, 11am-2pm & 4-7pm Tue-Sun Oct-Mar) is the Romanesque Catedral Vieja with the classic 13th-century cloister surrounding a trickling fountain and lemon trees, alongside the 16th-century Catedral Nueva, a Gothic-Renaissance blend with a handsome plateresque facade, soaring *retablo* and intricately carved choir stalls. Also in this double-barrelled cathedral is the soaring octagonal Capilla de San Pablo, with a dramatic 1569 Caravaggio painting of John the Baptist.

🛏 p73

DETOUR: PARQUE NACIONAL DE MONFRAGÜE

Start: ④ Plasencia

Spain's 14th and newest national park is a hilly paradise for birdwatchers and a wonderful place to enjoy Extremadura's diverse topography. Straddling the Tajo valley, the park is home to spectacular colonies of raptors and more than 75% of Spain's protected species. Among some 175 feathered varieties are around 300 pairs of black vultures (the largest concentration of Europe's biggest bird of prey) and small populations of two other rare large birds: the Spanish imperial eagle and the black stork. The best time to visit is between March and October, since many bird species winter in Africa.

Signed walking trails criss-cross the park, and gateways include the pretty hamlet of **Villareal de San Carlos**, from where most trails leave. The EX208 road also traverses the park and the hilltop **Castillo de Monfragüe** – a ruined 9th-century Islamic fort – has sweeping views. The castle can also be reached via an attractive 1½-hour walk from Villareal. Arguably the best spot is the **Mirador del Salto del Gitano**, a lookout point along the main road. From here, there are stunning views across the river gorge to the **Peña Falcón** crag.

To get to the park, drive south from Plasencia along the EX208. The park begins around 24km south of Plasencia.

RUTA DE LA PLATA

As you travel between Extremadura and Castilla y León, you may see signs designating the route as 'Autovía Ruta de la Plata'. The name of this ancient thoroughfare (aka Ruta de la Plata) probably derives not from the word for 'silver' (*plata* in modern Spanish), but the Arabic *bilath*, meaning tiled or paved. But it was the Romans in the 1st century who laid this artery that originally linked Mérida with Astorga and was later extended to the Asturian coast. Along its length moved goods, troops, travellers and traders – you're following in a fine, ancient tradition. Later, it served as a pilgrim route for the faithful walking from Andalucía to Santiago de Compostela and it's now increasingly a rival to the much more crowded Camino de Santiago. From Seville, it's a 1000km walk or cycle to Santiago or a similar distance to Gijón. Entering Extremadura south of Zafra, the well-marked route passes through Mérida, Cáceres and Plasencia, then heads for Salamanca in Castilla y León. Take a look at www.rutadelaplata.com or pick up the guide (€3) from tourist offices on the route.

The Drive » It's time to leave behind busy roads and disappear into the remote valleys of La Vera. Take the EX203 east of Palencia, and take the turn-off to Pasarón de la Vera after a rocking and rolling 25km.

⑤ Pasarón de la Vera

Pasarón de la Vera is a pretty, tranquil village nestled in a valley. It's a suitably gentle introduction to the charms of La Vera, with abundant stonework, a stone fountain in the main square and occasional half-timbered houses. Aside from a peaceful timeworn air, the standout attraction is the emotive 16th-century palace **Condes de Osorno**, featuring an open-arcaded gallery decorated with medallions.

The Drive » Twist down along the contours of La Vera's hills for around 8km to Jaraiz de la Vera.

⑥ Jaraiz de la Vera

Every Spanish cook knows that *pimentón de la Vera* (La Vera paprika, either sweet or spicy) has no peers, and Jaraiz de la Vera is where much of this fabled condiment comes from. With such success has come a certain prosperity; for this reason the buildings are a little grander and the atmosphere a touch less charming than other villages in the area. But do stop long enough to buy a tin of *pimentón* at the source. Your Spanish friends will be impressed indeed.

✕ p73

The Drive » Cuacos de Yuste lies just 8km northeast of Jaraiz along a particularly serpentine section of the EX203.

TRIP HIGHLIGHT

⑦ Cuacos de Yuste

Cuacos de Yuste ranks among the loveliest of La Vera's villages and it's here that you'll find one of the richest concentrations of La Vera's architectural speciality: half-timbered houses leaning at odd angles, their overhanging upper storeys supported by timber or stone pillars. In particular, seek out lovely Plaza Fuente Los Chorros, which surrounds a 16th-century fountain, and Plaza Juan de Austria, built on a rock, with its bust of Carlos I. And in a surprising twist, in a lovely setting 2km above the village, the **Monasterio de Yuste** (☎902 044 454; www.patrimonionacional.es; Carretera de Yuste, Cuacos de

EASTER SUFFERING

At midnight on the eve of Good Friday in Valverde de la Vera, Los Empalaos (literally 'the Impaled'), in the form of several penitent locals, strap their arms to a beam (from a plough) while their near-naked bodies are wrapped tight with cords from waist to fingertips. Barefoot, veiled, with two swords strapped to their backs and wearing a crown of thorns, these 'walking crucifixes' follow a painful Way of the Cross. Iron chains hanging from the timber clank sinisterly as the penitents make painful progress through the crowds. Guided by *cirineos* (who pick them up should they fall), the *empalaos* occasionally cross paths. When this happens, they kneel and rise again to continue their laborious journey. Doctors stay on hand, as being so tightly strapped does nothing good for blood circulation.

Yuste; adult/concession €7/4, guide €4, EU & Latin American citizens & residents Wed & last 3hr Sun free; ⊙10am-8pm Tue-Sun Apr-Sep, to 6pm Oct-Mar; **P**) is where Carlos I came in 1557 to prepare for death after abdicating his emperorship over much of Western and Central Europe. It's a soulful, evocative place amid the forested hills and a tranquil counterpoint to the grandeur of so many formerly royal buildings elsewhere in Spain.

The Drive ≫ Jarandilla de la Vera lies a winding 10km northeast of Cuacos de Yuste along the EX203.

❽ Jarandilla de la Vera

Jarandilla is one of the most appealing stops in La Vera. Its castle-like church, on Plaza de la Constitución, was built by the Templars and features an ancient font brought from the Holy Land. And it's almost worth coming

here just to stay in the magnificent, fortress-like *parador* (luxurious state-owned hotel), set against a backdrop of pretty wooded hillsides.

🛏 p73

The Drive ≫ The EX203 shows no signs of straightening out as it tracks east for 18km from Jarandilla to Valverde de la Vera.

❾ Valverde de la Vera

Valverde de la Vera is another classic La Vera hamlet – its lovely Plaza de España is lined with timber balconies, and water gushes down ruts etched into the cobbled lanes. It's also the scene for Extremadura's most haunting Easter celebrations, Los Empalaos.

The Drive ≫ Return back down the road to Cuacos de la Yuste (this is one road that's worth driving twice), then climb back up to the Monasterio de Yuste, from where a narrow road with fine views continues 7km further on to Garganta la Olla.

❿ Garganta la Olla

Garganta la Olla is a picturesque, steeply pitched village with ancient door lintels inscribed with its 16th-century date of construction and name of the original owner. Seek out the Casa de las Muñecas at No 3 on the main Calle Chorillo. The 'House of the Dolls' gets its name from the much-weathered carving of a woman on the stone archway. Painted in blue, the come-on colour of the time, it was a brothel under Carlos I and now houses a far drearier souvenir shop. Another distinctive house is the Casa de Postas Posada de Viajeros (look for the plaque at the top of the street), an inn for travellers and reputedly used by Carlos I.

The Drive ≫ From Garganta la Olla, take the spectacular drive over the Sierra de Tormantos and the 1269m Puerto de Piornal pass to the Valle del Jerte (around one hour). The road passes through thick forests with breaks in the trees opening out onto some lovely views on both sides of the pass.

---

⑪ Valle del Jerte

This valley reinforces northern Extremadura's claims as a foodie hub. For a start, Piornal (1200m), on the southeast flank of the valley and the first village you come to as you descend from the Puerto de Piornal, is famous for its *jamón serrano* (serrano ham). Further down the slopes, the Valle del Jerte grows half of Spain's cherries and is a sea of white blossom in early spring. Visit in May and every second house is busy boxing the ripe fruit. Continue northeast along the valley floor and you'll come to Cabezuela del Valle where the Plaza de Extremadura area has some fine houses with overhanging wooden balconies.

The Drive » A spectacular, winding 35km road leads from just north of Cabezuela over the 1430m Puerto de Honduras to Hervás in the Valle del Ambroz. From Hervás, it's around 25km west to Granadilla.

TRIP HIGHLIGHT

⑫ Granadilla

The ghost village of **Granadilla** (☎927 01 49 75; Carretera CC168; ⏰10am-1.30pm & 4-8pm Tue-Sun Apr-Oct, 10am-1.30pm & 4-6pm Tue-Sun Nov-Mar; P) is a beguiling reminder of how Extremadura's villages must have looked before the rush to modernisation. Founded by the Moors in the 9th century but abandoned in the 1960s when the nearby dam was built, the village's traditional architecture has been painstakingly restored as part of a government educational project. You enter the village through the narrow Puerta de Villa, overlooked by the sturdy castle. From here, the cobblestone Calle Mayor climbs up to the delightfully rustic Plaza Mayor. Some buildings function as craft workshops or exhibition

DETOUR:
SIERRA DE GATA & LAS HURDES

Start: ⑫ **Granadilla**

Remote and forgotten mountain ranges are a speciality in this corner of Extremadura and western Castilla y León, and they don't come much further off the beaten track than the Sierra de Gata and Las Hurdes in Extremadura's far north. The prettiest villages in the Sierra de Gata include Hoyos and San Martín de Trevejo, where people speak their own isolated dialect, a unique mix of Spanish and Portuguese. In Valverde del Fresno, **A Velha Fábrica** (☎659 113 673; www.avelhafabrica. com; Calle Carrasco 24, Valverde del Fresno; s/d incl breakfast €66/96; P ❀ 🛜 🐕) is a great small hotel set in a former textile mill.

The Las Hurdes region has taken nearly a century to shake off its image of poverty, disease, and chilling tales of witchcraft and even cannibalism. In 1922 the miserable existence of the *hurdanos* prompted Alfonso XIII to declare during a horseback tour, 'I can bear to see no more'. Head for villages like Casares and Ladrillar, with traditional stone, slate-roofed houses huddled in clusters, while the PR40 is a near-circular route from Casares that follows ancient shepherd trails.

From the N630, the EX205 runs west along the southern shore of the Embalse de Gabriel y Galán and into the Sierra de Gata. Close to the halfway point, the EX204 runs north into the heart of Las Hurdes.

centres in summer; make sure also to walk your way along the top of the Almohad walls, with evocative views of village, lake and pinewoods.

The Drive ≫ Return to the N630, the main and busiest road link between Extremadura and Castilla y León. Soon after crossing into the latter, follow the signs to Béjar and the climb up the steep, narrow and winding mountain road to Candelario (around an hour from Granadilla).

- - - - - - - - - - - - - - - -

⑬ Candelario

Candelario is your introduction to the Sierra de Béjar, which is home to more delightful villages and rolling mountain scenery; the peaks around here are normally snowcapped until well after Easter. Nudging against a steep rock face, tiny and charming Candelario is easily the pick of the villages, dominated as it is by mountain architecture of stone-and-wood houses clustered closely together to protect against the harsh winter climate. It is a popular summer resort and a great base for hiking.

The Drive ≫ Return to Béjar, cross the N630 and continue northwest along the marvellously serpentine SA515, passing small villages en route, such as Cristóbal and Miranda del Castañar. You'll see Mogarraz, high on a ridge, long before you arrive, around 45 minutes after leaving Candelario.

- - - - - - - - - - - - - - - -

⑭ Mogarraz

Mogarraz has some of the most evocative old houses in the region and is famous for its *embutidos* (cured meats), as well as the more recent novelty of over 400 portraits of past and present residents, painted by local artist Florencio Maillo and on display outside the family homes. The history of this extraordinary project dates from the 1960s when poverty was rife and many locals were seeking work, mainly in South America. They needed identity cards and it is these that inspired the portraits. Buy some *jamón*, admire the portraits and generally slow down to the pace of village life in this remote corner of the country.

DOLORES GIRALDEZ ALONSO/SHUTTERSTOCK ©

The Drive ≫ Roads wind along the walls of the Sierra de Francia's steep hills and by bearing generally north (losing yourself with the greatest of pleasure on occasion), you'll come to San Martín del Castañar. The whole trip shouldn't take longer than 30 minutes.

- - - - - - - - - - - - - - - -

⑮ San Martín del Castañar

If you dream of a village utterly unchanged by the passing years and retaining that sense of unspoiled community and blissful isolation, San Martín del Castañar could just be your place.

LA VERA FOOD BOUNTY

Surrounded by mountains often still capped with snow as late as May, the fertile La Vera region produces raspberries, asparagus and, above all, *pimentón* (paprika), sold in charming old-fashioned tins and with a distinctive smoky flavour.

Granadilla (p69)

It's the sort of village where old folk pass the day chatting on doorsteps and there's scarcely a modern building to be seen – it's all half-timbered houses, stone fountains, flowers cascading from balconies and there's a bubbling stream. At the top of the village there's a small rural bullring, next to the renovated castle and historic cemetery.

The Drive » Roads west of San Martín straighten out a little and there are fine views of the Peña de Francia (1732m), the Sierra's highest, craggiest point, up ahead. At the SA202, turn left and roll on into La Alberca. It should take 20 minutes all up.

----

16 La Alberca

La Alberca is one of the largest and most beautifully preserved of Sierra de Francia's villages, a historic and harmonious huddle of narrow alleys flanked by gloriously ramshackle houses built of stone, wood beams and plaster. Look for the date they were built (typically late 18th century) carved into the door lintels. Numerous stores sell local products such as *jamón,* as well as baskets and the inevitable tackier souvenirs. The centre is pretty-as-a-postcard Plaza Mayor; there's a market here on Saturday mornings. Our only word of warning: this is the busiest of the Sierra de Francia's towns, so try to avoid visiting on weekends when the tour buses roll in.

✕ ⊨ p73

The Drive » Return back up the SA202, then turn left (northwest) onto the C515 which takes you across less precipitous country into Ciudad Rodrigo (50km from La Alberca).

TRIP HIGHLIGHT

17 Ciudad Rodrigo

Close to the Portuguese border and away from well-travelled tourist routes, somnambulant Ciudad Rodrigo is one of the prettier towns in western Castilla y León and its walled old town is home to some of the best-preserved plateresque architecture outside of Salamanca.

The elegant, weathered sandstone **Catedral de Santa María** (www.catedralciudadrodrigo.com; Plaza de San Salvador 1; adult/concession €3/2.50, 4-6pm Sun free, tower €2; ☺church & museum 11.30am-2pm Mon, 11.30am-2pm & 4-7pm Tue-Sat, noon-2pm & 4-6pm Sun), begun in 1165, towers over the historic centre, while the long, sloping Plaza Mayor is another fine centrepiece – the double-storey arches of the Casa Consistorial are stunning, but the plaza's prettiest building is the **Casa del Marqués de Cerralbo**, an early-16th-century town house with a wonderful facade.

Elsewhere watch for the 16th-century

Palacio de los Ávila y Tiedra (Plaza del Conde 3; ☺9am-7pm Mon-Sat), and there are numerous stairs leading up onto the crumbling ramparts of the city walls that encircle the old town.

You can follow their length for about 2.2km around the town and enjoy fabulous views over the surrounding plains. And just for something different, there's the **Museo del Orinal** (Chamber Pot Museum; ☎952 38 20 87; www.museodelorinal. es; Plaza Herrasti; adult/child under 10yr €2/free; ☺11am-2pm Fri-Wed; ⛹), Spain's (possibly the world's) only museum dedicated to the not-so-humble chamber pot.

🍴 🛏 p73

The Drive » The quiet SA324 north from Ciudad Rodrigo passes through Castillejo de Martín Viejo (17km) and San Felices de los Gallegos (40km), with a pretty Plaza Mayor and a well-preserved castle. After Lumbrales, a further 10km north, the road (now the SA330) narrows and passes among stone walls – the big views lie just up ahead.

18 Parque Natural Arribes del Duero

One of the most dramatic landforms in Castilla y León, the Parque Natural Arribes del Duero is a little-known gem. Not far beyond Lumbrales, the **Mirador del Cachón de Caneces** (lookout) offers the first precipitous views. But it's at **Aldeadávila**, around 35km to the north, that you find the views that make this trip worthwhile. Before entering the village, turn left at the large purple sign. After 5.1km, a 2.5km walking track leads down to the **Mirador El Picón de Felipe**, with fabulous views down into the canyon.

Returning to the road, it's a further 1km down to the **Mirador del Fraile** – the views of the impossibly deep canyon with plunging cliffs on both sides are utterly extraordinary. This is prime birdwatching territory, with numerous raptors nesting on the cliffs and griffon vultures wheeling high overhead on the thermals. It's a wonderful way to end this wonderful journey.

Eating & Sleeping

Plasencia ④

🛏 Palacio Carvajal Girón
Historic Hotel €€

(📞927 42 63 26; www.palaciocarvajalgiron. com; Plaza Ansano 1; r €83-164; P ❄ 🛰 🏊) An impressive conversion job has transformed this formerly ruined palace in the heart of the old town into a chic address. Rooms have modern fittings, fresh white decor, plus original features, including fireplaces. The top-floor attic-style standard rooms have sloping ceilings and in-room concrete baths or showers, while the swish 1st-floor suite has an XXL bathroom with original tilework.

Jaraiz de la Vera ⑥

✗ Villa Xarahiz
Spanish €€

(📞927 66 51 50; www.villaxarahiz.com; Carretera EX203, Km 32.8, Jaraíz de la Vera; mains €10-23; ⏰1.30-3.45pm & 9-10.45pm Tue-Sat, 1.30-3.45pm Sun; 🛰 🏠) Offering spectacular *sierra* views from the terrace and the upmarket wood-beamed dining room, this hotel-restaurant 1km north of Jaraíz is one of La Vera's best bets for Spanish wines and smart regional pan-Spanish food, featuring local peppers, Torta del Casar cheese, Extremaduran *jamón* and stewed kid, among other quality Extremadura produce. The €12 weekday lunch *menú* is a hit.

Jarandilla de la Vera ⑧

🛏 Parador de Jarandilla
Historic Hotel €€

(📞927 56 01 17; www.parador.es; Avenida de García Prieto 1, Jarandilla de la Vera; d €90-210; P ❄ 🛰 🏊) Be king or queen of the castle at this 15th-century castle-turned-hotel with a warm, welcoming feel. Carlos I stayed here for a few months while waiting for his monastery digs to be completed. Within the stout walls and turrets lie period-furnished rooms that are wonderfully comfy without being ostentatiously grand, plus a classic courtyard where you can dine royally from the **restaurant** (📞927 56 01 17; www.parador.es; Avenida de García Prieto 1,

Jarandilla de la Vera; mains €12-26; ⏰1.30-4pm & 8.30-11pm; P 🛰 🍴) menu.

La Alberca ⑯

✗ La Taberna
Castilian €€

(📞923 41 54 60; www.latabernadelaalberca. com; Plaza Mayor 5; mains €9-19; ⏰1.30-4pm daily, plus 8pm-12.30am Fri & Sat; 🍴 🏠) Right on Plaza Mayor, with daily three-course menus plus gut-busting *parrilladas* (grills) of various meats (€12 per person) or – unusually – vegetables (€10). The upstairs dining room has views over the square. The *cabrito* (baby goat) is particularly good.

🛏 Hotel Doña Teresa
Hotel €€

(📞923 41 53 08; www.hoteldeteresa.com; Carretera de Mogarraz; r €63-99; P ❄ 🛰) Lovely Doña Teresa is a perfect modern fit for the village's old-world charm. The large rooms combine character (wooden beams and exposed stone) with all the necessary mod cons; some open onto a garden. The owners also run a spa 1.5km away, with various treatments available at reduced rates for guests.

Ciudad Rodrigo ⑰

✗ Zascandil
Tapas €

(📞665 63 58 84; Correo Viejo 5; pinchos €3, tostas €5.50-8; ⏰1-4pm & 7.30-11pm) A fashionable spot with an art-deco look to accompany the pretty-as-a-picture gastro tapas (such as sashimi and gourmet miniburgers). Organic veg come from the owner's *huerta* (market garden) and eco-wines are served. There's live music in summer.

🛏 Hospedería Audiencia Real
Historic Hotel €€

(📞923 49 84 98; Plaza Mayor 17; d €45-85; ❄ 🛰) Right on Plaza Mayor, this fine 16th-century inn has been beautifully reformed and retains a tangible historic feel with lovely exposed stone walls. Some rooms have wrought-iron furniture and several sport narrow balconies overlooking the square.

Spain's Interior Heartland

Take a journey through Spain's northern heartland, from the Bay of Biscay to Madrid, with some of inland Spain's most appealing towns to savour along the way.

4

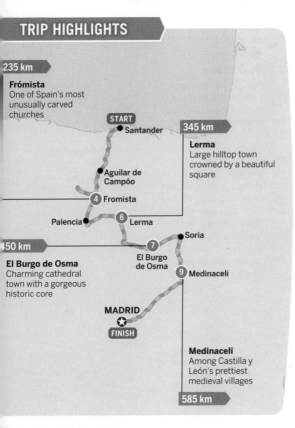

235 km

Frómista
One of Spain's most unusually carved churches

START
● Santander

345 km

Lerma
Large hilltop town crowned by a beautiful square

● Aguilar de Campóo

④ Fromista

● Palencia

⑥ Lerma

50 km

El Burgo de Osma
Charming cathedral town with a gorgeous historic core

⑦

● Soria

El Burgo de Osma

⑨ Medinaceli

MADRID
✪
FINISH

Medinaceli
Among Castilla y León's prettiest medieval villages

585 km

5–7 DAYS
748KM / 465 MILES

GREAT FOR...

BEST TIME TO GO

From April to May or September to October to avoid extremes of heat and cold.

ESSENTIAL PHOTO

Haunting riverside cloister of the Monasterio de San Juan de Duero.

BEST FOR HISTORY

Villa Romana La Olmeda, Spain's most intact Roman-era villa.

4 Spain's Interior Heartland

You *could* speed down the motorway and reach Madrid in a little over four hours from Santander. But unless you're in a hurry, why not detour via the stirring cathedral towns of Palencia, hilltop Lerma, and the catheral town of El Burgo de Osma. For much of the journey, the views of sweeping horizons and distant mountains make this one a real pleasure to drive.

1 Santander

Santander often plays second fiddle to the more-famous Basque cities further east, but this is one cool city, home as it is to the belle-époque elegance of El Sardinero neighbourhood and the best of seaside living Spanish-style. Just back from the water, there are good city beaches, bustling shopping streets and a heaving bar and restaurant scene.

✕ ⊨ p82, p149, p167

The Drive » The E5 is a multicarriageway road that climbs up and over the Cordillera Cantábrica, with some stunning mountain views in the early part of the journey. South of the mountains, track south until the turn-off to Aguilar de Campóo (110km).

2 Aguilar de Campóo

Aguilar de Campóo is a worthwhile stop, and the town and surrounding countryside offer some rather lovely views of the Montaña Palentina and the mountains you've just crossed to get here. The town is a pleasing place to wander, take in the fresh mountain air and soak up the bustle of a provincial northern Castilian town. On no account miss the **Monasterio de Santa María la Real** (☏979 12 30 53; www.santamarialareal.org; Carretera de Cervera; adult/child €5/3; ⏰10.30am-2pm & 4.30-8pm Jul-Sep, 4-7.30pm Tue-Fri, 10.30am-2pm & 4.30-7.30pm Sat & Sun Oct-Jun), a Romanesque monastery with a glorious 13th-century Gothic cloister with delicate capitals.

Bay of Biscay

Santander
① START
Solares
Torrelavega
Castro
Urdiales
San
Sebastián
Portugalete
Bilbao
Ramales de
la Victoria
Eibar
Durango
Arrasate
(Mondragón)
Cantábrica
einosa
Orbaneja del
Castillo
Vitoria-
Gasteiz
A1
Oña
Estella
(Lizarra)
Miranda
de Ebro
Pancorbo
Haro
Logroño
A12
Santo Domingo
de la Calzada
Burgos
N622
⑥ Lerma
Salas de los
Infantes
San Leonardo
de Yagüe
A1
Aranda de
Duero
El Burgo
de Osma
N122
⑧ Soria
⑦
N110
Ayllón
A15
Parque
Natural
del Hoz
Atienza
⑨
Medinaceli
N110
A1
govia
A2
Collado
Villalba
Madrid
⑩
FINISH
p60
Parla
Pastrana
Cuenca
Aranjuez
②

The Drive » Return to the E5 and follow it south as far as Abia de las Torres, then turn northwest along the P240, bound for Saldaña (65km, around one hour). The turn-off to Villa Romana La Olmeda is 3km south of Saldaña along the CL615.

③ Villa Romana La Olmeda

On the fertile plains south of the Montaña Palentina, **Villa Romana La Olmeda** (☏979 14 20 03; www.villaromanalaolmeda.com; off CL615; adult/child under 12yr €5/free; ⊙10.30am-6.30pm Tue-Sun; 🅿 🚻) is a stunning relic from the days when Spain stood at the crossroads of ancient civilisations. But it's worth the detour for far more than its historical significance – these are some of the most

LINK YOUR TRIP

1 Historic Castilla y León

This loop west and north of Madrid takes in historic towns and gorgeous villages all the way to Soria.

2 Back Roads Beyond Madrid

South and east of Madrid you'll encounter many historic towns and villages, from Toledo to Alcalá de Henares.

77

beautiful remnants of a Roman villa anywhere in the Iberian Peninsula. The villa was built around the 1st or 2nd century CE, but was completely overhauled in the middle of the 4th century. It was then that the simply extraordinary mosaics were added: the hunting scenes in El Oecus (reception room) are especially impressive. The whole museum is wonderfully presented – elevated boardwalks guide you around the floor plan of the 4400-sq-metre villa, with multimedia presentations in Spanish, English and French showing how the villa might once have appeared.

The Drive » Take the CL615 southeast of Villa Romana La Olmeda to the A231, then south along the A67 down into Frómista (57km).

TRIP HIGHLIGHT

❹ Frómista

Rather nondescript Frómista may seem like so many Castilian towns of northern Castilla y León. And then you find yourself alongside the **Iglesia de San Martín** (☎979 81 01 44; Plaza de San Martín, Frómista; adult/child €2/free; ◷9.30am-2pm & 4.30-8pm Apr-Sep, 10am-2pm & 3.30-6.30pm Oct-Mar). Perfectly proportioned, it dates from 1066 and has a veritable menagerie of human and zoomorphic

DETOUR: THE P980

Start: ❹ Frómista

The P980 between Frómista and Carrión de los Condes is a wonderful stretch of road. A couple of kilometres west of Frómista, at the entrance to the small hamlet of **Población de Campos**, the simplicity of the 13th-century **Ermita de San Miguel**, beneath its honour guard of trees, is a quietly beautiful Romanesque gem. Around 6km northwest of Frómista, quiet **Revanga de Campos** is home to the **Iglesia de San Lorenzo**, built between the 12th and 16th centuries. A couple of kilometres further on, in **Villalcázar de Sirga**, the **Iglesia de Santa María La Blanca** (☎979 88 08 54; Villalcázar de Sirga; €2; ◷11am-2pm & 5-8pm daily Jun–mid-Sep, 10.30am-2pm & 4-6pm Sat & Sun mid-Sep–Apr), an extraordinary fortress-church and important landmark along the Camino de Santiago, rises up from the Castilian plains. Begun in the 12th century and finished in the 14th, it spans both Romanesque and Gothic styles.

figures carved in the soft sandstone just below the eaves. It's one of those remarkable finds that turn up so often along the Camino de Santiago.

The Drive » Drive south along the A67, which takes you all the way into Palencia (33km).

----

❺ Palencia

Palencia is a quintessential Castilian town – subdued at first glance, it's a surprisingly lively town with some magnificent architectural creations.

Begin with a walk along the colonnaded main pedestrian street, Calle Mayor, which is flanked by shops and several other churches, then make your way to Palencia's immense Gothic **catedral** (☎979 70 13 47; www.catedraldepalencia. org; Calle Mayor Antigua 29; adult/child €5/2; ◷10am-1.30pm & 4-7.30pm Mon-Fri, 10am-2pm & 4-7.30pm Sat, 4.30-8pm Sun May-Oct, 10am-1.30pm & 4-6pm Mon-Fri, 10am-2pm, 4-5.30pm & 6.45-7.30pm Sat, 4-7pm Sun Nov-Apr), where the sober exterior belies the extraordinary riches that await within; it's widely known as 'La Bella Desconocida' (Unknown Beauty).

Inside, the Capilla El Sagrario is the pick with its ceiling-high altarpiece that tells the story of Christ in dozens of exquisitely carved and painted panels. Beyond the cathedral, Palencia is embellished with some real architectural gems, including the 19th-century **Modernista Mercado de Abastos** (Fresh Food Market) on Calle Colón, the eye-catching **Collegio Vallandrando** on Calle Mayor and the extraordinarily ornate neo-plateresque **Palacio Provincial** on Calle Burgos.

The Drive >> From Palencia, take the E80 motorway northeast towards Burgos, then detour off to the east along the N622 all the way into Lerma. The 77km drive should take just under an hour.

TRIP HIGHLIGHT

6 Lerma

Lerma rises from the Castilian plains like an Italian hill town, crowning the highest point for miles around. An ancient settlement, Lerma hit the big time in the early 17th century, when Grand Duke Don Francisco de Rojas y Sandoval, a minister under Felipe II, launched an ambitious project to create another El Escorial. He failed, but the cobbled streets and delightful plazas of the historic quarter are an impressive legacy nonetheless. High in the old town, the **Plaza Mayor** is fronted by the oversize **Parador**

ROMANESQUE DETOURS

Spain's northern interior is littered with outstanding examples of Romanesque architecture, most of which lie close by the main route. Aguilar de Campóo and its surrounds are strewn with Romanesque jewels. The Monasterio de Santa María la Real, just outside town on the highway to Cervera de Pisuerga, is the undoubted highlight. On the road between Villa Romana La Olmeda and Palencia, Frómista is known for its exceptional Iglesia de San Martín (p78). Further along the road, between Palencia and León, picturesque Sahagún is an important waystation for pilgrims en route to Santiago, particularly for the 12th-century Iglesia de San Tirso, with its pure Romanesque design and Mudéjar bell tower laced with rounded arches.

---

de Lerma (Palacio Ducal; ☎947 17 71 10; www.parador. es; Plaza Mayor 1; r €78-190; P ❄ @ 🛜), notable for its courtyards and 210 balconies. The square hosts a clothing and fresh-food market on Wednesday mornings.

 p82

The Drive >> The A1 whips you south from Lerma towards Aranda de Duero. Just shy of Aranda, follow the signs to the N622, in the direction of Soria. Soon enough, you're in El Burgo de Osma, 105km and one hour from Lerma.

TRIP HIGHLIGHT

7 El Burgo de Osma

Beautiful El Burgo de Osma is one of Castilla y León's most underrated towns. Once important enough to host its own university, the town is still partially walled, has some elegant,

---

colonnaded streetscapes and is dominated by a remarkable Gothic-baroque **catedral** (☎975 34 03 19; Plaza de San Pedro de Osma; adult/child €2.50/free; ⊙10.30am-1pm & 4-7.30pm Jul-Sep, 10.30am-1pm & 4-6pm Tue-Fri, 10.30am-1.30pm & 4-7pm Sat Oct-Jun) that dates back to the 12th century. The sanctuary is filled with art treasures, including the 16th-century main altarpiece and the Beato de Osma, a precious 11th-century codex (manuscript) displayed in the Capilla Mayor.

✕ 🏠 p82

The Drive >> The N622 goes all the way from El Burgo de Osma to Soria (57km). At the time of research, the journey took around 45 minutes, but that should change when they finally finish the motorway between Aranda de Duero and Soria.

8 Soria

Small-town Soria is one of Spain's smaller provincial capitals. Set on Río Duero in the heart of backwoods Castilian countryside, it has an appealing and compact old centre, and a sprinkling of stunning monuments. The narrow streets of the town centre on Plaza Mayor, with its attractive Renaissance-era *ayuntamiento* (town hall) and the **Iglesia de Santa María la Mayor**, with its unadorned Romanesque facade and gilt-edged interior. A block north is the majestic, sandstone, 16th-century **Palacio de los Condes Gomara** (Calle de Aguirre). Further north is the Romanesque **Iglesia de Santo Domingo** (🎧975 21 12 39; Calle de Santo Tomé Hospicio; ⏰7am-9pm), with a small but exquisitely sculpted portal of ferrous stone that seems to glow at sunset. Down the hill by the river east of the town centre, the 12th-century **Monasterio de San Juan de Duero** (🎧975 22 13 97; Camino Monte de las Ánimas; €1, Sat & Sun free; ⏰10am-2pm Sun year round, 10am-2pm & 4-8pm Tue-Sat Jul-Sep, 10am-2pm & 4-7pm Tue-Sat Feb-Jun & Oct, 10am-2pm & 4-6pm Tue-Sat Nov-Jan), has many gracefully interlaced arches in the partially ruined cloister. A lovely riverside walk south for 2.3km will take you past the 13th-century church of the former Knights Templar, the Monasterio de San Polo (not open to the public), and on to the fascinating

Medinaceli Arco Romano

baroque Ermita de San Saturio (p49).

✗ 🛏 p51, p82

The Drive › South of Soria, the A15 crosses low, bare hills with a stark beauty, passes the medieval town of Almazán, and then on into Medinaceli (78km).

- - - - - - - - - - - - - - - -

TRIP HIGHLIGHT

⑨ Medinaceli

One of Castilla y León's most beautiful *pueblos* (villages), Medinaceli lies draped along a high,

windswept ridge just off the A2 motorway. Its mix of Roman ruins, cobblestone laneways and terrific places to stay and eat that make it an excellent base for exploring this beautiful corner of Castilla y León.

The partly colonnaded **Plaza Mayor** is a lovely centrepiece to the village and one of the region's prettiest village squares. Not far away, the 1st-century **Arco Romano** watches over the entrance to the town.

✗ 🛏 p83

The Drive › From Medinaceli it's the A2 motorway all the way into Madrid. The 163km journey should take just under two hours.

- - - - - - - - - - - - - - - -

⑩ Madrid

Madrid is the start and end point for so many journeys but it's also a destination in its own right, with world-class art galleries, fabulous food and irresistible street life. Explore it on our walking tour (p60).

Eating & Sleeping

Santander ❶

🗙 Agua Salada   Fusion €€

(📞942 04 93 87; www.facebook.com/
aguasaladasantander; Calle San Simón 2; lunch
menú €14, mains €16-20; ⊙1.30-4pm Mon,
1.30-4pm & 8-11pm Wed-Sun) A labour of love
for owners Carlos García and Pilar Montiel,
this intimate corner bistro serves top-notch,
market-fresh cuisine that walks the line
between traditional and innovative. Indulge in
a superb tuna tartare with mustard ice cream,
local beef entrecôte with roasted peppers
and chips, or an endive salad with pears,
Gorgonzola and hazelnut pesto.

🛏 Jardín Secreto   Boutique Hotel €€

(📞942 07 07 14; www.jardinsecretosantander.
com; Calle de Cisneros 37; r €60-95; 🛜) Named
for its little back garden, this is a charming,
six-room world of its own, spread across a
200-year-old house near the city centre. It's
run by a welcoming, on-the-ball brother-and-
sister team, and designed by their mother in
a stylish blend of silvers, greys and pastels
with exposed stone, brick and wood. The
complimentary morning coffee hits the spot.

Lerma ❻

🗙 Asador Casa Brigante   Castilian €€

(📞947 17 05 94; www.casabrigante.com; Plaza
Mayor 5; mains €13-23, roast lamb for two €45;
⊙1.30-4pm) Our favourite *asador* in town is the
outstanding Asador Casa Brigante – you won't
taste better roast lamb anywhere. Ask about its
accommodation options nearby if you've eaten
so much you're unable to move.

🛏 Posada La
Hacienda de Mi Señor   Historic Hotel €€

(📞947 17 70 52; www.lahaciendademisenor.
com; Calle del Barco 6; s/d incl breakfast €49/72;
🌼 @🛜) This charming, quirky place near the
top of the town (it's a couple of blocks down the
hill from the square) is your best midrange bet,
with enormous rooms in a renovated, historic
building.

El Burgo de Osma ❼

🗙 Mesón Marcelino   Spanish €€

(📞975 34 12 49; Calle Mayor 71; mains €13-32,
set menu €35; ⊙1-4.30pm & 8.30-11.30pm)
A reliable choice along the main street,
Mesón Marcelino feeds the passions of this
unashamedly meat-loving town. It's all about
cordero or *cochinillo asado* – roast lamb or
suckling pig – with steaks and game meats
being what passes for variety in El Burgo de
Osma. Salads are an essential side order. It has
a good tapas bar next door.

🛏 Hotel Il Virrey   Hotel €

(📞975 34 13 11; www.virreypalafox.com; Calle
Mayor 2; r €50-65, ste €95-115; 🌼🛜) This
place is a curious mix of old Spanish charm
and contemporary flair; public areas remain
dominated by heavily gilded furniture, dripping
chandeliers and a sweeping staircase. Rates
soar on weekends in February and March,
when people flock here for the ritual slaughter
(*matanza*) of pigs, after which diners indulge in
all-you-can-eat feasts.

Soria ❽

🗙 Fogón del Salvador   Castilian €€

(📞975 23 01 94; www.fogonsalvador.com; Plaza
de El Salvador 1; mains €16-24; ⊙1.30-4pm &
9pm-midnight Mon, Tue & Thu-Sat, 1.30-4pm
Sun) A Soria culinary stalwart and fronted by
a popular bar, Fogón del Salvador has a wine
list as long as your arm – literally – and a
fabulous wood-fired oven churning out perfectly
prepared meat-based dishes such as *cabrito al
ajillo* (goat with garlic), as well as a variety of
steaks in all their red-blooded glory.

🗙 Crepería Lilot Du Ble Noir   French €

(📞651 495317; www.facebook.com/
CreperiaLilot; Calle Fueros de Soria 12; crêpes €7-
12; ⊙1-4.30pm & 9pm-midnight) This appealing
little French crêperie adds some much-needed
variety to Soria's culinary scene. Savoury
versions include minced meat with Camembert
and mushrooms, or Asian-spiced pork with rice
noodles. It also has sweet crêpes and salads,

and an English menu. Not surprisingly, it gets rave reviews from travellers and locals alike.

Hotel Leonor Centro Hotel €€

(☎975 23 93 03; www.hotelleonorcentro.com; Plaza Ramón y Cajal 5; s/d from €58/70; ❄ 📶) Just off the main pedestrian street through the historic centre, this fine four-star hotel has contemporary carpeted rooms with tasteful furnishings and a neutral colour scheme with splashes of burgundy and light-wood panels. The bathrooms have hydromassage tubs; there's also a small spa. If you're driving, ignore the signs to 'Hotel Leonor' – it's a different hotel.

Medinaceli 9

La Ceramica Spanish €€

(☎975 32 63 81; Calle de Santa Isabel 2; mains €8-21, set menus from €17; ⏰1-3.30pm & 9-11pm, closed mid-Dec–Jan) An intimate yet informal dining experience, La Ceramica serves excellent local specialities such as *migas del pastor* (shepherd's breadcrumbs) or *ensalada de codorniz* (quail salad), as well as the usual meats.

Asador de la Villa El Granero Castilian €€

(☎975 32 61 89; www.asadorelgranero.es; Calle de Yedra 10; mains €15-23; ⏰1.30-4pm & 9-11pm May-Sep, hours vary Oct-Apr) This well-signposted place, with a shop selling local food products at the front, is thought by many to be Medinaceli's best restaurant. The *setas de campo* (wild mushrooms) are something of a local speciality, though unsurprisingly, grilled and roasted meats dominate this bastion of hearty Castilian cooking. Book ahead on summer weekends and don't expect it to be open for dinner on winter weeknights.

Medina Salim Boutique Hotel €€

(☎975 32 61 72; www.hotelmedinasalim.com; Calle Barranco 15; s/d incl breakfast from €80/85; P ❄ 📶) A welcoming boutique hotel which sports large, airy rooms with fridges and terraces that overlook either the sweeping valley or medieval cobblestones out front. Decor is contemporary and light, with pale woodwork and excellent bathrooms. Perks include a small spa and a delightful breakfast room that overlooks part of the original Roman wall, where staff serve Medinaceli's best breakfast.

Route of Don Quixote

Follow the trail of Spain's favourite literary legend, El Quijote (Don Quixote in English), across the endless horizons and amid the castles and ancient windmills of Spain's interior.

5

TRIP HIGHLIGHTS

START
Toledo

67 km

Consuegra
Spain's most spectacular set of windmills

175 km

Belmonte
One of Spain's most dramatic castles

Alcázar de San Juan

123 km

Campo de Criptana
Whitewashed town crowned with more windmills

Ciudad Real

9

FINISH
Villanueva de los Infantes

Almagro
Beautiful town with fine plaza and theatrical pedigree

356 km

4–6 DAYS
424KM / 264 MILES

GREAT FOR...

BEST TIME TO GO

From March to May and September to November; summer and winter can be extreme across La Mancha.

ESSENTIAL PHOTO

Molinos de viento (windmills) lined up in a row above Consuegra.

BEST FOR HISTORY

Corral de Comedias in Almagro, Spain's oldest theatre.

---

5 Route of Don Quixote

Few literary landscapes have come to define an actual terrain quite like the Castilla-La Mancha portrayed in Miguel de Cervantes' *El ingenioso hidalgo don Quijote de la Mancha*. Here is where our noble knight tilted at windmills, fell for Dulcinea, and drove Sancho Panza and his trusty steed Rocinante across a land ripe for adventures. With this itinerary, you get to follow in their footsteps.

❶ Toledo

There's nothing to suggest that Don Quixote ever made his way through Toledo's streets, other than, perhaps, the numerous images of the knight in Toledo's souvenir shops, but it is in Toledo that most journeys through Castilla-La Mancha begin. This stunning city is awash in Christian, Islamic and Jewish architecture – its **catedral** (☎925 22 22 41; www.catedralprimada.es; Plaza del Ayuntamiento; €10,

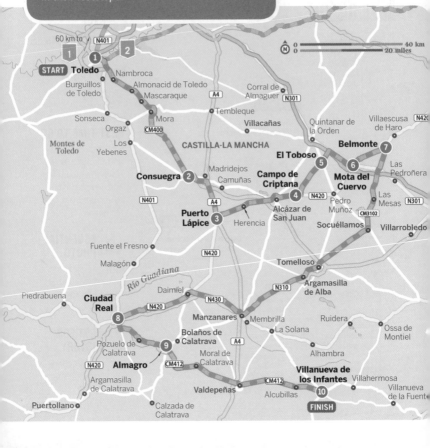

incl Torre de las Campanas €12.50; ⏰10am-6.30pm Mon-Sat, 2-6.30pm Sun) is one of Spain's most impressive, the **Mezquita del Cristo de la Luz** hints at Al-Andalus, and the **Sinagoga del Tránsito** (📞925 22 36 65; www.culturaydeporte.gob.es/msefardi; Calle Samuel Leví; adult/child €3/1.50, after 2pm Sat & all day Sun free; ⏰9.30am-7.30pm Tue-Sat Mar-Oct, to 6pm Nov-Feb, 10am-3pm Sun year-round) is superb. But this is a city to wander, a place of serpentine cobblestone laneways and a brooding atmosphere apt to fire the imagination.

🍴 🛏 p59, p92

The Drive » Drive southeast of Toledo along the CM400. On the final approach into

LINK YOUR TRIP

1 **Historic Castilla y León**

From Toledo, it's a 60km hop to Madrid, from where you can sweep through some of inland Spain's most beguiling cities and *pueblos* (villages).

2 **Back Roads Beyond Madrid**

This route through fabulous towns and villages passes through Toledo.

Consuegra (67km), watch for the line of windmills along a ridge of the kind that struck fear into the heart of El Quijote.

TRIP HIGHLIGHT

② Consuegra

Exactly where Don Quixote tilted at windmills and prepared to do honourable battle against these 'monstrous giants' is not clear from the book, but Consuegra is very much a leading candidate. Here, visible for miles around and strung out along a ridge, are nine *molinos de viento* (windmills) of the classic La Mancha variety. They're the most accessible of La Mancha's windmills (a well-signposted road leads up from the town) and the views from here seem to go on forever.

Adjacent to the windmills is a 12th-century **castle** (📞925 47 57 31; www.castillodeconsuegra.es; Cerro Calderico; adult/child incl Bolero windmill €4.50/2; ⏰10am-2pm & 3.30-6pm Mon-Fri, 10am-6pm Sat & Sun; 🅿) – Consuegra once belonged to the Knights of Malta; a few rooms in the castle have been re-created to give a good indication of how the knights would have lived. Down in the town, it's worth tracking down the Plaza Mayor, with its pretty 1st-floor balconies.

🛏 p92

The Drive » It's just under 7km east across pancake-flat plains to the N4 motorway, but you'll find yourself pulling over often to look back at Consuegra's windmills. Once on the N4, Puerto Lápice is 17km south and signposted just off the main highway.

③ Puerto Lápice

Many towns and villages in Castilla-La Mancha have tried to lay claim to an El Quijote pedigree, often basing their claims more upon wishful thinking than any close reading of the original text. In fact, few towns are actually mentioned by name in the book. One exception is the now-unremarkable town of Puerto Lápice. It was here that Don Quixote stayed in an inn that he mistook for a castle and, after keeping watch all night, convinced the innkeeper to knight him. It's the sort of town that shimmers in the summer heat, with only magic of the hallucinatory kind, so drive through town, nod to the noble knight, and keep on going.

The Drive » From Puerto Lápice, drive east along the N420, bypass Alcázar de San Juan (which some scholars have speculated may have been where El Quijote's journey began), and follow the signs to Campo de Criptana – the whitewashed town crowned by more windmills is unmissable north of the main road. Total journey time is around 30 minutes.

❹ Campo de Criptana

Campo de Criptana, one of the most popular stops on the El Quijote route, is Consuegra's main rival when it comes to windmills. And if you think its dramatic windmill crown is impressive, imagine how it must once have seemed – only 10 of Campo de Criptana's original 32 windmills remain. Local legend also maintains that Cervantes himself was baptised in the town's Iglesia de Santa María.

And, unusually for such a small town lost on the La Mancha plains, Campo de Criptana has another claim to fame, although it's one that many locals perhaps would rather forget: revered contemporary film-maker Pedro Almodóvar was born here, but left for Madrid in his teens, later remarking that in this conservative provincial town, 'I felt as if I'd fallen from another planet'.

✗ ⌷ p92

The Drive » Around 3km east of Campo de Criptana along the N420, turn left at the signpost for El Toboso, which is 19km further on along a quiet, flat road.

❺ El Toboso

To see the cult of El Quijote in full swing, come to El Toboso, a small town far from the main roads northeast of Campo de Criptana. The most entertaining of El Toboso's numerous Cervantes-influenced locations is the 16th-century **Casa-Museo de Dulcinea** (📞925 19 72 88; Calle Don Quijote 1; adult/child €3/1.50; ⏰10am-2pm & 3-6.30pm Tue-Sat, 10am-2pm Sun), which was apparently the home of Doña Ana, the *señorita* who inspired Cervantes' Dulcinea, the platonic

Belmonte Castillo de Belmonte

love of Quijote. Also scattered around the town are the obligatory Don Quixote statue and a library with more than 300 editions of the book in various languages.

The Drive » Drive northeast a short distance and then turn right (southeast) along the N301 – the next town you come to is Mota del Cuervo (20km).

- - - - - - - - - - - - - - - - - -

6 Mota del Cuervo

If there weren't any windmills here, you'd struggle to find a reason to stop. And if you've already had enough windmills, what are you doing on this trip? But we can't get enough of them and windmills there are (seven of them), standing in the fields around town. Position yourself in the right place on a good day and there are outstanding sunset photos to be had with the windmills in the foreground.

The Drive » Finding Belmonte couldn't be easier – drive northeast of Mota del Cuervo for 16km along the N420 and there you are. As elsewhere on Spain's high inland plateau, the horizons here are vast and you'll see Belmonte's castle well before you arrive.

- - - - - - - - - - - - - - - - - -

TRIP HIGHLIGHT

7 Belmonte

Quiet little Belmonte is notable for its fine castle, the 15th-century **Castillo de Belmonte** (☑678 646486; www.castillodebelmonte.com; Calle Eugenia de Montijo; adult/ child incl audio guide €9/5; ⏰10am-2pm & 4.30-8.30pm Tue-Sun May–mid-Sep, 10am-2pm & 4.30-6.30pm Tue-Sun mid-Sep–Apr; P). This is how castles *should* look, with turrets, intact walls and a commanding position over the village. It's been recently done up inside, and has a slick display with multilingual audio commentary. And the connection to Don Quixote? Some scholars believe that the castle served as inspiration for Cervantes when creating the knight's imaginary world and at least one film-maker agreed – the castle appeared in the 2002 Spanish production of *El caballero Don Quijote*. And while you're in town, stop by the **Iglesia Colegial de San Bartolomé** (La Colegiata; 967 17 02 08; Calle La Beltraneja; €3; ⏱11am-2pm & 4.30-7.30pm Tue-Sat, 4.30-7.30pm Sun Apr-Oct, shorter hours rest of the year), a magnificent golden-sandstone church with an impressive altarpiece.

🛏 p92

The Drive » The distances on this trip have so far been quite short, but today is a longer day in the saddle. From Belmonte, drive south along the quieter-than-quiet CM3102 for 56km to Tomelloso. Then join the N310 as far as Manzanares (42km), before changing to the N430 to Ciudad Real (55km).

- - - - - - - - - - - - - - -

❽ Ciudad Real

Despite being the one-time royal counterpart of Toledo, these days Ciudad Real is an unspectacular Spanish working town. The town centre has a certain charm its pedestrianised shopping streets and distinctive Plaza Mayor, complete with carillon clock (topped by Cupid), flamboyant neo-Gothic town-hall facade and modern tiered fountain.

The main reason to visit is to track down the museum-library, the **Museo del Quijote y Biblioteca Cervantina** (926 20 04 57; Ronda de Alarcos 1; ⏱10am-1.45pm & 5-7.45pm Mon-Sat, 10am-1.45pm Sun). The museum has audiovisual displays, while the Cervantes library is stocked with 3500 *Don Quixote* books, including some in Esperanto and Braille, with most of them now digitised, and others dating back

to 1724. It helps if you speak Spanish. Entry is by guided tour every half-hour.

🛏 p93

The Drive » Head south of Ciudad Real along the N412 and Almagro is just 28km southeast down a road that crosses the flat La Mancha plains.

- - - - - - - - - - - - - - -

TRIP HIGHLIGHT

❾ Almagro

Not even the marketing departments of local tourist authorities can come up with a Quijote connection for Almagro, but it's one of Castilla-La Mancha's prettiest towns and we recommend that you visit for that reason alone. The jewel in Almagro's crown is the extraordinary 16th-century Plaza Mayor, with its wavy tiled roofs, stumpy columns and faded bottle-green porticoes. Right on the square, the **Corral de Comedias** (926 88 24 58; www.corraldecomedias.com; Plaza Mayor 18; adult/child incl English audio guide €4/free; ⏱10am-2pm & 4-7pm) showcases a literary heritage of a different kind: this is the oldest theatre in Spain, an evocative 17th-century stage with rows of wooden balconies facing the original stage, complete with dressing rooms. Performances are still held here in July during the **Festival Internacional de Teatro Clásico** (www.festivalde

DON QUIXOTE

Few literary landscapes have come to define an actual terrain quite like the La Mancha portrayed in Miguel de Cervantes's *El ingenioso hidalgo don Quijote de la Mancha*, better known as El Quijote (in Spanish) or Don Quixote (in English). Published in two volumes in 1605 and 1615, El Quijote went on to become the most famous Spanish novel ever published; in 2002 the Norwegian Nobel Institute asked 100 leading authors from 54 countries to vote for the greatest novel of all time and El Quijote polled 50% more votes than any other book. It is also the most widely translated book on earth after the Bible.

Almagro Plaza Mayor

almagro.com; Corral de Comedias; ⊙Jul). **Just around the corner is the Museo Nacional de Teatro** (📞926 26 10 14; http://museoteatro.mcu.es; Calle Gran Maestre 2; adult/child €3/free; ⊙10am-2pm & 4-6.30pm Tue-Fri, from 10.30am Sat, 10.30am-2pm Sun), which has exhibits on Spanish theatre from the golden age of the 17th century displayed in rooms surrounding a magnificent 13th-century courtyard. Otherwise, the town is a delight to wander around, although it can be deathly quiet in the depths of winter.

✕ ⌖ p93

The Drive » Return to the N412, turn southeast and, 34km later, you'll cross the N4 motorway, pass the wine centre of Valdepeñas and continue east. Some 34km east of Valdepeñas is Villanueva de los Infantes.

- - - - - - - - - - - - - - - - -

⑩ Villanueva de los Infantes

'In a village in La Mancha whose name I cannot recall, there lived long ago a country gentleman...' Thus begins the novel and thus it was that the village where our picaresque hero began his journey had always remained a mystery. That was, at least, until 10 eminent Spanish

academics marked the 400th anniversary of the book's publishing in 1605 by carefully following the clues left by Cervantes. Their conclusion? That Villanueva de los Infantes, now with an ochre-hued Plaza Mayor surrounded by wood-and-stone balconies and watched over by the 15th-century Iglesia de San Andrés, was Don Quixote's starting point.

It's also the end point of our journey, unless, of course, you wish to retrace your steps and set out to follow once again the path trod by Spain's most quixotic knight.

⌖ p93

Eating & Sleeping

Toledo ❶

✗ Hacienda del Cardenal   Spanish €€€

(☏925 22 08 62; www.haciendadelcardenal.com; Paseo de Recaredo 24; mains €21-26; ⏱1-4pm & 8.30-11pm Tue-Sat, 1-4pm Sun) This hotel restaurant enjoys one of Toledo's most magical locations for dining alfresco: it's tucked into a private garden entered via its own gate in the city walls. The food is classic Spanish, with roast meats to the fore – suckling pig and lamb are the prime dishes. It's a bit touristy, but the location is unforgettable on a balmy summer's night.

▦ Casa de Cisneros   Boutique Hotel €€

(☏925 22 88 28; www.hospederiacasade cisneros.com; 12 Calle del Cardenal Cisneros; r €65-191; ✽🖥) Across from the cathedral, this seductive hotel is built on the site of an 11th-century Islamic palace, which can be best appreciated by visiting the basement restaurant. In comparison, this building is a 16th-century youngster, with pretty stone-and-wood beamed rooms and exceptionally voguish bathrooms. A rooftop terrace offers stunning views of the cathedral and beyond.

▦ Parador Conde de Orgaz   Hotel €€€

(☏925 22 18 50; www.parador.es; Cerro del Emperador; r €140-225; P✽🖥≋) High above the southern bank of Río Tajo, Toledo's low-rise *parador* has a classy interior and sublime views (ask for a room with a balcony!). Rooms are relatively spacious and not as heritage-heavy as other *paradores*. You'll need a car or a taxi ride (around €8) to get here from the old town. Be prepared: it's popular with tour groups.

Consuegra ❷

▦ La Vida de Antes   Hotel €€

(☏925 48 21 33; www.lavidadeantes.com; Calle de Colón 2; s €55, d €75-90, apt €118; P✽@🖥≋) The best digs in Consuegra

are encased in a noble old house with tiled floors, antique furnishings and a pretty patio that evokes a bygone era. The duplex rooms are particularly cosy and there's interesting art exhibited throughout the building.

Campo de Criptana ❹

✗ Las Musas   Spanish €€

(☏926 58 91 91; www.facebook.com/RestauranteLasMusas; Calle Barbero 3; mains €18-22, weekday lunch menu €15; ⏱1.30-4pm & 8.30-11pm) Across from the windmills, Las Musas is hands down the best restaurant in town, and one of the top dining spots in the region. Painstakingly prepared dishes of high-quality Manchegan ingredients, a first-rate wine list and exceptional service make for a surprising find in small-town Campo de Criptana.

▦ Casa los Tres Cielos   Guesthouse €€

(☏926 56 37 90; www.casalos3cielos.com; Calle Libertad 11; r €60-70; ✽🖥≋) On a winding lane in the village, this nine-room guesthouse makes a great base for taking in the windmill-studded scenery of the rolling countryside nearby. The wi-fi is weak, but the welcome is warm, and the pleasantly furnished rooms don't lack for comfort (the best have small terraces with pretty views). Bonuses include the good cooked breakfast and the pool.

Belmonte ❼

▦ Palacio Buenavista Hospedería   Boutique Hotel €€

(☏967 18 75 80; www.palaciobuenavista. es; Calle Párroco Luis Andújar 2; s/d/ste incl breakfast €50/80/115; P✽🖥) Palacio Buenavista Hospedería is a classy boutique hotel set in a 16th-century palace next to the town's iconic Iglesia Colegial de San Bartolomé. Stylish rooms are positioned around a balconied central patio with historic columns; request a room with a castle view, if possible. There's an excellent restaurant and a pretty outside terrace where the buffet breakfast is served (weather permitting).

Ciudad Real ⑧

🛏 Palacio de la Serna   Hotel €€

(📞926 84 22 08; www.hotelpalaciodelaserna. com; Calle Cervantes 18, Ballesteros de Calatrava; r €115-170, ste €200-270; P ❄ 🛜 ♿ 🐾) Just a 20-minute drive south of bustling Ciudad Real in the sleepy village of Ballesteros de Calatrava, this superb hotel feels a world away. Set around a courtyard, it combines rural comfort with appealing design; the owner's evocative modern sculptures feature heavily. The modern rooms are bursting with character, with lots of mirrors, spot lighting, bright colours and edgy contemporary paintings. There's also a good on-site restaurant.

Almagro ⑨

🍴 Restaurante Abrasador   Castilian €€

(📞652 332410; www.abrasador.com; Calle San Agustín 18; mains €12-25; ⌚11.30am-4pm & 8.30-11.30pm Mon-Wed, Fri & Sat, 11.30am-4pm Sun) Thoughtfully prepared cooking including perfectly grilled meats dominates the restaurant out the back. Snaffle the table next to the open fire in winter if you can. Out the front, you'll find some of the most creative tapas in Almagro – the famed local aubergine features prominently and it's our pick of the orders, whatever guise it's in. The €15 lunchtime menu is great value.

🛏 La Casa del Rector   Hotel €€

(📞926 26 12 59; www.lacasadelrector.com; Calle Pedro de Oviedo 8; r €80-180; ❄ @ 🛜 ♿) A three-way marriage between modern rooms, 'design' rooms and traditional historical rooms, the Rector is, in a word, magnificent. It's difficult to imagine what taste isn't being catered for in its lush interior set around three courtyards with elegant fountains, retro antiques (sewing machines!) and a streamlined cafe.

🛏 Casa Rural Tía Pilar   Guesthouse €€

(📞650 860475; www.tiapilar.com; Calle de los Carrascos 1; r €65-110; P ❄ 🛜 ♿) This beautiful 18th-century house is a delight with four patios, a lovely common room and a small but elegant swimming pool. Rooms are decorated with antiques and are well heated and/or air-conditioned. The owners live on-site to provide warm but discreet service. Excellent value.

Villanueva de los Infantes ⑩

🛏 La Morada de Juan de Vargas   Hotel €€

(📞926 36 17 69; www.lamoradadevargas. com; Calle Cervantes 3; d €65-85; ❄ 🛜 ♿) Exceptionally welcoming and thoughtful hosts combined with a prime location in the historic centre, just off the main square, make La Morada de Juan de Vargas the best of the town's appealing rural hotel options. The rooms and common areas are full of lovely antiques and artful flourishes, and the hosts happily advise on activities in the area. Note that at weekends there is a minimum stay of two nights.

Ancient Extremadura

6

This journey traverses Spain's ancient past, from stirring Roman ruins to tight tangles of medieval old quarters and castles that evoke a picaresque past.

TRIP HIGHLIGHTS

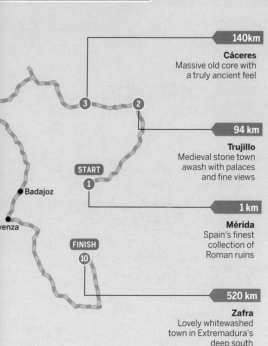

140km

Cáceres
Massive old core with a truly ancient feel

94 km

Trujillo
Medieval stone town awash with palaces and fine views

START
①

● Badajoz

enza

FINISH
⑩

1 km

Mérida
Spain's finest collection of Roman ruins

520 km

Zafra
Lovely whitewashed town in Extremadura's deep south

5–7 DAYS
520KM / 323 MILES

GREAT FOR...

BEST TIME TO GO
From March to May or September to October, when you should enjoy milder weather.

 ESSENTIAL PHOTO
On stage at Mérida's Teatro Romano.

BEST FOR FAMILIES
Wandering slowly through the Ciudad Monumental in Cáceres.

Teatro Romano (p96)

6 Ancient Extremadura

Extremadura is one of Spain's least-visited corners, but that would surely change if only people knew what was here. This is a land where the stories of ancient civilisations, the golden age of Spanish exploration and untold medieval riches are written in stone, with so many magnificent old cities and villages strung out across a splendid terrain of rolling hills and big horizons.

TRIP HIGHLIGHT

❶ Mérida

Mérida, capital of Extremadura, is a marvellous place to begin your journey, home as it is to the most impressive set of Roman ruins in all Spain. Once capital of the Roman province of Lusitania, Emerita Augusta (the Roman forerunner to Mérida) has so much to turn the head. The glittering jewel is the 1st-century-BCE **Teatro Romano** (Paseo Álvarez Sáez de Buruaga; adult/

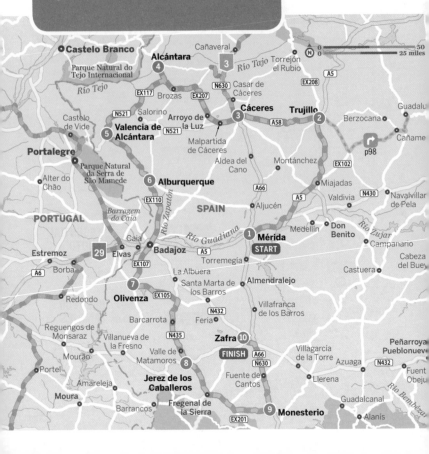

child incl Anfiteatro €12/6, combined 6-site ticket adult/concession/child €15/7.50/free; ⏰9am-9pm Apr-Sep, 9.30am-6.30pm Oct-Mar), a classical theatre still used for performances during the summer **Festival del Teatro Clásico** (www.festivaldemerida.es; €15-45; ⏰Jul-Aug), and the adjacent **Museo Nacional de Arte Romano** (☎924 31 16 90; www.culturaydeporte.gob.es/mnromano/home.html; Calle de José Ramón Mélida; adult/child €3/free, after 2pm Sat & all day Sun free; ⏰9.30am-8pm Tue-Sat, 10am-3pm Sun Apr-Sep, 9.30am-6.30pm Tue-Sat, 10am-3pm Sun Oct-Mar). But in Mérida such splendours are just the beginning. There's the 60-arch **Puente Romano** that

LINK YOUR TRIP

3 The Forgotten West

Begin in Cáceres then disappear off the map through some of the loveliest, least-known villages in the country.

29 Medieval Jewels in the Southern Interior

It's a 110km drive northwest from Zafra to Elvas, where you'll find striking landscapes and medieval lore in Portugal's southern interior.

spans the Río Guadiana, the **Templo de Diana** (Calle de Sagasta) that rises improbably from the modern city centre, and the **Alcazaba** (Calle Graciano; adult/child €6/3, combined 6-site ticket adult/concession/child €15/7.50/free; ⏰9am-9pm Apr-Sep, to 6.30pm Oct-Mar), a fortress that has been occupied by just about everyone down through the ages, from Visigoths and Romans to the enlightened Muslims of Al-Andalus.

✖ 🛏 p101

The Drive » Getting from Mérida to Trujillo couldn't be easier – take the N5 motorway heading northeast of the city and Trujillo lies just 94km up the road.

- - - - - - - - - - - - - - - - - -

TRIP HIGHLIGHT

2 Trujillo

The core of Trujillo is one of the best-preserved medieval towns in Spain. It begins in the Plaza Mayor, which is surrounded by towers and palaces. The splendour continues up the hillside with a labyrinth of mansions, leafy courtyards, churches and convents all enclosed within 900m of walls circling the upper town and dating back to the 16th century when Trujillo's favourite sons returned home as wealthy conquistadors. At the top of the hill, Trujillo's impressive **Alcazaba** (adult/child €1.50/

free; ⏰10am-2pm & 5-8pm Apr-Sep, 10am-2pm & 4-7pm Oct-Mar) has 10th-century Muslim origins. Patrol the battlements for magnificent 360-degree sweeping views. From just about any vantage point up here, whether bathed in the warm light of a summer sunset or shrouded in the mists of winter, Trujillo can feel like a magical place.

✖ 🛏 p101

The Drive » The A58 connects Trujillo with Cáceres, just 46km to the west.

- - - - - - - - - - - - - - - - - -

TRIP HIGHLIGHT

3 Cáceres

The old core of Cáceres, its Ciudad Monumental (Old Town), is truly extraordinary. Narrow cobbled streets twist and climb among ancient stone walls lined with palaces and mansions, while the skyline is decorated with turrets, spires, gargoyles and enormous storks' nests. Protected by defensive walls, it has survived almost intact from its 16th-century heyday and so much of the monumental beauty is clustered around three connected squares, the Plaza de Santa María, Plaza de San Jorge, and the Plaza de San Mateo. At dusk or after dark, when the crowds have gone, you'll feel like you've stepped back into the Middle Ages.

Stretching at the feet of the old city, the lively and arcaded Plaza Mayor is one of Spain's finest public squares.

🛏 p101

The Drive » Drive 13km west of Cáceres along the N521, then turn right (northwest) onto the EX207 (the sign will say Arroyo de la Luz). Some 17km further on, turn left onto the EX207 – Alcántara is 26km away to the northwest.

----

④ Alcántara

Out in Extremadura's wild, remote and rarely travelled west, Alcántara is best known for its magnificent Roman bridge. The bridge – 204m long, 61m high and much reinforced over the centuries – spans the Río Tajo below a huge dam. The town itself retains old walls, a ruined castle, several

imposing mansions and the enormous Renaissance **Convento de San Benito** (☎927 39 00 81; Calle Regimiento de Argel; ⊙tours hourly 10.15am-1.15pm & 5-7pm Mon-Fri, 11.15am-1.15pm & 5-7pm Sat, 11.15am-1.15pm Sun Apr-Oct, hours vary Nov-Mar). The highlights of the down-at-heel monastery, built in the 16th century to house the Orden de Alcántara (an order of Reconquista knights), include the Gothic cloister and the perfectly proportioned three-tier loggia. Admission is by free hourly guided visits.

The Drive » Leaving Alcántara, return along the EX207 for around 6km, then take the EX117. Where that road ends, just after Membrío, turn right onto the N521. Just when you think you're headed for Portugal, Valencia de Alcántara appears up ahead. Total distance: 60km.

⑤ Valencia de Alcántara

Not many travellers stop out here, 7km from the Portuguese border, and its well-preserved old centre is a curious labyrinth of whitewashed houses and mansions. One side of the old town is watched over by the ruins of a medieval castle and the 17th-century **Iglesia de Rocamador**. The surrounding countryside is known for its cork industry and some 50 ancient dolmens (stone circles of prehistoric monoliths).

The Drive » Unless you plan on crossing the border, return a few clicks back up the N521 heading northeast, then turn right (southeast) onto the EX110 along which, 32km later, you'll encounter Alburquerque.

DETOUR: GUADALUPE

Start: ② Trujillo

Guadalupe's revered **Real Monasterio de Santa María de Guadalupe** (☎927 36 70 00; www.monasterioguadalupe.com; Plaza de Santa María de Guadalupe; church free, monastery by guided tour adult/child €5/2.50; ⊙church 9am-7.30pm, monastery 9.30am-1pm & 3.30-6pm) is located, according to legend, on the spot where a shepherd found an effigy of the Virgin, hidden years earlier by Christians fleeing the Muslims. A sumptuous church-monastery (complete with works attributed to El Greco, Goya, Zurbarán and even Michelangelo) was built on the site and this is still one of Spain's most important pilgrimage sites. Hour-long guided tours leave every half-hour. While the monastery is the obvious highlight, take some time to wander the picturesque streets off the Plaza Mayor.

Guadalupe is a nearly-two-hour drive along narrow mountain roads. Take the EX208 for 27km southeast of Trujillo, then the EX102 for 50km into Guadalupe.

Trujillo Alcazaba (p97)

6 Alburquerque

Looming large above this small town, 38km north of Badajoz, is the intact **Castillo de Luna** (☎924 40 12 02; ⊙tours 11am, noon, 1pm, 5pm & 6pm Tue-Sun last Sun in Mar-last Sat in Oct, 11am, noon, 1pm, 4pm & 5pm Tue-Sun rest of year). The centrepiece of a complex frontier defence system of forts, the castle was built on the site of its Islamic antecedent in the 13th century and subsequently expanded. From the top, views take in the Portuguese frontier (the Portuguese actually took the town for a few years in the early 18th century).

The Drive » Head roughly south along the EX110, shadowing the Portuguese border, crossing low hills and quiet farmlands all the way into Badajoz. This provincial capital has little to recommend it – carry right on through, looking for the EX107 and the signs to Olivenza. The journey is 72km.

7 Olivenza

Pretty Olivenza, 24km south of Badajoz, clings to its Portuguese heritage – it has only been Spanish since 1801. The cobbled centre is distinctive for its whitewashed houses, typical turreted defensive walls and penchant for blue-and-white ceramic tile work. Smack-bang in its centre is the 14th-century castle, dominated by the **Torre del Homenaje**, 36m high, from which there are fine views. The most impressive section of the original defensive walls is around the 18th-century Puerta del Calvario, on the western side of town.

The Drive » It's 29km east-southeast along the EX105 to the N435 at Barcarrota – after all this time in the backblocks, the sudden rush of traffic may come as a surprise. From there it's 25km south into Jerez de los Caballeros

8 Jerez de los Caballeros

Walled and hilly Jerez de los Caballeros was a cradle of conquistadors. It has a 13th-century castle that was built by

Zafra Plaza Grande

the Knights Templar. You can wander around at will, but it's basically just the impressive walls that are preserved. There are several handsome churches scattered across the town, three with towers emulating the Giralda in Seville.

The Drive » Take the N435 southeast to Fregenal de la Sierra, then the EX201, then the EX103 over the hills, watching for signs to Monesterio (and black pigs fattening up in stone-walled fields). It's a 66km journey to Jerez de los Caballeros.

- - - - - - - - - - - - - - - - -

9 Monesterio

Since the completion of the A66 motorway, many bypassed towns have disappeared into quiet obscurity, but not Monesterio, because this is one of Spain's (and certainly Extremadura's)

most celebrated sources of *jamón*. Occupying pride of place at the southern end of the town is the outstanding **Museo del Jamón** (924 51 67 37; www.museodeljamondemonesterio.com; Paseo de Extremadura 314; 9.30am-2pm & 4.30-7pm Mon-Sat, 10am-2pm Sun; P), arguably the best of its kind in Spain. Its exhibits take visitors through the process of *jamón* production, from ideal pig habitats, to the *matanza* (killing of the pigs) right through to the finished product.

The Drive » It's 40km north from Monesterio to Zafra, either along the motorway or the quieter N630 that shadows it.

- - - - - - - - - - - - - - - - -

TRIP HIGHLIGHT

10 Zafra

Looking for all the world like an Andalucian *pueblo*

blanco (white town), gleaming-white Zafra is a serene, attractive place to rest at journey's end. Originally a Muslim settlement, Zafra's narrow streets are lined with baroque churches, old-fashioned shops and traditional houses decorated by brilliant red splashes of geraniums. Zafra's 15th-century castle, a blend of Gothic, Mudéjar and Renaissance architecture, is now a *parador* and dominates the town's roofscape. Plaza Grande and the adjoining Plaza Chica, arcaded and bordered by bars, are the places to see Zafra life. The southern end of the Plaza Grande, with its palm trees, is one of Extremadura's prettiest corners.

p101

Eating & Sleeping

Mérida ❶

✕ Tábula Calda   Spanish €€

(📞924 30 49 50; www.tabulacalda.es; Calle
Romero Leal 11; mains €13-22, set menu
€13-25; 🕐1-4.30pm & 8.30pm-midnight)
This inviting yellow-washed space, filled with
tilework and greenery, serves well-priced,
quality meals encompassing Spain's favourite
staples. Everything either comes from its
garden or is sourced from within 100km of
the kitchen. Before your food arrives, you'll
enjoy a complimentary tapa, house salad
(orange, sugar and olive oil, reflecting the
family's Jewish roots) and olives. Manuel is a
welcoming host.

🛏 Hotel Ilunion
Mérida Palace   Historic Hotel €€

(📞924 38 38 00; www.ilunionmeridapalace.com;
Plaza de España 19; r €80-210; P ❄ 🛜 🛄)
Set across two linked 18th- and 19th-century
buildings flanking the palm-dotted Plaza de
España, five-star Mérida Palace is smart,
efficient and wonderfully characterful. Swish
pastel-painted rooms sport Roman-themed
touches such as mosaic-print bedheads,
black-and-white ancient-Mérida drawings and
decorative Roman coins. Enter through the
beautiful arched, blue-toned atrium and, in
summer, enjoy the rooftop pool overlooking the
plaza's palms and fountain.

Trujillo ❷

✕ Mesón La Troya   Spanish €

(📞927 32 13 64; www.mesonlatroya.es; Plaza
Mayor 10; mains €7-22, set menus €16-25;
🕐1-4pm & 8-11pm; 🚼) Famous across Spain
for its copious servings of no-frills *comida
casera* (home-style cooking), Troya enjoys a
prime location on Trujillo's main square. The
food is decent, but it's more about quantity. At
lunchtime, you'll be directed to one of several
dining areas, where plates of tortilla and
lettuce-and-tomato salad materialise before
you've even ordered your three-course *menú*.
Weekend queues stretch out the door.

❨ Eurostars
Palacio de Santa Marta   Hotel €€

(📞927 65 91 90; www.eurostarshotels.com; Calle
de los Ballesteros 6; d standard/premium from
€60/90; P ❄ 🛜 🛄) Above Plaza Mayor, the
refurbished 16th-century Santa Marta Palace
combines slick, wood-floored chambers with
original features such as exposed stone walls
and high ceilings. There's a summer-only pool.
For prime vistas over the square, book a superior
or premium room. Spacious room 208, with
its little pillared balcony, is stunning, as is two-
balconied 206. Outstanding breakfasts, too.

Cáceres ❸

🛏 Hotel Soho Boutique
Casa Don Fernando   Boutique Hotel €€

(📞927 62 71 76; https://en.sohohoteles.com/
hotel-boutique-casa-don-fernando-in-caceres;
Plaza Mayor 30; s/d from €55/70; P ❄ 🛜)
Cáceres' smartest midrange choice sits on
Plaza Mayor right opposite the Arco de la
Estrella. Boutique-style rooms, spread over four
floors, are tastefully modern, with gleaming
bathrooms through glass doors. Pricier
'superiors' enjoy the best plaza views (though
weekend nights can be noisy), and attic-style
top-floor rooms are good for families. Service
hits that perfect professional-yet-friendly note.

Zafra ❿

🛏 Hotel Plaza Grande   Hotel €

(📞924 56 31 63; www.hotelplazagrande.es;
Calle Pasteleros 2; incl breakfast s €32-42, d
€55; P ❄ 🛜) Right on the Plaza Grande, this
friendly, sparkling gem of a hotel is an excellent
deal. Modern-rustic decor accentuates
terracotta with cream paintwork, exposed
brick, floral prints and soft pastels. Go for room
108, with its corner balconies overlooking the
plaza; room 208 is the same but with windows
instead of balconies. The lively downstairs
cafe-restaurant (📞924 56 31 63; www.
hotelplazagrande.es; Calle Pasteleros 2;
tapas €4.50-7, raciones €9-19, mains €14-21;
🕐12.30pm-midnight; 🛜 🍴) is reliably good.

Northern Spain & the Basque Country

THIS IS THE SPAIN THAT MOST INTERNATIONAL VISITORS ARE YET TO DISCOVER. The north coast and its bright-green hinterland are home to some of the most dramatic scenery in the country, from snow-speckled mountains to a cliff-strung coastline peppered with long sandy beaches and pastel-painted villages.

Few parts of the Iberian peninsula are more rewarding for drivers. Many roads are quiet and wend slowly through small fishing ports, across mountain pastures and along ancient pilgrim trails. The scenic and cultural variety awaiting road trippers here is astounding. Pause in food-obsessed cities, climb castle turrets, stand among rolling vineyards, explore magical cave art, and peer over the edge of southern Europe's highest ocean cliffs.

La Rioja Vineyards
ALBERTO LOYO/SHUTTERSTOCK ©

Northern Spain & the Basque Country

A map showing locations including:

Cabo Ortegal, Punta da Estaca de Bares, O Barqueiro, Ferrol, Valdoviño, San Cosme, Ribadeo, Navia, **12**, Avilés, Gijón, Ribades, A Coruña, Baio, Betanzos, Vilalba, Cangas del Narcea, Oviedo, Arriondas, **13**, Santiago de Compostela, Lugo, San Antolín de Ibias, El Cornón (2194m), Peña Ubiña (2417m), Torrecerred (2648m), Fisterra, Sarria, Alto do Poio (1335m), Parque Natural de Somiedo, Parque Natural de Redes, Parque Nacion los Picos de Eu, Ribeira, Monforte de Lemos, Pedrafita do Cebreiro, La Magdalena, Guard, **7**, Pontevedra, Ourense, A Rúa, Ponferrada, León, **7**, Saha, ATLANTIC OCEAN, Baiona, Vigo, A Gudiña, Astorga, Río Porma, A Guarda, Parque Nacional da Peneda-Gerês, Verín, Puebla de Sanabria, Viana do Castelo, Parque Natural de Montesinho, Benavente, Vallado, Braga, Chaves, Bragança, Guimarães, Mirandela, Miranda do Douro, Zamora, Tordesillas, Vila Real, Porto, PORTUGAL, Río Duero, Río Tormes, Salamanca

7 Northern Spain Pilgrimage 5–7 Days
Follow pilgrims along roads that criss-cross the Camino de Santiago walking route.

8 Roving La Rioja Wine Region 2–3 Days
Discover the wealth of the grape on this peaceful countryside drive.

9 Lofty Roads: the Picos de Europa 2–4 Days
Change into low gear and head into Spain's most spectacular mountain range.

10 Cantabria's Eastern Valleys 2–4 Days
Get well off the beaten track on this journey through remote farming hamlets.

11 Along the Río Ebro 2–4 Days
Wine, cave churches, Islamic palaces, desert...it's all along the Río Ebro.

12 North Coast Beaches & Culture 4–6 Days
Hop between glorious sandy strands, sophisticated cities and slow-paced fishing villages.

13 Coast of Galicia 5–7 Days
Take a fearful drive along the Costa da Morte (Coast of Death).

Food

Northern Spain's varied people unite over a love of food. Find the freshest shellfish, artistic tapas or succulent steaks on Trips 8 10 11 12 13

Wine Tasting

La Rioja is home to the best red wines in Spain. Tours, tastings and museums inform as you imbibe on Trip 8

Coastal Villages

Sheltered fishing ports like Cedeira and Cudillero add a gentle touch to Spain's wildly dramatic northern coasts on Trips 12 13

Meeting God

Rock-cut churches, the Camino de Santiago and Islamic monuments: there's always somewhere to commune with your god along Trips 7 8 11 12 13

Art

From the Guggenheim to Goya and caves of Altamira to the sculptures of Santiago's cathedral, there's artistic genius aplenty on Trips 7 11 12 13

Cudillero (p166)

Classic Trip

Northern Spain Pilgrimage

Travel in the footprints of millions of pilgrims past and present as you journey along the highroads and backroads of the legendary Camino de Santiago pilgrimage trail.

7

TRIP HIGHLIGHTS

191 km

Santo Domingo de la Calzada
Get to know small-town Spain at its very best

259 km

Burgos
Pray before the altar of the Unesco-listed Burgos Cathedral

START
Roncesvalles

FINISH 20

Astorga 13

9 8

Puente la Reina

Santiago de Compostela
The magic of Santiago de Compostela cannot but overwhelm

786 km

León
León has stunning historical architecture and irresistible energy

449 km

5–7 DAYS
786KM / 488 MILES

GREAT FOR...

BEST TIME TO GO

From April to June for fields of poppies, September and October for golden leaves.

 ESSENTIAL PHOTO

Standing outside the cathedral of Santiago de Compostela.

☑ **BEST FOR A SENSE OF ACHIEVEMENT**

Reaching Santiago de Compostela.

7 Northern Spain Pilgrimage

For over a thousand years pilgrims have marched across the top of
Spain on the Camino de Santiago (Way of St James) to the tomb of
St James the Apostle in Santiago de Compostela. Real pilgrims walk,
but by driving you'll enjoy religious treasures, grand cathedrals, big
skies and wide open landscapes – and no blisters.

❶ Roncesvalles

History hangs thick in the air of the **Roncesvalles monastery complex** (📞948 79 04 80; www.roncesvalles.es; Carretera de Francia; guided tours adult/child €5.20/2.50; ⏱10am-2pm & 3.30-7pm Apr-Oct, 10am-2pm & 3-6pm Mar & Nov, 10.30am-2.30pm Thu-Tue Feb & Dec), where pilgrims give thanks for a successful crossing of the Pyrenees. The monastery contains a number of different buildings of interest,

including the 13th-century Gothic **Real Colegiata de Santa María** (📞948 79 04 80; www.roncesvalles. es; Carretera de Francia; ⏱9am-8.30pm) which houses a much-revered, silver-covered statue

of the Virgin beneath a modernist-looking canopy. Also of interest is the cloister, containing the tomb of King Sancho VII (El Fuerte) of Navarra, leader of one of the victorious Christian armies in the

LINK YOUR TRIP

13 Coast of Galicia
With the Camino de Santiago ticked off, carry on to Fisterra and a spectacular trip along Galicia's awe-inspiring coast.

1 Historic Castilla y León
From Burgos you can head south to discover the rich heritage of the cities of the Spanish plain.

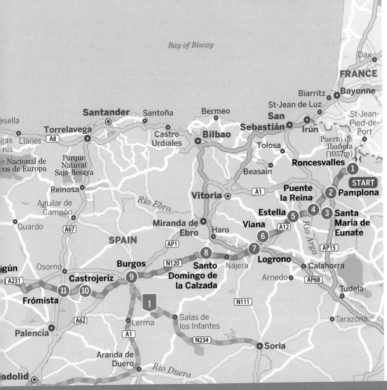

battle of Las Navas de Tolosa, fought against the Muslims in 1212.

📑 p227

The Drive >> It's 49km (one hour) basically downhill to Pamplona – a pretty drive along the N135 through mountainscapes, forests and gentle farmland. Innumerable hamlets and villages are painted in the red and white Basque colours and centred on old stone churches, many of them crammed with religious treasures.

- - - - - - - - - - - - - - - - - -

❷ Pamplona

Renowned across the world for the Sanfermines festival (6 to 14 July), when bulls tear through the streets at 8am causing chaos as they go (and alcohol-fuelled revellers cause chaos for the remainder of the day – and night), Pamplona (Iruña in Basque) is a quiet, low-key city at any other time of the year. Animal welfare groups condemn the bull-running as a cruel tradition. Pamplona's history stretches back to Roman times, and is best traced in the fantastic **Museo de Navarra** (📞848 42 64 93; www.navarra. es; Calle Cuesta de Santo Domingo 47; adult/child €2/ free, Sat afternoon & Sun free; ⏰9.30am-2pm & 5-7pm Tue-Sat, 11am-2pm Sun), whose highlights include huge Roman mosaics. Another Pamplona highlight is the tour of the **catedral** (www. catedraldepamplona.com; Calle Dormitalería; adult/child €5/3; ⏰10.30am-7pm Mon-Sat Apr-Oct, to 5pm Mon-Sat Nov-Mar, closed Sun, tower climb 11.15am), a late-medieval Gothic gem with a neoclassical facade. The tour takes you into the

WHAT IS THE CAMINO DE SANTIAGO

The Camino de Santiago (Way of St James) originated as a medieval pilgrimage. For more than a millennium people have taken up the challenge of the Camino and walked to Santiago de Compostela. It all began in the 9th century when a remarkable event occurred in the poor Iberian hinterlands: following a shining star, a religious hermit named Pelayo unearthed the tomb of St James the Apostle (Santiago in Spanish). The news was confirmed by the local bishop, the Asturian king and later the pope.

Compostela became the most important destination for Christians after Rome and Jerusalem. Its popularity increased with an 11th-century papal decree granting it Holy Year status: pilgrims could receive a plenary indulgence (a full remission of your life's sins) during a Holy Year. These occur when Santiago's feast day (25 July) falls on a Sunday: 2021 is such a year and the next is 2027 – but driving there doesn't count...

The 11th and 12th centuries marked the heyday of the pilgrimage. The Reformation was devastating for Catholic pilgrimages and by the 19th century the Camino had nearly died out. In its startling late-20th-century reanimation, which continues today, it's equally popular as a personal and spiritual journey of discovery as for primarily religious motives. These days over 350,000 people a year arrive in Santiago on foot, or sometimes bicycle and occasionally horseback, having completed one of the many Caminos de Santiago that lead to the city from all points of the Iberian Peninsula and beyond. The most popular route has always been the Camino Francés, which in its full extent crosses some 770km of northern Spain from the Pyrenees, and attracts walkers of all backgrounds and ages from across the world. For pilgrims, it's equal to visiting Jerusalem, and by finishing it you can expect a healthy chunk of time off purgatory.

cloisters and a museum displaying the remains of a Roman-era house and the tiny skeleton of a seven-month-old baby found there. The 11.15am tour also goes up the bell tower to see (and possibly hear) the second-largest church bell in Spain.

 p120

The Drive » Take the A12 southwestward. After about 10 minutes take exit 9 onto the driver-friendly NA1110. Drive through Astraín and continue along this country road for 15 minutes to Legarda and Muruzábal, then it's 2km southeast to Santa María de Eunate. Total 22km; about 40 minutes.

③ Santa María de Eunate

Surrounded by corn-fields and brushed by wildflowers, the near-perfect octagonal Romanesque chapel of **Santa María de Eunate** (www.santamariadeeunate.es; Carretera de Campanas; adult/child €1.50/1; ◷10.30am-1.30pm Tue-Fri, 11am-1.30pm & 4.30-6.30pm Sat & Sun Apr-Jun, Sep & Oct, 10.30am-1.30pm & 5-6.30pm Wed-Mon Jul & Aug) is one of the most picturesque churches along the Camino. It dates from around the 12th century but its origins – and the reason why it's located in the middle of nowhere – are a mystery.

The Drive » From the chapel it's just a 5km drive along the NA6064 and NA1110 to gorgeous Puente la Reina.

④ Puente la Reina

The chief calling card of Puente la Reina (Basque: Gares) is the spectacular six-arched **medieval bridge** dominating the western end of town, but Puente la Reina rewards on many other levels.

A key stop on the Camino de Santiago, the town's pretty streets throng with the ghosts of a multitude of pilgrims. Pilgrims' first stop here is the late-Romanesque **Iglesia del Crucifijo**. Erected by the Knights Templar, it contains one of the finest Gothic crucifixes in existence.

The Drive » The fastest way between Puente la Reina and Estella is on the A12 (20km, 20 minutes), but the more enjoyable drive is along the slower, more rural, NA1110, taking about half an hour. You'll probably spy a few Camino pilgrims striding along.

⑤ Estella

Estella (Basque: Lizarra) was known as 'La Bella' in medieval times because of the splendour of its monuments and buildings, and though the old dear has lost some of its beauty to modern suburbs, it still has charm. During the 11th century, Estella became a main reception point for the growing flood of pilgrims along the Camino. Today most visitors are continuing that same tradition.

The attractive old quarter has a couple of notable churches, including the 12th-century **Iglesia de San Pedro de la Rúa**, whose cloisters are a fine example of Romanesque sculptural work. Across the river and overlooking the town is the **Iglesia de San Miguel**, with a fine Romanesque north portal. The countryside around Estella is littered with monasteries. Two of the most impressive

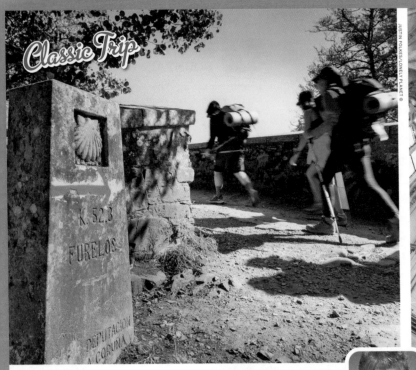

Classic Trip

WHY THIS IS A CLASSIC TRIP
JOHN NOBLE, AUTHOR

Millions of people following the Camino de Santiago over 1200 years have given rise to an unrivalled heritage of monumental cathedrals, tiny chapels, ancient inns and other landmarks. To follow the pilgrims' path today is to breathe the aura of countless journeys and to sense the excitement of those doing it on foot. You might even be inspired to come back and walk it yourself one day!

Above: Waymarker, Camino de Santiago (p110)
Left: Pilgrim passport, Camino de Santiago (p110)
Right: **Burgos** Chapel of Purification, Catedral (p48)

are **Monasterio de Iratxe** (off Carretera NA1110, Ayegui; 🕐10am-1.15pm & 4-6pm Wed-Sun mid-Jan–mid-Nov), 2.5km southwest near Ayegui, and **Monasterio de Irantzu** (off Carretera NA7135, Abárzuza; €2.50; 🕐10am-2pm & 4-8pm Apr-Sep, to 6pm Oct-Mar), 11km north near Abárzuza.

The Drive ≫ It's a 40km (50 minute) drive to Viana. Take the A12 westward and turn onto the NA1110 at junction 58. Follow the NA1110 through the sleepy villages of Los Arcos, Sansol and Torres del Río. In hillside Torres you'll find a remarkably intact eight-sided Romanesque chapel, the Iglesia del Santo Sepulcro.

- - - - - - - - - - - - - - -

6 Viana

Overlooked by many non-pilgrim tourists, Viana, the last town in Navarra, started life as a garrison town defending the kingdom of Navarra from Castilla. The old part of the town, which sits atop a hill, is still largely walled and is an interesting place to wander about for a couple of hours. Work started on the **Iglesia de Santa María** in the 13th century and it's one of the more impressive religious structures on this eastern part of the Camino. Viana's former **bullring** is now a plaza in the middle of town, where children booting footballs are considerably more common than bulls.

113

The Drive » It's 10km to Logroño. The first half of the drive is through open, big-sky countryside; the last part through the city suburbs. There's a large car park under Paseo del Espolón on the south edge of Logroño's old town.

----

❼ Logroño

Logroño, capital of La Rioja – Spain's wine-growing region par excellence – doesn't feel the need to be loud and brash. Instead it's a stately town with a heart of tree-studded squares, narrow streets and a monumentally good selection of *pintxos* (tapas) bars. It's the sort of place where you can't help feeling contented. And it's not just the wine. The superb **Museo de la Rioja** (📞941 29 12 59; www.museodelarioja.es; Plaza San Agustín 23; ⏰10am-2pm & 4-9pm Tue-Sat, 10am-2pm Sun) in the centre takes you on a wild romp through Riojan history and culture, from the days when dinner was killed with arrows to recreations of the kitchens that many a Spanish granny grew up using. The other major attraction is the **Catedral de Santa María de la Redonda** (www.laredonda.org; Calle de Portales 14; ⏰8.30am-1pm & 6-8.45pm Mon-Sat,

8.30am-2pm Sun); it started life as a Gothic church before maturing into a full-blown cathedral in the 16th century.

🍴 🛏 p120, p126, p131

The Drive » For the 45km (35-minute) hop to Santo Domingo de la Calzada, the Camino walking trail parallels – mostly at a respectful distance – the fast, and dull, A12. There's not much reason for you to veer off the motorway (none of the quieter roads really follow the Camino).

TRIP HIGHLIGHT

❽ Santo Domingo de la Calzada

Santo Domingo is small-town Spain at its very best. A large number of the inhabitants still live in the partly-walled old quarter, a labyrinth of medieval streets where the past is alive and the sense of community is strong. The **Catedral de Santo Domingo de la Calzada** (📞941 34 00 33; www.catedralsantodomingo.com; Plaza del Santo 4; adult/child €7/2; ⏰10am-8pm Mon-Fri, to 7pm Sat, 10am-noon & 2-8pm Sun Apr-Oct, shorter hours Nov-Mar) and its attached museum glitter with the gold that attests to the great wealth the Camino has bestowed on otherwise backwater towns. The cathedral's most eccentric feature is the white rooster and hen that forage in a glass-fronted cage opposite the entrance to the crypt.

Their presence celebrates a long-standing legend, the Miracle of the Rooster, which tells of a young man who was unfairly executed only to recover miraculously, while the broiled cock and hen on the plate of his judge suddenly leapt up and chickened off, fully fledged.

🍴 🛏 p131

The Drive » It's 68km (one hour) to Burgos. Again, you're sort of stuck with using the main road, the N120.

TRIP HIGHLIGHT

❾ Burgos

On the surface, conservative Burgos seems to embody all the stereotypes of a north-central Spanish town, with sombre grey stone architecture, the fortifying cuisine of the high *meseta* (plateau) and a climate of extremes. But Burgos is a city that rewards. The historic centre is austerely elegant, guarded by monumental gates and with the **cathedral** (p48) as its centrepiece – a World Heritage–listed masterpiece that started life as a modest Romanesque church, but over time became one of the most impressive cathedrals in a land of impressive cathedrals. Read more about Burgos in Trip 1: Historic Castilla y León (p41).

✕ 🛏 p51, p120

The Drive » It's 48km (45 minutes) to castle-topped Castrojeriz. Head southwest on the A62 to junction 32 and turn off northwest along the minor BU400.

---

⑩ Castrojeriz

With its mix of old and new buildings huddled around the base of a hill that's topped with what's left of a crumbling **castle**, Castrojeriz is a typical small *meseta* town. It's worth a climb up to the castle if only for the views. The town's church, **Iglesia de San Juan**, is worth a look as well.

The Drive » From Castrojeriz it's 26km (30 minutes) along the BU403 and P432 to Frómista. The scenery is classic *meseta* and if you're lucky you'll catch a glimpse of such evocative sights as a flock of sheep being led over the alternately burning or freezing plateau by a shepherd.

---

⑪ Frómista

The main (and some would say only) reason for stopping here is the village's exceptional **Iglesia de San Martín** (📞979 81 01 44; Plaza de San Martín, Frómista; adult/child €2/free; 🕑9.30am-2pm & 4.30-8pm Apr-Sep, 10am-2pm & 3.30-6.30pm Oct-Mar). Dating from 1066 and restored in the early 20th century, this harmoniously proportioned church is one of the premier Romanesque churches in

rural Spain, adorned with human and animal forms below the eaves. The capitals within are also richly decorated.

The Drive » Take the P980 (the Camino runs alongside it) to Carrión de los Condes, then the more major A231 west to Sahagún. (56km; 45 minutes).

---

⑫ Sahagún

Despite appearances, Sahagún was an immensely powerful and wealthy Benedictine centre by the 12th century. The brick Romanesque churches, some with later Mudéjar additions, merit a visit.

The Drive » The 60km (50-minute) stretch from Sahagún to León along the A231

and A60 isn't a memorable drive. Still, you have to feel for those walking the Camino: some pilgrims bus between Burgos and León because so much of the route is next to busy roads.

TRIP HIGHLIGHT

⑬ León

León is a wonderful city, combining stunning historical architecture with an irresistible energy. Its standout attraction is the 13th-century **catedral** (📞987 87 57 70; www.catedralleon.org; Plaza Regla; adult/concession/under 12yr €6/5/free, combined ticket with Claustro & Museo Catedralicio-Diocesano €9/8/free; 🕑9.30am-1.30pm & 4-8pm Mon-Fri, 9.30am-noon & 2-6pm Sat, 9.30-11am & 2-8pm Sun

WHO WAS ST JAMES THE APOSTLE

St James, or James the Greater, was one of the 12 disciples of Jesus. He may even have been the first disciple. He was also probably the first to be martyred, by King Herod in 44 CE. So, if St James was living in the Holy Lands 2000 years ago, an obvious question persists: what were his remains doing in northwest Spain 800 years later? The legend (and we're not standing by its historical accuracy) suggests that two of St James' own disciples secreted his remains on a stone boat which sailed across the Mediterranean and passed into the Atlantic to moor at present-day Padrón (Galicia). After various trials and tribulations, they buried his body in a forest named Libredón (present-day Santiago de Compostela). All was then forgotten until about 820 CE, when a religious hermit found the remains. Further legends attest that during his lifetime St James preached in various parts of Spain, including Galicia, which might explain why his remains were brought here.

Classic Trip

May-Sep, 9.30am-1.30pm & 4-7pm Mon-Sat, 9.30am-2pm Sun Oct-Apr), one of the most beautiful cathedrals in Spain and arguably the country's premier Gothic masterpiece. Whether spotlit at night or bathed in glorious sunshine, it exudes an almost luminous quality. The showstopping facade has a radiant rose window, three richly sculpted doorways and two muscular towers. Inside, an extraordinary gallery of stained-glass windows awaits.

The even older **Real Basílica de San Isidoro** (📞987 87 61 61; Plaza de San Isidoro; ⏰7.30am-11pm) provides a stunning Romanesque counterpoint to the cathedral's Gothic strains. Fernando I and Doña Sancha founded this church in 1063 to house the remains of San Isidoro, and of themselves and 21 other early Leonese and Castilian monarchs. The main basilica is a hotchpotch of styles, but the two main portals on the southern facade are pure Romanesque.

The attached **Real Colegiata de San Isidoro** (Panteón Real; 📞987 87 61 61; www.museosanisidorodeleon.com; Plaza de San Isidoro; adult/child €5/free; ⏰10am-2pm & 4-7pm Mon-Sat,

10am-2pm Sun) houses royal sarcophagi, which rest with quiet dignity beneath a canopy of some of the finest Romanesque frescoes in Spain. Motif after colourful motif of biblical scenes drench the vaults and arches of this extraordinary hall.

🍴 🛏 p120

The Drive » Taking the N120 to Astorga will keep you on the route of the Camino, which runs alongside the road for long stretches. It's a 50km (one-hour) drive. The AP71 is much faster, but what's the point in coming all this way to drive on a road like that?

🕦 Astorga

Perched on a hilltop on the frontier between the bleak plains of northern Castilla and the mountains that rise west towards Galicia, Astorga is a fascinating small town with a wealth of attractions way out of proportion to its size. The most eye-catching sight is the **Palacio Episcopal**, a rare flight of fancy in this part of the country, designed by Antoni Gaudí. There's also a smattering of Roman ruins (Astorga was once an important Roman settlement called Astúrica Augusta), a fine Gothic and plateresque **catedral** (Plaza de la Catedral; incl museum & cloister €5; ⏰10am-8.30pm Mon-Sat, 10-11.15am & 1-8.30pm Sun Apr-Oct, 10.30am-6pm Nov-Mar) and even a **Museo del Chocolate** (📞987 61 62 20; Avenida de la Estación 16; adult/child €2.50/free, incl Museo Romano adult/child €4/free; ⏰10.30am-2pm & 4.30-7pm Tue-Sat, 10.30am-2pm Sun; 👶), dedicated to the town's long chocolate-making tradition.

Less sinfully, the town sees a steady stream of pilgrims passing through along the Camino de Santiago.

León Catedral (p115)

The Drive » It's just 8km (15 minutes) along the rural LE142 to Castrillo de los Polvazares. Non-residents are not allowed to drive into Castrillo, so park in one of the parking areas on the edge of the village.

----

15 Castrillo de los Polvazares

One of the prettiest villages along the Camino – if a little twee – is Castrillo de los Polvazares. It consists of little but one main cobbled street, a small church and an array of well-preserved 18th-century stone houses.

If you can be here before the tour buses arrive, or after they have left, then it's an absolute delight of a place and one in which the spirit of the Camino can be strongly felt.

The Drive » Continue along the LE142 to Ponferrada (53km; 1¼ hours). It runs pretty much beside the Camino and you'll pass through attractive stone villages, most of which have churches topped with storks' nests. Rabanal del Camino, with its 18th-century church Ermita del Bendito Cristo de la Vera Cruz, is worth a quick stop.

Classic Trip

16 Ponferrada

Ponferrada is not the region's most enticing town, but its castle and remnants of the old town centre (around the stone clock tower) make it worth a brief stop. Built by the Knights Templar in the 13th century, the walls of the fortress-monastery **Castillo Templario** rise high over the Río Sil with a lonely and impregnable air, and its square, crenellated towers ooze romance and history.

The Drive » If you're not in a huge hurry, take the NVI to Villafranca del Bierzo (24km, 30 minutes). It's slower but gentler than the A6 motorway.

17 Villafranca del Bierzo

Villafranca del Bierzo has a very well preserved old core and a number of interesting churches and other religious buildings. Chief among these are **San Nicolás El Real**, a 17th-century convent with a baroque altarpiece, and the 12th-century **Iglesia de Santiago**. The northern doorway of this church is called the 'door of forgiveness'. Pilgrims who were sick, or otherwise unable to continue to Santiago de Compostela, were granted the same godly favours as if they'd made it all the way.

The Drive » It's 32km (45 minutes) uphill to O Cebreiro using the NVI, or a bit quicker via the A6. On the NVI you can admire or pity the pilgrims making the Camino's longest, hardest climb, right beside the road on several stretches. Turn off at Pedrafita do Cebreiro and take the LU633 for the last 4km.

18 O Cebreiro

O Cebreiro, 1300m high, is the first village in Galicia on the Camino. It's an atmospheric and picturesque little place, busy with pilgrims happy to have completed the climb from Villafranca. O Cebreiro contains several *pallozas* (circular, thatched dwellings known in Galicia since pre-Roman times). A former village priest here, Elías Valiño (1929–89), is considered to have been the driving force behind the revival of the Camino de Santiago in the late 20th century.

The Drive » The marvellous 33km drive to Samos winds down the LU633 through refreshingly

THE PÓRTICO DE LA GLORIA

Santiago cathedral's artistically unparalleled **Pórtico de la Gloria** features 200 Romanesque sculptures by Maestro Mateo, who was placed in charge of the cathedral-building programme in the late 12th century. These detailed and remarkably lifelike sculptures add up to a comprehensive review of major figures and scenes from the Bible. The Old Testament and its prophets (including a famously smiling Daniel) are on the north side; the New Testament, Apostles and Last Judgement are on the south; and glory and resurrection are depicted in the central archway.

Visits are limited to 25 people at a time. Spanish-language **guided visits** (45 minutes; adult/concession/child €10/8/free) are given several times daily, with tickets sold up to 90 days ahead through the cathedral website or on the same day (if available) at the **Pazo de Xelmírez** adjoining the cathedral, where the visit starts. Fifteen-minute **unguided visits** happen from 7pm to 8pm Monday to Saturday; 50 tickets for these (free) are given out between 7pm and 8pm the day before at the Fundación Catedral office in the **Casa do Deán** (Rúa do Vilar 3). For Monday visits go on Saturday. Take your ID document.

green countryside with great long-distance views, frequently criss-crossing the Camino.

19 Samos

A pretty village in the Río Sarria valley, Samos is built around the very fine Benedictine **Mosteiro de Samos** (📞982 54 60 46; www.abadiadesamos.com; tours €5; 🕐tours hourly 9.30am-12.30pm & 4.30-6.30pm Mon-Sat, 12.45pm & hourly 4.30-6.30pm Sun May-Oct, hourly 10am-noon, 4.30pm & 5.30pm Mon & Wed-Sat, 12.45pm, 4.30pm, 5.30pm Sun Nov-Apr; 🅿). This monastery has two beautiful big cloisters – one Gothic, with distinctly unmonastic Greek nymphs adorning its fountain, the other neoclassical and filled with roses.

🍴 p121

The Drive » Follow the LU633 and N547 to stay fairly close to the Camino and pass through attractive villages and small towns such as Portomarín. There's no avoiding the A54 motorway to get past Santiago airport. Follow 'Centro Histórico' signs towards the city centre (137km, 2¾ hours from Samos). Private vehicles are barred from the Old Town; underground car parks around its fringes charge around €15 per 24 hours. Cheaper are Aparcadoiro Xoan XXIII (€11) and open-air Aparcadoiro Belvís (€7.50).

TRIP HIGHLIGHT

20 Santiago de Compostela

This, then, is it. The end of The Way. And what

DETOUR: CABO FISTERRA

Start: 20 Santiago de Compostela

This spectacular, cliff-girt, wave-lashed cape has, in popular imagination, long been considered the western edge of Spain, and in days way before satnav it was believed to be the very end of the world. The name Fisterra (Finisterre in Castilian Spanish) means 'Land's End'. In fact, Spain's real westernmost point is Cabo Touriñán, 20km north, but that doesn't lessen Fisterra's magnetic appeal. The end point of a highly popular extension to the Camino de Santiago, the cape is an 82km, 1½-hour drive west from Santiago. Camino pilgrims ritually burn smelly socks, T-shirts and the like on the rocks just past the lighthouse. Many people come for sunset but it's a magnificent spot at any time (unless shrouded in fog or rain). Fisterra town, 3.5km before the cape, is a fishing port with a picturesque harbour and some beautiful beaches nearby.

a spectacular finish. Santiago de Compostela, with its granite buildings and frequent drizzle, is one of the most beautiful, fascinating cities in Spain.

With more than 350,000 pilgrims arriving annually, Santiago has a busy, festive atmosphere throughout the warmer half of the year (May to October). The magnificent **Catedral de Santiago de Compostela** (www.catedraldesantiago. es; Praza do Obradoiro; 🕐9am-8pm) soars above the city centre in a splendid jumble of spires and statues. Its beauty is a mix of the original Romanesque structure (built between 1075 and 1211) and later Gothic and baroque flourishes. The tomb of Santiago beneath the main altar

is a magnet for all who arrive. The artistic high point is the **Pórtico de la Gloria** inside the west entrance.

Grand **Praza do Obradoiro**, in front of the cathedral's west facade, is traffic- and cafe-free and has a unique atmosphere. From here you can start exploring Santiago's other fine squares and churches. At the square's northern end, the **Hostal dos Reis Católicos** (📞981 58 22 00; www.parador.es; Praza do Obradoiro; adult/child €3/ free, Mon free; 🕐noon-2pm & 4-6pm Sun-Fri) was built in the 16th century as a refuge for exhausted pilgrims. Today it's a *parador* (luxurious state-owned hotel), but its four courtyards are open to visitors.

🍴🛏 p121

Eating & Sleeping

Pamplona ➋

🍴 Bar Gaucho   Pintxos €

(☏948 22 50 73; Calle Espoz y Mina 7; pintxos €2-4.50; ⏰8.30am-12.30am) This bustling bar's multi-award-winning *pintxos* are among the finest in the city. Highlights include smoked eel with tomato jelly, filo pastry–calf's tongue, a shot glass of truffled egg, mushroom crème and crispy ham, and sea urchin mousse served in the shell.

Logroño ➐

🍴 La Cocina de Ramón   Spanish €€€

(☏941 28 98 08; www.lacocinaderamon. es; Calle de Portales 30; mains €18-27; ⏰1.30-4pm & 8.30-11pm Mon, Tue & Thu-Sat, 1.30-4pm Wed) It looks unassuming from the outside, but Ramón's high-quality, locally grown produce and tried-and-tested family recipes, such as chargrilled lamb cutlets or beef tenderloin cooked with wines from La Rioja, has earned him a lot of fans. The fine cooking is matched by the top service and white tablecloths; Ramón likes to come and explain the dishes to guests.

Burgos ➒

🍴 La Favorita   Tapas €€

(☏947 20 59 49; www.lafavoritaburgos.com; Calle de Avellanos 8; tapas from €4; ⏰10am-midnight Mon-Fri, noon-12.30am Sat & Sun) Away from the main Burgos tapas hub but still close to the cathedral, La Favorita has an appealing, barn-like interior of exposed brick and wooden beams. The emphasis is on local cured meats and cheeses (try the cheese platter for €15); wine by the glass starts at €2. The tapas menu includes beef sirloin with foie gras.

🛏 Hotel Norte y Londres   Historic Hotel €

(☏947 26 41 25; www.hotelnorteylondres.com; Plaza de Alonso Martínez 10; s/d from €40/45; 🅿 @ 🛜) Set in a former 16th-century palace and decorated with understated period charm, this fine, family-run hotel promises spacious rooms with antique furnishings and polished wooden floors. All rooms have pretty balconies and double-glazed windows; those on the 4th floor are more modern. The bathrooms are exceptionally large and the service friendly and efficient.

León ⓭

🍴 Restaurante Cocinandos   Modern Spanish €€€

(☏987 07 13 78; www.cocinandos.com; Calle de las Campanillas 1; set menus €50-90; ⏰1.45-3.15pm & 9.30-10.30pm Tue-Sat) The proud owner of León's first Michelin star, Cocinandos brings creative flair to the table with a menu that changes weekly with the seasons and market availability. The atmosphere is slightly formal so dress nicely and book in advance, but the young team puts diners at ease and the food is exceptional (in that zany new-Spanish-cuisine kind of way).

🛏 La Posada Regia   Historic Hotel €€

(☏987 21 31 73; www.regialeon.com; Calle de Regidores 9-11; s €54-70, d €59-130; 🛜) This place has the feel of a *casa rural* (village or farmstead accommodation) despite being in the city centre. The secret is a 14th-century building, magnificently restored (with wooden beams, exposed brick and understated antique furniture), with individually styled rooms and supremely comfortable beds and bathrooms. As with anywhere in the Barrio Húmedo, weekend nights can be noisy.

Samos 🅑

🛏 Casa de Díaz   Heritage Hotel €

(📞982 54 70 70; www.hotelcasadediaz.com;
Vilachá; r €42-68, breakfast €4-8; ⊗Apr-Oct;
🅿 @ 🛜 ⌖) Samos has plenty of inexpensive
lodgings, but a good option is to continue 3.5km
west to the welcoming Casa de Díaz, an 18th-
century farmhouse turned rural hotel at Vilachá.
It has 12 comfy rooms in olde-worlde style and
(except Sundays) serves three-course dinners
(€18) by reservation. The spacious gardens,
pool and games room make it a good place to
hang out if you're with children.

Santiago de Compostela 🅒

🍴 Mercado de Abastos   Market €

(www.mercadodeabastosdesantiago.com;
Rúa das Ameas 5-8; ⊗8am-2pm Mon-Sat)
Santiago's food market is a fascinating, always
lively scene. It's very clean, with masses of
fresh produce from the seas and countryside
displayed at 300-odd stalls. Saturday is
particularly festive, with Galician folk musicians
sometimes playing in the surrounding bars.

Stock up on *tetilla* cheese, cured meats,
sausage, fruit, *empanada* (pastry pie) or the
terrific home-made, take-away dishes of
Cocina María (www.cocinamaria.es; Mercado
de Abastos, Nave 1, Posto C61; items €1.50-15;
⊗9.30am-3pm Mon-Sat) for a picnic.
Bars and restaurants line the street outside,
but there are also good options within the
market itself, especially **Nave 5 Abastos**
(www.facebook.com/nave5abastos; Mercado
de Abastos, Nave 5; dishes €4-16; ⊗11.30am-
4.30pm Mon-Sat), where chefs in Aisle 5 cook up
top-class fresh seafood and fish, *filloas* (Galician
crêpes), Mexican tacos and more, and you sit
at long tables or stools to enjoy it. Drinks too,
at equally reasonable prices. Also in Nave 5,
popular **Mariscomanía** (Mercado de Abastos,

Nave 5, Posto 81; ⊗9am-3pm Tue-Sat) will, for
€5 per person, cook up seafood or meat that
you buy elsewhere in the market (though it
doesn't do octopus or fish).

Around the outside of the buildings you'll
find stallholders selling the produce of their
orchards or veggie gardens.

🍴 A Moa   Galician €€

(📞981 07 18 18; www.amoa32.com; Rúa de
San Pedro 32; mains €15-18, tapas €3-7, lunch
menú Tue-Fri €10-15; ⊗1-4pm & 8pm-midnight
Tue-Sat, 1-4pm Sun; 🍴) A Moa produces a great
mix of trad Galician and more international fare
in its street-level wine bar and stone-walled
downstairs restaurant opening onto a verdant
garden area. Starters and tapas range over
octopus croquettes, a great lemony ceviche,
falafel and vegetarian salads. Main dishes are
mostly a little more conventional: roast lamb,
BBQ pork ribs, fish of the day.

It's all great, and enhanced by service which
manages to be efficient, friendly and relaxed all
at the same time.

🛏 Altaïr Hotel   Boutique Hotel €€

(📞981 55 47 12; www.altairhotel.net; Rúa dos
Loureiros 12; s €50-85, d €60-130; ⊗closed
Jan; ❄ 🛜) The Altaïr combines stone walls
and solid oak floors with cosy comfort,
attentive staff, soft furnishings and splashes
of contemporary design. Breakfast (€8.50) is
a gourmet affair, and there are great city views
from some rooms.

🛏 San Francisco
Hotel Monumento   Historic Hotel €€€

(📞981 58 16 34; www.sanfranciscohm.com;
Campillo de San Francisco 3; incl breakfast s
€105-138, d €154-334; 🅿 ❄ @ 🛜 ⌖) The
three cloister-courtyards and low-lit hallways
recall the hotel's former life as a Franciscan
monastery. But the rooms are large and all
about contemporary comfort, and there's
a great indoor pool as well as a huge grassy
garden, cafe, and good restaurant.

Classic Trip

Roving La Rioja Wine Region

8

Learn about the gift of the grape on this quiet road trip through vine-studded countryside. Along the way, visit wineries and wine museums and admire stunning architecture.

TRIP HIGHLIGHTS

95 km

Vivanco Wine Museum
Obtain wine-fuelled knowledge in this space-age museum

125 km

Laguardia
Spin back the wheels of time in this wine-soaked fortress town

Haro

6

8

Santo Domingo de la Calzada

Nájera

START/ FINISH

1

San Millán de Cogolla

Santo Domingo de la Calzada
The old town buzzes with Camino pilgrims

6 km

Logroño
Delve into the fabulous culinary scene of this understated city

1 km

2–3 DAYS
145 KM / 90 MILES

GREAT FOR...
🍷 📖

BEST TIME TO GO
September and October when the grapes are being harvested.

📷 ESSENTIAL PHOTO
Waving at the camera from in front of the Hotel Marqués de Riscal.

✓ BEST FOR FOOD
Logroño has some of the best tapas bars in Spain.

Hotel Marqués de Riscal, designed by architect Frank Gehry (p129)

Classic Trip

8 Roving La Rioja Wine Region

La Rioja is home to the best wines in Spain and on this short and sweet road trip along unhurried back roads you'll enjoy gorgeous vine-striped countryside and asleep-at-noon villages of honey-coloured stone. But the overriding interest is reserved for food and drink: winery tours, cutting-edge museums and some of the best tapas in Spain make this drive an essential for any food and wine lover.

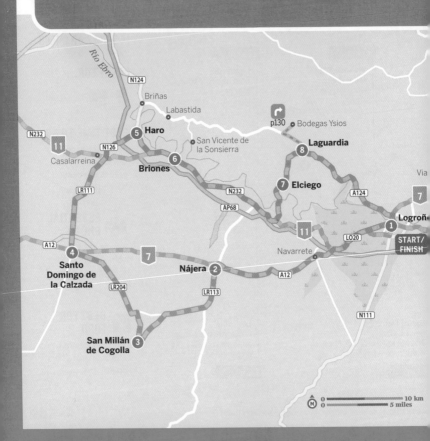

① Logroño

Small, low-key Logroño is the capital of La Rioja. The city doesn't receive all that many tourists and there aren't all that many things to see and do, but the historic centre makes for pleasant strolling and there is a monumentally good selection of *pintxos* (tapas) bars. In fact, Logroño is quickly gaining a culinary reputation to rival anywhere in Spain.

Rioja Trek (☏941 58 73 54; www.riojatrek.com; Calle Francisco de Quevedo 12), based 2.5km southeast of the city centre, offers a wide range of customisable winery tours (which can include visiting a traditional vineyard and bodega and even doing some wine-making yourself), as well as wine tastings, tapas tours, hikes along some of La Rioja's fabulous mountain trails and activities for families with children.

✕ ⛺ p120, p126, p131

The Drive » It's only a short drive of 28km (25 minutes) from Logroño to Nájera, starting along the LO20, which transforms into the A12 motorway around the halfway point.

---

② Nájera

The main attraction of this otherwise unexciting town, which lies on the Camino de Santiago, is the Gothic **Monasterio de Santa María la Real** and, in particular, its fragile-looking, early-16th-century cloisters. The monastery was built in 1032, but was significantly rebuilt in the 15th century.

The Drive » The dry landscapes around Nájera become greener and more rolling as you head southwest along the LR113 and LR205 for 18km (20 minutes) to San Millán de Cogolla. In the far distance rise the 2000m-plus mountains of the Sierra de la Demanda – snow-capped in winter.

---

③ San Millán de Cogolla

The hamlet of San Millán de Cogolla is home to two remarkable monasteries, which between them helped give birth to the Castilian (Spanish) language. On account of their linguistic heritage and artistic beauty, they have been recognised by Unesco as World Heritage sites.

The **Monasterio de Yuso** (☏941 37 30 49; www.monasteriodesanmillan.com/yuso; Calle Convento; adult/child €7/3; ⊙10am-1.30pm & 4-6.30pm Tue-Sun Apr-Sep, also open Mon Aug, to 5.30pm Tue-Sun Oct-Mar) contains numerous treasures in its museum. You can only visit as part of a guided tour (in Spanish, with English and French information sheets available). Tours last 50 minutes and run every half-hour or so.

A short distance away is the **Monasterio de Suso** (☏941 37 30 82; www.monasteriodesanmillan.com/suso; Calle de Suso; €4; ⊙9.30am-1.30pm & 3.30-6.30pm Tue-Sun Apr-Sep, to 5.30pm Oct-Mar). It's believed that in the 13th century a monk named Gonzalo de Berceo wrote some of the first Castilian words here. Again, it can only be visited on a guided tour. Tickets include a short bus ride up to the monastery from the Monasterio de Yuso, whose reception area sells them; you can't arrive independently.

The Drive » It's a 20km (20-minute) drive along the delightfully quiet LR206 and LR204 to Santo Domingo de la

LINK YOUR TRIP

7 Northern Spain Pilgrimage

Follow the path of pilgrims on the road to Santiago de Compostela. You can join The Way in Logroño.

11 Along the Río Ebro

From Logroño you can join this tour and explore deserts and Islamic palaces, churches carved into rock and castles with hanging gardens.

Classic Trip

Calzada. The scenery is a mix of vast sunburnt fields, red-tinged soils, vineyards and patches of forest.

TRIP HIGHLIGHT

④ Santo Domingo de la Calzada

The small, walled old town of Santo Domingo is the kind of place where you can be certain that the baker knows all his customers by name and that everyone will turn up for María's christening. Santiago-bound pilgrims have long been a part of the

fabric of this town, and that tradition continues to this day, with most visitors being foot-weary pilgrims. All this helps to make Santo Domingo one of the most enjoyable places in La Rioja. The biggest attraction in town, aside from the very worthwhile pursuit of just strolling the streets and lounging in the main old-town plaza, is a visit to the monumental **catedral** (☏941 34 00 33; www.catedralsantodomingo. com; Plaza del Santo 4; adult/ child €7/2; ⏱10am-8pm Mon-Fri, to 7pm Sat, 10am-noon & 2-8pm Sun Apr-Oct, shorter hours Nov-Mar).

✕ ⛏ p131

The Drive ≫ The LR111 (becoming the N126) goes in an almost ruler-straight line across fields of crops and under a big sky to the workaday town of Haro (20km, 20 minutes).

---

⑤ Haro

Despite its fame in the wine world, there's not much of a heady bouquet to Haro, La Rioja's premier wine-producing town. But it has a cheerful pace, and the compact old quarter, leading off Plaza de la Paz, has some intriguing alleyways with bars and wine shops aplenty.

There are plenty of wine bodegas in the vicinity of the town,

---

LOCAL KNOWLEDGE:
TAPAS IN LOGROÑO

Make no mistake about it: Logroño is an eater's delight. There are several very good restaurants, and then there are the tapas (which here are often called by their Basque name, *pintxos*). Few cities have such a dense concentration of excellent tapas bars. Most of the action takes place on Calle Laurel and Calle San Juan. *Pintxos* cost around €2 to €4, and most of the bars are open from about 8pm to midnight Tuesday to Sunday. Here are some of our favourites:

Bar Torrecilla (☏608 344694; Calle Laurel 15; pintxos €2-3.50; ⏱1-4pm & 8pm-12.30am Wed-Sun) The best *pintxos* in town? You be the judge. Go for the melt-in-your-mouth foie gras or the mini-burgers, or anything else that takes your fancy, at this modern bar on buzzing Calle Laurel.

Tastavin (www.facebook.com/tastavinbardepinchos; Calle San Juan 25; pintxos €2.50-4; ⏱8-11pm Tue, 1-4pm & 8-11pm Wed-Sun; 🛜) On *pintxos* bar–lined San Juan, stylish Tastavin whips up some of the tastiest morsels in town, including smoked trout and lemon cream cornets, fried artichokes, tuna tataki and braised oxtail. The wines are outstanding.

Bar Soriano (Travesía de Laurel 2; tapas €1.50; ⏱11.45am-3pm & 7-11.45pm Mon, Tue, Thu & Fri, 11am-3pm & 6-11pm Sat, 11am-10pm Sun) This venerable bar has been serving just one tapa, a mushroom stack topped with a prawn, since 1972.

THE WEALTH OF THE GRAPE

La Rioja, and the surrounding areas of Navarra and the Basque province of Álava, comprise Spain's best-regarded wine-producing region. The principal grape of Rioja is the tempranillo. The first taste of a tempranillo is of leather and cherries and the wine lingers on the tongue.

The Riojans have had a long love affair with wine. There's evidence that both the Phoenicians and the Celtiberians produced and drank wine here and the earliest written evidence of grape cultivation in La Rioja dates to 873 CE. Today, some 250 million litres of wine bursts forth from the grapes of La Rioja annually. Almost all of this (around 85%) is red wine, though some quality whites and rosés are also produced. The Riojan love of wine is so great that in the town of Haro they even have a fiesta devoted to it. It culminates with a messy 'wine battle', in which thousands of litres of wine gets chucked around, turning everyone's clothes red in the process. This takes place on 29 June.

How to find a good bottle? Spanish wine is subject to a complicated system of classification, similar to the ones used in France and Italy. La Rioja is the only wine region in Spain classed as *Denominación de Origen Calificada* (DOC), the highest grade and a guarantee that any wine labelled as such was produced according to strict regional standards. The best wines are often marked with the designations 'Crianza' (aged more than two years, with at least one year in an oak barrel), 'Reserva' (aged for at least three years, at least one of them in an oak barrel) or 'Gran Reserva' (aged for at least two years in an oak barrel and three years in the bottle).

some of which are open to visitors (but almost always with advance reservation). One of the more receptive to visitors is **Bodegas Muga** (📞941 31 18 25; www. bodegasmuga.com; Barrio de la Estación; 1hr winery tour €15, 2½-hour hot-air balloon tour €170; 🕐 by reservation Mon-Sat), which is just after the railway bridge on the way out of town to the north. It gives guided tours and tastings, in Spanish and English, daily except Sunday.

The Drive » Briones is almost within walking distance of Haro. It's just 9km away (10 minutes) along the N124 and N232.

TRIP HIGHLIGHT

6 Briones

One man's dream has put the small, obscenely quaint village of Briones firmly on the Spanish wine and tourism map. The sunset-gold village crawls gently up a hillside and offers commanding views over the surrounding vine-carpeted plains. It's on these plains where you will find the fantastic wine museum **Vivanco** (Museo de la Cultura del Vino; 📞941 32 23 23; www. vivancoculturadevino.es; Carretera Nacional, Km 232; museum only adult/child €16.50/free, guided visit with wine tasting €45-97; 🕐10am-6pm Tue-Fri & Sun, 10am-8pm Sat). Over several floors you will learn all about the history and culture of wine and the various processes that go into its production. All of this is done through interesting displays brought to life with computer technology. The treasures on display include Picasso-designed wine jugs, Roman and Byzantine mosaics, and gold-draped, wine-inspired religious artefacts. Various guided tours take you behind the scenes of the winery and include tastings.

🛏 p131

Classic Trip

WHY THIS IS A CLASSIC TRIP
JOHN NOBLE, AUTHOR

How can anyone not love an area sloshing in wine, and with fine restaurants and plenty of tempting tapas bars too? There's a soothingly slow pace and sense of space that adds an extra dimension to touring La Rioja, Spain's premier wine-producing region, with broad, vine-carpeted plains, big skies, sleepy honey-toned *pueblos* (villages) and plenty of sunshine, even in winter when the distant hills are capped with snow.

Above: **Santo Domingo de la Calzada** Catedral (p126)
Above right: **Logroño** Patatas (p125)

The Drive >> It's 23km (30 minutes) along the N232, LR211 and A3210 to Elciego. The scenery, which is made up of endless vineyards, will delight anyone who enjoys wide open spaces (and vine leaves). In the distance are strange, sheer-faced, table-topped mountains.

7 Elciego

Rioja wine's most flamboyant flourish lurks in the village of Elciego (Eltziego in Basque) in the showstopping form of the Hotel Marqués de Riscal (p131) – not unlike a rainbow-hued Guggenheim museum (not surprising, perhaps, as both buildings were designed by Canadian Frank Gehry). Casual visitors are not welcome at the hotel, but if you want to see it, you have three options. The easiest is to join one of the **Marqués de Riscal winery tours** (Vinos de los Herederos del Marqués de Riscal; ☎945 18 08 88; www.marquesderiscal.com; Hotel Marqués de Riscal, Calle Torrea 1,

129

Elciego; tours €12; ☾tours 10.30am-1pm & 4-6pm) – there's at least one English-language tour a day, but it's best to book in advance. You won't get inside the building, but you will get to see its exterior from some distance. A much closer look can be obtained by reserving a table at one of the two superb in-house restaurants: the Michelin-starred **Restaurante Marqués de Riscal** (☎945 18 08 80; www.restaurantemarques deriscal.com; Hotel Marqués de Riscal, Calle Torrea 1, Elciego; 14-/21-course menu €110/140; ☾8-10pm Tue, 1.30-3.30pm & 8-10pm Wed-Sun) or the **1860 Tradición** (☎945 18 08 80; www.hotel-marquesderiscal.com; Hotel Marqués de Riscal, Calle Torrea 1, Elciego; mains €22-36; ☾1.30-3.30pm & 8-10pm). For the most intimate look at the building, you'll need to reserve a hotel room for the night.

🛏 p131

The Drive » It's only 10 minutes (7km) along the A3210 from Elciego to wonderful Laguardia, which rises up off the otherwise flat, vine-striped countryside.

↱ DETOUR: BODEGAS YSIOS

Start: ⑧ **Laguardia**

Just a couple of kilometres north of Laguardia is **Bodegas Ysios** (☎945 60 06 40; www.bodegasysios. com; Camino de la Hoya; 90-minute tour & tasting €25; ☾tours 11am daily), architecturally perhaps the most gobsmacking bodega in Spain. Designed by Santiago Calatrava as a 'temple dedicated to wine', it features a cedar exterior with an aluminium wave for a roof that matches the flow of the rocky mountains behind it – and looks best after dark when pools of light flow out of it. Tours provide an insight into wine production; book ahead.

TRIP HIGHLIGHT

⑧ Laguardia

It's easy to spin back the wheels of time in the medieval fortress town of Laguardia, or the 'Guard of Navarra' as it was once appropriately known, sitting proudly on its rocky hilltop. As well as memories of long-lost yesterdays, the town further entices visitors with its wine-producing present. **Bodegas Palacio** (☎945 60 00 57; www.bodegaspalacio.com; San Lazaro 1; 90-minute tour & tasting from €25; ☾by appointment), just 800m south of Laguardia, arranges tours and tastings by appointment. Check the website

for details of its wine courses (from €35 for one hour).

On the southeast edge of town is the **Centro Temático del Vino Villa Lucía** (☎945 60 00 32; www.villa-lucia.com; Carretera de Logroño; 90-minute tour €12; ☾9am-2pm & 4-8pm Tue-Sat, 9am-2pm Sun), a wine museum and shop selling high-quality wine from a variety of small, local producers. Museum visits are by guided tour only and finish with a 4D film and wine tasting.

✕ 🛏 p131

The Drive » From Laguardia, it's a short 18km (20 minutes) down the A124 back to Logroño where you started this tour.

Eating & Sleeping

Logroño ❶

🛏 Hotel Calle Mayor   Hotel €€

(📞941 23 23 68; www.hotelcallemayor.com;
Calle Marqués de San Nicolás 71; s/d/ste from
€95/125/235; 🅿❄🛜) Set within a restored
16th-century building, classy Hotel Calle Mayor
has a dozen large, comfortable rooms bathed in
light, some with wooden beams and balconies,
and modern neutral-toned bathrooms.

Santo Domingo de la Calzada ❹

🍴 Los Caballeros   Spanish €€€

(📞941 34 27 89; www.restauranteloscaballeros.
com; Calle Mayor 56; mains €18-32; 🕐1-3.30pm
& 7.30-10.30pm Tue-Sat, 1-3.30pm Sun) Beside
the cathedral in a classy dining room set with
exposed brick, wood-beamed ceiling and
stained-glass details, Los Caballeros serves
suckling pig and lamb, among other classic
Navarran fare. Don't miss house speciality
cinnamon and vanilla *nuestra tarta del abuelito*
('our grandfather's pudding') for dessert.
Advance reservations are a must at busy times.

🛏 Parador de Santo
Domingo de la Calzada   Historic Hotel €€

(📞941 34 03 00; www.parador.es; Plaza del
Santo 3; d from €100; 🅿🛜) Occupying the
town's 12th-century former hospital opposite
the cathedral, this palatial hotel has spacious
rooms (some with canopied beds and small
balconies) and magnificent public areas,
including the in-house restaurant (mains €11
to €19).

Briones ❻

🛏 Los Calaos de Briones   Hotel €€

(📞941 32 21 31; www.loscalaosdebriones.com;
San Juan 13; d from €65) At this lovely hotel,
some rooms have romantic four-poster beds;
those facing east have beautiful views over the
countryside. The attached restaurant (mains
€11 to €17), in an old wine cellar, specialises in
local lamb and seasonal vegetables.

Elciego ❼

🛏 Hotel Marqués
de Riscal   Design Hotel €€€

(📞945 18 08 80; www.hotel-marquesderiscal.
com; Calle Torrea 1, Elciego; d from €371;
🅿❄🛜) When the owner of Elciego's Bodegas
Marqués de Riscal decided he wanted to create
something special, he didn't hold back. The
result is the spectacular Frank Gehry–designed
Hotel Marqués de Riscal, which opened in 2006.
Costing around €85 million, the building is a
flamboyant wave of multicoloured titanium
sheets that stand in utter contrast to the village
behind.

Laguardia ❽

🍴 Restaurante Amelibia   Spanish €€

(📞945 62 12 07; www.restauranteamelibia.com;
Barbacana 14; mains €15-22; 🕐1-3.30pm Mon
& Wed-Sun, 8.30-10.30pm Fri & Sat; 👶) Gaze
out the windows at a view over the scorched
plains and distant mountain ridges while
dining on sublime traditional cuisine, such as
oxtail and wild mushrooms in red wine sauce
with seasonal vegetables, or pig's trotters in a
sherry reduction. Half-portions are available
for kids.

🛏 Posada Mayor
de Migueloa   Historic Hotel €€

(📞945 60 01 87; www.mayordemigueloa.com;
Calle Mayor 20; s/d incl breakfast from €83/106;
❄🛜) This 17th-century mansion-hotel has
seven atmospheric rooms that evoke a bygone
age with old stone walls, low-beamed ceilings
and polished antique furnishings. Be sure to
pay a visit to the hotel's wine cellar. The on-site
restaurant (mains €18 to €24.50) is also top
notch.

Lofty Roads: the Picos de Europa

9

These jagged, deeply fissured mountains dotted with small stone villages and crystal-clear lakes amount to some of the most spectacular country in Spain.

TRIP HIGHLIGHTS

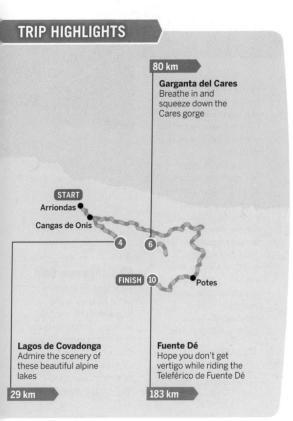

80 km

Garganta del Cares
Breathe in and squeeze down the Cares gorge

START
Arriondas

Cangas de Onís

4   **6**

FINISH **10**

Potes

Lagos de Covadonga
Admire the scenery of these beautiful alpine lakes

29 km

Fuente Dé
Hope you don't get vertigo while riding the Teleférico de Fuente Dé

183 km

2–4 DAYS
183KM / 114 MILES

GREAT FOR...

BEST TIME TO GO

From June and September have the best combination of reliable(ish) weather and fewer crowds.

 **ESSENTIAL PHOTO**

The gorgeous blue Lagos de Covadonga.

BEST FOR AN ADRENALINE RUSH

Swaying in the breeze on the Teleférico de Fuente Dé.

9 Lofty Roads: the Picos de Europa

Rising snow-capped and majestic off the coastal plain, the Picos de Europa mark the greatest, most dramatic heights of the Cordillera Cantábrica. The awe-inspiring mountainscapes make this not just some of Spain's finest hill-walking country but also some of its most exciting for car touring. You can drive along precipitous gorges and up to alpine lakes, and when the road runs out you never have to walk far for magnificent vistas.

1 Arriondas

The little town of Arriondas, on the northwest fringe of the Picos de Europa, is the starting point for hugely popular and fun canoe trips down the tree-lined Río Sella (7km to 15km, 1½ to four hours). Numerous agencies hire out canoes and gear, show you how to paddle and bring you back to Arriondas at the end. The river has a few entertaining minor rapids, but isn't a serious white-water affair. Anyone from about eight years old can enjoy the outing. The standard charge, including a picnic lunch, is €25/15 per adult/child. You can normally start any time between 11am and 1.30pm. Bring a change of clothes.

Just don't come on the first Saturday after 2 August, when tens of thousands of people converge for the **Descenso Internacional del Sella** (www.descensodelsella.com), an international canoeing event that sees 1000-plus serious paddlers racing off downriver to Ribadesella at noon.

📑 p141

The Drive >> It's a simple 8km journey southeast along the N625 to Cangas de Onís.

2 Cangas de Onís

This largely modern town bustles with Picos-related tourism activity throughout the summer months. It's a decent base for Picos explorations, with plenty of accommodation and eating options in

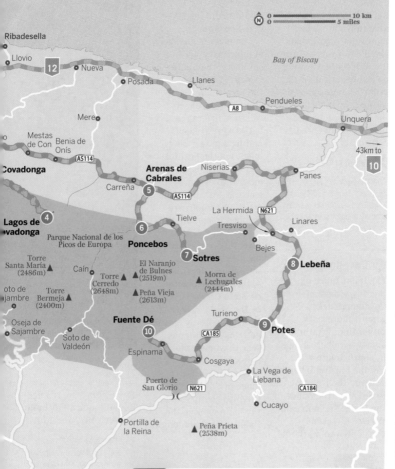

and around the town. If you want organised activities, numerous agencies will take you hiking, climbing, canoeing, rafting, horse riding or canyoning. The so-called **Puente Romano** (Roman Bridge) spans the

LINK YOUR TRIP

10 Cantabria's Eastern Valleys

Rural paradise your thing? After finishing this trip, head to Santander and start meandering Cantabria's eastern valleys.

12 North Coast Beaches & Culture

Swap the mountains for the allure of golden beaches and cultured cities. Join the coastal route anywhere between Santander and Ribadesella.

Río Sella, arching like a cat in fright. In fact there's nothing Roman about it – it was built in the 13th century – but it's no less beautiful for that. From it hangs a copy of the Cruz de la Victoria, the symbol of Asturias that resides in Oviedo's cathedral.

 p141

The Drive » It's just 9km (15 minutes) along the AS114 and AS262 to Covadonga, with the scenery becoming increasingly impressive.

----

❸ Covadonga

The importance of the tiny village of Covadonga lies in what it represents rather than what it is. Somewhere hereabouts, in approximately 722 CE, the Muslim invaders suffered their first defeat in Spain, at the hands of the Visigothic nobleman Pelayo – an event considered to mark the beginning of the 800-year Reconquista.

The place is an object of pilgrimage, for in a cave here, the **Santa Cueva** (🕙9am-7pm), the Virgin supposedly appeared to Pelayo's warriors before the battle. On weekends and in summer, long queues of the faithful and curious line up to enter the cave, now with a chapel installed. The cave's two tombs are claimed to contain the remains of Pelayo and several of his family members including son-in-law Alfonso I of Asturias. The **Fuente de Siete Caños** spring, by the pool below the cave, supposedly ensures marriage within one year to women who drink from it.

Landslides destroyed much of Covadonga in the 19th century and the main church, the **Basílica de Covadonga**

KSL/SHUTTERSTOCK ©

(www.santuariodecovadonga.com; 🕙9am-7pm), is a neo-Romanesque affair built between 1877 and 1901.

The Drive » It's 12km (30 minutes) up a narrow, winding and scenic mountain road to the main car park at the Lagos de Covadonga. For three weeks over Easter and from June to September, and on the early November and early December holiday weekends, private vehicles may only continue past Covadonga before 8.30am or after 9pm, but can drive back down at any time. A shuttle bus runs from Cangas de Onís and three car parks along the Cangas–Covadonga road.

✓ **TOP TIP: WARNING**

The weather in and around the Picos can change very fast, and sudden bouts of mist, rain, cold and snow are common. If you're motoring around higher roads anytime between late October and early May, be prepared for sudden snowfall, which can block routes and even leave you stranded. If you get out on foot, go properly equipped for sudden weather changes. For mountain weather forecasts, see www.mountain-forecast.com (select 'Cantabrian Mountains'), or www.aemet.es/en/eltiempo/prediccion/montana.

Poncebos Garganta del Cares (p138)

TRIP HIGHLIGHT

④ Lagos de Covadonga

Summer crowds don't distract from the beauty of these two little lakes. Most of the trippers don't get past snapping selfies near the water, so walking here is as nice as anywhere else in the Picos.

Lago de Enol is the first lake you reach, with the main car park just past it. It's linked to **Lago de la Ercina**, 1km away, not only by the paved road but also by a footpath via the **Centro de Visitantes Pedro Pidal** (☏985 84 86 14; ⏰10am-6pm Easter & Jun–Oct), which has displays on Picos flora and fauna. There are rustic restaurants near both lakes (closed in winter).

A marked circuit walk, the **Ruta Lagos de Covadonga** (PRPNPE2; 5km, about 2½ hours), takes in the two lakes, the visitors centre and an old mine, the Minas de Buferrera. Other trails will take you further afield.

When mist descends, the lakes, surrounded by the green pastures and bald rock that characterise this part of the Picos, take on an eerie appearance.

The Drive » After you've finished delighting in the lakes, backtrack all the way down to the AS114 and head east along the northern fringe of the Picos to Arenas de Cabrales (45km, one hour). The drive is through rollicking farmland with a daunting mountain backdrop.

137

⑤ Arenas de Cabrales

Arenas lies at the confluence of the bubbling Ríos Cares and Casaño. The busy main road is lined with hotels, restaurants and bars, and just off it lies a little tangle of quiet squares and back lanes, with several more local *sidrerías* (cider bars). You can learn all about and sample the fine, smelly, blue Cabrales cheese at Arenas' **Cueva del Queso de Cabrales** (📞985 84 67 02; www.fundacioncabrales. com; Carretera AS264; adult/child €4.50/3; ☺tours hourly 10.15am-1.15pm & 4.15-7.15pm), a cheese-cave museum on the Poncebos road 500m from Arenas' centre. There are 45-minute guided visits in Spanish.

Working hours may be shorter from November to Easter.

🛏 p141

The Drive 》 Head south for 6km (10 minutes) along the AS264 to Poncebos.

TRIP HIGHLIGHT

⑥ Poncebos

Poncebos, a tiny straggle of buildings at the northern end of the incredible Cares gorge, is set amid already spectacular scenery. A side road uphill from here leads 1.5km to the hamlet of **Camarmeña**, where there's a lookout with views to the gigantic rock pillar El Naranjo de Bulnes in the Picos' central massif.

The **Garganta del Cares Walk** is one of the most spectacular day walks in Spain. Even if you don't normally like to get out of the car, this one's well worth the huff and puff.

The Drive 》 From Poncebos the minor CA1 winds its way 11km (20 minutes) up to small and often chilly Sotres.

⑦ Sotres

If you want a room with a view, then Sotres, the highest village in the Picos (altitude: 1045m) and the starting point for a number of good walks, is where you should head to. The setting, under a shaft of bare limestone mountain peaks, is breathtaking.

Many walkers head west along the PRPNPE21 trail to the

GARGANTA DEL CARES WALK

Ten kilometres of well-maintained path (the PRPNPE3) high above the Río Cares between Poncebos and Caín constitutes the **Garganta del Cares walk**, the most popular mountain walk in Spain. In August the experience can feel like Saturday morning on London's Oxford St, but this is still a spectacular – and at times vertiginous – excursion along the gorge separating the Picos' western and central massifs. It's possible to walk the whole 10km and return in one longish day's outing of six to seven hours plus stops. There are restaurants in Caín where you can lunch before heading back (though you can't be sure to find anything open from November to February). There's no drinkable water along the route, so bring your own. A number of agencies in Picos towns offer transport support, such as a drive back from Caín to Poncebos for around €30 per person.

The beginning of the walk from Poncebos involves a steady climb in the gorge's wide, mostly bare early stages; you're over the highest point after about 3km. As you approach the regional boundary with Castilla y León, the gorge becomes narrower and its walls thick with vegetation, creating greater contrast with the alpine heights above. The last stages of the walk are possibly the prettiest and, as you descend nearer the valley floor, you pass through a series of low, wet tunnels to emerge at the end of the gorge in Caín.

Collado de Pandébano
pass (1212m), a 4km
walk (one to 1½ hours).
At Pandébano, the
massive rock pillar
El Naranjo de Bulnes
comes into view and
you can continue up to
its base in 2½ to three
hours. Another popular
walking route goes east
to the village of Tresviso
and on down to Urdón
in the Desfiladero de la
Hermida gorge on the
Potes–Panes road. As
far as Tresviso (11km)
it's a paved road, but
the final 6km is a
dramatic walking trail,
the **Ruta Urdón-Tresviso**
(PRPNPE30), snaking
825m down to the floor
of the gorge.

The Drive » Head back to
Arenas de Cabrales and follow
the AS114 east to its junction
with the north–south N621
at the humdrum town of
Panes. South of Panes, the
N621 to Potes follows the Río
Deva upstream through the
impressive Desfiladero de la
Hermida gorge before reaching
the turn-off to Lebeña (1km).
Total journey distance 60km
(1¼ hours).

- - - - - - - - - - - - - - - - - -

⑧ Lebeña

The fascinating little
**Iglesia de Santa María
de Lebeña** (adult/child
€2/free; ⊙10am-1.30pm &
4-7.30pm Tue-Sat, 10am-
1.30pm Sun Jun-Sep, to
6pm Oct-May; **P**) dates
back to the 9th or 10th
century. The horseshoe
arches in the church
are a telltale sign of its
Mozarabic style, rarely

seen this far north in
Spain. The floral motifs
on the columns are
Visigothic, and a Celtic
engraved stone supports
the altarpiece with its
15th-century image of the
breastfeeding Virgen de
la Buena Leche (Virgin of
the Good Milk). Outside
the church stands the
stump of a beloved,
centuries-old yew tree
destroyed by a storm in
2007. A sapling grown
from a cutting from the
tree was planted beside it
in 2017.

The Drive » Keep following
the N621 south to Potes for 9km
(10 minutes).

- - - - - - - - - - - - - - - - - -

⑨ Potes

Potes is a popular
staging post on the
southeastern edge of
the Picos, with the
range's eastern massif
rising close at hand. The
Quiviesa and Deva rivers

meet here and the heart
of town is a cluster of
bridges, towers and
quaint back streets
restored in traditional
slate, wood and red
tile after considerable
damage during the
civil war.

Christian refugees,
fleeing from Muslim-
occupied Spain to
this remote Christian
enclave in the 8th
century, brought with
them the **Lígnum Crucis**,
purportedly the single
biggest chunk of Jesus'
cross. The **Monasterio
de Santo Toribio de
Liébana** (☎942 73 05 50;
www.santotoribiodeliebana.
org; CA885; ⊙10am-1pm
& 4-7pm May-Sep, to 6pm
Oct-Apr; **P**), 3km west of
Potes, has housed this
holy relic ever since,
making it a significant
pilgrimage goal. The
monastery is also
famous as the home

POTES FIREWATER

The potent liquor *orujo,* made from grape pressings, is drunk throughout northern Spain and is something of a Potes speciality, often made using traditional copper stills. People here like to drink it as an after-dinner aperitif as part of a herbal tea called *té de roca* or *té de puerto.* Plenty of shops around town sell *orujo,* including varieties flavoured with honey, fruits and herbs, and most will offer you tastings if you're thinking of buying. Potes' jolly **Fiesta del Orujo** (www.facebook.com/fiestaorujo; Potes; ⊘Nov) happens on the second weekend in November, with practically every bar in town setting up a stall selling *orujo* shots for a few cents. The proceeds go to charity. Of course, you'll have to decide in advance whose turn it is to drive...

of medieval monk and theologian Beato de Liébana, celebrated across Europe for his *Commentary on the Apocalypse.*

You can drive 500m past the monastery to the tiny **Ermita de San Miguel**, a chapel with great valley and Picos views.

✕ ⊨ p141

The Drive » It's a beautiful 23km (30 minutes) along the CA185 to Fuente Dé, following the Río Deva upstream through several small villages – some of them, such as Cosgaya and Espinama, with attractive sleeping and eating options. This route is best outside high summer, when you can really get a better feel for the majesty of the Picos.

TRIP HIGHLIGHT

⑩ Fuente Dé

At 1078m, Fuente Dé lies at the foot of the stark southern wall of the Picos' central massif. In four minutes the dramatic (and frankly rather terrifying!) **Teleférico de Fuente Dé cable car** (☎942 73 66 10; www.cantur.com; Fuente Dé; adult/child return €18/7, one way €11/4; ⊘10am-6pm early Feb-Jun & mid-Sep–early Jan, 8am-7pm Jul–mid-Sep, hours may vary; P) whisks people 753m up to the top of that wall, from where walkers and climbers can make their way deeper into the mountains.

It's an easy 3.5km, one-hour walk from the top of the *teleférico* to the Hotel Áliva, open from June to mid-October, where you can get refreshments. From here several other walks of varying length will reveal the beauty of the mountains to you. You can walk back down to Fuente Dé by the PRPNPE24 'Puertos de Áliva' trail, through contrasting landscapes of stark limestone peaks and lush alpine pastures. It starts off along the track that goes down to Espinama on the CA185, then branches off about halfway down to reach Fuente Dé (11km, about 3½ hours from the hotel).

Be warned that during the high season (especially August) you can wait an hour or more for a place in the cable car, going up or down. Good job the scenery is worth lingering for.

Eating & Sleeping

Arriondas ❶

🛏 Posada del Valle   Hotel €€

(☎985 84 11 57; www.posadadelvalle.com; Collía; s €60-70, d €75-98; ☺Apr-Oct; 🅿🛜) This remarkable, English-run spot, in a beautiful valley 3km north of Arriondas, is not only a charming 12-room rural retreat and a wonderful walking base, but also a working organic farm. Design and decor emphasise local art and artistry, and all rooms have valley views. Excellent breakfasts (€9) and four-course dinners (€28; nonguests by reservation only) always include vegetarian options.

Cangas de Onís ❷

🍴 El Molín de la Pedrera   Asturian €€€

(☎985 84 91 09; www.elmolin.com; Calle Río Güeña 2; mains €19-30; ☺1-4.30pm & 8.30-11.30pm Thu-Tue early Feb-late Dec, closed last week Jun & Sun-Tue evenings approx Oct-May) This stone-and-brick-walled, family-run restaurant wins with both its traditional Asturian dishes – such as *fabada* (bean, meat and sausage stew) and *tortos de maíz* (maize pancakes) – as well as delicious homemade desserts. Welcoming service and good wines complete a top dining experience.

🛏 Parador de Cangas de Onís   Historic Hotel €€€

(☎985 84 94 02; www.parador.es; Villanueva de Cangas; r €90-234; ☺Mar-early Jan; 🅿❄@🛜) Cangas' *parador* (luxurious state-owned hotel) overlooks the Río Sella, 3km northwest of town. The main building, originally a monastery founded in the 12th century on the site of early Asturian King Favila's palace, houses 11 gorgeously characterful rooms (some of them former monks' cells, now suitably upgraded).

Arenas de Cabrales ❺

🛏 Hotel Rural El Torrejón   Hotel €

(☎985 84 64 28; www.hotelruraleltorrejon.es; Calle del Torrejón; r incl breakfast €50-71; ☺mid-Feb–mid-Jan; 🅿🛜) This friendly, family-run country house welcomes travellers with flower-filled balconies, gorgeous gardens and tastefully decorated rooms in a cosy rural style. The setting is idyllic, overlooking fields beside the Río Casaño.

Potes ❾

🍴 La Soldrería   International €€

(☎942 73 81 22; www.facebook.com/lasoldreria; Calle El Sol 13, Potes; mains €12-22; ☺1-3.45pm & 8-11.30pm Wed-Mon) Lively, tavern-like La Soldrería is blessed with several diverse spaces: the back patio is a brilliant place to kick back on a sunny day, sipping local cider and sampling the half-Cantabrian, half-international menu. Specialities include veggie couscous, cider-simmered scallops, grilled mushrooms, teriyaki tenderloin and spinach-and-Picón-cheese croquettes.

🛏 Posada San Pelayo   Hotel €€

(☎942 73 32 10; www.posadasanpelayo.com; San Pelayo; s €50-60, d €70-90; ☺Mar-Dec; 🅿🛜🏊) A welcoming, family-run rural hotel of recent construction in traditional country style, in a pretty hamlet 5km west of Potes. Spacious modern-rustic rooms are decorated in cheerful, earthy colours; there are plenty of cosy common areas, and a gorgeous garden and pool with exquisite mountain views. Breakfast (€8) is a good buffet.

Cosgaya

🛏 Hotel del Oso   Hotel €€

(☎942 73 30 18; www.hoteldeloso.es; CA185, Cosgaya; s €61-73, d €73-92; ☺mid-Mar–early Dec; 🅿🛜🏊) The ever-popular, flower-fringed Oso comprises majestic twin stone houses facing each other across the Río Deva and the road. Spacious, rustic-style rooms with timber floors and floral decor are very inviting, and there's a lovely big pool. The **restaurant** (☎942 73 30 18; www.hoteldeloso.es; CA185, Cosgaya; mains €10-24, menú €21; ☺1-3.45pm & 8.30-10.30pm mid-Mar–early Dec; 🅿) is one of the area's finest, with top-quality meat, stews and desserts in huge portions.

Cantabria's Eastern Valleys

10

Rich in unspoiled rural splendour, Cantabria's little-visited eastern valleys will delight anyone who enjoys driving country roads between old-fashioned villages set deep between verdant hills.

1 km

Santander
Enjoy the buzzing food scene of Cantabria's capital

136 km

Cueva de Covalanas
Admire the 20,000-year-old paintings found in this cave system

START/FINISH

Santoña

Vega de Pas

Cuevas de Monte Castillo
Compare hand prints with your ancestors in these caves

28 km

Puerto de la Sía
Re-enter Cantabria via this breathtaking 1200m mountain pass

99 km

2–4 DAYS
245KM / 152 MILES

GREAT FOR...

BEST TIME TO GO

In May, June and September, temperatures are up, rainfall and prices are down, and crowds are away.

 ESSENTIAL PHOTO

Snap the breathtaking views from the Puerto de la Sía pass.

 BEST FOR ANCIENT ART

The prehistoric paintings of Cueva de Covalanas.

de Pas Capital of the Valles Pasiegos (p146)

143

10 Cantabria's Eastern Valleys

This route is one for art lovers. Nature itself has painted a grand canvas of brilliantly green river valleys reaching up to panoramic passes and down to a coast where pretty beaches alternate with wave-lashed cliffs. Humanity has added a sprinkling of stone-and-terracotta villages that enhance the landscape's charms. This is also where people did some of their first painting, depicting prehistoric animals on cave walls tens of thousands of years ago.

TRIP HIGHLIGHT

❶ Santander

Cantabria's busy capital enjoys a superb setting along the northern side of the Bahía de Santander, and has good city beaches, a heaving bar and restaurant scene, and some intriguing cultural attractions.

On the waterfront, the futuristic-looking **Centro Botín** (☎942 04 71 47; www.centrobotin.org; Jardines de Pereda; galleries adult/child €8/free; ☉10am-9pm Tue-Sun Jun-Sep, to 8pm Oct-May) arts

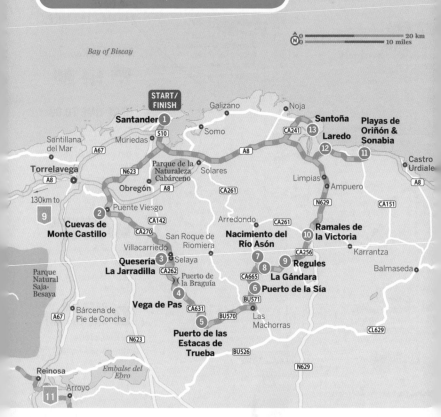

centre opened in 2017. Designed by Italian Renzo Piano, it includes 2500 sq metres of exhibition space and a bright cafe where you can stop in for a drink or bite to eat.

The parklands of the **Península de la Magdalena**, 3km east of the centre, are perfect for a stroll. Kids will enjoy the seals and penguins and the little train that choo-choos around the headland. The English-inspired **Palacio de la Magdalena** (☑942 20 30 84; www.palaciomagdalena.com; tours €3; ☺tours hourly 11am-1pm & 4-6pm Mon-Fri, 10am-noon Sat & Sun Oct–mid-Jun, 10am-noon Sat & Sun mid-Jun–Sep) was built between 1908 and 1912 as a gift from Santander to Spain's royal family: you can get inside on 45-minute Spanish-language guided tours.

LINK YOUR TRIP

11 **Along the Río Ebro**

It's simple enough to join this trip up with the leisurely drive along the mighty Río Ebro.

9 **Lofty Roads: the Picos de Europa**

Mountainscapes – and driving routes – don't get much more dramatic than those found on the Picos de Europa drive.

🍴 🛏 p82, p149, p167

The Drive » It's 27km (40 minutes, depending on the traffic leaving Santander) along the busy S10 and the less hectic N623 to Puente Viesgo. Once you reach the town, turn right at the 'Cuevas del Monte Castillo' sign and go 1.5km uphill.

- - - - - - - - - - - - - - - - - -

TRIP HIGHLIGHT

② Cuevas de Monte Castillo

The valley town of Puente Viesgo lies at the foot of the conical Monte Castillo. Part-way up this hill are the **Cuevas de Monte Castillo** (☑942 59 84 25; http://cuevas.culturadecantabria.com; Puente Viesgo; adult/child per cave €3/1.50; ☺10am-2.30pm & 3.30-7pm Tue-Sat, 10am-3.30pm Sun mid-Jun–mid-Sep, reduced hours rest of year; **P**), a series of caves frequented by humans since 150,000 years ago. Four of them are World Heritage–listed and two of these, **El Castillo** and **Las Monedas**, are open for 45-minute guided visits (in Spanish). Booking ahead is highly advisable, especially for the more spectacular El Castillo, whose 275 paintings and engravings of deer, bison, horses, goats, aurochs, handprints, mysterious symbols and a mammoth (very rare) date from around 39,000 to 11,000 BCE. One red symbol, believed to be 40,800 years old, is Europe's oldest known cave art.

Las Monedas has less art (black animal outlines from around 10,000 BCE) but contains an astounding labyrinth of stalactites and stalagmites.

The Drive » Turn east off the N623 3km south of Puente Viesgo and follow the CA270 and CA142 southeast to Selaya. Here, turn right on the CA625 and follow signs 800m to Quesería La Jarradilla. Total distance 21km.

- - - - - - - - - - - - - - - - - -

③ Quesería La Jarradilla

Milk from cattle grazed on the rich green pastures of northern Spain is made into a wide variety of tasty cheeses. The cheeses of the Valles Pasiegos (the parallel valleys of the Ríos Pas, Pisueña and Miera) are notably young, soft and creamy – the damp climate means they can't mature. At the family-run dairy **Quesería La Jarradilla** (☑942 59 03 42, 652 779660; www.quesoslajarradilla.com; Barcenilla 246, Tezanos de Villacarriedo; ☺tours noon Sat, shop 11am-2pm & 6-8pm Mon-Sat Jul-Sep, 11am-2pm & 4.15-6.15pm Mon-Sat Oct-Jun), just outside Selaya in the Pisueña valley, you can taste, buy and find out all about these tempting cheeses. The shop opens daily except Sunday; tours (free) run once weekly (occasionally in English, depending on demand), usually with an extra one at 5pm Wednesday or Thursday from July to September.

The Drive » From Selaya follow the CA262 south for 16km to Vega de Pas. The views from the Puerto de la Braguía pass are stunning – pull over by the bus stop to admire them. This is a popular cycling route.

④ Vega de Pas

Vega de Pas is the 'capital' of the Valles Pasiegos (www.valles pasiegos.org), which are among Cantabria's (and therefore Spain's) most traditional rural areas. The small town has a handsome central plaza of stone houses with wooden galleries and flowery window boxes. Look for shops advertising *quesadas* and *sobaos*, two local food specialities that are favourites throughout Cantabria. *Quesadas* are a kind of dense cheesecake; *sobaos* are rich sponge cakes prepared with lots of butter. The countryside is outrageously picturesque: it's all deep greens and steep-sided hills with minuscule villages of

stone houses. There are plenty of opportunities to get out for a walk all around here.

The Drive » Climb southeast for 14km on the CA631 up the lovely, green Yera valley with a few switchbacks to the Puerto de las Estacas de Trueba.

⑤ Puerto de las Estacas de Trueba

Stop to take in the panoramas from this 1154m-high mountain pass where your route leaves Cantabria and enters Castilla y León. It's a lonely but exhilarating spot with a few scattered stone barns and the cliffs of Castro Valnera (1718m) looming over to the east.

The Drive » Continue into Castilla y León on the BU570. Turn north just after Las Machorras onto the BU571 which heads up to the Puerto de la Sía (19km, 30 to 40 minutes).

TRIP HIGHLIGHT

⑥ Puerto de la Sía

Wonderful views of green Cantabrian valleys open out below you as you cross the 1200m Puerto de la Sía mountain pass back into Cantabria.

The Drive » Zigzag down into Cantabria on the CA665. At a T-junction after 9km, go left for 3km to the viewpoint over the Nacimiento del Río Asón.

⑦ Nacimiento del Río Asón

The Río Asón, the main river of Cantabria's easternmost reaches, begins life as a 50m waterfall pouring straight out of a cliff into a deep, thickly wooded valley – a beautiful sight easily taken in from the *mirador* (viewpoint) across the valley on the CA265.

**TOP TIP:
WEATHER WISDOM**

Check the weather before setting out on this drive. You'll be crossing mountain passes where cloud or fog sometimes make the going difficult, and snow occasionally makes it impossible.

Santander Palacio de la Magdalena (p145)

The Drive » Head 3km back up the CA265 to the T-junction where it meets the CA665, and continue 2km straight on to La Gándara on the CA256.

---

8 La Gándara

La Gándara is a scattered high-valley village with mountain vistas all around, and a couple of restaurant-bars for refreshments. The **Centro de Interpretación Collados del Asón** (☏942 64 94 38, 619 892634; www. redcantabrarural.com/ naturea-3; CA256, La Gándara; ⏰10am-5pm Wed-Fri, to 7pm Sat & Sun Apr-Jun & Oct, to 7pm Jul-Sep, to 3.30pm

Wed-Fri, to 6pm Sat & Sun Nov-Mar) offers information on this upland area (protected as a *parque natural*). A 400m walk behind the office leads to a viewpoint over the beautiful **Cascada La Gándara** waterfall.

The Drive » Continue 10km down the CA256 to Regules.

---

9 Regules

In a lovely, tranquil spot beside the tree-lined Río Gándara, Regules is a mere pinprick on many a map. The country around here provides lots of opportunities for walking and generally moseying

about at a slow pace. There's also a wonderful hotel beside the bridge, with a good restaurant.

🛏 p149

The Drive » Head on down the CA256, which feeds into the marginally more major N629 for the final couple of kilometres into Ramales de Victoria (10km, 15 minutes from Regules).

TRIP HIGHLIGHT

10 Ramales de la Victoria

The easygoing small valley town of Ramales de la Victoria is the 'capital' of the Alto Asón district, which stretches from the mountains almost to the

147

coast and claims more than half of Cantabria's 9000 known caves. There are two outstanding visitable caves here. The **Cueva de Cullalvera** (📞942 59 84 25; http:// cuevas.culturadecantabria. com/cullalvera-2; Ramales de la Victoria; adult/child €3/1.50; ⏰10am-2.30pm & 3.30-7pm Tue-Sat, 10-3.30pm Sun mid-Jun–mid-Sep, reduced hours rest of year) is a jaw-droppingly vast cavity but its prehistoric art is off-limits. The **Cueva de Covalanas** (📞942 59 84 25; http:// cuevas.culturadecantabria. com/covalanas-2; adult/child €3/1.50; ⏰10am-2.30pm & 3.30-7pm Tue-Sat, 10am-3.30pm Sun mid-Jun–mid-Sep, reduced hours rest of year), 2km up the N629 south from Ramales, then 650m up a footpath, is World Heritage–listed for its stunning depictions of deer and other animals, executed around 20,000 BCE using an unusual dot-painting technique. Visits to either cave are guided and last 45 minutes; it's advisable to book ahead online. Ramales' **tourist office** (📞942 64 65 04; www. cantabriaorientalrural.es/ turismo; Paseo Barón de Adzaneta 8, Ramales de la Victoria; ⏰9.30am-2pm & 4-7.30pm Jul-Sep, 9am-3.30pm Mon, 9.30am-2pm & 4-7pm Sat, 9.30am-2pm Sun Oct-Jun) can tell you all about the area's attractions.

🛏 p149

The Drive » From Ramales head 18km north down the N629, then go 13km east along the A8 motorway to junction 160, from which it's a 1.5km drive down to Playa Oriñón – 30 to 40 minutes total.

⑪ Playas de Oriñón & Sonabia

After your mountain wanderings it's time for the beach! The broad sandy strip of **Playa de Oriñón** is set deep between protective headlands, making the water calm and *comparatively* warm. The settlement here consists of ugly holiday flats and caravan parks. For a smaller but wilder strand continue 1km past Oriñón to the hamlet of Sonabia, and turn left 100m after the church to reach a parking area. It's then a 200m walk down to **Playa de Sonabia**, a little, clothing-optional beach tucked into a rock-lined inlet beneath high crags, above which huge griffon vultures circle the sky. There are a couple of seasonal bar-restaurants by the car park.

The Drive » It's 15km (15 minutes) along the A8 to Laredo.

⑫ Laredo

Laredo's very long, sandy and normally very calm beach is backed by ugly 20th-century blocks. But at the east end of town the cobbled streets of the old **Puebla Vieja**

slope down from the impressive 13th-century **Iglesia de Santa María**, with the remains of the 16th-century **Fuerte del Rastrillar** fortress spread over the scenic La Atalaya hill above. The Puebla Vieja has a lively food and drinks scene.

The Drive » It's a 20-minute (15km) hop around the bay on the A8 and CA241 to Santoña. Alternatively, between March and November, park near El Puntal, the northwestern end of Laredo's beach, and take the Excursiones Marítimas passenger ferry to Santoña (one-way/return €2/3.50, five minutes) and explore on foot.

⑬ Santoña

The engaging fishing port of Santoña is famed for its anchovies, which are bottled or tinned here, with olive oil to preserve them, and sold all over town. At the eastern end of the seafront promenade and also at the foot of the hilly headland **Monte Buciero** are two old fortresses: the **Fuerte de San Martín** and, further along, the abandoned **Fuerte de San Carlos**. Monte Buciero has five hiking paths for a stretch of the legs. You could also head 2.5km north along the CA141 and CA907 to **Playa de Berria**, a magnificent sweep of sand and surf on the open sea.

🛏 p149

The Drive » To get back to Santander, head along the A8 and S10 for 47km (40 minutes).

Eating & Sleeping

Santander ➊

✕ Agua Salada Fusion €€

(📞942 04 93 87; www.facebook.com/agua
saladasantander; Calle San Simón 2; lunch menú
€14, mains €16-20; 🕐1.30-4pm Mon, 1.30-4pm
& 8-11pm Wed-Sun) A labour of love for owners
Carlos García and Pilar Montiel, this intimate
corner bistro serves top-notch, market-fresh
cuisine that walks the line between traditional
and innovative. Indulge in a superb tuna tartare
with mustard ice cream, local beef entrecôte
with roasted peppers and chips, or an endive
salad with pears, Gorgonzola and hazelnut
pesto.

🛏 Jardín Secreto Boutique Hotel €€

(📞942 07 07 14; www.jardinsecretosantander.
com; Calle de Cisneros 37; r €60-95; 🛜) Named
for its little back garden, this is a charming,
six-room world of its own, spread across a
200-year-old house near the city centre. It's run
by a welcoming, on-the-ball brother-and-sister
team, and designed by their mother in a stylish
blend of silvers, greys and pastels with exposed
stone, brick and wood. The complimentary
morning coffee hits the spot.

🛏 Eurostars Hotel Real Luxury Hotel €€€

(📞942 27 25 50; www.eurostarshotelcompany.
com; Paseo Pérez Galdós 28; incl breakfast r €84-
539, ste €237-749; 🅿 ❄ 🛜) The Real was built,
on a panoramic hilltop, in 1917 to house the
royal family's guests. Following a full makeover
it again offers a regal-style experience from the
brilliantly white lounge, opening to a columned
bay-view terrace, to the 123 updated classical-
style rooms with rich chestnut-wood furnishings
and blue-and-gold trim. An additional draw is
the thalassotherapy spa with its ample seawater pool.

Regules ➒

🛏 La Casa del Puente Hotel €€

(📞645 820418, 942 63 90 20; www.lacasa
delpuente.es; Regules; r incl breakfast €79-199;
🅿 🛜) In little Regules village, 10km southwest
of Ramales, stands this beautifully restored
casa de indianos (mansion built by a returned
emigrant from the Americas). It's in a fantastic,
tranquil riverside position: a step further and
you'd be in the Río Gándara. Rooms follow a very
comfy, multicoloured, modern-rustic design,
with exposed stonework and, in most, king-size
beds and large hot tubs.

Ramales de la Victoria ➓

🛏 Hotel Palacio Torre de Ruesga Heritage Hotel €€

(📞942 64 10 60; www.torrederuesga.com;
Barrio de la Bárcena, Valle; incl breakfast d
€79-129, ste €99-179, family bungalow €99-220;
🅿 ❄ 🛜 ♨) This two-towered stone mansion
dating from 1610, 6km west of Ramales de la
Victoria, has been remodelled into a deluxe
hotel without losing its wonderful historical
ambience, with thick stone walls, wood beams,
antique furniture and fascinating 19th-century
frescoes. The sizeable, stylish rooms (many
with large, up-to-date hot tubs) range from
four-poster affairs in the main house to family
bungalows in the extensive gardens.

Santoña ⓭

🛏 Hotel Juan de la Cosa Hotel €€

(📞942 66 12 38; www.hoteljuandelacosa.com;
Playa de Berria 14; s €45-85, d €60-175; 🕐Apr-
Oct; 🅿 ❄ 🛜 ♨) The Juan de la Cosa may be
an unsympathetic-looking building, but about
two-thirds of its spacious, blue-hued, maritime-
inspired rooms have full-on beach views. It
also offers a good restaurant with a seafood
emphasis, and plain self-catering apartments
designed for families.

Along the Río Ebro

Follow Spain's most voluminous river, the mighty Ebro, on a journey that reveals something of almost everything the country has to offer.

11

TRIP HIGHLIGHTS

55 km

Santa María de Valverde
Magical millennium-old church hewn out of solid rock

START
● Fontibre
③

340 km

Olite
Welcome to the fairy-tale fantasy of turret-filled Olite

⑥   ⑦

🏛 Parque Natural de las Bárdenas Reales

FINISH
⑨

Logroño
Eat, drink and take it easy in the Rioja wine capital

254 km

Zaragoza
Fabulous tapas and aeons of history in this truly underrated city

482 km

2–4 DAYS
482KM / 300 MILES

GREAT FOR...

📖 🍷 🌳

BEST TIME TO GO
In May when the poppies are in bloom and the weather pleasing.

📷 **ESSENTIAL PHOTO**
Framing a Wild West backdrop in the Parque Natural de las Bárdenas Reales.

✓ **BEST FOR KNIGHTS IN ARMOUR**
Rescuing a princess from the castle of Olite.

11 Along the Río Ebro

Stand on top of a castle turret in Olite and think back over everything you have seen – and will see – on this stunning drive and you'll probably end up agreeing that this is perhaps the single most diverse and fascinating drive you can cover in northern Spain. Just look at what there is: mountain springs and deserts, underground churches and Islamic palaces, wine and superb tapas. This is a drive you won't forget.

1 Fontibre

Where else to start your Ebro odyssey but at the **Nacimiento del Río Ebro** (Fontibre; P), where the baby Ebro spills out of a rock to begin its 930km meander from the remote hills of southern Cantabria to the Mediterranean. Five kilometres west of the area's main town, Reinosa, this is a stunningly serene spot in its own tree-shaded park, with a big pool of deep-turquoise water, a tiny shrine and a few

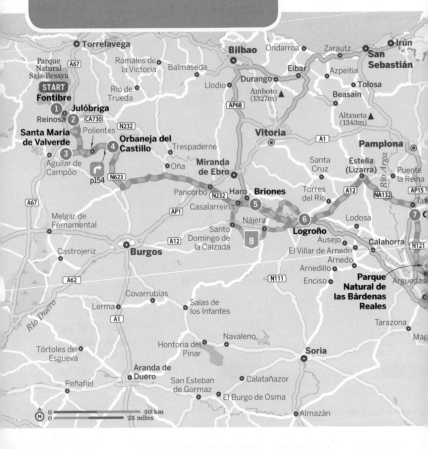

ducks splashing around. Wander up into the village to scrutinise a large open-air map-model of the river's entire course.

🛏 p157

The Drive » It's just 10km east to Julióbriga but navigation round Reinosa needs attention. Entering Reinosa on the CA183, go left at a roundabout following 'A67 Santander Palencia' signs. After 2km go right at another roundabout ('CA171 Requejo'). Turn left ('CA171 Corconte') after 500m, then right ('CA731 Bolmir') after 1km. In Bolmir (1.5km) go left on the CA730. After 500m take the 'Julióbriga' turn-off for the final 1km.

② Julióbriga

On the edge of the hamlet of Retortillo you'll discover the remains of Cantabria's most significant Roman town, **Julióbriga** (📞942 59 84 25; http://centros.culturadecantabria.com; Retortillo; adult/child €3/1.50; ⏱10am-2.30pm & 3.30-7pm Tue-Sat, 10am-3.30pm Sun mid-Jun–mid-Sep, shorter hours rest of year; P).

Hourly guided visits (45 minutes, in Spanish) lead you through the Museo Domus, a full-scale recreation of one of Julióbriga's houses. You're free to explore independently the excavated parts of the town (about 10% of the total), with a 12th-century Romanesque church built over the Roman forum.

🔗 LINK YOUR TRIP

8 Roving La Rioja Wine Region

Once you hit Logroño, take a couple of days to enjoy the gift of the grape on the La Rioja Wine Region drive.

19 Barcelona to Valencia

Head on south from Zaragoza to uncover more of Aragón's unsung secrets.

The Drive » It's 45km through woodlands and countryside to Santa María de Valverde, with the now much larger Ebro often your companion. From Julióbriga head back to the CA730, go 7.5km east to Arroyo, then 4km south along the CA735 to turn right onto the CA741. Head 9km along this to meet the CA272. Turn left and go 13km to a roundabout, then 9km west along the CA273.

TRIP HIGHLIGHT

③ Santa María de Valverde

The beautiful little **Iglesia Rupestre de Santa María de Valverde** (Santa María de Valverde; ⏱10am-2pm & 4-7pm Sat & Sun mid-Mar–Jun & Sep–mid-Dec, Tue-Sun Jul-Aug, Mass 1pm Sun year-round), hewn out of solid rock, is the most impressive of several remarkable *iglesias rupestres* (rock-cut churches) along the Ebro valley in the extreme south of Cantabria.

The churches date from the 7th to 10th centuries, the early days of Christianity in the region. Santa María retains a magical beauty, with irregular stone arches and rough-cut stone floors suffused in ghostly subterranean light. Visits are in conjunction with visits to the adjacent **Centro de Interpretación del Rupestre** (📞942 77 61 46; Santa María de Valverde; adult/child €1/free; ⏱10am-2pm

& 4-7pm Tue-Sun Jul & Aug, 10am-2pm & 4-7pm Sat & Sun mid-Mar–Jun & Sep–mid-Dec; P), which gives an excellent introduction (with photos, videos and maps) to the Ebro valley's rock church phenomenon.

The Drive » Head east along the CA273 and CA272 to Polientes (22km from Santa María de Valverde), the biggest village in this part of the world and a possible refreshments stop. Continue 18km east along the Ebro valley following the CA274, CA275 and BU643 to Orbaneja del Castillo.

4 Orbaneja del Castillo

The quaint stone-and-terracotta village of Orbaneja is the first settlement that the Ebro reaches after threading a deep gorge as it flows from Cantabria into Castilla y León. It's a perfect halt for its gorgeous multi-tailed waterfall, views of fantastic karstic rock formations and, not least, some good country restaurants specialising in grilled meats and *cocidos* (meat-bean-sausage stews).

The Drive » Continue 6km southeast on the BU643 to meet the N623 and follow this south for 27km, between imposing rock-topped bluffs, then turn east along the CL633. Crossing mostly flatter, more arable land, this becomes the CL663 leading to Cornudilla. From Cornudilla head east on the more major N232 for 58km to Briones – altogether 123km (about two hours) from Orbaneja.

5 Briones

Even without the marvel that is the Vivanco wine museum (p127), Briones, in the heart of La Rioja's world-renowned wine-growing country, would be worth a stop. From its hillside perch above a loop of the Ebro, the village commands views over the surrounding vine-striped plains. There's a cute little church and a small park built around the remains of a castle.

🛏 p131

The Drive » Seeing as the navigator is likely to have tried to satisfy their wine cravings in Briones, you'll probably be pleased to know that it's just a straightforward 36km cruise down the N232 to the capital of Spain's wine country: Logroño. Lucky navigator!

DETOUR:
EL TOBAZO

Start: 3 Santa María de Valverde

The pretty little riverside village of **Villaescusa de Ebro** is the starting point for an exhilarating short hike up to **El Tobazo**, one of the smallest but most superbly located of the Ebro rock-cut churches. The village sits just across the Ebro from the CA275 on the way from Santa María de Valverde to Orbaneja del Castillo.

Eleven kilometers past Polientes there's a sizeable parking area on the left side of the road. Walk across the bridge into Villaescusa and follow 'El Tobazo' signs up out of the village.

It's 1km gradually uphill to the top of a beautiful **waterfall**, where you'll find the **cave-church** (three small caves) and some natural caves behind the falls. Just above is the *surgencia* (spring) where the crystal-clear stream flows out of the rock before tumbling down the hillside – a magical spot where you can easily imagine a few *anjanas*, Cantabria's legendary water nymphs, skipping around the rocks. Heading back down, after 200m you can take the path signed 'Cascada del Tobazo Zona Inferior' down to the **lower falls**, then return to Villaescusa along an Ebro-side track. From Villaescusa, continue 7km along the CA275 and BU643 to Orbaneja del Castillo.

Olite Palacio Real

TRIP HIGHLIGHT

6 Logroño

Logroño, the capital of La Rioja, is one of those towns that on the surface doesn't have much to attract visitors, yet everyone who comes here does seem to end up having a good time. The food (p126) and, of course, the wine are exceptional, and there's a superb museum (p114) in the attractive old centre.

✕ 🛏 p120, p126, p131

The Drive » With the navigator now likely singing songs about wine in the seat next to you, they won't be disappointed to know there's a fermented-grape-juice theme at the next stop too. It's an easy 86km drive east across wine and crop country via the A12, NA132 and N121 to Olite.

TRIP HIGHLIGHT

7 Olite

The turrets and spires of Olite are filled with stories of kings and queens, brave knights and beautiful princesses – it's as if it has burst off the pages of a fairy tale. This honey-coloured village was once the home of the royal families of Navarra, and the walled old quarter is crowded with their memories. It's Carlos III that we must thank for the exceptional **Palacio Real** (Castillo de Olite; 📞948 74 12 73; www.guiartenavarra. com; Plaza Carlos III; adult/child €3.50/2; 🕙10am-8pm Jul-Aug, 10am-7pm Mon-Fri, 10am-8pm Sat & Sun May, Jun & Sep, shorter hours Oct-Apr), which towers over the village. Back in Carlos' day, the castle's inhabitants included not just princes and jesters but also lions and other exotic pets, as well as Babylon-inspired hanging gardens. Don't miss the **Museo de la Viña y el Vino de Navarra** (Navarra Vineyard and Wine Museum; 📞948 74 12 73; Plaza de los Teobaldos 10; adult/

Zaragoza

child €3.50/2; ⏲10am-2pm & 4-7pm Mon-Sat, 10am-2pm Sun Mar-Oct, shorter hours Nov-Feb), a fascinating journey through wine and wine culture.

🛏 p157

The Drive » Start dressing like Lawrence of Arabia as you head south along the N121 to Arguedas on the edge of the semidesert Parque Natural de las Bárdenas Reales. It's a pleasant 42km drive.

❽ Parque Natural de las Bárdenas Reales

In a region largely dominated by fertile farmland and wet mountain slopes, the last thing you'd expect is a sunburnt desert, but in the Bárdenas Reales a

desert is exactly what you'll find. The weirdly eroded sandstone hills and snakelike gorges may look like an almost pristine wilderness, but it's actually a human creation: the Bárdenas Reales were once forest, but people chopped it all down and let their livestock eat all the lower growth. There are a couple of dirt motor tracks and numerous hiking and cycling trails, but most people come to drive the park's 34km loop road. The **park information office** (☎948 83 03 08; www.bardenasreales. es; Carretera del Parque Natural Km 6, off Carretera NA8712; ⏲9am-2pm & 4-7pm Apr-Aug, 9am-2pm & 3-5pm Sep-Mar), on the main route into the park from

Arguedas, can supply information.

The Drive » Head south to Tudela (its old quarter is worth a quick stop if time allows) and join the A68 then the AP68 tollway for the final push to Zaragoza. Total distance 100km (1¼ hours).

TRIP HIGHLIGHT

❾ Zaragoza

Few foreign tourists find their way to Zaragoza, which is a real pity for them but a bonus for those who do, because this city with 11 bridges straddling the Ebro is truly one of the most interesting and beautiful in northern Spain. For more on Zaragoza, see Trip 19: Barcelona to Valencia (p229).

🍴 🛏 p131, p236-7

Eating & Sleeping

Fontibre ❶

🛏 Posada Fontibre   Inn €€

(📞942 77 96 55; www.posadafontibre.com;
El Molino 23, Fontibre; s €50-65, d €62-92;
📶) A tranquil haven in little Fontibre village,
this old stone *posada* offers six very well-kept
rooms just steps from the source of the
Río Ebro. Decor is comfortably rustic, with
beamed ceilings, stone walls, colourful rugs,
and interesting historical curios and photos
dotted around. Breakfast is €5.50 and there
are a couple of good dinner options in the
village, including the enticing **Restaurante
Fuentebro** (📞942 77 96 45; www.
restaurantefuentebro.com; Fontibre; mains
€14-22; ⏲1.30-4pm & 9-11pm, closed Sun,
Tue, Wed & Thu lunchtime & all day Mon Sep–
mid-Jun) overlooking the Nacimiento.

Polientes

🛏 Molino Tejada   Design Hotel €€€

(📞675 153340, 623 019059; www.molinotejada.
com; Valdeperal 1, Polientes; incl breakfast ste
for 2 €115-225, for 4-6 €195-275; ⏲closed
Mon-Wed Oct-Feb; 🅿📶🏊) A wonderful
place to kick back, this 16th-century watermill
amid extensive riverside gardens, 1km east of
Polientes, has been stunningly renovated by its
owner, locally born but now California-based
designer Celia Tejada. A black-and-white theme
runs throughout the property, with its spacious
common areas, soft furnishings and varied art
and ethnic-flavoured artisanry.

The nine large, TV-free apartments sport
well-equipped kitchens and big comfy beds.
There's normally a two-night minimum stay
but this is a fabulous base for a break in your
travels.

Olite ❼

🛏 Parador de Olite   Historic Hotel €€

(📞948 74 00 00; www.parador.es; Plaza de los
Teobaldos 2; s/d from €100/115; ❄📶) The
most spectacular lodging option in town is set
in a wing of Olite's restored medieval castle
(though some rooms are in a newer extension).
Part of the Parador chain and a national
monument, this photogenic hotel has plenty of
atmosphere with its heavy wood furniture, gilt-
framed prints and, in some rooms, balconies
with views over the countryside. There's a
superb regional restaurant (mains €13.50 to
€24) open to guests and nonguests.

Zaragoza ❾

🍴 La Clandestina Café   Cafe €€

(📞876 28 11 65; Calle San Andrés 9; brunch €15,
light dishes €7-16; ⏲10am-midnight or later
Tue-Fri, from 11am Sat & Sun; 📶🖊) There's an
eye-catching huge pair of red lips painted on
one white brick wall, but this place is as much
about gastronomy as style, particularly in the
brunch (11.30am to 3.30pm, including a glass
of *cava*) and coffee-and-cake departments. The
cold-pressed juices are divine on hot days, and
the cheesecake with fruits of the forest may just
be the best cheesecake you've ever tasted.

🛏 Hotel Sauce   Hotel €

(📞976 20 50 50; www.hotelsauce.com; Calle de
Espoz y Mina 33; s €42-70, d €45-80; ❄📶) This
stylish family-run hotel with a central location
provides fresh, cheerful, contemporary rooms
with walk-in showers, tasteful watercolours,
outstandingly friendly and helpful staff, and
a pleasant 24-hour cafe serving excellent
breakfasts, cakes and cocktails. Prices are very
reasonable given everything the hotel provides.

North Coast Beaches & Culture

Wend your way along a scenic, cliff-strung coastline dividing your time between spectacular beaches, pretty fishing villages and lively cultured cities with superb eating.

12

TRIP HIGHLIGHTS

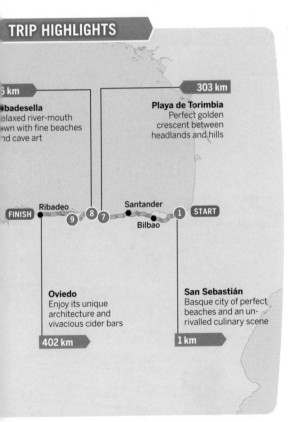

5 km

Ribadesella
Relaxed river-mouth town with fine beaches and cave art

303 km

Playa de Torimbia
Perfect golden crescent between headlands and hills

FINISH — Ribadeo ⑨ ⑧ ⑦ — Santander ① START
Bilbao

Oviedo
Enjoy its unique architecture and vivacious cider bars

402 km

San Sebastián
Basque city of perfect beaches and an unrivalled culinary scene

1 km

**4–6 DAYS
551KM / 348 MILES**

GREAT FOR...

BEST TIME TO GO

July and August have most sunshine and a festive atmosphere; June and September have decent weather and fewer crowds.

ESSENTIAL PHOTO

Ocean breakers rolling in to glorious Playa Oyambre.

BEST FOR FOOD

San Sebastián's *pintxos* (Basque tapas) bars.

Oyambre 2km of golden beach (p164)

12 North Coast Beaches & Culture

Just turn off the A8 motorway and you're straight on to rural lanes winding down through green countryside to hundreds of sandy strands that alternate with the high rocky capes and cliffs of this surprisingly untamed coast. You'll discover breathtaking ocean-facing expanses like Playa Oyambre, perfect headland-bounded crescents like Playa de Torimbia, and places of awe-inspiring geology like the rock 'cathedrals' of Praia As Catedrais.

TRIP HIGHLIGHT

1 San Sebastián

With golden beaches, a world-famous culinary scene and a packed cultural calendar, San Sebastián may well tempt you to reschedule the following stages of your trip. When it comes to cooking, no other city quite compares, whether you're snacking on delectable *pintxos* (Basque tapas) in the Parte Vieja, or lingering over a multicourse feast in a Michelin-starred dining room.

Playa de la Concha is a 1.5km stretch of golden sands curving gently around a protected bay. Complete with calm seas, a picturesque promenade and wonderful vistas, it's one of Europe's most perfect city beaches.

Behind the beach and the *pintxos* bars stands a city of great design. Elegant art-nouveau buildings, ornate bridges and beautifully manicured parks and plazas are an integral part of San Sebastián. The showpiece cultural attraction is **San Telmo Museoa** (☎943 48 15 80; www.santelmomuseoa.eus; Plaza de Zuloaga 1; adult/child €6/free, Tue free; ◷10am-8pm Tue-Sun), a thought-provoking collection that explores Basque history and culture in all its complexity.

 p167, 227

The Drive » It's a straight-forward 102km, mostly along the AP8 motorway, from San Sebastián to Bilbao (about 1½ hours, depending on traffic, from city centre to city centre).

 LINK YOUR TRIP

8 Roving La Rioja Wine Region

Treat yourselves to a couple of days touring Spain's premier wine region.

9 Lofty Roads: the Picos de Europa

Head inland to explore the most spectacular of the mountains lining the southern horizon.

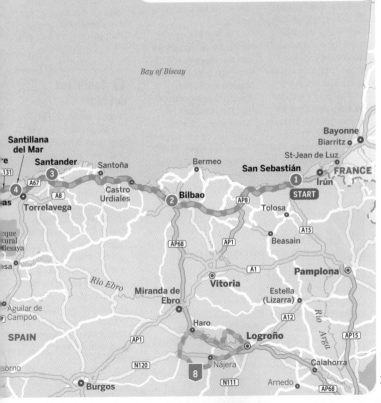

Bay of Biscay

Santillana del Mar

Santander · Santoña · Bermeo · San Sebastián · Bayonne · Biarritz · St-Jean de Luz · Irún · FRANCE · START

131 · A67 · 3 · A8 · Castro Urdiales · Bilbao · AP8 · Tolosa

4 · Torrelavega · 2 · A15

AP68 · AP1 · Beasain

rque tural Besaya

Río Ebro · Miranda de Ebro · Vitoria · A1 · Pamplona · Estella (Lizarra) · A12

Aguilar de Campóo · Haro · Logroño · AP15 · Río Arga

SPAIN · AP1 · N120 · 8 · Nájera · N111 · Arnedo · Calahorra · AP68

orno · Burgos

❷ Bilbao

The Basque Country's biggest city is famed for its contemporary architecture and enjoys a dining scene just as varied and mouth-watering as San Sebastián's. Buzzing *pintxos* bars, venerable family-run restaurants and temples of fine dining offer endless different takes on Basque cuisine, especially in the cobbled lanes of the atmospheric **Casco Viejo** (Old Town).

Frank Gehry's shimmering titanium **Museo Guggenheim** (944 359 080; www. guggenheim-bilbao.eus; Avenida Abandoibarra 2; adult/student & senior/child €15/7.50/free; 10am-8pm, closed Mon Sep-Jun), itself a byword for contemporary architecture, is packed with art treasures inside and out, has lost none of its ability to captivate more than two decades after its opening. Today it stands among other great architectural works, like the nearby **Zubizuri**, a soaring bridge designed by Santiago Calatrava.

p167

The Drive ›› Hop on to the A8 motorway for the 100km drive to the north's next major city – Santander. The drive should take about 1¼ hours, traffic permitting.

---

❸ Santander

Capital of the Cantabria region, Santander has a fabulous setting along the north side of the broad Bahía de Santander. The waterfront arts centre, the Centro Botín (p144), is the city's latest showpiece, while the parklands of the **Península de la Magdalena** (off Avenida Reina Victoria; 8am-10pm) are great for a relaxing wander.

For beaches, you're spoilt for choice. **Playa del Sardinero**'s 1.5km-long stretch of gorgeous golden sand faces the open sea north of the Península de la Magdalena. Surfers emerge in force when the waves are right, mainly in autumn and winter. **Playa del Puntal**, a 2km-long finger of sand jutting

across the bay towards Santander, is idyllic on calm days (but beware of the currents). Ferries sail there from the city through the day from May or June to October. An 18km drive west, the exquisite, 3km-long **Playa de Valdearenas** (Playa de Liencres; Liencres; P) has a delightful natural feel and is hugely popular with surfers and beach-lovers alike.

p82, p149, p167

The Drive ›› It's 30km (about half an hour) west from Santander to Santillana del Mar, along the S20, A67 and CA131. Only village residents or guests in hotels with garages may take vehicles into the old heart of Santillana. Other hotel guests may drive to unload luggage and then return to the car park at the village entrance.

---

❹ Santillana del Mar

Despite its name, Santillana is not by the *mar* (sea), but don't let that deter you from visiting this medieval jewel of a village. It's in such a perfect state of preservation with its bright cobbled streets, flower-filled balconies and huddle of tanned stone and brick buildings that it almost seems like a film set. At the end of the main street, past solemn 15th-to 18th-century nobles' houses, rises the beautiful 12th-century **Colegiata de Santa Juliana** (Plaza

> ✓ **TOP TIP:**
> **BILBAO FROM ABOVE**
>
> Bilbao's setting among rolling green hills comes as a pleasant surprise to many. For a change of pace and mesmerising views, take a ride on the old-fashioned **Funicular de Artxanda** (Plaza Funicular; adult/child one-way €2/0.31; every 15min 7.15am-10pm Mon-Thu, to 11pm Fri & Sat, 8.15am-10pm Sun Jun-Sep, 7.15am-10pm Oct-May).

Altamira Museo de Altamira (p164)

del Abad Francisco Navarro; adult/child €3/free; ☉10am-1.30pm & 4-7.15pm, to 6.15pm Nov-Mar, closed Mon Oct-Jun). This ex-monastery's big drawcard is the cloister, a formidable storehouse of Romanesque handiwork, with the capitals of its columns finely carved into a huge variety of figures.

🔖 p167

The Drive » Drive 16km west along the CA131 through verdant countryside to Comillas.

---

5 Comillas

The small town of Comillas is crowned by some of the most original and beautiful buildings on the north coast. The Marqués de Comillas (1817–83), born here as plain Antonio López, was the financier; in Cuba he profited as a planter, banker and slave trader, before returning to commission leading Catalan Modernista architects to reimagine his home town.

A particularly flamboyant example is the **Capricho de Gaudí** (📞942 72 03 65; www.elcaprichodegaudi.com; Barrio de Sobrellano; adult/child €5/2.50; ☉10.30am-8pm Mar-Jun & Oct, to 9pm Jul-Sep, to 5.30pm Nov-Feb), a summer play-pad for the marquis' sister-in-law's brother, designed by a young Antoni Gaudí.

Next door is the **Palacio de Sobrellano** (📞942 72 03 39; http://centros.culturadecantabria.com; Barrio de Sobrellano; adult/child €3/1.50, grounds free; ☉9.30am-6.30pm Tue-Sun Apr–mid-Jun & mid-Sep–Oct, 9.45am-7.30pm mid-Jun–mid-Sep, 9.30am-3.30pm Tue-Fri, to 5.30pm Sat & Sun Nov-Mar), an imposing neogothic affair by Joan Martorell. The spooky **cemetery** (off Paseo de Garelly; ☉hours vary) is overlooked by a chilling white-marble statue of the exterminating angel by sculptor Josep Llimona.

The Drive » Continue west on the CA131, then turn north on the CA236 to reach Playa Oyambre, 5km from Comillas.

ALTAMIRA

Spain's finest prehistoric art, the wonderful carbon-and-ochre paintings of bison, horses, deer and other animals in the Cueva de Altamira, 2.5km from Santillana del Mar, was discovered in 1879 by Cantabrian historian and scientist Marcelino Sanz de Sautuola and his eight-year-old daughter María Justina. By 2002, Altamira had attracted so many visitors that the cave was closed to stop deterioration of the art. Today, a replica cave in the **Museo de Altamira** (☏942 81 80 05; www.culturaydeporte. gob.es/mnaltamira; Avenida Marcelino Sanz de Sautuola; adult/senior, student & child €3.50/free, Sun & from 2pm Sat free; ☉9.30am-8pm Tue-Sat, to 3pm Sun May-Oct, 9.30am-6pm Tue-Sat, to 3pm Sun Nov-Apr; Ⓟ🚻) enables everyone to appreciate the inspired, 13,000- to 35,000-year-old paintings. The museum is incredibly popular, so you should book well ahead online, especially from Easter to September.

⑥ Playa Oyambre

The 2km-long, soft-blonde Playa Oyambre, 5km west of Comillas, is a sandy dream protected by the Parque Natural Oyambre. It has surfable waves and a dash of intriguing history as the emergency landing spot of the first ever USA–Spain flight (1929) – commemorated by the Pájaro Amarillo (Yellow Bird) monument towards the beach's west end. Waves and wind can be strong: swim only when the green flags fly.

The Drive » It's 50km west to spectacular Playa de Torimbia, about a 40-minute drive if you use the A8 motorway, approached through San Vicente de la Barquera. Exit at junction 300 and go southwest to Balmori. Here turn right to follow the LLN11 to Niembro, from where it's 2km (signposted) to the beach car park.

TRIP HIGHLIGHT

⑦ Playa de Torimbia

A beautiful gold crescent bounded by rocky headlands and a bowl of green hills, clothing-optional Torimbia is truly spectacular. You have to walk the last kilometre or so to reach it, which keeps the crowds down.

A 1km walk back over the headland from Torimbia (or 500m from Niembro village) brings you to the also attractive **Playa de Toranda**, 250m of sand backed by green fields and a forested headland. Both beaches have appealing *chiringuitos* (informal seasonal bar-restaurants) serving drinks and food from about mid-June to early September.

The Drive » Head back to Niembro then west on the LLN11 to join the A8 westbound at junction 303. Exit at junction 319 on to the N632 which follows the Río Sella into Ribadesella (23km, about 30 minutes).

TRIP HIGHLIGHT

⑧ Ribadesella

This low-key fishing town and seaside resort straddles the estuary of the Río Sella. The western part (with most of the best hotels) has an expansive golden beach, **Playa de Santa Marina**, lined by handsome early-20th-century *casas de indianos* (houses built by emigrants returned from the Americas). To see some of Spain's finest prehistoric cave art, including superb horse paintings probably done between 15,000 and 10,000 BCE, book ahead for Ribadesella's World Heritage–listed **Cueva de Tito Bustillo** (☏985 18 58 60, 902 306600; www.centrotitobustillo.com; Avenida de Tito Bustillo; adult/child €4.14/2.12, Wed free; ☉tours 10.15am-5pm Wed-Sun Mar-Oct; Ⓟ). The one-hour visits are guided in Spanish. If you miss the cave itself, the displays of the adjacent **Centro de Arte Rupestre Tito Bustillo** (☏985 18 58 60, 902 306600; www.centrotitobustillo.com; Avenida de Tito Bustillo; adult/child €5.45/3.29, Wed free; ☉10am-6pm Wed-Fri, to 7pm Sat & Sun Mar-Jun & Sep-Oct, to 7pm Wed-Sun Jul & Aug, to 6pm

Wed-Sun Nov-Dec & Feb; [P])
are well worth your time.

The broad, 1.5km-long sands of **Playa de Vega**, 8km west of Ribadesella, are among the least known of northern Spain's finest beaches. There are three or four relaxed restaurant-bars (most closed in winter) at the east end, and it's a surfing beach – but it's big enough, and just hard enough to reach, that it never feels crowded. To find it, go west from Ribadesella on the N632, turn off at Km 9.3 and go 1.6km to the beach.

🛏 p167

The Drive » Leave Ribadesella westbound on the N632. At a roundabout after 5km turn left to join the A8 westbound after 1km. After 34km, at A8 junction 360, take the A64, joining the A66 for the final couple of kilometres into Oviedo (total 76km, one hour).

TRIP HIGHLIGHT

⑨ Oviedo

Forsake the coastal vistas briefly for a breath of urban sophistication in Asturias' civilised capital. Oviedo is endowed with a lively Old Town of stone-paved, traffic-free streets and plazas, a stash of intriguing sights and some excellent restaurants

and bars. The imposing **Catedral de San Salvador** (📞985 21 96 42; www.catedral deoviedo.com; Plaza de Alfonso II; adult/child incl audio guide €7/free; ⏰10am-1pm & 4-6pm or 7pm Mar-Jun & Oct, 10am-7pm Jul-Aug, to 6pm Sep, 10am-1pm & 4-5pm Nov-Feb, closed Sun & from 5pm Sat year-round) was built mainly in Gothic and baroque styles between the 13th and 18th centuries but its origins and greatest interest lie in the **Cámara Santa**, a pre-Romanesque chapel begun in the 8th century to house important holy relics. Nearby are two excellent museums, the **Museo Arqueológico de Asturias** (📞985 20 89 77;

PRE-ROMANESQUE OVIEDO

Largely cut off from the rest of Christian Europe by the Muslim invasion of 711 CE, the tough and tiny kingdom that emerged in 8th-century Asturias engendered a unique style of art and architecture known as pre-Romanesque. The buildings, taking some inspiration from Roman and Visigothic styles, are typified by straight-line profiles, semicircular arches, and a triple-naved plan for churches.

Of the surviving buildings of the genre, several of the best are found in and near Oviedo. The **Iglesia de San Julián de los Prados** (Iglesia de Santuyano; 📞687 052826; Calle de Selgas 1; adult/child €2/0.50; ⏰10am-12.30pm Mon, 10am-12.30pm & 4-6pm Tue-Sat May-Jun, 10am-1pm Mon, 9.30am-1pm & 4-6pm Tue-Fri, 9.30am-12.30pm & 4-6pm Sat Jul-Sep, 10am-noon Mon-Sat Oct-Apr), 1km northeast of the city centre, is the largest remaining pre-Romanesque church, constructed in the early 9th century under Alfonso II. Its interior is covered with wonderfully preserved, brightly coloured frescoes. On the slopes of Monte Naranco, 3.5km northwest of central Oviedo, the **Iglesia de San Miguel de Lillo** (Iglesia de San Miguel de Lliño; Monte Naranco; guided visit adult/child incl Palacio de Santa María del Naranco €3/2; ⏰9.30am-1pm & 3.30-7pm Tue-Sat, 9.30am-1pm Sun Apr-Sep, 10am-2.30pm Tue-Sat, 10am-12.30pm Sun Oct-Mar) and the **Palacio de Santa María del Naranco** were built by Ramiro I (r 842–50 CE). The beautifully proportioned Santa María was probably a royal hunting lodge. Of San Miguel, only the western end remains (the rest collapsed centuries ago), but what's left has a singularly pleasing form. Visits inside all three of these buildings are by guided tour, in Spanish only.

A short walk below Santa María, the **Centro de Interpretación del Prerrománico** (📞985 18 58 60, 902 306600; www.prerromanicoasturiano.es; Monte Naranco; ⏰10am-2pm & 3.30-7pm Jul & Aug, 9.30am-1.30pm & 3.30-6pm Wed-Sun Mar-Jun, Sep & Oct, 9.30am-2.30pm Wed-Sun Nov, Dec & Feb; [P]) has informative displays on the pre-Romanesque phenomenon.

www.museoarqueologico
deasturias.com; Calle de San
Vicente 3-5; ☺9.30am-8pm
Wed-Fri, 9.30am-2pm & 5-8pm
Sat, 9.30am-3pm Sun), houses
the region's archaeological
riches, and the **Museo de
Bellas Artes de Asturias**
(📞985 21 30 61; www.museo
bbaa.com; Calle de Santa Ana
1; ☺10.30am-2pm & 4-8pm
Tue-Sat, 10.30am-2.30pm Sun
Jul & Aug, 10.30am-2pm & 4.30-
8.30pm Mon-Fri, 11.30am-2pm
& 5-8pm Sat, 11.30am-2.30pm
Sun Sep-Jun), which features
many Spanish greats.

✖ ▶ p167

The Drive » Make your way
out on to the A66 running north
past the east side of Oviedo.
Branch on to the A8 westbound
and follow this to junction 425,
where you exit and drive the last
6km down into Cudillero by the
N632 and CU2. It's a 60km trip,
taking 45 minutes (barring wrong
turns when extricating yourself
from Oviedo's one-way system).

- - - - - - - - - - - - - - - - -

⑩ Cudillero

Cudillero is the most
picturesque fishing village
on the Asturian coast,
with houses cascading
down to a port on a
narrow inlet. The main
activities in town are
watching the fishing
boats unload (3pm to
8pm), then sampling fish
and crustaceans at local
sidrerías (cider bars)
and restaurants. The
coastline is a dramatic
sequence of sheer cliffs
and fine beaches, with
Playa del Silencio (15km
west) outstanding for its
beauty: a long, silver-sand
cove backed by a natural

rock amphitheatre. It isn't
great for swimming due to
underwater rocks, but it's
a stunning spot for a stroll
and some sun-bathing.
To find it, take exit 441
off the A8, then head
2.5km west on the N632
to Castañeras, where the
beach is signposted. The
last 500m is on foot.

The Drive » Leave Cudillero
westward by the CU1 to join
the A8 westbound. Exit at
junction 474 to drive the last
4km down to Puerto de Vega
(49km, 40 minutes).

- - - - - - - - - - - - - - - - -

⑪ Puerto de Vega

Puerto de Vega, 15km
west of bigger Luarca, is a
lovely fishing village with
a colourful harbour and
several inviting seafood-
focused restaurants. It's
also the starting point
for scenic walks along
the **Senda Costa Naviega**
coastal footpath to two
beautiful, undeveloped,
sandy beaches. **Playa
de Barayo** (🅿), 5km
east of town, stretches
along a pretty bay with
a river winding through
wetlands and dunes.
Playa de Frejulfe, 4km
west (2.5km if you drive),
stretches 750m along the
ocean shore in front of
thick eucalyptus woods.
Surfers might catch a
wave here in spring or late
summer.
    The pick of the eateries
is **Mesón El Centro** (www.
facebook.com/Meson-El-
Centro-303872116336839;
Plaza de Cupido, Puerto de
Vega; mains €15-27, set menu

€35; ☺1.30-3.30pm & 8-11pm,
closed Mon evening), on a
tiny plaza just up from
the port, preparing good
fresh seafood with a
touch of flair and without
scrimping on the portions.

The Drive » Return to the
A8 and head west. Just after
crossing the bridge high above
the Ría de Ribadeo, exit at
junction 506 for the final 2km
into Ribadeo town (40km,
about 40 minutes).

- - - - - - - - - - - - - - - - -

⑫ Ribadeo

This lively port town
on the Ría de Ribadeo
– a sun-seeker magnet
in summer – is your
introduction to Galicia,
Spain's northwestern
region. The Old Town
between the central
Plaza de España and the
harbour is an attractive
mix of handsome old
galleried and stone
houses. **Praia As
Catedrais** (Cathedrals Beach;
http://ascatedrais.gal; 🅿 🚻),
10km west, is perhaps
the north's most spectacular
beach and a perfect
place to finish your
drive. This 1.5km sandy
stretch is strung with
awesome Gothic-looking
rock towers, arches and
chambers. Such is As
Catedrais' popularity that
during Easter week, July,
August, September and
some holiday weekends,
permits (free from http://
ascatedrais.xunta.gal) are
required to go onto the
beach. Avoid the hour or
two either side of high
tide when the beach is
under water.

Eating & Sleeping

San Sebastián ①

✕ Bar Borda Berri   Pintxos €

(☎943 43 03 42; Calle de Fermín Calbetón 12; pintxos €2-4; ⏰12.30-3.30pm & 7.30-11pm Wed-Sat, 12.30-3.30pm Sun Sep-Jun, also Mon & Tue Jul & Aug) Perennially popular Bar Borda Berri is an old-school *pintxo* bar – with black-and-white chequerboard floors and mustard-coloured walls hung with old photos and strands of garlic – that really lives up to the hype. Hungry diners crowd in for house specials such as braised veal cheeks in wine, mushroom and Idiazabal sheep's cheese risotto, and beef-rib skewers.

Bilbao ②

✕ Miró Hotel   Design Hotel €€€

(☎946 61 18 80; www.mirohotelbilbao.com; Alameda Mazarredo 77; d/ste from €168/283; ✳🛜) This hip hotel facing the Museo Guggenheim Bilbao is the passion project of fashion designer Antonio Miró. It's filled with photography and art, books, and minimalist decor – a perfect fit with art-minded Bilbao.

Santander ③

✕ Bodega del Riojano   Spanish €€

(☎942 21 67 50; www.bodegadelriojano.com; Calle Río de la Pila 5; mains €14-23; ⏰1.30-4pm & 8.30pm-midnight) The Riojano's high-ceilinged, wood-pillared dining room and bar, adorned with colourfully painted wine barrels, make an atmospheric setting for a fine range of northern Spanish favourites.

Santillana del Mar ④

✕ Casa del Organista   Hotel €€

(☎942 84 03 52; www.casadelorganista.com; Calle de Los Hornos 4; s €50-77, d €60-98; ⏰closed approx 7-31 Jan; Ⓟ🛜) The 14 rooms at this elegant 18th-century house, once home to the Colegiata's organist, are particularly attractive, with plush rugs, antique furniture, plenty of exposed oak beams and stonework,

and up-to-date bathrooms. Some have balconies looking across fields to the Colegiata. Expect a warm welcome and excellent breakfasts (€6.90). Parking is free.

Ribadesella ⑧

✕ Villa Rosario   Historic Hotel €€€

(☎985 86 00 90; www.hotelvillarosario.com; Calle de Dionisio Ruisánchez 3-6; r incl breakfast €81-285; ⏰Mar–mid-Jan; Ⓟ✳@🛜) Occupying a century-old *casa de indianos* (house built by an emigrant returned from the Americas), this luxurious, history-filled hotel overlooks Playa de Santa Marina. Interiors are pleasingly styled with wood floors, rich-toned carpets and an original cherry-wood staircase, while the 17 white-on-white rooms are tastefully contemporary. The buffet breakfast is excellent. The Villa Rosario 2 block out back is also comfortable, and cheaper, but lacks historical character.

Oviedo ⑨

✕ Tierra Astur   Asturian €€

(☎985 20 25 02; www.tierra-astur.com; Calle de la Gascona 1; mains €9-25, set menus €15-25; ⏰1-4.30pm & 7.30pm-midnight; 🛜) This particularly atmospheric *sidrería*-restaurant is famous for its prize-winning cider and good-value lunchtime *menús*. People queue for tables; settle for tapas at the bar or just buy traditional products for home. Try enormous salads, Asturian *cachopo* (stuffed breaded veal), giant grilled-veg platters or assorted seafood.

✕ Barceló Oviedo Cervantes   Hotel €€

(☎985 25 50 00; www.barcelo.com; Calle de Cervantes 13; r €75-120; Ⓟ✳@🛜) Comprising a revamped century-old mansion and two modern smoked-glass wings, the Barceló is just two blocks northwest of the central Campo de San Francisco. Impeccably contemporary style runs throughout, from the cocktail-lounge-style lobby bar to the 72 spacious, luxurious rooms, with their chain curtains, multiple mirrors and glass-partitioned bathrooms. Service is simultaneously warm and professional.

Coast of Galicia

13

Drive along Spain's most spectacular coast, a succession of long, snaking rías (inlets) with perpendicular cliffs, sandy beaches, picturesque fishing ports and some of the best seafood around.

TRIP HIGHLIGHTS

7 km

Cabo Ortegal
Be dwarfed by these enormous cliffs

FINISH
18

0 km

Cabo Fisterra
Peer over the cliffs that stand at the end of the world

A Coruña
Betanzos

Camariñas

10

7 km

7
6

Cambados
Enjoy the wineries and taverns of the albariño wine capital

129 km

Pontevedra
Walk the stone-paved streets of Pontevedra's old quarter

Vigo

A Guarda
START

**5–7 DAYS
654KM / 406 MILES**

GREAT FOR...

BEST TIME TO GO

June to September for beach weather (normally!), and November to February for wild storms.

ESSENTIAL PHOTO

Cabo Fisterra – the end of the world.

BEST FOR GHOSTS

The shipwreck-haunted Costa da Morte (Coast of Death).

Fisterra Western edge of Spain (p174)

169

Rocky headlands, winding inlets, small fishing towns, narrow coves, wide sweeping bays and many a sandy beach – this is the beautiful coastline of Galicia and it's a world away from the clichéd images of Spain. Relatively heavily populated in the south (known as the Rías Baixas – Lower Rías), the coast becomes wilder as you work your way north to the Rías Altas (Upper Rías).

ATLANTIC OCEAN

Malpic
Bergant
Camelle
14
Laxe
Camariñas 13   Ba
Muxía 12   Vimianzo   Za
Lires 11
Cée
Fisterra 10   Monte Pind
O Pindo   (627m)
Carnota 9
AC550
8
Muros
Porto do Son   R
Xuño   Boirc
Corrubedo   A Pc
Cambad
O Grov
Sanx

Cabo de Home

Baior

A Guard
START
Ca

Viana
Cast

❶ A Guarda

A fishing port just north of where the Río Miño spills into the Atlantic, A Guarda (Castilian: La Guardia) has a pretty harbour and good seafood restaurants, but its unique draw is the beautiful **Monte de Santa Trega** (adult/child in vehicle Tue-Sun mid-Feb–Dec €1/0.50, Mon & Jan-mid-Feb free; P 👫), whose summit is a 4km drive or 2km uphill walk (the PRG122) from town. On the way up, poke around the partly restored **Castro de Santa Trega** (*castros* were the fortified settlements of circular stone huts inhabited by Galicians' Celtic ancestors). At the top, you'll find a

16th-century chapel, an interesting small **archaeological museum** (🕑9am-9pm Jul & Aug, 10am-8pm Apr-Jun & Sep, to 7pm Mar & Oct, 11am-5pm 2nd half Feb, Nov & Dec; P), a couple of cafes – and truly majestic panoramas up the Miño, across to Portugal and out over the Atlantic.

🍴 🛏 p179

The Drive » Follow the PO552 north along its fairly straight coastal route to Baiona (30km, 35 minutes). Enjoy not fighting the steering wheel much – this is almost the last straight stretch of road you're going to encounter!

❷ Baiona

Baiona (Castilian: Bayona) is a popular resort with an inviting

casco histórico (historic centre) of tangled lanes, and its own little place in history: the shining moment came on 1 March 1493, when one of Columbus' small fleet, the *Pinta,* stopped in for supplies, bearing the remarkable news that the explorer had made it to the (West) Indies.

You can't miss the pine-covered promontory **Monte Boi**, dominated by the **Fortaleza de Monterreal** (approx Jun-Sep; pedestrian/car €1/5, rest of year free; ⏱10am-10pm; **P**). This fortress is protected by a 3km circle of walls, and an enjoyable 40-minute walking trail loops round the promontory's rocky shoreline, which is broken up by a few small beaches.

 LINK YOUR TRIP

7 **Northern Spain Pilgrimage**

The beaches and cliffs of Galicia's coast are the perfect follow-up to the inland trip along the Camino de Santiago.

30 **The Minho's Lyrical Landscapes**

The Atlantic beaches, historic cities and verdant landscapes of northern Portugal have a lot in common with Galicia, but also fascinating contrasts.

The Drive » It's 25km (45 minutes) along the PO552 to Vigo. It's best to use one of the several signposted underground car parks around the centre.

❸ Vigo

Vigo is both a historic city and a gritty industrial port that's home to Europe's largest fishing fleet. Its central areas make for good strolling, and it's the main departure point for summer ferries (45 minutes one-way) to the beautiful **Illas Cíes**, the three islands in the mouth of the Ría de Vigo that are home to some of Galicia's most splendid beaches. Vigo's citizens really know how to enjoy life, especially after dark in the many buzzing tapas bars, restaurants and clubs.

The Casco Vello (Old Town) climbs uphill from the cruise-ship port; at the heart of its jumbled lanes is elegant **Praza da Constitución**, a perfect spot for a drink. To the east spreads the heart of the modern city, with

the parklike **Praza de Compostela** a welcome green space in its midst.

The Drive » Head east out of central Vigo past Guixar train station, following A9 (or AP9) Pontevedra signs. From the far end of the Puente de Rande bridge (spanning the Ría de Vigo), follow the AG46, CG4.1 and VG4.6 westward. Where the VG4.6 ends at a roundabout, go left. Just after Aldán village, turn right along the narrow EP1008 for 1km to Hío – 33km (40 minutes) from Vigo.

❹ Hío

Little Hío village is home to Galicia's most famous *cruceiro* (carved wayside cross, a traditional Galician art form). The **Cruceiro de Hío**, standing outside the Romanesque San Andrés de Hío church, was sculpted in the 1870s by Ignacio Cerviño. Its delicate, detailed carvings narrate key passages of Christian teachings, from Adam and Eve to the taking down of Christ from the cross.

The Drive » Take the winding EP1006 from Hío through

woodlands and Donón village (following occasional signs to Cabo Home or Facho) until ocean views open out before you, with a couple of cafes on the right. You can park nearby (5km, 10 minutes).

❺ Cabo de Home

Windswept Cabo de Home is a rocky cape with walking trails, three lighthouses and great views of the offshore Illas Cíes. It's an excellent area to spend a few hours exploring. The partly excavated Iron Age *castro* **Berobriga** sits atop panoramic Monte Facho nearby. There are

**TOP TIP:
BRING YOUR
UMBRELLA**

Swept by one rainy Atlantic front after another, Galicia has, overall, twice as much rain as the Spanish national average. Galicians have more than 100 words to describe different kinds of rain, from *babuxa* (a variety of drizzle) to *xistra* (a type of shower) and *treboada* (a thunderstorm).

Pontevedra Old town

some beautiful beaches in the area as well (some nudist).

The Drive ⟫ It's 36km (45 minutes) along the south side of the Ría de Vigo from Cabo de Home to appealing Pontevedra. Return to Aldán, then follow the PO551, VG4.4 and PO12. There's a convenient car park underneath the Mercado Municipal on the northern edge of Pontevedra's Old Town, and plenty of free open-air parking just across the river there.

- - - - - - - - - - - - - - - -

TRIP HIGHLIGHT

6 Pontevedra

Back in the 16th century Pontevedra was Galicia's biggest city.

Columbus' flagship, the *Santa María,* may have been built here. Today this is an inviting, small, riverside city that combines history, culture and style into a lively overnight stop. It's a pleasure to wander the narrow, traffic-free streets and the dozen or so small plazas of the Old Town, abuzz with shops, markets, cafes, taverns and tapas bars.

The eclectic **Museo de Pontevedra** (☎986 80 41 00; www.museo.depo. gal) is scattered over six city-centre buildings. The **Edificio Sarmiento**

(Rúa Sarmiento; ⏰10am-9pm Tue-Sat, 11am-2pm Sun), in a renovated 18th-century Jesuit college, houses a particularly absorbing collection encompassing Galician Sargadelos ceramics, modern art, prehistoric gold jewellery and much more. The adjoining **Sexto Edificio** (Rúa de Padre Amoedo; ⏰10am-9pm Tue-Sat, 11am-2pm Sun) has three floors of Galician and Spanish art from the 14th to 20th centuries.

The Drive ⟫ Head north on the AP9 then west on the AG41 and VG2 to Cambados (28km, 30 minutes).

⑦ Cambados

The capital of **albariño wine country**, the pretty little *ría*-side town of Cambados is a delightful stop. Its old streets are lined by stone architecture and dotted with inviting taverns and eateries. Cambados' **tourist office** (📞986 52 07 86; www.cambados.es; Edificio Exposalnés, Paseo da Calzada; ⊘10am-2pm & 5-8pm Mon-Sat, 10.30am-2pm Sun Jun-Sep, 10am-1.30pm & 4-7pm Mon-Sat, 10.30am-1.30pm Sat Oct-May) has details on all visitable wineries. The best-known ones are in the countryside, including the innovative **Mar de Frades** (📞986 68 09 11; www.mardefrades. es; Finca Valiñas, Arosa; tour incl 3-wine tasting €12; ⊘closed Mon & Tue Feb-Mar, Sun-Tue afternoons all year), 9km east (book visits via the website or by phone). Don't miss **Gil Armada** (📞660 078252; www.bodegagilarmada.com; Praza de Fefiñáns; tours €7-12; ⊘tours noon, 12.30pm, 5.30pm, 6.30pm Mon-Sat, 12.30pm Sun Jun-Sep, noon, 12.30pm & 5.30pm Mon-Sat Oct-May) in the town: the handsome 17th-century Pazo de Fefiñáns mansion in which it's housed steals the show here. Pay a visit to the ruined 15th-century church, the **Igrexa de Santa Mariña Dozo** (Rúa do Castro; ⊘24hr), now roofless but still

with its four roof arches intact. It's surrounded by a well-kept cemetery – particularly atmospheric after dark! The five-minute walk up to the **Mirador de A Pastora**, behind, is well worth it for expansive views over the Ría de Arousa.

🛏 p179

The Drive ›› It's a longish hop to Muros, so it makes sense to take the easiest route. Head east from Cambados to join the AP9 motorway northbound. Exit at junction 93 on to the AG11, then almost immediately turn north on the AC301. This brings you to the CG1.5. Follow this then the AC554 and AC550 to Muros (95km, about 1½ hours from Cambados).

⑧ Muros

The small fishing port of Muros is an agreeable halt en route to the Costa da Morte. Behind the bustling seafront extends a web of stone-paved lanes dotted with taverns and lined with dignified stone houses. The medieval **Igrexa de San Pedro** is a fine example of a Galician 'maritime Gothic' church, typified by a single very wide nave.

The Drive ›› As you leave Muros, the real excitement of this drive begins (can you believe that everything so far was a mere taster?) as you start along the famed Costa da Morte. It's so named because of the number of shipwrecks it has claimed. To get to Carnota follow the AC550 round the coast (17km, 20 minutes).

⑨ Carnota

Carnota village is renowned as home to Galicia's largest *hórreo* (traditional grain store on stilts) – 34.5m long and constructed in an 18th-century *hórreo*-building contest with nearby Lira. However, many people come here not for the grain store but for the spectacular, if exposed, 7km curve of nearby **Praia de Carnota**. The more protected sections are at its south end, signposted (all with separate names) from Lira.

The Drive ›› Driving to the end of the world has never been so easy. Just follow the AC550 and AC445 to Fisterra (37km; 45 minutes), enjoying some great views over the Ría de Corcubión as you go.

⑩ Fisterra

Cabo Fisterra (Cabo Finisterre; 🅿) is the western edge of Spain, at least in popular imagination. The real westernmost point is Cabo Touriñán, 20km north, but that doesn't stop throngs of people from heading out to this beautiful, windswept cape, which is also the end-point of an 86km extension of the Camino de Santiago. It's crowned by a lighthouse, the Faro de Fisterra.

The cape is a 3.5km drive past the town of

Fisterra. On the edge of town you pass the 12th-century **Igrexa de Santa María das Areas**. Some 600m past the church, a track signed 'Conxunto de San Guillermo' heads up the hill to the right, Monte Facho. This provides a longer but even more scenic alternative walking route to the cape on which you can visit the mysterious **Ermida de San Guillerme** – a ruined medieval chapel and rock shelter, possibly the location of a legendary pre-Christian *ara solis* (altar of the sun).

Fisterra itself is a fishing port with a picturesque harbour. **Praia da Mar de Fora**, over on the ocean side of the promontory, is spectacular but not safe for swimming. For calmer waters, head to sandy, 2km-long **Praia de Langosteira** north of town.

🛏 p179

The Drive » Fisterra to Lires is an easy 12km drive. Head north on the AC445 and turn left after 2.5km (500m after Hotel Playa de Langosteira). The rest of the way is along very minor country roads, with some glimpses of Praia do Rostro.

⓫ **Lires**

Pretty Lires village sits just inland from the coast, above the little Ría de Lires, amid typically green, wooded Costa da Morte countryside. It's a popular stop for walkers on both the Camino de Santiago and the coastal Camiño dos Faros trail, but with wonderful beaches nearby, it's a fine stop even if you're not following any *camino*.

The beautiful, 1.5km sandy curve of **Praia de Nemiña**, stretching north from the mouth of the Ría de Lires, attracts surfers in

LOCAL KNOWLEDGE: GALICIA SEAFOOD TIPS

Galicia's ocean-fresh seafood, from *pulpo á feira* (tender, spicy octopus slices) to melt-in-the-mouth *lubiña* (sea bass), is a reason in itself to come here. In any coastal town or village (and many inland) you can get a meal to remember. Tuck into any of these and you'll never want to eat red meat again.

Pulpo á feira is Galicia's signature dish (known as *pulpo a la gallega* elsewhere in Spain): tender slices of octopus tentacle sprinkled with olive oil and paprika. It's even better when accompanied by *cachelos* (sliced boiled potatoes).

Percebes (goose barnacles) is Galicia's favourite shellfish delicacy, pulled off coastal rocks at low tide (a sometimes dangerous pursuit) and looking like miniature dragon claws. To eat them you hold the 'claw' end, twist off the other end and eat the soft, succulent bit inside.

Shellfish fans will also delight in **ameixas** (clams), **mexillons** (mussels), **vieiras** (scallops), **zamburiñas** (small scallops), **berberechos** (cockles) and **navajas** (razor clams). These will be on the menu in every coastal town.

Other delicacies include **bogavantes** or **lubrigantes**, types of mini-lobster with two outsized claws, and various crabs, from little **nécoras** and **santiaguiños** to huge **centollos** (spider crabs) and the enormous **buey del mar** ('ox of the sea').

Shellfish in restaurants is often priced by weight: around 250g per person usually makes a fairly large serving. Simple steaming or hotplate-grilling (*a la plancha*) is almost always the best way to prepare shellfish, maybe with a dash of olive oil, garlic and herbs to enhance the natural flavour.

numbers from roughly April to November. The *ría* mouth can be crossed from Lires at low tide in summer, but otherwise it's a 2.5km walk (or a roundabout drive of 9km) from village to beach. **Praia do Rostro** is a broad 2km stretch of unbroken sand beginning about 4km south of Lires. It's a particularly magnificent sight from the headlands at either end, with the Atlantic surf pouring in. Unfortunately it's not good for swimming, but it's a wonderful walk.

📖 p179

The Drive » Take the long route to Muxía via scenic Cabo Touriñán, mainland Spain's most westerly point, great for a breezy walk. Follow Touriñán signs off the CP2301 3km east of Lires, and head northwest to the cape through woodlands and Frixe and Touriñán villages. Afterwards, return 5km the way you came, then turn north along the DP5201 for 12km to Muxía. Total 31km (45 minutes' driving).

⑫ Muxía

Muxía is a photogenic little fishing port with a handful of cosy bars and restaurants, and, like Cabo Fisterra, a popular onward destination for pilgrims from Santiago de Compostela. The **Santuario da Virxe da Barca** (🕐Mass 7pm Mon-Fri, noon & 7pm Sat & Sun; 🅿) on the rocky seashore marks the spot where (legend attests) the Virgin Mary arrived in a stone boat and appeared to Santiago (St James) while he was preaching here. Two of the rocks strewn on the foreshore, the **Pedra dos Cadris** and **Pedra d'Abalar**, are, supposedly, the boat's sail and keel. Crawling under the former nine times is said, improbably, to be good for back problems.

The Drive » Camariñas is just 4km northeast of Muxía across the Ría de Camariñas, but 25km (40 minutes) by road. Fortunately it's a pretty drive, via the inviting beach Praia do Lago, the hórreo-studded hamlet Leis and the riverside villages of Cereixo and Ponte do Porto.

⑬ Camariñas

Wrapped around its colourful fishing harbour, Camariñas is the starting point for the scenic Ruta Litoral drive.

The Drive » The Ruta Litoral to Camelle is one of the most beautiful stretches of the Costa da Morte, but if you don't like the sound of its unpaved sections you can head inland from Camariñas along the AC432, then turn left on to the DP1601 as you leave Ponte do Porto. It's 15km (20 minutes) this way.

⑭ Camelle

Camelle has no outstanding charm, but it does have two touching mementos of 'Man' (Manfred Gnädinger), a long-time German resident who died in 2002, only weeks after the *Prestige* oil tanker went down just offshore.

RUTA LITORAL DRIVE

It takes longer than the inland road but don't miss the scenic coastal route (part paved, part dirt/gravel) from Camariñas to Camelle. You start by going 5km northwest to **Cabo Vilán lighthouse** (with a cafe and an exhibition on shipwrecks and lighthouses), then head east to Camelle, a further 19km. The route winds past secluded beaches, across windswept hillsides and past weathered rock formations, and there are several places to stop along the way. **Praias da Pedrosa**, **da Balea** and **da Reira** are a picturesque set of short sandy strands a couple of kilometres past Cabo Vilán; then there's the **Cemiterio dos Ingleses** (English Cemetery), the sad burial ground from an 1890 shipwreck that took the lives of 172 British naval cadets. Signposting after the cemetery is poor: go left at forks after 2km and 3km, straight on at the junction after 5.7km, and left at the fork after 8.5km. This takes you into Camelle through pretty Arou village.

The resulting oil slick devastated this fragile coastline and, some people say, caused Man to die of a broken heart. His hut and quirky sculpture garden made from rocks and ocean bric-a-brac, beside the pier, are now labelled the **Museo Xardín de Man** (view from outside only); the **Museo Man de Camelle** (☑981 71 02 24; www.mandecamelle. com; Rúa do Muelle 9, Camelle; adult/child €1/free; ☺11am-2pm & 5-8pm Tue-Sun mid-Jun–mid-Sep, 11am-2pm & 5-7pm Sat & Sun mid-Sep–mid-Jun; P), back along the waterfront, exhibits some of his sketchbooks, notebooks and objets trouvés.

Praia de Traba, a little-frequented 2.5km stretch of sand with dunes and a lagoon, is a lovely 4km walk east along the coast.

The Drive » Head inland on the DP1601 and AC432 to Vimianzo, then east along the AC552 and the quick AG55 to A Coruña (85km, 1¼ hours).

----

⑮ A Coruña

Coruña (Castilian: La Coruña) is a port city, beachy hot spot and cruise-ship stop; a busy commercial centre and a cultural enclave; a historic city and a modern metropolis. The Ciudad Vieja (Old City) has shady plazas, charming old churches, hilly cobbled lanes and a good smattering of

cafes and bars. The Unesco-listed **Torre de Hércules** (Tower of Hercules; www.torredeherculesacoruna. com; Avenida Doctor Vázquez Iglesias; adult/child €3/1.50, Mon year-round & Sat Oct-Jun free; ☺10am-9pm Jun-Sep, to 6pm Oct-May; P) sits near the windy northern tip of the city. It was actually the Romans who originally built this lighthouse in the 1st century CE – a beacon on what was then the furthest edge of the 'civilised' world.

Kids love the seal colony and the under-water Nautilus room (surrounded by sharks and 50 other fish species) at the excellent **Aquarium Finisterrae** (☑981 18 98 42; www.coruna.gal/mc2/es/aquarium-finisterrae; Paseo Marítimo 34; adult/child €10/4; ☺10am-8pm Jul & Aug, shorter hours rest of year; P 👶) on the city's northern headland.

There's a great tapas scene along the streets west of the central Plaza de María Pita – Calles de la Franja, Barrera, Galera, Olmos and Estrella. Moving westward along these lanes the vibe mutates from old-style *mesones* (taverns) to contemporary tapas bars.

The Drive » The straight, yes straight, drive to Betanzos takes just 20 minutes if you're lucky with the traffic. Take the AP9 motorway then the A6, exiting at junction 567.

⑯ Betanzos

Once a thriving estuary port rivalling A Coruña, Betanzos is renowned for its welcoming taverns and a well-preserved medieval Old Town that harmoniously combines galleried houses, old-fashioned shops and some monumental architecture. Take Rúa Castro up into the oldest part of town. Handsome **Praza da Constitución** is flanked by a couple of appealing cafes along with the Romanesque/Gothic **Igrexa de Santiago**. A short stroll northeast, two beautiful Gothic churches, **Santa María do Azougue** and **San Francisco** (Rúa San Francisco; adult/child €2/free; ☺10.30am-1.30pm & 4.30-7pm Mar-Sep, to 6pm Oct-Feb), stand almost side by side. The latter is full of particularly fine stone carving, including many sepulchres of 14th- and 15th-century Galician nobility.

The Drive » Take the N651 north from Betanzos and join the AP9 motorway after Pontedeume. The AP9 takes you across the Ría de Ferrol; now navigation becomes tricky due to poor signage. Turn north at junction 34F, 2km after the bridge, then go right at a roundabout after 6km, then left at another roundabout after 1.5km. You're now on the AC566 which leads all the way to Cedeira (65km, one hour from Betanzos).

DETOUR: BEST BANK OF THE WORLD

Start: ⑱ Cabo Ortegal

At Km 63.1 of the AC682, 20km east of Ponte Mera, turn north (signed to Praia do Picón) and go 3km north along narrow country lanes to Picón village, set above a cliff-foot beach. One kilometre west along the clifftops stands the bench that has acquired celebrity status under the English name 'Best Bank of the World' (thanks to a confusion about the Spanish word *banco*, meaning both bench and bank). It affords magnificent panoramas along the jagged coast all the way from Cabo Ortegal to the Punta da Estaca de Bares. From here return to the AC682 and continue towards the Estaca de Bares.

⑰ Cedeira

The fishing port and very low-key resort of Cedeira has a cute little old town sitting on the west bank of the Río Condomiñas, while **Praia da Magdalena** fronts the modern, eastern side of town. Around the headland to the south (a 7km drive) is the wilder **Praia de Vilarrube**, a long, sandy beach with shallow waters between two river mouths, in a protected area of dunes and wetlands.

For a nice stroll of an hour or two, walk along the waterfront to the fishing port, climb up to the 18th-century **Castelo da Concepción** above it, and walk out to **Punta Sarridal**, overlooking the mouth of the Ría de Cedeira.

Weather permitting, you can take a scenic boat trip north past the spectacular Herbeira cliffs and Cabo Ortegal as far as Cariño and back (per person €30, 1¾ hours, adults only) with **Rutas Cedeira** (☏722 615382; www.facebook.com/rutascedeira; Puerto de Cedeira; ⊙mid-Jun–mid-Sep). The ride can be bumpy. A minimum six people are required.

🛏 p179

The Drive ›› This 28km drive is the most spectacular of the whole trip. Heading northeast from Cedeira, take the DP2204 then the DP2205. The road crosses the Serra da Capelada and has incredible views. The Garita de Herbeira lookout, after 4km, is 615m above sea level and the best place to be wowed over southern Europe's highest sea cliffs. Continue to Cariño then north to Cabo Ortegal.

TRIP HIGHLIGHT

⑱ Cabo Ortegal

The Atlantic Ocean meets the Bay of Biscay at the mother of all Spanish capes, Cabo Ortegal, where great stone shafts drop sheer into the ocean from such a height that the waves crashing on the rocks below seem pitifully benign.

The Drive ›› Head south to Ponte Mera and turn east along the AC682. At O Barqueiro, after 25km, head north on the AC100. After Vila de Bares (Vares), follow signs to the Faro and/or Estaca de Bares. Park just before the lighthouse and follow the trail to the tip of the peninsula, the Punta da Estaca de Bares (47km, one hour, from Cabo Ortegal).

⑲ Estaca de Bares

The Bares Peninsula is a marvellously scenic spur of land jutting north into the Bay of Biscay, with walking trails, beaches, cliffs and a few delightfully low-key spots to stay over. From the lighthouse near the tip of the peninsula, a 400m path follows the spine of a rock outcrop to the Punta da Estaca de Bares, Spain's most northerly point, a satisfying place to complete your drive, with awe-inspiring cliffs and fabulous panoramas.

Eating & Sleeping

A Guarda ❶

✕ Casa Chupa Ovos   Seafood €€

(☎986 61 10 15; Rúa A Roda 24; mains &
raciones €8-26, lunch menú €10; ◷1.30-
3.30pm Tue, 1.30-3.30pm & 8.30-11pm Thu-Mon,
closed 3 weeks Oct/Nov) It's up a flight of steps
from the harbourfront, and it doesn't have a sea
view, but Chupa Ovos is a deserved favourite with
locals and visitors alike for its perfectly prepared
fresh seafood, friendly and prompt service, bright
atmosphere and good wines.

🛏 Hotel Convento de San Benito   Historic Hotel €€

(☎986 61 11 66; www.hotelsanbenito.es; Rúa
Concepción Arenal; s €42-61, d €54-99; ◷closed
mid-Dec–early Jan; [P][❀][📶]) A real treat, the San
Benito is housed in a 16th-century former convent
near the harbour. Its 33 rooms are elegant and
very comfortable, and the whole place is like a
mini-museum. Great breakfast (€7.50) too.

Cambados ❼

🛏 Quinta de San Amaro   Boutique Hotel €€

(☎630 877590; www.quintadesanamaro.com;
Rúa San Amaro 6, Meaño; incl breakfast s €95-130,
d €110-190; [P][❀][📶][⛱][🐾]) A dream base for
enjoying the Rías Baixas, this hotel is surrounded
by vineyards 12km south of Cambados. With
inspired traditional-meets-contemporary design,
first-class service and a relaxed atmosphere, it
unites 14 different rooms with diverse common
spaces, including an inviting pool and lovely
gardens. An important part of the magic is the
panoramic **restaurant** (mains €13-21; ◷1.30-
4pm & 8.30-11pm, closed Mon-Thu mid-Oct–Mar),
serving delicious updates on traditional Galician
cuisine (open to all; reservations recommended).

Fisterra ❿

🛏 Hotel Mar da Ardora   Design Hotel €€

(☎667 641304; www.hotelmardaardora.com;
Rúa Mar de Fora 17; incl breakfast s €75-110, d
€85-110; ◷closed mid-Dec–Jan; [P][@][📶][⛱]）
This delightful family-run hotel sits at the top of
town, with fantastic westward ocean views from
the big windows and terraces of its six rooms.
Everything is impeccably contemporary and
comfortable. Downstairs is a good spa and gym
with solar-heated pool and Turkish bath.

Lires ⓫

🛏 Casa Fontequeiroso   Hotel €€

(☎617 490851; www.casafontequeiroso.com;
Hotel Rural Fontequeiroso, Lugar de Queiroso; s/d
incl breakfast Jul-Sep €65/80, Oct-Jun €55/70;
[P][📶]) This restored, century-old stone house,
2km above Praia de Nemiña, is a welcoming and
very well-run place to stay, with six thoughtfully
designed rooms and a wonderfully tranquil rural
situation. Owner Mari Carmen prepares superb
dinners (from €20) based around traditional
Galician country recipes.

Cedeira ⓱

🛏 Hotel Herbeira   Design Hotel €€

(☎981 49 21 67; www.hotelherbeira.com;
Cordobelas; s €50-105, d €55-135; ◷closed 20
Dec-12 Jan; [P][❀][@][📶][⛱]) As sleek as Galicia
gets, welcoming, family-run Herbeira offers
16 large, thoughtfully designed rooms with
glassed-in galleries, well-equipped bathrooms
and stunning views over the *ría* – a perfect
combination of design, comfort and practicality.
There's a beautiful pool at the front and a
spacious cafe and sitting area for the good
breakfasts (€4 to €9).

Barcelona & Eastern Spain

WILD AND GORGEOUS COASTLINE, CHISELLED MOUNTAIN PEAKS AND ENCHANTING CITYSCAPES set the stage for awe-inspiring drives around Catalonia and eastern Spain. Barcelona makes a fine gateway, with its madcap architecture and brilliant restaurants. The Costa Brava is studded with picture-perfect villages and pretty beaches against curving headlands topped with pine forests. West of Barcelona, the coastal plains give way to lowland mountains, with medieval towns set over the vineyards of the Penedès region. The views only get more spectacular as you roll past the old stone villages and flower-strewn meadows of the Pyrenees, with the mountains all around you.

Barcelona Park Güell (p226)
S-F/SHUTTERSTOCK ©

Barcelona & Eastern Spain

Aurillac

Bergerac

Sarlat-la-Canéda

Bordeaux

Figeac

Villeneuve-sur-Lot

Rodez

Me

Caussade

Villefranche de Rouergue

Millau

A62

Montauban

Mont-de-Marsan

Albi

Béz

Aire-sur-l'Adour

Auch

Castres

Toulouse

Mazamet

Colomb

Biarritz

Bayonne

St-Palais

Pau

Tarbes

Montréjeau

Carcassonne

Bilbao

San Sebastián

Irún

St-Jean Pied de Port

Foix

Ax-les-Thermes

Perpig

Soraluze

AP68

A15

N135

Burguete

Hecho (Echo)

Vignemale (3298m)

Parque Nacional de Ordesa y Monte Perdido

Vielha

ANDORRA

Vitoria

A1

Pamplona

Yesa

Jaca

Mt Perdido (3355m)

⊕ **ANDORRA LA VELLA**

Estella

AP15

N240

18

N260

Sort

Adrall

N260

Figueres

Cadac

Miranda de Ebro

Logroño

Sos del Rey Católico

Ayerbe

Alquézar

17

Tremp

Ripoll

Olot

Girona

15

Calahorra

Huesca

Barbastro

Benabarre

Cardona

16

Vic

AP7

Pala

N111

Tudela

A23

N240

19

A2

Manresa

Sant Celoni

Tossa de

Soria

AP68

Sariñena

Lleida

Igualada

18

A15

SPAIN

Zaragoza

AP2

Barcelona

Paracuellos de Jiloca

A2

Bujaraloz

N211

AP2

Medinaceli

Daroca

Azaila

Río Ebro

Móra la Nova

Reus

Vilanova i la Geltrú

N211

Molina de Aragón

Caminreal

A23

Alcañiz

N420

Tarragona

Cambrils

Río Tajo

Pastrana

Albarracín

Utrillas

Alcorisa

Tortosa

Sant Carles de la Ràpita

AP7

Balearic Sea

Teruel

N420

Mora de Rubielos

Peñíscola

Cuenca

19

Benicàssim

Castellón de la Plana

A23

Río Júcar

Sagunto

Golfo de Valencia

Inca

Palma de Mallorca

Mallorca

Ma

A3

A3

Aldaya

Valencia

Tomelloso

A31

N330

Alginet

Sueca

Munera

Albacete

Xàtiva

Gandia

Ibiza

Parque Natural Sierras de Cazorla, Segura y las Villas

Almansa

Ontinyent

Dénia

Ibiza Town

AP36

A30

A31

A7

Villena

Alcoy

Calpe (Calp)

Formentera

Hellín

Elda

Ibi

AP7

Benidorm

Beas de Segura

Novelda

Alicante

Río Segura

Elche

MEDITERRANEAN SEA

Puebla de Don Fadrique

Cieza

Murcia

Huéscar

Alhama de Murcia

Torrevieja

A7

San Pedro del Pinatar

Cúllar

Lorca

Los Alcázares

Baza

Puerto Lumbreras

14

Cartagena

Huércal-Overa

AP7

Águilas

A7

Mojácar

0 — 100 k
0 — 50 miles

Cadaqués (p199)

DON'T MISS

The palm groves of Elche
Take a refreshing walk along the wandering paths of this surprising oasis in Murcia. See it on Trip **14**

Cadaqués
Wander the rocky shores and hilly streets that inspired the great artist Salvador Dalí. Stroll in the surrealist's footsteps on Trip **15**

Estany de Sant Maurici
Enjoy spectacular views on a hike past this mountain lake in Catalonia's only national park. Experience it on Trip **17**

Teruel
Visit the tombs of two star-crossed lovers from the 13th century in a stirring but kitschy display. Catch it on Trip **19**

Zugarramurdi
Walk through the caves where witches once held covens and pagan rituals in the 17th century. See it on Trip **18**

Unsung Wonders of Murcia & Alicante

14

This ramble takes you from old-fashioned villages to picturesque shorelines, with a vibrant mix of culture, history and outdoor adventure in one easy-going journey.

TRIP HIGHLIGHTS

FINISH
● Villena

338 km

Elche
Strolling through enchanting groves of date palms

40 km

Parque Natural de Sierra Espuña
Walking trails amid dramatic highlands

⑨

● Murcia
START

② ● Lo Pagán

③ ● Cabo de Palos

● Cartagena

④

Águilas
Exploring picturesque coves

108 km

Lorca
Seeing the world in blue and white

72 km

2–4 DAYS
402KM / 241 MILES

GREAT FOR...

BEST TIME TO GO
From March to June or September to November to escape the heat and crowds.

ESSENTIAL PHOTO

Limestone cliffs in Parque Natural de Sierra Espuña.

BEST FOR WILDLIFE

Spotting birds in the lagoons of the Salinas de San Pedro.

14 Unsung Wonders of Murcia & Alicante

This winding route through Murcia and Alicante provinces takes you to some of the unsung wonders of southeast Spain. You'll find great hiking amid rocky forests, striking coastal scenery and a trove of historical treasures (Roman ruins, Gothic cathedrals and Modernista architecture). This 402km journey offers plenty of surprises, from strolling among ancient groves of date palms to swimming in untouched coves in the Mediterranean.

---

1 Murcia

Bypassed by most tourists and treated as a country cousin by many Spaniards, this laid-back provincial capital nevertheless more than merits a visit.

Murcia's most striking site is the **Real Casino de Murcia** (968 21 53 99; www.realcasinomurcia.com; Calle de la Trapería 18; adult/child €5/3; 10.30am-7pm Sep-Jul, to 2.30pm Mon-Sat Aug), which first opened as a gentlemen's club in 1847. Painstakingly restored to its original glory, the building is a fabulous combination of historical design and opulence. A few blocks south, the **Catedral de Santa María** (968 21 63 44; www.catedralmurcia.com; Plaza del Cardenal Belluga; adult/child €5/3; 10am-5pm Tue-Sat & services at other times) was built in 1394 on the site of a mosque. It has a stunning facade facing on to Plaza Belluga.

North of the centre, the **Museo Arqueológico** (968 23 46 02; www.museoregiondemurcia.es; Avenida Alfonso X El Sabio 7; 10am-2pm Tue-Fri, 11am-2pm Sat & Sun Jul & Aug, 10am-2pm & 5-8pm Tue-Fri, 11am-2pm & 5-8pm Sat, 11am-2pm Sun Sep-Jun) has exceptionally well-laid-out and well-documented exhibits spread over two floors, focusing mostly on prehistory. The trendy cafe with pleasant outdoor seating is a popular spot.

✕ p191

The Drive » It's a short and easy 37km drive west along the toll-free A7 from Murcia to Alhama de Murcia, gateway to the national park.

TRIP HIGHLIGHT

❷ Parque Natural de Sierra Espuña

The Sierra Espuña is an island of pine forest and limestone formations rising high above an ocean of heat and dust down below. The natural park that protects this fragile and beautiful environment has more than 250 sq km of unspoilt highlands covered with trails and is popular with walkers and climbers.

Access to the park is best via Alhama de Murcia. The informative Ricardo Codorniu Visitors Centre is located in the heart of the park.

 LINK YOUR TRIP

20 **Mediterranean Meander**

For a longer drive, join up with this trip at Cartagena, and take in the splendour of coastal Spain.

19 **Barcelona to Valencia**

From Villena, take the A7 90km north to Valencia, to hook up with this memorable route between two great cities.

187

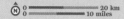

A few walking trails leave from here, and it can provide good maps for picturesque hikes.

🛏 p191

The Drive » It's a straight shot (30 minutes or so) along the A7 from Alhama de Murcia to Lorca, 36km to the southwest.

TRIP HIGHLIGHT

③ Lorca

The market town of Lorca has long been known for its historic centre crowned by a 13th-century castle and for hosting one of Spain's most flamboyant Holy Week celebrations.

Among the highlights of Lorca is **Castillo de Lorca** (☎968 95 96 46; www.lorcatallerdeltiempo. com; Carretera de la Parroquia; adult/child €6/5; ☺10.30am-dusk; 🚗), the castle that looms high over Lorca. In the old town, take a stroll through the **Plaza de España**. It's surrounded by a group of baroque buildings, including the **Pósito**, a 16th-century former granary, and the golden limestone **Colegiata de San Patricio**.

Peculiar to Lorca are various small museums exhibiting the magnificent Semana Santa costumes. The big two are the **Museo de Bordados del Paso Azul** (MASS; ☎968 47 20 77; www. museoazul.com; Calle Cuesta de San Francisco; adult/child €3/1.50; ☺10am-2pm &

5-7.30pm Mon-Sat, 10.30am-2pm Sun Oct-Mar, 10am-2pm & 5.30-8pm Mon-Sat, 10.30am-2pm Sun Apr-Sep, mornings only Aug), which competes in splendour with the **Museo de Bordados del Paso Blanco** (muBBla; ☎968 46 18 13; www.mubbla. org; Calle Santo Domingo 8; adult/child €2.50/free; ☺10.30am-2pm & 5-8pm Mon-Sat, 10.30am-2pm Sun).

The Drive » The journey takes you from the southern slopes of the Sierra del Caño down to to the coast. It's a speedy 37km ride along the RM11 from Lorca to Águilas.

TRIP HIGHLIGHT

④ Águilas

This easy-going waterfront town is beautiful, and still shelters a small fishing fleet. Town beaches are divided from each other by a low headland topped by an 18th-century fortress. The real interest, though, are the Cuatro Calas a few kilometres south of town. These four coves are largely unmolested by tourist development (though they get very busy in summer) and have shimmering waters which merge into desert rock. Take RM33 to get there.

🛏 p191

The Drive » Take the Carretera de Lorca (RM11) 2.5km northward, then head east some 70km along the toll-road AP7. Take exit 815 toward Cartagena Oeste and continue onto RM332.

CSABA HENRIKSEN/500PX ©

⑤ Cartagena

Inhabited for over 2000 years, Cartagena wears its history with pride. From ancient Roman ruins to Modernista architecture, the city has a dazzling array of eye candy, made all the more photogenic against its magnificent mountain-fringed harbour.

Set alongside the Molinete hill, the **Barrio del Foro Romano** (www. cartagenapuertodeculturas. com; Calle Honda; adult/child €5/4; ☺10am-8pm Jul–mid-Sep, to 7pm Tue-Sun mid-Mar–Jun & mid-Sep–Oct, to 5.30pm Tue-Sun Nov–mid-Mar) are

Águilas

the evocative remains
of a whole town block
and street linking the
port with the forum,
dating from the 1st
century BCE.

🍴 🛏 p191, p258

The Drive » From Paseo
Alfonxo XIII, take the A30
towards Murcia. After 3km, take
exit 190 onto CT32. Continue
for 5km then take Autovía de La
Manga/RM12 20km east. It's a
30-minute drive in total.

- - - - - - - - - - - - - - - - -

6 Cabo de Palos

The Mar Menor is a
170-sq-km saltwater
lagoon. Its waters are
a good 5°C warmer

than the open sea and
excellent for water
sports. Cabo de Palos,
at the southern base
of a narrow 22km
peninsula, is delightful
with a picturesque
small harbour filled
with pleasure boats. The
waters around the tiny
protected Islas Hormigas
(Ant Islands) are great
for scuba diving and the
harbour is lined with
dive shops.

The Drive » Start off this
50km journey by retracing your
route (heading west) along
RM12. After 20km, take exit
1 onto AP7. After 25km take
exit 774 toward San Pedro del
Pinatar. Go straight through

the roundabout as it leads you
down to Lo Pagán.

- - - - - - - - - - - - - - - - -

7 Lo Pagán

At the northern end of
the lagoon, Lo Pagán
is a mellow, low-rise
resort with great water
views, a long promenade,
pleasant beach and
plenty of bars and
restaurants. Get locals to
show you where to walk
out on jetties for natural
mud treatments.

The Drive » It's just 2.5km
up to the salt pans. Take
Carretera Quintín north and
turn right on Avenida de las
Salinas.

LOCAL KNOWLEDGE:
ADDING COLOUR TO SEMANA SANTA

In Lorca locals tend to see things in blue and white – the colours of the two major brotherhoods that have competed every year since 1855 to see who can stage the most lavish Semana Santa display.

Lorca's Easter parades move to a different rhythm, distinct from the slow, sombre processions elsewhere in Murcia. While still deeply reverential, they're full of colour and vitality, mixing Old Testament tales with the Passion story.

If you hail from Lorca, you're passionately *Blanco* (White) or *Azul* (Blue). Each brotherhood has a statue of the Virgin (one draped in a blue mantle, the other in white, naturally), a banner and a spectacular museum. The result of this intense and mostly genial year-round rivalry is just about the most dramatic Semana Santa you'll see anywhere in Spain.

8 Salinas de San Pedro

Just east of Lo Pagán lie the Salinas de San Pedro (San Pedro salt pans), where you can follow the well-signposted Sendero de El Coterillo.

This relatively easy walk of just under 4km passes by a lagoon favoured by various bird species (including flamingos), dunes and a pristine beachfront.

The Drive » Skip the high-speed AP7 and take the more scenic coastal route (60km in total). Head back to San Pedro del Pinatar and take the N332 north.

You'll pass sea-fronting but overdeveloped beach towns such as Torrevieja on the way. A few kilometres after the Dunas de Guadamar (a fine beach for swimming), exit onto CV853 and follow signs north to Elche.

TRIP HIGHLIGHT

9 Elche

Thanks to Moorish irrigation, Elche (Valenciano: Elx) is an important fruit producer and also a Unesco World Heritage site twice over: for the *Misteri d'Elx*, its annual mystery play, and for its extensive palm groves, Europe's largest, planted by the Phoenicians. The palms, the mosque-like churches, and the historic buildings in desert-coloured stone give it a North African feel. Around 200,000 palm trees, each with a lifespan of some 250 years, make the heart of this busy industrial town a veritable oasis. A 2.5km walking trail leads from the **Museu del Palmerar** (965 42 22 40; Porta de la Morera 12; adult/child €1/0.50, Sun free; 10am-2pm & 3-6pm Tue-Sat, 10am-2pm Sun) through the groves.

p191

The Drive » Take Calle San Fulgencio west and turn right onto CV8510. Merge onto AP7 and after 3.5km take A31 north toward Alicante. Take exit 185 toward Villena. The 55km drive takes about 45 minutes.

10 Villena

Villena, between Alicante and Albacete, is the most attractive of the towns along the corridor of the Val de Vinalopó. Plaza de Santiago is at the heart of its old quarter.

Perched high above the town, the 12th-century **Castillo de Atalaya** (www.turismovillena. com; Calle Libertad; adult/child €3/1.50; guided tours 11am, noon, 1pm, 4pm & 5pm Tue-Sat, 11am, noon & 1pm Sun) is splendidly lit at night.

p191

Eating & Sleeping

Murcia ①

✕ Los Zagales   Spanish €

(☎968 21 55 79; www.facebook.com/bar
loszagales.murcia; Calle Polo de Medina 4;
dishes €3-12; ⏰9.30am-4pm & 7pm-midnight
Mon-Sat) Handy to stop by after a cathedral
visit, the old-style, traditional Los Zagales,
run by the same family for nearly 100 years,
dishes up superb, inexpensive tapas, *raciones*,
platos combinados (mixed platters), homemade
desserts...and homemade chips. It's popular
locally so you may have to wait for a table, or
just graze at the bar.

Parque Natural de Sierra Espuña ②

🛏 Bajo el Cejo   Boutique Hotel €€

(☎968 66 80 32; www.bajoelcejo.com; Calle
El Paso; s incl breakfast €81, d €105-140;
🅿 ❄ 🛜 🏊 🐾) For luxurious relaxation, you
can't beat this delicious countryside hideaway
in El Berro. It's located inside a converted
watermill under a bluff and is an away-from-it-
all heaven. Rooms are spacious and superb,
but it's the terrace, pool and delightful setting
overlooking citrus groves and valley that are
utterly memorable. There's an exceptional
personal welcome and brilliant organic food,
much of it produced here.

Águilas ④

🛏 Hotel Mayarí   Hotel €€

(☎964 41 97 48; www.hotel-mayari.com; Calle
Río de Janeiro 14, Calabardina; s/d incl breakfast
€65/98; ⏰Mar-Nov; 🅿 ❄ 🛜) In the seaside
settlement of Calabardina, 7km from Águilas,
this airy villa offers exceptional hospitality
among dry, handsome hillscapes. Rooms are
simple, comfortable and all different, with cool,
fresh decor. Some have sea views, and brilliant
home-cooked dinners are available by request,
as well as helpful hill-walking advice and bikes to
explore the area.

Cartagena ⑤

🛏 LoopINN   Hostel €

(☎868 45 17 60; www.loopinnhostels.com;
Calle San Crispín 34; dm €22-26, d €48-63;
❄ 🛜) On a backstreet near the train and bus
stations, this modern hostel is a cheery place
with a variety of comfortable dorms and rooms,
including family options. White walls, wood and
the odd quirky feature give it a summery feel,
while a gym, kitchen and sundeck are among the
facilities. Don't miss the slide between floors!

Elche ⑨

✕ El Granaino   Spanish €€

(☎966 66 40 80; www.mesongranaino.com;
Carrer Josep María Buck 40; mains €14-24;
⏰10am-4pm & 8pm-midnight Mon-Sat; 🛜)
Across the river from the centre, El Granaino,
with its bar lined with quiet, well-dressed people
scarfing down a quick, quality lunch, is worth
the 10-minute walk. Top seafood, delicious
stews and a fine range of tapas showcase a
classic, quintessentially Spanish cuisine. Fuller
meals can be enjoyed outside or in the adjacent
dining room. Excellent service and quality.

Villena ⑩

🛏 La Casa de los Aromas   B&B €

(☎666 475612; www.hotelcasadelosaromas.
com; Calle Arco 1; s/d €35/55; ❄ 🛜) In the
heart of the old centre, this place offers a
genuine welcome and five sweet rooms, all
with an individual aroma. It's got lots of charm,
and staff can arrange winery visits and other
activities. You get access to a fridge and
microwave as well as an appealing common
room with a vinyl collection to play.

Artistic Inspiration on the Costa Brava

Classic Trip

15

This seaside stunner takes you to some of Spain's prettiest beaches, with unspoilt coves, flower-trimmed villages and sweeping panoramas lurking around nearly every bend.

TRIP HIGHLIGHTS

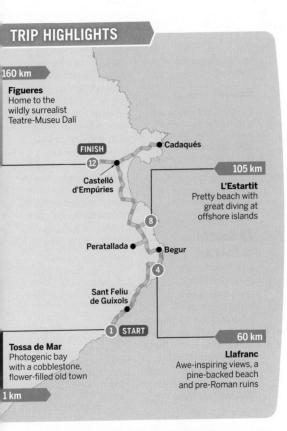

160 km

Figueres
Home to the wildly surrealist Teatre-Museu Dalí

FINISH
12

Cadaqués

105 km

L'Estartit
Pretty beach with great diving at offshore islands

Castelló d'Empúries

8

Peratallada • • Begur

4

Sant Feliu de Guíxols

1 **START**

Tossa de Mar
Photogenic bay with a cobblestone, flower-filled old town

1 km

60 km

Llafranc
Awe-inspiring views, a pine-backed beach and pre-Roman ruins

2–4 DAYS
160KM / 99 MILES

GREAT FOR...

BEST TIME TO GO
May or September for beach weather with fewer crowds.

ESSENTIAL PHOTO
The weird and wonderful Teatre-Museu Dalí in Figueres.

BEST FOR FAMILIES
Playing in the sand on pretty Llafranc beach.

Teatre-Museu Dalí showcases Salvador Dalí's life and works (p200)

193

Classic Trip

15 Artistic Inspiration on the Costa Brava

Just north of Barcelona, the Costa Brava has long captivated visitors with its beautiful bays, dramatic headlands and quaint, cobblestone villages just inland from the surf. Great views aside, there's much to do in this picturesque corner of Catalonia: you can visit ancient Roman ruins, clamber around medieval castles, go eye-to-eye with marbled rays off the Iles Mendes, and wander wide-eyed through fantastical Salvador Dalí creations.

TRIP HIGHLIGHT

1 Tossa de Mar

Curving around a boat-speckled bay and guarded by a headland crowned with impressive defensive medieval walls and towers, Tossa de Mar is a picturesque village of crooked, narrow streets onto which tourism has tacked a larger, modern extension.

The deep-ochre, fairy-tale walls and towers on the pine-dotted headland, **Mont Guardí**, at the end of the main beach, were built between the 12th and 14th centuries. The area they girdle is known as the Vila Vella – or Old Town – full of steep little cobbled streets and picturesque whitewashed houses, garlanded with flowers.

🛏 p201

The Drive » A snaking road hugs the spectacular ups and downs of the Costa Brava for the 23km from Tossa de Mar to Sant Feliu de Guíxols with – allegedly – a curve for each day of the year. From Tossa de Mar take Carretera Blanes a Sant Feliu and stick to the shoreline.

2 Sant Feliu de Guíxols

Sant Feliu has an attractive waterside promenade and a handful of curious leftovers from its long past, the most important being the so-called **Porta Ferrada** (Iron Gate): a wall and entrance, which is all that remains of a 10th-century monastery.

The gate lends its name to an annual music festival held here every July since 1962.

Just north along the coast is **S'Agaró**, with each of its Modernista houses designed by Gaudí disciple Rafael Masó. Leave your wheels behind and walk the shoreline Camí de Ronda to **Cala Sa Conca** – one of the most attractive beaches in the area.

The Drive » Take the Carretera de Palamós (located just a few blocks north of the marina) east. After 1.5km take the Carretera Castelo d'Aro and follow this north onto C31. After 17km on C31, take exit 331. Continue through the historic village of Mont-Ras, skirting the southern edge of bigger Palafrugell. Then take Avinguda del Mar into Calella de Palafrugell. It takes about a half-hour to do the 28km drive.

❸ Calella de Palafrugell

Halfway up the coast from Barcelona to the French border begins one of the most beautiful stretches of the Costa Brava. Start off in Calella, the southernmost of Palafrugell's crown jewels. The settlement is strung Aegean-style around a bay of rocky points and small, pretty beaches, with a few fishing boats still hauled up on the sand. The seafront is lined with year-round restaurants serving the fruits of the sea. Perched high above the sea, 2.5km from the centre, the verdant **Jardins de Cap Roig**

LINK YOUR TRIP

16 Central Catalonia's Wineries & Monasteries

After ending in Figueres, travel 44km south to Girona to the start of this scenic drive around Catalonia's interior.

18 The Pyrenees

From Figueres it's just 25km west to Besalú, where you can drive the Pyrenees trip in reverse, traveling across the mountains to San Sebastián.

Classic Trip

(📞972 61 45 82; http://fundacionlacaixa.org/ca/centros/jardines-de-cap-roig; Cap Roig; adult/senior & student/child €10/5/free; 🕙10am-8pm Apr-Sep, to 6pm Oct-Mar, weekends only Jan & Feb) contain some 1000 floral species, set around an early-20th-century castle-palace. From mid-July to late August, the gardens host over two dozen open-air concerts, featuring big-name performers (tickets from €30).

🍴 p201

The Drive » The next stop is barely 2km northeast of Calella. If you need to stretch your legs, you can also walk to Llafranc along coastal footpaths. Driving, take Avinguda Joan Pericot i García east. Go straight through the roundabout at Plaça Doctor Trueta, then veer to the right on Carrer de Lluís Marquès Carbó.

TRIP HIGHLIGHT

④ Llafranc

Llafranc has a smaller bay but a longer, handsome stretch of sand, cupped on either side by pine-dotted craggy coastline. Above the east side of town, the **Cap de Sant Sebastià** is a magical spot that offers fabulous views in both directions and out to sea. There's a lighthouse and an

excellent restaurant here, as well as a defensive tower and chapel now incorporated into a hotel. You can also check out the ruins of a pre-Roman Iberian settlement with multilingual explanatory panels. It's a 40-minute walk up: follow the steps from the harbour and the road up to the right.

The Drive » From Llafranc, head north along Camí de la Font d'En Xecu towards Palafrugell and follow the signs to Tamariu. You'll pass through piney forest on the way. Again, if you'd prefer to walk, it's a magnificent (but hilly) 4km walk along the coast.

----

⑤ Tamariu

Tamariu is a fabulous, small, crescent-shaped cove redolent with the scent of pine. Its beach has some of the most translucent waters on Spain's Mediterranean coast. The gently sloping sands and shallow waters are a great place for small children to play.

🛏 p201

The Drive » It's around 8km to Begur. Take narrow Carrer Aigublava north on a scenic forested uphill journey, then turn right on GIP6531 and follow this to Begur.

----

⑥ Begur

Attractive little Begur, with its quaint cobblestone lanes, is dotted with tempting restaurants and cafes

and topped by a 10th-century *castell* (castle), towering above the village. The sublime coastline around Begur, with its pocket-sized coves hemmed in by pine trees and subtropical flowers and lapped by azure water, is magical. There are some lovely **walking trails** around Begur, including to several attractive beaches and an 11.5km hike south to Tamariu (five hours) along GR92.

🛏 p201

The Drive » Head west out of Begur along GI653. In Regencós, take C31, then a few kilometres north of the village of Pals, turn left onto GI651. Drive time to Peratallada is about 20 minutes.

----

⑦ Peratallada

One of Catalonia's most gorgeous villages, Peratallada is blessed with beautifully preserved narrow lanes, heavy stone arches, a 12th-century Romanesque church and an 11th-century castle-mansion (now a luxury hotel and restaurant). It's a wonderfully characterful spot, particularly at night.

The Drive » Get back on GI651 and retrace the drive to C31. But this time turn north onto C31 and continue for 6km. You'll cross the attractive medieval town of Torroella de Montgrí, then continue on Carretera de L'Estartit. At the

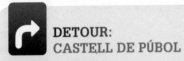

DETOUR:
CASTELL DE PÚBOL

Start: **7** Peratallada

Northwest of Peratallada, the **Castell de Púbol** (www.salvador-dali.org; Plaça de Gala Dalí, Púbol; adult/student €8/6; ⏰10am-8pm mid-Jun–mid-Sep, to 6pm Tue-Sun mid-Mar–mid-Jun & mid-Sep–Oct, to 5pm Tue-Sun Nov-early Jan) forms the southernmost point of the 'Salvador Dalí triangle', other elements of which include the Teatre-Museu Dalí (p200) in Figueres and his home in Portlligat (p200).

Having promised to make his wife Gala, his muse and the love of his life, 'queen of the castle', in 1969 Dalí finally found the ideal residence to turn into Gala's refuge, since at the age of 76 she no longer desired Dalí's hectic lifestyle – a semi-dilapidated Gothic and Renaissance stronghold which included a 14th-century church in the quiet village of Púbol.

The sombre castle, its stone walls covered with creepers, is almost the antithesis to the flamboyance of the Teatre-Museu Dalí or Dalí's seaside home: Gala had it decorated exactly as she wished and received only whom she wished. Legend has it that Dalí himself had to apply for written permission to visit her here.

The interior reflects her tastes, though Dalí touches creep in here and there. In the dining room is a replica of *Cua d'oreneta i violoncels* (Swallow's Tail and Cellos) – his last painting, completed here in 1983 during the two years of mourning following Gala's death.

The Castell is 2km from the village of La Pera, just south of the C66 and 15km northwest of Peratallada.

roundabout continue straight, along GI641. The 18km drive takes about 25 minutes.

TRIP HIGHLIGHT

8 L'Estartit

L'Estartit has a long, wide beach of fine sand but it's the diving that stands out. The protected **Illes Medes**, a spectacular group of rocky islets barely 1km offshore, are home to some of the most abundant marine life on Spain's Mediterranean coast. Eateries serving fresh seafood as well as standard Spanish fare are plentiful along the seafront.

The Drive » Retrace the drive back through Torroella de Montgrí, then continue onto C31 northwest. After about 3km turn right onto GI632, which leads straight into town (depositing you at the town hall if you so wish). The 19km drive takes about 22 minutes.

---

9 L'Escala

Travel back millennia to the ancient Greco-Roman site of **Empúries** (☎972 77 02 08; www.mac.cat; Carrer Puig i Cadafalch; adult/child €6/free; ⏰10am-8pm Jun-Sep, to 6pm Oct–mid-Nov & mid-Feb–May, to 5pm & closed Mon mid-Nov–mid-Feb), set behind a near-virgin beach facing the Mediterranean. Its modern descendant, L'Escala, 11km north of Torroella de Montgrí, is a sunny and pleasant medium-sized resort on the often-windswept southern shore of the Golf de Roses.

The Empúries is a picturesque two-part site that was an important Greek, and later Roman, trading port, though the site was originally used by Phoenicians. There are fine pieces – including mosaics – in the museum here, which gives good background information. Empúries is 2km northwest of the L'Escala town centre along the coast.

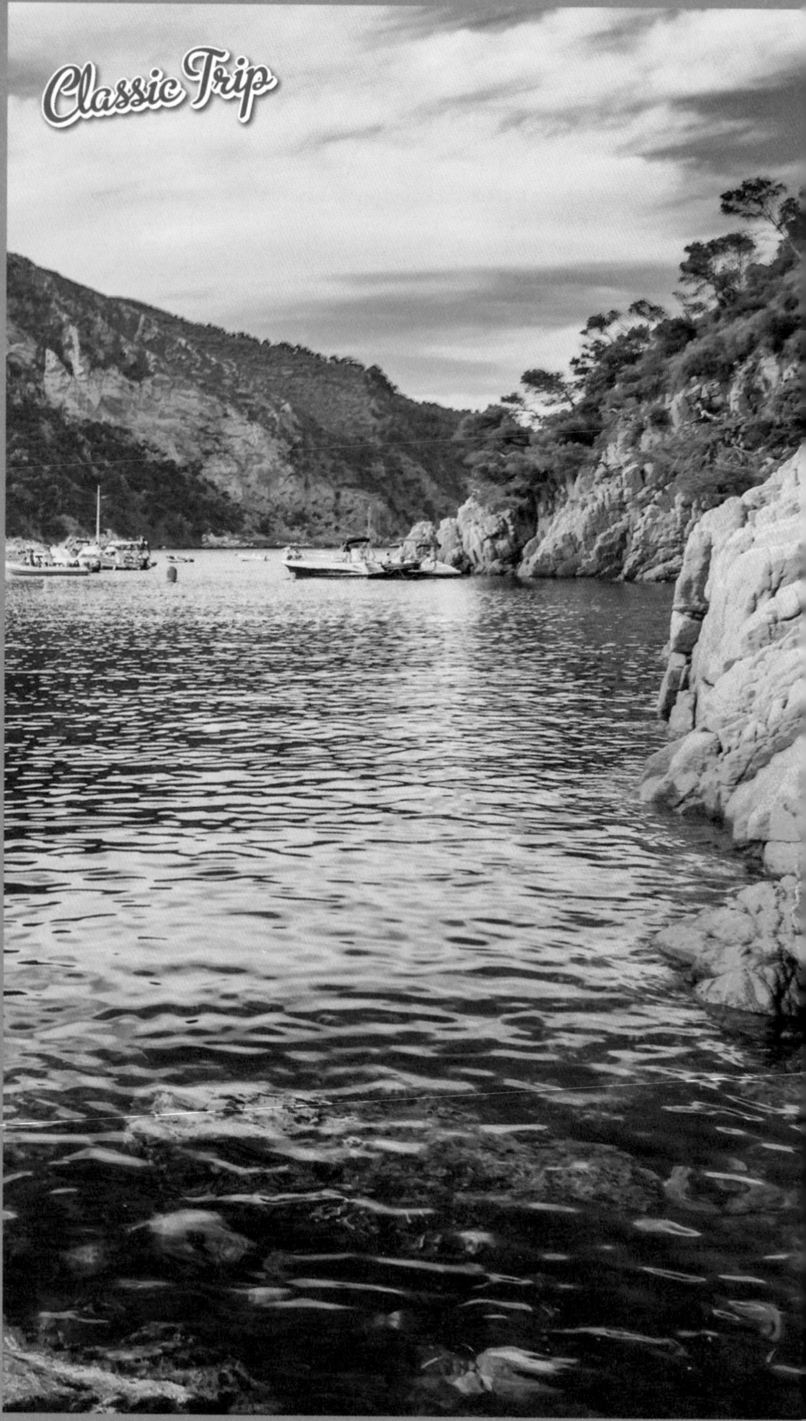
Classic Trip

The Drive » Start this half-hour drive by taking Carretera Sant Martí d'Empúries to Sant Pere Pescador. After crossing a small river, look for GIV6216 leading north. From here, it's a straight shot 8km or so to Castelló d'Empúries.

---

⑩ Castelló d'Empúries

This well-preserved ancient town was once the capital of Empúries, a medieval Catalan county that maintained a large degree of independence up to the 14th century. Today it makes a superb base for birdwatching at the nearby **Parc Natural dels Aiguamolls de l'Empordà** (☎972 45 42 22; www.gencat.cat/parcs/aiguamolls_emporda; GIV6216 Sant Pere Pescador-Castelló d'Empúries Km 4.2; parking motorbike or car €5, van €10; ⏰El Cortalet information centre 9am-6.30pm Easter-Sep, to 4pm Oct-Easter), as well as a number of wind-blown but peaceful beaches. The park lies 4km to the northeast along Carretera Castelló d'Empúries. Away from the avian allure of the natural park, architectural beauty can be found in the town centre's 14th-century **Basílica de Santa Maria**. A short stroll southwest of there, the Museu d'Historia Medieval de la Cúria-Presó provides fascinating insight into Castelló's medieval history (with centuries-old graffiti in a few creepy prison cells).

🛏 p201

The Drive » It's 23km to Cadaqués – a 30-minute trip, though you could take much longer, with stops to admire the panoramic views on this stunning drive. From Castelló d'Empúries, take Carrer Santa Clara to C260. Pass through La Garriga and get on curvy, narrow GI614, which will take you the rest of the way.

---

⑪ Cadaqués

A whitewashed village around a rocky bay, Cadaqués' narrow, hilly streets are perfect for wandering. The iconic town and its surrounding area have a special magic – a fusion of wind, sea, light and rock – that isn't dissipated even by the throngs of summer visitors.

A portion of that magic owes itself to

WHY THIS IS A CLASSIC TRIP
REGIS ST LOUIS, AUTHOR

As a lifelong admirer of the strange and captivating works of Salvador Dalí, I've always felt a deep affinity for the wild coastal scenery around Cadaqués where Dalí spent his formative (and later) years. Yet the whole Costa Brava easily passes for artistic inspiration, with its serene bays, rugged headlands and golden beaches. This coastal drive is pure magic.

JORDI GARRIO/SHUTTERSTOCK ©

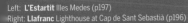

Left: **L'Estartit** Illes Medes (p197)
Right: **Llafranc** Lighthouse at Cap de Sant Sebastià (p196)

Classic Trip

THE COSTA BRAVA WAY

The 255km-long stretch of cliffs, coves, rocky promontories and pine groves that make up the signposted Costa Brava Way, stretching from Blanes to Colliure in France, unsurprisingly offers some of the best walks in Catalonia, ranging from gentle rambles to high-octane scrambles (or one long, demanding hike if you want to do the whole thing).

For the most part, the trail follows the established GR92, but also includes a number of coastal deviations. A choice route runs from Cadaqués to Cap de Creus Lighthouse (2½ hours each way). This relatively easy 7km walk from the centre of Cadaqués passes Portlligat before continuing along windswept, scrub-covered, rocky ground past several isolated beaches before it reaches the lighthouse – there's an appealing restaurant-cafe (Bar Restaurant Cap de Creus) next door.

Salvador Dalí, who spent family holidays here during his youth, and lived much of his later life at Portlligat, 1km northeast of Cadaqués: there the **Casa Museu Dalí** ([☎]972 25 10 15; www. salvador-dali.org; adult/senior & student/child under 14yr €14/8/free; [⊙]9.30am-9pm mid-Jun–mid-Sep, 10.30am-6pm mid-Sep–early Jan & mid-Feb–mid-Jun, closed early Jan–mid-Feb, plus Mon Nov–mid-Mar) is a mishmash of cottages and sunny terraces, linked by narrow labyrinthine corridors and an assortment of offbeat Dalí-esque flourishes. Access is by semi-guided eight-person tour; it's essential to book well ahead.

[✖] p201

The Drive » Backtrack to Castelló d'Empúries. Stay on C260 as it skirts the southern edge of town, and follow it all the way to Figueres. Total drive time is about 45 minutes for the 35km drive.

- - - - - - - - - - - - - - - -

TRIP HIGHLIGHT

⑫ Figueres

Twelve kilometres inland, Figueres is a busy town with a French feel and an unmissable attraction: Salvador Dalí. The artist was born in Figueres in 1904 and although his career took him to Madrid, Barcelona, Paris and the USA, he remained true to his roots. In the 1960s and '70s he created here the extraordinary **Teatre-Museu Dalí** (www. salvador-dali.org; Plaça de Gala i Salvador Dalí 5; adult/ child under 9yr €15/free; [⊙]9am-8pm Apr-Jul & Sep, 9am-8pm & 10pm-1am Aug, 9.30am-6pm Tue-Sun Oct & Mar, 10.30am-6pm Tue-Sun Nov-Feb) – a monument to surrealism and a legacy that outshines any other Spanish artist, both in terms of popularity and sheer flamboyance.

This red castle-like building, topped with giant eggs and studded with plaster-covered croissants, is an entirely appropriate final resting place for the master of surrealism. 'Theatre-museum' is an apt label for this trip through the incredibly fertile imagination of one of the great showmen of the 20th century. The inside is full of surprises, tricks and illusions, and contains a substantial portion of Dalí's life's work.

Eating & Sleeping

Tossa de Mar ①

🛏 Cap d'Or   Hotel €€

(📞972 34 00 81; www.hotelcapdor.com; Passeig del Mar 1; incl breakfast s/d/tr €92/142/180; ⊙Easter–early Oct; ❄🛜) Get wrapped up in Tossa's history at this family-run spot right below the old-town walls. The 10 rooms are simple but lovingly decorated with vintage-feel pictures and quaint marine miscellany; the best look straight onto the beach. There's a cheery all-day cafe-restaurant serving seafood, salads, omelettes and snacks (€7 to €14) overlooking the sand.

Calella de Palafrugell ③

🍴 La Blava   Catalan €€

(📞972 61 40 60; www.lablava.com; Carrer de Miramar 3; mains €16-24; ⊙1-3.45pm & 8-10.45pm Jun-Oct, weekends only Apr & May) In a former fisher's house overlooking the beach, La Blava has earned a loyal following for its exquisite seafood, best enjoyed at outdoor tables overlooking the lapping waves. The small, well-curated menu ensures you can't go wrong, whether opting for the simple perfection of braised octopus with smoked paprika, or something richer like black rice with squid, cuttlefish and clams. Reservations essential.

Tamariu ⑤

🛏 Hotel Tamariu   Hotel €€

(📞972 62 00 31; www.tamariu.com; Passeig del Mar 2; incl breakfast s €85-110, d €115-185; ⊙late Feb–early Nov; ❄🛜) A former fisher's tavern, the jolly Hotel Tamariu has been family-run for four generations. It has spacious rooms with a clean, minimalist design, oversized windows and maritime-themed artwork on the walls. Some rooms have a balcony offering views of this little beach town. The owners also rent apartments nearby.

Begur ⑥

🛏 Cluc Hotel   Boutique Hotel €€€

(📞972 62 48 59; www.cluc.cat; Carrer del Metge Pi 8; d incl breakfast €123-210; ❄🛜) One of old-town Begur's chicest, yet friendliest, hotels unfolds across this ravishing, revamped 1800 *casa d'indians* (house built by a returned colonist). The 12 rooms are on the small side, but decorated in elegant vintage style with restored furniture and tile-covered floors. Expect an honesty bar, a library and homemade breakfasts on a charming terrace. No kids under 12.

Castelló d'Empúries ⑩

🛏 Hostal Casa Clara   Hostal €€

(📞972 25 02 15; www.hostalcasaclara.com; Plaça de les Monges; d incl breakfast €90; ⊙Mar-Dec; 🅿❄🛜) Genial service and cosy rooms make this colourful *hostal* a splendid midrange option in the heart of old-town Castelló d'Empúries. All eight spacious rooms feature natural light, comfortable beds and individual colour schemes. There's a pleasant lounge with books, board games and birdwatching information.

Cadaqués ⑪

🍴 Lua   Fusion €€

(📞972 15 94 52; www.facebook.com/lua.cdqs; Carrer Santa Maria 1; dishes €9-20; ⊙1-4pm & 8pm-midnight May-Sep, closed Tue Oct-Apr, may close Jan-Mar; 🍴) A mango-yellow door sets the jazzy tone for delicious, creative Mediterranean-Asian 'soul food' at this laid-back, Italian-run eatery with beer-barrel tables and benches on an old-town alley. It's perfect for vegetarians; try a Veggie Venus bowl of black rice, hummus and babaganoush, or lighter bites like cheese platters and original ceramic-bowl salads. Excellent seafood too (tuna tartare and salmon poke bowls).

Central Catalonia's Wineries & Monasteries

16

On this dramatic drive into Catalonia's hinterland, you'll see age-old monasteries, wander through lamplit medieval quarters and take in picturesque vineyards.

TRIP HIGHLIGHTS

km

Girona
Gothic architecture, riverside strolling and great restaurants

START 1

Cardona ●

INISH
Vallbona de les Monges

Santes Creus

4

6

209 km

Montserrat
Mountain monastery with breathtaking views

265 km

Vilafranca del Penedès
Historic village in the heart of wine country

**2–4 DAYS
380KM / 236 MILES**

GREAT FOR...

BEST TIME TO GO
Any time, but March to November for warmer days.

ESSENTIAL PHOTO
Montserrat against its dramatic mountainous backdrop.

BEST FOR HISTORY
Strolling the medieval Jewish quarter in Girona.

---

16 Central Catalonia's Wineries & Monasteries

You'll experience many of Catalonia's lesser known charms on this memorable inland drive. The wonderful medieval town of Girona is crammed with historic sites, while a wander along Vic's cobblestone streets reveal countless architectural treasures. You'll find a photogenic castle in Cardona and atmospheric monasteries along the Cistercian route. The trip ends at the town of Vilafranca del Penedès, in the heart of magnificent wine country.

TRIP HIGHLIGHT

1 Girona

Northern Catalonia's largest city, Girona is a tight huddle of ancient arcaded houses, grand churches and climbing cobbled streets. It's home to Catalonia's most extensive and best-preserved medieval Jewish quarter, all enclosed by defensive walls, with the lazy Río Onyar meandering along the edge of town. The excellent **Museu d'Història dels Jueus de**

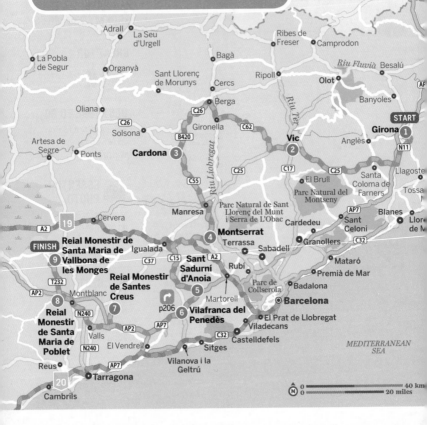

Girona (www.girona.cat/call; Carrer de la Força 8; adult/child €4/free; ⏱10am-8pm Mon-Sat, to 2pm Sun Jul & Aug, 10am-6pm Tue-Sat, to 2pm Mon & Sun Sep-Jun) shows genuine pride in Girona's Jewish heritage. Nearby, the stunning 800-year-old **catedral** (www.catedraldegirona.cat; Plaça de la Catedral; adult/concession incl Basílica de Sant Feliu €7/5; ⏱10am-7.30pm Jul & Aug, to 6.30pm Apr-Jun, Sep & Oct, to 5.30pm Nov-Mar) provides a window into medieval Christendom.

🍴🛏 p209

The Drive ⟫ From Girona, it's about one hour (70km) to Vic. Take Carrer del Carme east out of town. At the roundabout (2.7km further), turn onto GIV6703. Merge onto the N11. Take exit 702 onto the C25. Follow this 50km through lush mountainous scenery, before taking exit 187 onto N141, which takes you into Vic.

LINK YOUR TRIP

19 **Barcelona to Valencia**

After finishing this trip, head 56km west to Lleida for historic villages and outdoor adventures.

20 **Mediterranean Meander**

From the last monastery, drive 64km south on C14 to Tarragona for a highlight-filled drive along Spain's south coast.

② Vic

Vic is one of Catalonia's gems. The enchanting old quarter is crammed with Roman remnants, medieval leftovers, a grand Gothic cloister, an excellent art museum and a glut of good-value restaurants.

Plaça Major, the largest of Catalonia's central squares, is lined with medieval, baroque and Modernista mansions. It's still the site of the huge twice-weekly market (Tuesday and Saturday mornings). Around it swirl the narrow serpentine streets of medieval Vic, lined by mansions, churches, chapels, a Roman temple and a welcoming atmosphere.

The **Museu Episcopal** (www.museuepiscopalvic.com; Plaça Bisbe Oliba 3; adult/child €8/5; ⏱10am-7pm Tue-Sat Apr-Sep, 10am-1pm & 3-6pm Tue-Fri, 10am-7pm Sat Oct-Mar, 10am-2pm Sun year-round) holds a marvellous collection of Romanesque and Gothic art, including works by key figures like Lluís Borrassà and Jaume Huguet.

🍴 p209

The Drive ⟫ From Vic, take a northern, slightly longer, route to Cardona for stunning mountain scenery. Take C25 west from town. After about 6km, take exit 170 onto C651, then take C62. Around La Plana, take E9 north, then take the C26 southwest. Stay on this until the B420, and follow signs to Cardona.

③ Cardona

Long before arrival, you spy in the distance the outline of the impregnable 18th-century fortress high above Cardona, which itself lies next to the Muntanya de Sal (Salt Mountain). The castle – follow the signs uphill to the Parador de Cardona, a lovely place to stay overnight – was built over an older predecessor. The single-most remarkable element of the buildings is the elegant Romanesque **Canònica de Sant Vicenç**.

🍴🛏 p209

The Drive ⟫ It's a one-hour drive south to Montserrat. The scenic route along C55 passes over forested slopes and around the old village of Manresa (a pilgrimage site). About 20km south of there, take BP1121 and follow the signs to Montserrat.

TRIP HIGHLIGHT

④ Montserrat

Montserrat is a spectacular 1236m-high mountain of strangely rounded rock pillars, shaped by wind, rain and frost. With the historic Benedictine Monestir de Montserrat, this is one of Catalonia's most important shrines. Its caves and many mountain paths offer spectacular rambles, reachable by funiculars.

You can explore the mountain above the monastery on a web of paths leading to some of the peaks and to 13 empty hermitages. The **Funicular de Sant Joan** (www.cremallerademontserrat. cat; one-way/return €9.10/14; ⏱ every 12min 10am-4.50pm Nov-Mar, to 5.50pm Apr-Jun & mid-Sep–Oct, to 6.50pm Jul–mid-Sep, closed 3 weeks Jan) will carry you up the first 250m from the monastery. To see the chapel on the spot where the holy image of the Virgin was discovered, it's an easy walk down, followed by a stroll along a precipitous mountain path with fabulous views

The Drive >> The drive from the monastery offers magnificent views from clifftop heights, particularly along BP1103, which merges onto B110. A few kilometres further, take the ramp onto A2 and stay on it for 9km. Take exit 559 towards Vilafranca del Penedès, then take C15 south, and BP2151 into Sant Sadurní d'Anoia.

⑤ Sant Sadurní d'Anoia

Some of Spain's finest wines come from the Penedès plains southwest of Barcelona. Sant Sadurní d'Anoia, located about a half-hour west of Barcelona, is the capital of *cava*, a sparkling, champagne-style wine popular worldwide, and drunk in quantity in Spain over Christmas.

The headquarters of **Codorníu** (☎938 91 33 42; www.visitascodorniu.com; Avinguda de Jaume Codorníu, Sant Sadurní d'Anoia; adult/child €16/12; ⏱ tours 10am-5pm Mon-Fri, to 1pm Sat & Sun) are in a beautiful Modernista cellar at the entry to Sant Sadurní d'Anoia. Next to the Sant Sadurní train station, **Freixenet** (☎938 91 70 96; www.freixenet.es;

Carrer de Joan Sala 2, Sant Sadurní d'Anoia; adult/child €15/10; ⏱ tours 9am-4pm Mon-Sat, to 1pm Sun) is the biggest *cava*-producing company in Penedès. Visits include a tour of its 1920s cellar, a spin on the tourist train around the property and samples of its *cava*. Chocolate lovers shouldn't miss a visit to **Espai Xocolata Simón Col** (☎938 91 10 95; www.simoncoll.com; Carrer de Sant Pere 37; adult/child €5.50/4; ⏱9am-7pm Mon-Fri, to 3pm Sat & Sun; 🚗), a family-run, bean-to-bar chocolate maker, which has been going strong since 1840.

The Drive >> It's an easy 15km drive to the next stop. To avoid the AP7 toll road, take the Rambla de la Generalitat southwest and follow it onto C243a. Stay on this all the way to Vilafranca del Penedès.

TRIP HIGHLIGHT

⑥ Vilafranca del Penedès

Vilafranca del Penedès is an attractive historical town and the heart of the Penedès Denominación de Origen (DO; Denomination of Origin) region, which produces noteworthy light white wines and some very tasty reds.

Vilafranca has appealing narrow streets lined with medieval mansions. The mainly Gothic **Església de Santa Maria** stands

---

↱ DETOUR: TORRES

Start: ⑥ Vilafranca del Penedès

Just 3km northwest of Vilafranca del Penedès on the BP2121, **Torres** (☎938 17 74 00; www.torres.es; Pacs del Penedès; tours from €15; ⏱9am-6pm Mon-Sat, to noon Sun) is the area's premier winemaker, with a family winemaking tradition dating from the 17th century and a strong emphasis on organic production and renewable energy. Apart from a shop, tasting room and high-end restaurant, there's also a small (free) museum containing ancient amphorae, a massive wine press and videos on the craft of barrel making. Tours in various languages explore the vineyards and several bodegas. Reserve ahead.

Girona (p204)

at the heart of the old town. Nearby, you can delve into the history and cultural significance of wine at the **Vinseum** (Museu de les Cultures del Vi de Catalunya; www.vinseum. cat; Plaça de Jaume I; adult/child €7/free; ⏱10am-7pm Tue-Sat May-Sep, 10am-2pm & 4-7pm Tue-Sat Oct-Apr, 10am-2pm Sun year round), housed in the medieval Palau Reial. Admission includes an audio guide and a glass of wine in the attached bar.

✕ p209

The Drive » Leave town via Avinguda de Tarragona. Follow this onto the AP7. Take the E90/AP2 exit towards Lleida.

After 17km on this road, take exit 11 and get onto TP2002, which leads up to Santes Creus. All told it's about a 45-minute drive.

- - - - - - - - - - - - - - -

❼ Reial Monestir de Santes Creus

Cistercian monks settled here in the 12th century and from then on this **monastery** (☎977 63 83 29; www.larutadelcister. info; Plaça de Jaume el Just, Santes Creus; adult/senior & student €6/4; ⏱10am-7pm Jun-Sep, to 5.30pm Oct-May) developed as a major centre of learning and a launch pad for the repopulation of the surrounding territory.

Behind the Romanesque and Gothic facade lies a glorious 14th-century sandstone cloister, austere chapter house, cavernous dormitory and royal apartments where the count-kings often stayed when they popped by during Holy Week.

The Drive » Take TP2002 south and turn onto C51 about 7km south of Santa Creus. Stay on C51 for a few kilometres before taking N240. Fine views await as you cross the Tossal Gros mountain, part of Catalonia's pre-coastal range. Exit onto TV7001 towards L'Espluga de Francolí. You'll pass through this small town along T700 en route to the monastery.

207

Vilafranca del Penedès (206)

8 Reial Monestir de Santa Maria de Poblet

This fortified **monastery** (☎977 87 00 89; www.poblet. cat; Plaça Corona d'Aragó 11, Poblet; adult/student €12/8; ⏱10am-12.30pm & 3-5.25pm Mon-Sat, 10.30am-12.25pm & 3-5.25pm Sun), now a A Unesco World Heritage site, was founded in 1150. It became Catalonia's most powerful monastery and the burial place of many of its rulers. Poblet was sacked in 1835 by marauding peasants as payback for the monks' abuse of their feudal powers, which included imprisonment and torture.

High points include the mostly Gothic main cloister and the alabaster sculptural treasures of the Panteón de los Reyes (Kings' Pantheon). The raised alabaster sarcophagi contain eight Catalan kings, including such greats as Jaume I (the conqueror of Mallorca and Valencia) and Pere III.

The Drive » The last stop is another 30km north. You'll take the T700 back through L'Espluga de Francolí, then hop onto the T232. You'll take the L220 as you reach Els Omells de na Gaia. Follow this north, about another 1km, then look for the signed right turn leading to Valbona de les Monges.

9 Reial Monestir de Santa Maria de Vallbona de les Monges

This **monastery** (☎973 33 02 66; www.monestirvallbona. cat; Carrer Major, Vallbona de les Monges; €5; ⏱visit by guided tour in Spanish 10.45am-5pm) was founded in the 12th century and is where a a handful of *monges* (nuns) still live and pray. The monastery has undergone years of restoration, which has finally cleared up most of the remaining scars of civil war damage. Visits are by hourly 40-minute guided tour (Spanish or Catalan).

Eating & Sleeping

Girona ❶

✕ La Fábrica
Cafe €€

(www.lafabricagirona.com; Carrer de la Llebre 3; dishes €3-9; ☺9am-3pm; 🐌📶) Girona's culinary talents morph into top-quality coffee and Catalan-inspired brunchy favourites starring local ingredients at this energetic German-Canadian–owned cycle-themed cafe. Pillowy artisan *torrades* (toasts) – perhaps topped with avocado, feta and peppers – arrive on wooden sliders, washed down with expertly poured brews made with beans sourced from eco-conscious suppliers.

🛏 Bells Oficis
B&B €€

(📞972 22 81 70; www.bellsoficis.com; Carrer dels Germans Busquets 2; d incl breakfast €45-102; ❄📶) A lovingly restored 19th-century apartment towards the old town's southern end, Bells Oficis makes a stylish, ultra-welcoming base. It's the former home of Catalan artist Jaume Busquets i Mollera (a fresco he painted in 1921 adorns one room). Period details survive in the five very different rooms (one of which is a teeny two-bunk pad).

Three rooms share a bathroom; one en-suite room has no bathroom door.

Vic ❷

✕ Boira
Catalan €€

(📞93 886 70 80; www.boiradevic.com; Carrer Sant Miquel dels Sants 3; menu weekday €15, weekend €27-37; ☺1-3.30pm Wed, Thu & Sun, 1-3.30pm & 8-11pm Fri & Sat) Original tiling and stonework adorn Boira's elegant multiroom interior, where tables are sprinkled across an atmospheric old-town house. It's the perfect old-meets-new backdrop for a multi-course feast of Catalan ingredients and international flourishes: think grilled scallops with parmesan and mushrooms, lamb chops with mustard and mint, and black pasta with cuttlefish, prawns and romesco sauce.

Cardona ❸

✕ La Volta del Rector
Catalan €€

(📞938 69 16 37; www.lavoltadelrector.cat; Carrer de les Flors 4; mains €12-18; ☺8am-5pm Tue-Thu & Sun, to midnight Fri & Sat; 📶) Twelfth-century stone walls mix with wild violet decor at La Volta del Rector, in the heart of medieval Cardona. The atmosphere is rustic, romantic and fashionable all at once, while dishes – from grills and wild game to the house special: mountain potatoes with free-range fried eggs and/or chorizo – are whipped up with flair.

🛏 Parador de Cardona
Historic Hotel €€

(📞938 69 12 75; www.parador.es; Castell de Cardona; d €110-140; P ❄ 📶) Rooms occupy an adjoining modern building, but that doesn't dim the magic of sleeping like a lord at this *parador* (luxurious state-owned hotel) within Cardona's medieval castle. Lodgings are spacious and comfortable, in old-world style, many with exceptional views. Common areas are resplendent with antique furnishings and displays of historical finery. The highlight is breakfasting under Gothic arches in a converted monks' refectory.

Vilafranca del Penedès ❻

✕ Cal Ton
Catalan €€€

(📞938 90 37 41; www.restaurantcalton.com; Carrer Casal 8; mains €18-29, tasting menus €32-55; ☺1-3.30pm Tue & Sun, 1-3.30pm & 8.30-10.30pm Wed-Sat; 📶) An evening of gastronomic wonder awaits at Cal Ton, going strong since 1982. From feather-light potato-and-prawn ravioli to oxtail in red wine with pears, meals at this crisp modern restaurant exhaust superlatives.

The unpretentious yet knowledgeable service ensures the perfect local wine to complement any dish. Don't miss the quivering chocolate soufflé with passion-fruit ice cream.

Peaks & Valleys in Northwest Catalonia

Get off the beaten path in this jaw-dropping drive through Catalonia. Memorable hikes, white-water rafting and picturesque mountain villages are all part of the allure.

17

TRIP HIGHLIGHTS

85 km

Espot
Gateway to hiking amid stunning glacially carved valleys

Arties   Salardú

Erill la Vall

Parc Nacional d'Aigüestortes i Estany de Sant Maurici

7

3

2

66 km

Llavorsí
Scenic spot for white-water rafting

 START
La Seu d'Urgell

196 km

Taüll
Mountain village and setting for two historic Romanesque churches

8

INISH

Congost de Mont-rebei
Jaw-dropping river gorge on the edge of Aragón

258 km

**2–4 DAYS
258KM / 160 MILES**

GREAT FOR...

BEST TIME TO GO
From May to October for hiking and rafting.

ESSENTIAL PHOTO
Mountain-fringed Lake Sant Maurici in Parc Nacional d'Aigüestortes i Estany de Sant Maurici.

BEST FOR OUTDOORS
White-water rafting from Llavorsí to Rialp.

Parc Nacional d'Aigüestortes i Estany de Sant Maurici (p213)

211

17 Peaks & Valleys in Northwest Catalonia

This zigzagging journey through northwest Catalonia takes you back through the centuries, as you roll through stone villages and past Romanesque churches sitting pretty against a backdrop of pine-covered peaks. This is also a major draw for adventure lovers, with white-water rafting along the pristine Riu Noguera Pallaresa and scenic walks amid wildflower-strewn valleys, craggy summits and one breathtaking river gorge.

1 La Seu d'Urgell

The lively valley town of La Seu d'Urgell (la *say*-oo dur-*zhey*) has an attractive medieval centre, watched over by an admirable Romanesque cathedral. When the Franks evicted the Muslims from this part of the Pyrenees in the early 9th century, they made La Seu a bishopric and capital of the counts of Urgell; it remains an important market and cathedral town.

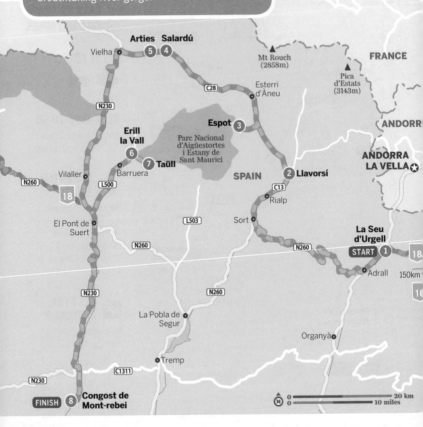

Much of town is dominated by the enormous 19th-century seminary above the cathedral. On the southern side of Plaça dels Oms, the 12th-century **Catedral de Santa Maria** (Plaça dels Oms; adult/child €4/free; 10am-1.30pm & 4-7pm Mon-Sat Jun-Sep, to 6pm Oct-May) is one of Catalonia's outstanding Romanesque buildings, with a gorgeous cloister full of characterful carved capitals.

 p217

The Drive >> Get ready for magnificent mountain scenery on this winding 66km drive. From La Seu take the N260 about 51km northwest to Sort. From there, switch to the C13 for

LINK YOUR TRIP

18 **The Pyrenees**
At the trip's end in Taüll, drive 58km back to Vielha to intersect with the magnificent drive across the Pyrenees.

16 **Central Catalonia's Wineries & Monasteries**
From Taüll it's about 185km south to Monestir de Santa Maria de Vallbona, where you can make this memorable drive in reverse.

the final 15km. It will take you straight in to Llavorsí.

TRIP HIGHLIGHT

2 Llavorsí

The Riu Noguera Pallaresa, running south through a dramatic valley about 50km west of La Seu d'Urgell, is Spain's best-known white-water river. The village of Llavorsí (along with Rialp and Sort) is a good place to organise a white-water trip.

The Riu Noguera Pallaresa's grade-IV drops attract a constant stream of white-water fans between mid-March and mid-October. It's usually at its best in May and June.

The best stretch is the 12km from Llavorsí to Rialp, on which the standard raft outing costs around €45 per person for two hours. In town, there are several rafting operators, including **Rafting Llavorsí** (973 62 21 58; www.raftingllavorsi.cat; Carrer Vilanova, Llavorsí; 2hr rafting €41; mid-Mar–mid-Oct). Longer rides to Sort and beyond will cost more, and Sort is the jumping-off point for the river's tougher grade-IV rapids. You can also arrange other summer activities including kayaking, canyoning, horse riding, rock climbing and canoeing.

p217

The Drive >> More lush scenery including rolling pine-dappled hillsides spread beneath you on this easy 20km drive. From Llavorsí go 12km north along C13. At the tiny stone village of Berrós Jussà, switch to the winding LV5004 for the final 7.5km.

TRIP HIGHLIGHT

3 Espot

Espot is a principal gateway to the stunning **Parc Nacional d'Aigüestortes i Estany de Sant Maurici**, Catalonia's only national park. Although small – just 20km east to west, and 9km north to south – the rugged terrain positively sparkles with more than 400 lakes and countless streams and waterfalls. This combined with a backdrop of pine and fir forests, and open bush and grassland, bedecked with wildflowers in spring, creates a wilderness of rare splendour.

Created by glacial action over two million years, the park is essentially two east–west valleys at 1600m to 2000m altitudes lined by jagged 2600m to 2900m peaks of granite and slate. The park is crisscrossed by paths. Numerous good walks of three to five hours return will take you up into spectacular side valleys from Estany de Sant Maurici or Aigüestortes.

NATAN RUBIO/SHUTTERSTOCK ©

Espot is 4km east of the park's eastern boundary and 8km away from the huge Estany de Sant Maurici lake.

✗ 🛏 p217

The Drive » The scenery just keeps getting better as you travel through the mountains. From Espot, go east along the LV5004 to C28, and take this north 37km, passing sleepy villages and ski resorts along the way.

- - - - - - - - - - - - - - - - - -

④ Salardú

Salardú's nucleus of old houses and narrow streets has largely resisted the temptation to sprawl. In the apse of the village's 12th- and 13th-century Sant Andreu church, you can admire the 13th-century Crist de Salardú crucifixion carving. The 1858 **Refugi Rosta** houses a tiny museum (admission €5 for non-guests) covering the seminal explorers, photographers and map-makers who brought

renown to the Pyrenees in the 19th century.

🛏 p217

The Drive » It's a quick hop (3.5km) west along C28 to Arties, with green peaks looming above you.

- - - - - - - - - - - - - - - - - -

⑤ Arties

This village on the southern side of the highway sits astride the confluence of the Garona and Valarties rivers. Among its cheerful stone houses is the Romanesque **Església de Santa Maria**, with its three-storey belfry and triple apse. Arties has cachet, and is packed with upmarket restaurants and bars. You can also visit the **Banys d'Arties** (C28 Km 28; adult/child €3/ free; ⏰10.30am-2.30pm & 4.30-8pm Tue-Sun Jul & Aug, 10am-5pm Tue-Sun Sep-Jun, hours vary) for a soak in a small open-air thermal pool a short walk from the village.

The Drive » Begin this 70-minute drive by going west towards Vielha along C28. From there drive 38km south along N230, which skirts the boundary between Aragon and Catalonia. About 17km after passing the mountain-fringed Baserca Reservoir, you'll turn onto the L500 and follow signs to La Vall de Boí.

- - - - - - - - - - - - - - - - - -

⑥ Erill la Vall

The sublime Vall de Boí is dotted with some of Catalonia's loveliest little Romanesque churches – unadorned stone structures sitting in the crisp alpine air, constructed between the 11th and 14th centuries

TOP TIP:
FOOD MATTERS

Quality dining options are limited in this sparsely inhabited corner of Catalonia, so stock up on picnic fare before hitting the road. A good place to start is the expansive green market that takes over the streets of La Seu d'Urgell's historic centre on Tuesdays and Saturdays. You'll find over 70 vendors, selling a mix of seasonal fruits and vegetables, farm-fresh cheeses, olives, breads, preserves and other temptations.

Taüll Sant Climent de Taüll

– which together were declared a Unesco World Heritage site in 2000. Start off in the **Centre del Romànic de la Vall de Boí** (☎973 69 67 15; www.centreromanic. com; Carrer del Batalló 5, Erill la Vall; €2; ◷9am-2pm & 5-7pm). Here you'll find a small Romanesque art collection; it's also where you can organise guided tours of the churches.

The Drive » It's a short (5.5km) but scenic drive, past pine forests and the tiny village of Boí, to Taüll. Take L500 1km north and turn onto the L501 heading south. After about 3.5km you'll see Sant Climent de Taüll on the left.

TRIP HIGHLIGHT

7 Taüll

Continue the journey back in time at **Sant Climent de Taüll** (www. centreromanic.com; €5; ◷10am-2pm & 4-7pm Sep-Jun, to 8pm Jul & Aug). Located at the entrance to Taüll, this church, with its slender six-storey bell tower, is a gem, not only for its elegant, simple lines but also for the art that once graced its interior. The central apse contains a copy of a famous 1123 mural that now resides in Barcelona's

Museu Nacional d'Art de Catalunya; at its centre is a Pantocrator, whose rich Mozarabic-influenced colours and expressive but superhuman features have become an emblem of Catalan Romanesque art. It's worth timing your visit for the outstanding audiovisual projection (five times daily) that casts the original art onto the church walls.

In the old village centre of Taüll you can see the **Santa Maria de Taüll** (www.centreromanic. com; ◷10am-7pm Sep-Jun, to

LOCAL KNOWLEDGE:
HIKING IN THE VALL DE BOÍ

There are some spectacular hikes in the Parc Nacional d'Aigüestortes i Estany de Sant Maurici, but one long-time favourite is the **Marmot Trail** – a round trip of 3½ hours – which begins next to the impressive Cavallers dam and passes a series of waterfalls. The hike ends at **Estany Negré** (Black Lake), close to this trail's first *refugi* (mountain shelter), **Ventosa i Calvell**; you spend a half-day among the beautiful mountains with breathtaking views of the Vall de Boí. There is also a nice three-hour trail from Taüll that takes in the entire valley and passes through the four villages along the way – Boí, Durro, Barruerra, Boí again, and back to Taüll.

You can also plan longer multiday hikes and spend the night in a *refugi*. Keep in mind that these can get quite crowded in July and August. Things are much more comfortable in May, June, September and October.

Many people wonder when is the best season to visit the park. In spring the valley is at its greenest, and the rivers are running the fastest from the snowmelt; in autumn the colours are at their best, and both spring and autumn are great times for hiking as there are not too many visitors.

8pm Jul & Aug) church, with its striking five-storey tower. The central fresco is reproduced here (again the original is preserved in Barcelona).

🛏 p217

The Drive » Start this 70-minute drive by heading back to the L500 and going south. After 15km, you'll merge onto the N230, which later runs alongside the Escales Reservoir. Turn left onto the C1311 towards Tremp, and look for the turn-off to the right onto the narrow road signed for Reserva del Congost de Mont-rebei.

TRIP HIGHLIGHT

8 Congost de Mont-rebei

Hidden along the western fringes of Catalonia, on the border of Aragón, the spectacular river gorge of Mont-rebei offers a dazzling vision of Catalan wilderness.

Carved by the sinewy Rio Noguera Ribagorçana through the pre-Pyrenean mountain range of Montsec, the narrow gorge has walls reaching some 500m with a width of just 20m

in some places. A small path cut into the cliff face follows along the gorge, offering dramatic views (and sometimes precipitous descents) along the way.

Allow around four hours to cover the 9.2km out-and back hike. Parking is limited. On weekends and from mid-June to mid-September, it's wise to reserve a parking space (€5) through the website www.fundaciocatalunya-lapedrera.com. At other times, arrive early to beat the crowds.

Eating & Sleeping

La Seu d'Urgell ❶

Arbeletxe — Catalan €€

(☎973 36 16 34; www.arbeletxe.com; Carrer de Sant Ermengol 22; mains €14-20; ⏰1-3pm Sun-Tue, 1-3pm & 9-11pm Thu-Sat; 🌶) One of La Seu d'Urgell's best-loved dining destinations is this elegant but unpretentious, two-room restaurant just west of the Plaça Catalunya. Service is warm, and the price-quality ratio is excellent for plates of perfectly cooked *magret* (duck), *entrecot* (rib-eye steak), *xipirons farcits* (stuffed squid) and a flavour-packed vegetable lasagna.

Groc Rooms — Apartment €€

(☎627 429908; www.grocrooms.com; Carrer Major 59; d €57-90; P 📶) Vintage mirrors, antique fireplaces and original-period tiled floors meet colourful, contemporary styling at these four 'boutique apartments' in a gorgeously revamped old-town house. The massive kitchen-equipped Loft apartment sleeps up to five, while others are more like cosy-chic rooms; the Suite features an in-room bathtub.

Llavorsí ❷

Hostal Noguera — Hostal €€

(☎973 62 20 12; www.hostalnoguera.info; Carretera Vall d'Aran, Llavorsí; s/d incl breakfast €39/70; ⏰Apr-Nov; P 📶) This stone building on the southern edge of town has 15 pleasant rooms, nine with balconies overlooking the rushing river. The three wood-beamed top-floor rooms have a dash more charm, while the downstairs restaurant serves filling local specialities like grilled meats and fried eggs swimming in ratatouille.

Espot ❸

Restaurant Juquim — Catalan €€

(☎973 62 40 09; Plaça Sant Martí 1; mains €10-19; ⏰1-4pm & 7.30-10.30pm; 🌶) Spread over two levels, this popular place on Espot's main street focuses on filling country fare like grilled wild-boar leg, lamb ribs with fried potatoes and vegetarian-friendly mushroom cannelloni. Eat in the atmospheric stone-walled dining room downstairs or on the front terrace on sunny days.

Roca Blanca — Hotel €€

(☎973 62 41 56; www.hotelrocablanca.com; Carrer Església; incl breakfast d €80-90, ste €120-125; P 📶) From the 16 gleaming, impressively spacious rooms with modern bathrooms to the polished lounge with fireplace, this hotel is one of the region's most welcoming and inviting. Contemporary art adorns the walls, service is attentive and personal, and breakfast is a feast. Extra touches include a gym, sauna and gorgeous garden – plus Teo, the resident English sheepdog.

Salardú ❹

Hotel Seixes — Hotel €€

(☎973 64 54 06; www.hotelseixes.com; Carretera Ta Bagergue 3; s/d/tr/q from €42/70/90/110; ⏰Dec-Mar & Jun-Oct; P 📶) This efficiently run hikers' favourite, perched within tinkling distance of the pealing bell of Sant Feliu church in tiny Bagergue (2km northeast of Salardú), has simply furnished rooms, many with gorgeous valley views. The location will appeal to nature lovers and seclusion seekers. Ask staff for tips on local hikes.

Taüll ❽

Alberg Taüll — Hostel €

(☎645 750600; elalberguetaull@gmail.com; Avinguda Feixanes 5-7; dm/d/tr incl breakfast €38/49/100; P 📶) This is everything a hostel should be: stylish rooms for two to seven guests feature large beds with orthopaedic mattresses, the suite has a hot tub, there's underfloor heating for crisp mornings, and the lounge includes a large park map for planning hikes. Families are welcome and you'll get great walking advice. Sheets and a towel cost €5.50. Cheaper midweek.

The Pyrenees

Great food, spectacular scenery and frozen-in-time villages perched high in the mountains are among the big draws of this exhilarating drive across the Pyrenees.

18

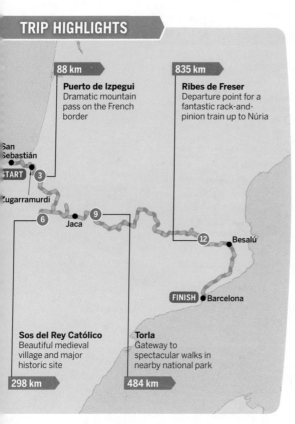

TRIP HIGHLIGHTS

88 km

Puerto de Izpegui
Dramatic mountain pass on the French border

835 km

Ribes de Freser
Departure point for a fantastic rack-and-pinion train up to Núria

San Sebastián

START 3

Zugarramurdi

6 Jaca 9

12 Besalú

FINISH ● Barcelona

Sos del Rey Católico
Beautiful medieval village and major historic site

298 km

Torla
Gateway to spectacular walks in nearby national park

484 km

5–7 DAYS
1040KM / 646 MILES

GREAT FOR...

BEST TIME TO GO
From May to October for warm weather and outdoor activities.

ESSENTIAL PHOTO

A mouthwatering plate of *pintxos* (tapas) at a San Sebastián eatery.

BEST FOR OUTDOORS

Hiking through breath-taking mountain scenery near Núria.

18 The Pyrenees

The rolling, mist-covered hills and snow-plastered mountains that make up the Pyrenees are a playground for outdoor enthusiasts. Aside from hiking, skiing and simply admiring the view, the Pyrenees are home to old-fashioned villages that are rich in history. Foodies will delight in the abundant Basque, Aragonese and Catalan produce – not to mention two world-class dining cities (San Sebastián and Barcelona) bookending the drive.

❶ San Sebastián

San Sebastián (Basque: Donostia) is a stunning city that loves to indulge. With Michelin stars apparently falling from the heavens onto its restaurants and a *pintxos* culture almost unmatched anywhere else in Spain, San Sebastián frequently tops lists of the world's best places to eat. But just as good as the food is the summer fun in the sun. For its setting, form and attitude, Playa de la Concha is the equal of

any city beach in Europe. Then there's Playa de Gros (also known as Playa de la Zurriola), with its surfers and sultry beachgoers.

About 700m from Playa de la Concha, the Isla de Santa Clara is accessible by boats that run every half-hour from the fishing port. At low tide the island gains its own tiny beach and you can climb its forested paths to a small lighthouse. For great views over the city, head up to **Monte Igueldo**, just west of town. The best way to get there is via the old-world **funicular railway** (www.monteigueldo. es; Plaza del Funicular; return adult/child €3.75/2.50; ⏱10am-10pm Jun-Aug, shorter hours Sep-May) to the Parque de Atracciones.

🍴 🛏 p167, p227

The Drive ❯❯ Start this 50km journey by taking the GI20 east and continuing onto the AP8. Just before hitting France, take N121 south, then switch to the peaceful country road NA4410 near Bera. As it crosses into France, the road becomes D406. Cut back south and into Spain, before reaching Sare.

② Zugarramurdi

Just before the French border is the pretty village of Zugarramurdi, home to the decidedly less pretty Cuevas de Las Brujas. These caves were once, according to the Inquisition, the scene of evil debauchery. Having established this, the perverse masters of the Inquisition promptly tortured and burned scores of alleged witches. Playing on the flying-broomstick theme is the **Museo de las Brujas** (📞948 59 90 04; www.turismozugarramurdi. com; Calle Beitikokarrika 22, Zugarramurdi; adult/child €4.50/2; ⏱11am-7.30pm Tue-Sun mid-Jul–mid-Sep, to 6pm Wed-Sun mid-Sep–mid-Jul), a fascinating dip into

louse
Castres
Mazamet
Castelnaudary
Béziers
Carcassonne
Fanjeaux
Le Cap d'Agde
Limoux
Narbonne
Montgaillard
Sigean
Tarascon-sur-Ariège
Quillan
Port Barcarès
FRANCE
ORRA ELLA
Perpignan
Mont Canigou ▲ (2784m)
Puig Neulós ▲ (1256m)
25
Puigcerdà
AP7
N260 ⑫ Ribes de Fraser
Figueres
Cadaqués
Bellver de Cerdanya
⑬
⑭ Besalú
Castelló d'Empúries
Ripoll
Olot
C66
L'Escala
Gironella
Sarrià de Ter
L'Estartit
Vic
Girona
Palafrugell
Maçanet de la Selva
Palamós
Sant Feliu de Guíxols
nresa
Sant Celoni
AP7
Cardedeu
Tossa de Mar
ada
Mollet del Vallès
Blanes
Rubí
Mataró
ca del ès
Premià de Mar
MEDITERRANEAN SEA
FINISH ⑮
Barcelona p238
ges

LINK YOUR TRIP

7 Northern Spain Pilgrimage

At Roncesvalles, join pilgrims on the Camino de Santiago for a drive through stunning scenery and history-rich villages.

17 Peaks & Valleys in Northwest Catalonia

You can add on to this trip by connecting in Vielha (just west of Arties) with a scenic drive around northwest Catalonia.

the mysterious cauldron of witchcraft in the Pyrenees.

The Drive » Drive east of town then take the N121B south. After 18km or so, take windy NA2600 east. The 52km drive takes about 75 minutes, and passes through stunning mountain scenery with great views lurking around every turn.

❸ Puerto de Izpegui

The road here meanders dreamily amid picturesque farms, villages and hills before climbing sharply to the French border pass of Puerto de Izpegui, where the world becomes a spectacular collision of crags, peaks and valleys. At the pass, you can stop for a short, sharp hike up to the top of Mt Izpegui. You'll find a good number of *casas rurales* (village or farmstead accommodation) throughout the area.

The Drive » To avoid lengthy backtracking, continue into France towards the pretty town of Saint-Jean Pied de Port. From there take the D933, which turns into the N135 as it crosses south back into Spain. The 48km drive takes a little over an hour.

❹ Roncesvalles

Roncesvalles (known in Basque as Orreaga) has a fascinating history. Legend has it that it was here that the armies of Charlemagne

were defeated and Roland, commander of Charlemagne's rearguard, was killed by Basque tribes in 778. In addition to violence and bloodshed, though, Roncesvalles is also a pivotal stop on the road to Santiago de Compostela, where Camino pilgrims visit the famous monastery before continuing the eastward journey. Don't miss the Real Colegiata de Santa María, an atmospheric monastery with an iconic statue of the Virgin Mary.

 p227

The Drive » It's a scenic 70km drive to the next stop. Head south out of Roncesvalles to get on to the NA140 east. Follow this to the NA137 south, which takes you into Roncal.

❺ Roncal

Navarra's most spectacular mountain area is around Roncal, a charming village of cobblestone alleyways that twist and turn between dark stone houses and meander down to a river full of trout. Roncal is renowned for its Queso de Roncal, a sheep's-milk cheese that's sold in the village.

The Drive » Start this 70km drive by taking NA137 south, then turn onto A21 west, which offers fine views of the Yesa reservoir (the shoreline-hugging NA2420 is even more scenic). At Liédena, take NA127 south, which turns into A127.

❻ Sos del Rey Católico

Sos del Rey Católico is one of Aragón's most beautiful villages. The old medieval town is a glorious maze of twisting, cobbled lanes that wriggle between dark stone houses with deeply overhung eaves.

Fernando II of Aragón is said to have been born in the **Casa Palacio de Seda** (Plaza de la Hispanidad; adult/child €2.90/1.90; ☺10am-1pm & 4-7pm Mon-Fri, 10am-2pm & 4-7pm Sat & Sun, closed Mon Sep-Jun) in 1452.

Sos del Rey Católico

It's an impressive noble mansion, which now contains an interpretative centre, with fine exhibits on the history of Sos and the life of the king. The Gothic **Iglesia de San Esteban** (Calle Salud; €1; ⊙10am-1pm & 4-6pm Mon-Sat, 10am-12.30pm Sun), with a weathered Romanesque portal, has a deliciously gloomy crypt decorated with medieval frescoes. Above the central Plaza de la Villa, the Renaissance-era town hall is one of the grandest public buildings in Sos. Duck inside to admire the magnificent central courtyard.

🛏 p227

The Drive ≫ Retrace the drive back to N240 and continue east. At Puente de la Reina de Jaca, take the A176 north. Plan on 75 minutes or so to complete the 90km drive.

- - - - - - - - - - - - - - - -

7 Hecho

The verdant Hecho valley is mountain magic at its best, beginning with gentle climbs through the valley and the accumulating charms of old stone villages punctuating slopes of dense mixed woods of beech, pine, rowan, elm and hazel. As the valleys narrow to the north, 2000m-plus peaks rise triumphantly at their heads. Lovely Hecho (Echo), the largest village in the valley, is an attractive warren of solid stone houses with steep roofs and flower-decked balconies. It's also endowed with a large collection of contemporary sculpture, with over 40 pieces, mostly in stone, scattered around the village.

The Drive ≫ Take A176 back south, cross the bridge at Puente de la Reina de Jaca, and continue east along the N240. It takes about 40 minutes to do the drive, which takes in rolling green hillsides and wide open fields.

LOCAL KNOWLEDGE: WHAT'S COOKING IN ARAGÓN

The kitchens and tables of Aragón are dominated by meat. The region's cold harsh winds create the ideal conditions for curing *jamón* (ham), a top tapa here; some of the best can be found in no-frills bars. Likewise, another meaty favourite, *jarretes* (hock of ham or shanks), is available in simple village restaurants like Torla's **La Brecha** (📞974 48 62 21; www.lucienbriet.com; Calle A Ruata; set menu €17; ⏰2-3.30pm & 8.30-10.30pm Easter-early Dec; 🐾), while heartier *ternasco* (suckling lamb) is generally served as a steak or ribs with potatoes – try it at **Bodegón de Mallacán** (📞974 50 09 77; Plaza Mayor 6; mains €17-21, set menus €22; ⏰noon-4pm & 7-11pm) in Aínsa.

Other popular dishes include *conejo a la montañesa* (rabbit mountain-style) served with gusto (and sometimes with snails) at Hecho's **Restaurante Gaby** (📞974 37 50 07; www.casablasquico.es; Plaza La Fuente 1; mains €13-20, set menu €25; ⏰1.30-3.30pm & 8.30-10pm Mar-Dec; 🐾), while (phew!) vegetarians can seek out tasty *pochas viudas* (white-bean stew with peppers, tomatoes and onion), a popular starter at restaurants like **La Cocina del Principal** (📞948 88 83 48; www.lacocinadelprincipal.es; Calle Fernando el Católico 13; mains €19-26, set menu €28; ⏰1.30-3.30pm & 8.30-10.30pm Tue-Sat Mar-Nov, by reservation Dec-Feb) in Sos del Rey Católico.

8 Jaca

A gateway to the western valleys of the Aragonese Pyrenees, Jaca has a compact and attractive old town dotted with remnants of its past as the capital of the nascent 11th-century Aragón kingdom. These include an unusual fortress and a sturdy cathedral, while the town also has some great places to eat.

Jaca's 11th-century **Catedral de San Pedro** (Plaza de la Catedral; ⏰11am-1.30pm & 4.15-8pm) is a formidable building, its imposing facade typical of the sturdy stone architecture of northern Aragón.

There are some lovely old buildings in the streets of the *casco*

historico (old town) that fans out south of the cathedral, including the 15th-century **Torre del Reloj** and the charming little **Ermita de Sarsa**.

The star-shaped, 16th-century **Ciudadela** (Citadel; www.ciudadeladejaca.es; Avenida del Primer Viernes de Mayo; adult/senior & child €5/4, incl Museo de Miniaturas Militares €8/5; ⏰10.30am-1.30pm & 4-8pm Apr-Jun & Sep–mid-Oct, 10.30am-1.30pm & 4.30-8.30pm Jul-Aug, 10.30am-1.30pm & 3.30-7.30pm mid-Oct–Mar) is Spain's only extant pentagonal fortress. Inside, you can explore the bastions, casemates, powder magazines and chapel as well as the broad central Patio de Armas.

🍴 p227

The Drive ≫ Take the E7 east. At Sabiñánigo, take the N260 north. Keep following the N260 as it loops east around Biescas and continues towards Torla, with winding roads offering spectacular panoramas. The 60km drive takes a little over an hour.

TRIP HIGHLIGHT

9 Torla

This is where the Spanish Pyrenees really take your breath away. At the heart of it all is a dragon's back of limestone peaks skirting the French border.

Torla is gateway to spectacular walking in the **Parque Nacional de Ordesa y Monte Perdido**, located 3km northeast. This lovely Alpine-style village has stone houses with slate roofs, and a delightful setting above Río Ara under a backdrop of the national park's mountains. In your ramblings around town, make for the 13th-century **Iglesia de San Salvador**; there are fine views from the small park on the church's northern side.

The Drive » It's a 45km drive to Aínsa along the N260. You'll pass sunlit streams with forested conical peaks on either side of you on this straightforward trip.

- - - - - - - - - - - - - - - - - -

🔟 Aínsa

The beautiful hilltop village of medieval Aínsa, which stands above the modern town of the same name, is one of Aragón's gems, a stunning village hewn from uneven stone. From its perch, you'll have commanding panoramic views of the mountains.

The **Castillo** and fortifications off the western end of the Plaza de San Salvador contain a fascinating ecomuseum on Pyrenean fauna and an exhibition space covering the region's geology.

🛏 p227

The Drive » Take N260 east. Around Castarnés, switch to the N230 north. Allow about 1¾ hours to cover the 105km drive.

- - - - - - - - - - - - - - - - - -

⓫ Vielha

Vielha is Aran's junction capital, a sprawl of holiday housing and apartments straggled along the valley and creeping up the sides, crowded with skiers in winter. The tiny centre retains some charm in the form of the **Església de Sant Miquèu**, which houses some notable medieval artwork, namely the 12th-century *Crist de Mijaran*.

The Drive » This 214km drive takes about four hours, owing to curving mountain roads. From Vielha take C28 down to Sort, continue east on N260 to Ribes de Freser.

- - - - - - - - - - - - - - - - - -

TRIP HIGHLIGHT

⓬ Ribes de Freser

Sheltered within the Vall de Ribes is small, well-equipped Ribes de Freser, a stone village that makes a great base for exploring the pine forests, plummeting dales and spectacular rugged hills of the Vall de Núria. From Ribes de Freser, you can hop aboard a narrow-gauge rack-and-pinion railway (*cremallera*) that ascends some 1000m on its 12km journey to mountain-ringed Núria, which is equal parts pilgrimage site and ski resort.

Once there, you'll find some fabulous marked trails throughout the valley and up nearby peaks; one of the best is the Camí Vell, an 8km walk down through the gorge from Núria to Queralbs (which is also a stop on the railway).

DETOUR: ANDORRA

Start: ⓫ **Vielha**

If you're on the lookout for great hiking or skiing, or just want to say you've been in a different country, then don't miss the curious nation of Andorra, just 10km north of La Seu d'Urgell – and a little over halfway along the drive from Vielha to Ribes de Freser.

At only 468 sq km, it's one of Europe's smallest countries and, though it has a democratic parliament, the nominal heads of state are two co-princes: the bishop of Urgell in Spain and the president of France. Catalan is the official tongue, though Spanish, French and, due to a large immigrant workforce, Portuguese, are widely spoken. Make sure you fuel up in Andorra, as it's significantly cheaper. There's rarely any passport control, though you may be stopped by customs on the way back into Spain, so don't go over the duty-free limit.

The Drive >> Take N260 south to Ripoll and east to Olot. The 50km drive, which passes over forested hillsides and offers fine views, takes about an hour.

- - - - - - - - - - - - - - - - - -

⓭ Olot

Olot is the spread-out capital of La Garrotxa region, with wide, tree-lined walkways (with the exception of its serpentine medieval heart) and plenty of options for rambling in the surrounding countryside. This area has been shaped by the ancient activity of now-dormant volcanoes. Four hills of volcanic origin stand sentry on the fringes of Olot. You can follow a 2km (45-minute) trail up the **Volcà del Montsacopa**, north of the centre.

✖ p227

The Drive >> It's a quick drive to the next stop, which is 22km east along the fast-moving A26. Take exit 67 to reach Besalú.

- - - - - - - - - - - - - - - - - -

⓮ Besalú

The tall, crooked 11th-century Pont Fortificat (Fortified Bridge) over Río Fluvià in medieval Besalú, with its two tower gates and heavy portcullis, is an arresting sight, leading you into the coiled maze of cobbled narrow streets that make up the core of this delightfully well-preserved town.

Besalú's thriving Jewish community fled the town in 1436 after relentless Christian persecution, leaving behind a **miqvé** (Baixada de Miqvé; guided tours €2.25-4.80) – a 12th-century ritual bath – the only survivor of its kind in Spain. Access to the *miqvé* is by guided tour with the **tourist office** (📞972 59 12 40; www.besalu.cat; Carrer del Pont 1; 🕐10am-2pm & 4-7pm), but you can see the square and ruin exterior independently.

The Drive >> The journey to Barcelona ends with a 130km drive (1¾ hours) from the mountains down to the sea. Take C66 south. At Montegut, take the AP7 and follow signs to Barcelona.

- - - - - - - - - - - - - - - - - -

⓯ Barcelona

After rolling through remote mountain villages, the buzzing metropolis of Barcelona may come as a shock. But don't delay, dive in. One way into the city's heart is through its celebrated food scene. Start the culinary journey at the **Mercat de Sant Antoni** (📞93 426 35 21; www.mercatdesantantoni. com; Carrer del Comte d'Urgell 1; 🕐8am-8.30pm Mon-Sat; Ⓜ Sant Antoni), a glorious 19th-century market with some fine tapas bars.

Afterwards, stop by the nearby **MACBA** (Museu d'Art Contemporani de Barcelona; 📞93 412 08 10; www.macba. cat; Plaça dels Àngels 1; adult/concession/child under 14yr €11/8.80/free, 4-8pm Sat free; 🕐11am-7.30pm Mon & Wed-Fri, 10am-8pm Sat, 10am-3pm Sun & public holidays; Ⓜ Universitat) for a look at some of the city's best contemporary exhibitions. The building, designed by Richard Meier, is a work of art in itself. Barcelona is justly famous for its Modernista architecture. You can wander through a Gaudí-designed fairy tale in spacious **Park Güell** (📞93 409 18 31; www. parkguell.barcelona; Carrer d'Olot 7; adult/child €10/7; 🕐8am-9.30pm May-Aug, to 8.30pm Apr, Sep & Oct, to 6.15pm Nov–mid-Feb, to 7pm mid-Feb–Mar; 🚌H6, D40, V19, Bus Güell, Ⓜ Lesseps, Vallcarca, Alfons X), which is located north of downtown. End the day with a meal in one of the atmospheric restaurants in **El Born**.

✖ p236, p259

Eating & Sleeping

San Sebastián ❶

✘ La Cuchara de San Telmo Pintxos €€

(☎943 44 16 55; Calle 31 de Agosto 28; pintxos €3-5; ⏰7.30-11pm Tue, 12.30-5.30pm & 7.30-11.30pm Wed-Sun) This bustling, always packed bar offers miniature *nueva cocina vasca* (Basque nouvelle cuisine) from a supremely creative kitchen. Unlike many San Sebastián bars, this one doesn't have any *pintxos* laid out on the bar top; instead you must order from the blackboard menu behind the counter.

🛏 Pensión Altair Pension €€

(☎691 810403; www.pension-altair.com; Calle Padre Larroca 3; s/d from €85/115; 🛜) This *pensión* occupies a beautifully restored Gros townhouse, with arched windows and modern, minimalist rooms that are a world away from the fusty decor of the old-town *pensiones*. Interior rooms lack the grandiose windows but are much larger. There's a minimum three-night stay at peak times.

Roncesvalles ❹

🛏 Casa de Beneficiados Hotel €€

(☎948 76 01 05; www.casadebeneficiados. com; Carretera de Francia; s/d/tr €80/90/115, apt €90-150; ⏰mid-Mar–Dec; 🛜) In a former life this was an 18th-century monks' residence. Today it has modernised rooms, some overlooking the countryside, and the atmospheric common areas make fine places to unwind after a day's hike. You can also dine on local game, cheese and mountain trout at the good-value restaurant (mains €9 to €22), hire bicycles or arrange horse-riding trips.

Sos del Rey Católico ❻

🛏 Ruta del Tiempo Boutique Hotel €€

(☎948 88 82 95; www.rutadeltiempo.es; Plaza de la Villa; incl breakfast s €50, d €70-110; ❄🛜) Evocatively located under the arches of the central plaza, this little family-run hotel has 1st-floor rooms themed around three Aragonese kings, while the four 2nd-floor rooms are dedicated to

different continents. They all have charm, but spacious 'Asia' and 'Africa' are the best.

Jaca ❽

✘ La Tasca de Ana Tapas €

(Calle de Ramiro I 3; tapas €1.80-3.60, raciones €3-9; ⏰12.30-3.30pm & 7.30pm-midnight Jul-Sep, 7-11.30pm Mon-Fri, 12.30-3.30pm & 7-11.30pm Sat & Sun Oct-Jun; 🛜) One of Aragón's best tapas bars (hence the crowds) La Tasca has tempting options lined up along the bar, more choices cooked to order and a well-priced list of local wines. Check out its blackboard of *tapas mas solicitados* (most popular orders). Top contenders include the *tostada* (toast) topped with goat's cheese, *trigueros* (asparagus) and a hard-boiled egg.

Aínsa ❿

🛏 Hotel Los Siete Reyes Boutique Hotel €€

(☎974 50 06 81; www.lossietereyes.com; Plaza Mayor; d €95-120; ❄🛜) Tucked under an arcade on Aínsa's ancient main square and exhibiting a style best described as historical-boutique, the Siete Reyes offers six rooms fit for kings (and queens). Modern art hangs on old stone walls, mood lighting shines from ceilings crossed by wooden beams, and the wonderful subterranean bodega is great for breakfast.

Olot ⓭

✘ La Deu Catalan €€

(☎972 26 10 04; www.ladeu.es; Carretera La Deu; 3-course menú €15-23, mains €6-25; ⏰1-4pm & 8-10.30pm Mon-Sat, 1-4pm Sun; 🅿) Down a tree-lined road with a volcanic stone fountain bubbling away in its terrace dining area, family-run La Deu has been perfecting its filling *cuina volcànica* since 1885. Service is charmingly efficient, and there's huge culinary variety, including slow-cooked lamb, pork with sweet chestnuts, oven-baked hake, asparagus 'cake' lashed with basil oil, and the house spin on classic *patates d'Olot*.

Barcelona to Valencia

On this memorable drive, you'll experience some of Eastern Spain's prettiest villages, explore lush natural scenery and enjoy the heady sights of two very vibrant cities.

19

TRIP HIGHLIGHTS

250 km

Alquézar
Go canyoning outside this tiny village

Huesca ③

⑤

Lleida

Barcelona

START

375 km

Zaragoza
Lively river town with good dining and nightlife

allocanta

⑧ Teruel

FINISH ⑪

767 km

Valencia
Paella feasts and dazzling architecture

Albarracín
Picturesque village with a magnificent castle

588 km

5–7 DAYS
767KM / 477 MILES

GREAT FOR...

BEST TIME TO GO

Any time, but March to May and October to November to beat the summer crowds.

📷 ESSENTIAL PHOTO

A flock of cranes flying over the Laguna de Gallocanta.

✅ BEST FOR CULTURE

Exploring the fascinating Islamic-era Aljafería in Zaragoza.

a de Gallocanta Cranes flying over the lake (p233)

229

19 Barcelona to Valencia

Some of Spain's great unsung wonders are on display on this looping drive between coast and mountain. You'll find architectural and culinary treasures courtesy of Valencia and Barcelona, Unesco World Heritage gardens, Spain's largest lake (a birdwatcher's delight) and adrenaline-fuelled canyon adventures near Alquézar. There are also fascinating relics from the past, from Roman ruins and an Islamic-era palace to Gothic and Modernista masterpieces.

❶ Barcelona

Home to historical treasures, brilliantly inventive architecture, and a boundless dining and drinking scene, Barcelona is one of Europe's most enchanting cities. Start off with a visit to the **Barri Gòtic**, the old medieval quarter of Barcelona, which is packed with quaint squares, cobblestone lanes with old shops and looming churches. Delve into the past at the **Museu d'Història**

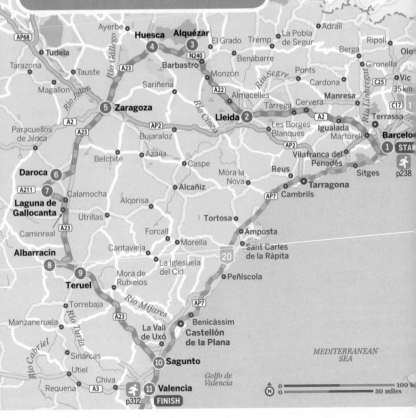

de Barcelona (MUHBA; 📞93 256 21 00; http://ajuntament.barcelona.cat/museuhistoria; Plaça del Rei; adult/concession/child €7/5/free, 3-8pm Sun & 1st Sun of month free; 🕙10am-7pm Tue-Sat, to 8pm Sun; Ⓜ Jaume I). This fascinating museum takes you back through the centuries to the very foundations of Roman Barcino. Afterwards, stop in the palm-filled **Plaça Reial** (Ⓜ Liceu), where you'll find eateries and bars with outdoor tables on the square. You can't leave Barcelona without touring at least one building designed by Antoni Gaudí. A good starting point is Casa Batlló; see p238 for a walking tour that takes in this strange and fantastical building.

🍴 🛏 p236, p259

LINK YOUR TRIP

15 Artistic Inspiration on the Costa Brava

From Barcelona, go 90km up the coast for a drive past sunny beaches, rugged coves and Dalí theatrics.

20 Mediterranean Meander

Once you hit Valencia, keep going! Follow this sea-lover's drive all the way to Málaga.

The Drive » In Barcelona take the waterfront Passeig de Colom southwest and get onto the B10. After 7km continue onto the A2. Stay on this for 165km then take exit 474 for Lleida. It's about two hours' drive total from Barcelona to Lleida.

---

② Lleida

The mighty fortress-church on top of the hill in the town centre – Lleida's major historical landmark – is one of the most spectacular in Spain and is in itself reason enough to visit. Enclosed within a fortress complex, Lleida's 'old cathedral', **La Seu Vella** (www.turoseuvella.cat; adult/child incl Castell del Rei €6/5; 🕙10am-7.30pm Tue-Sat May-Sep, 10am-1.30pm & 3-5.30pm Tue-Fri, 10am-5.30pm Sat Oct-Apr, 10am-3pm Sun year-round), towers above the city. The cathedral is a masterpiece with beautiful cloisters, the windows of which are laced with exceptional Gothic tracery. Lleida has several intriguing museums, including the **Museu de Lleida** (📞973 28 30 75; www.museudelleida.cat; Carrer del Sant Crist 1; adult/child €5/free; 🕙10am-2pm & 4-6pm Tue-Sat Oct-May, 10am-2pm & 5-7pm Tue-Sat Jun-Sep, 10am-2pm Sun year-round). This expansive collection encompasses artefacts reaching back to the Stone Age, Roman remains, Visigothic relics, medieval art and works by 19th-century Catalan artists.

🍴 p236

The Drive » Take Av Alcalde Rovira Roure (just north of Plaça Cervantes) to the N240, which merges into the A22. Stay on this for 50km then take exit 51 onto the N240. From here you'll pass through the winemaking center of Somontano. Around Barbastro (the epicentre of this winery region), follow signs to A1232 and follow this to Alquézar.

TRIP HIGHLIGHT

③ Alquézar

Picturesque Alquézar is a handsome village that's famed for its canyoning *(descenso de barrancos),* which involves following canyons downstream by whatever means available – walking, abseiling, swimming, even diving. There are many local outfitters that lead tours, including **Vertientes** (📞974 31 83 54; www.vertientesaventura.com; Paseo San Hipólito; 🔗).

Alquézar is crowned by the large castle-monastery of the **Colegiata de Santa María** (€3; 🕙11am-2pm & 4-7pm Sep-Jun, 10.30am-2pm & 4.30-7.30pm Jul-Aug). Originally built as an *alcázar* (fortress) by the Arabs in the 9th century, it was subsequently conquered and replaced by an Augustinian monastery in 1099.

🛏 p236

The Drive ›› It's a short drive (50 minutes or so) to Huesca. From Alquézar take the A1233, then switch to the A1229 around Adahuesca. After 11km get onto the A22 towards Huesca.

❹ Huesca

Huesca is a provincial capital in more than name, a town that shutters down during the afternoon hours and stirs back into life in the evenings. That said, its old centre retains considerable appeal. The Gothic **Catedral de Santa María** (www.museo. diocesisdehuesca.org; Plaza de la Catedral; adult/child €4/free; ⏱10.30am-2pm & 4-6pm Mon-Fri, 10.30am-2pm Sat Mar-Jun & Sep-Oct, 10.30am-2pm & 4-7pm Mon-Sat Jul-Aug, 10.30am-2pm Mon-Sat Nov-Jan) is one of Aragón's great surprises.

The richly carved main portal dates from 1300, the attached Museo Diocesano contains some extraordinary frescoes, and you can round off your visit by climbing the 180 steps of the bell tower for 360-degree views.

✕ p236

The Drive ›› Zaragoza is about an hour's drive (75km). From Huesca, take Av Martínez de Velasco west. Hop onto the E7 heading southwest. Stay on this for 59km, then take exit 298 onto N330 toward Zaragoza.

TRIP HIGHLIGHT

❺ Zaragoza

Zaragoza (Saragossa) is a vibrant, elegant and fascinating city. Located on the banks of the mighty Río Ebro, the residents comprise over half of Aragón's population and enjoy a lifestyle that revolves around some of the best tapas bars in the province, as well as superb shopping and a vigorous nightlife. The restoration of the riverbank has created footpaths on either side of the Río Ebro, resulting in an 8km circular route. It's superb birdwatching territory, with herons, kingfishers and many other species.

Brace yourself for the great baroque cavern of Catholicism known as the **Basílica de Nuestra Señora del Pilar** (www. basilicadelpilar.es; Plaza del Pilar; ⏱6.45am-8.30pm Mon-Sat, to 9.30pm Sun). The faithful believe that it was here on 2 January 40 CE that Santiago saw the Virgin Mary descend atop a marble *pilar* (pillar). A lift whisks you most of the way up the north tower from where you climb to a superb viewpoint over the city.

The 11th-century **Aljafería** (☎976 28 95 28; www.cortesaragon.es; Calle de los Diputados; adult/child €5/free, Sun free; ⏱10am-2pm &

LUIS OVERLANDER/SHUTTERSTOCK ©

4.30-8pm Apr–mid-Oct, 10am-2pm & 4-6.30pm Mon-Sat, 10am-2pm Sun mid-Oct-Mar) is Spain's finest Islamic-era edifice outside Andalucía.

✕ ⌂ p157, p236-7

The Drive ›› From Zaragoza take Avenida de Valencia west. Turn right onto Avenida Séptimo Arte and follow this as it merges onto the A23. Follow the A23 for 68km and take exit 210 near Romanos onto the A1506. From here follow signs into Daroca. The 87km drive takes just over an hour.

❻ Daroca

Daroca, a sleepy medieval town, was

a one-time Islamic stronghold and, later, a Christian fortress town in the early medieval wars against Castilla. Its well-preserved old quarter is laden with historic references and the crumbling old city walls encircle the hilltops; the walls once boasted 114 military towers. The pretty **Plaza de España**, at the top of the village, is dominated by an ornate Romanesque Mudéjar Renaissance–style church, which boasts a lavish interior and organ.

🛏 p237

The Drive » From Daroca, take Avenida de Madrid southwest and merge onto the A211. Follow this 23km then follow signs to Gallocanta, another 1km south of the A211.

- - - - - - - - - - - - - - - - - - - -

❼ Laguna de Gallocanta

This is Spain's largest natural lake, with an area of about 15 sq km (though it can almost dry up in summer). It's a winter home for tens of thousands of cranes, as well as many other waterfowl – more than 260 bird species have been recorded here. The cranes arrive in

mid-October and leave for the return flight to their breeding grounds in Scandinavia in March. Unpaved roads of over 30km encircle the lake, passing a series of hides and observation points, and can be driven in normal vehicles except after heavy rain. The **Centro de Interpretación Laguna de Gallocanta** (☎976 80 30 69; www. facebook.com/oficinaturismo. gallocanta; Gallocanta; adult/ child €2/1; ⏰9am-1.30pm & 3.30-6.30pm Oct-Mar, 10am-2pm & 4-7.30pm Wed-Sun Apr-Jun, 10am-2pm & 4.30-8pm Sat & Sun Jul–mid-Sep; **P**), at the lake's northeast

LOCAL KNOWLEDGE:
THE LOVERS OF TERUEL

In the early 13th century, Juan Diego de Marcilla and Isabel de Segura fell in love, but, in the manner of other star-crossed historical lovers, there was a catch: Isabel was the only daughter of a wealthy family, while poor old Juan Diego was, well, poor. Juan Diego convinced Isabel's reluctant father to postpone plans for Isabel's marriage to someone more appropriate for five years, during which time Juan Diego would seek his fortune. Not waiting a second longer than the five years, Isabel's father married off his daughter in 1217, only for Juan Diego to return, triumphant, immediately after the wedding. He begged Isabel for a kiss, which she refused, condemning Juan Diego to die of a broken heart. A final twist saw Isabel attend the funeral in mourning, whereupon she gave Juan Diego the kiss he had craved in life. Isabel promptly died and the two lovers were buried together. You can see their tombs at the **Fundación Amantes**.

corner, has binoculars and picture windows for lake viewing.

The Drive » Take the A1507 east. Around Calamocha, get on the N234, then merge onto the A23. Stay on this for 53km, before taking exit 131 onto A2515. Around Cella switch to the TEV 9011 and follow signs towards Albarracín. The drive takes about 90 minutes.

TRIP HIGHLIGHT

8 Albarracín

Built on a steep, rocky outcrop and surrounded by a deep valley carved out by the Río Guadalaviar, Albarracín is one of Spain's most beautiful villages. It's famous for its half-timbered houses with dusky-pink facades, reminiscent of southern Italy.

Crowning the old town is a castle that dates from the 9th century when Albarracín was an important Islamic military post.

Visits are by hour-long Spanish-language tours starting at the **Museo de Albarracín** (Calle San Juan; €3; ⏱10.30am-1pm & 4.30-7pm, closed Sun afternoon mid-Sep–Jun). Albarracín's highest point, the **Torre del Andador**, has enviable views over town. Reach it by heading uphill alongside the imposing *murallas* (walls) that once protected the village.

✕ 🏠 p237

The Drive » From Albarracín get back on the A1512, and follow it for 37km to Teruel. It's a scenic 40-minute drive that takes in forest and rocky foothills, before descending into the wide open plains outside Teruel.

9 Teruel

Lovely, compact Teruel is an open-air museum of ornate Mudéjar monuments. But this is very much a living museum where the streets are filled with life – a reflection of a city with

serious cultural attitude. Teruel's **Catedral de Santa María de Mediavilla** (Plaza de la Catedral; incl Museo de Arte Sacro adult/child €5/3; ⏱11am-2pm & 4-8pm Apr-Oct, to 7pm Nov-Mar) is a rich example of the Mudéjar imagination at work with its kaleidoscopic brickwork and colourful ceramic tiles.

The curious **Fundación Amantes** (www.amantes deteruel.es; Calle Matías Abad 3; complete visit adult/senior/student €10/8.50/6; ⏱10am-2pm & 4-8pm) pulls out the stops on the city's famous legend of Isabel and Juan Diego. Here, the 13th-century couple lie beneath modern alabaster effigies, their hands almost (but not quite) touching.

The most impressive of Teruel's Mudéjar towers is the **Torre de El Salvador** (www.teruelmudejar.com; Calle El Salvador 7; adult/child €2.50/2; ⏱11am-2pm Mon, 11am-2pm & 4.30-7.30pm

Albarracín

Tue-Sun Feb-Jul & Sep-Oct, 10am-2pm Aug, 11am-2pm Mon, 11am-2pm & 4.30-6.30pm Tue-Sun Nov-Jan), an early-14th-century extravaganza of brick and ceramics built around an older Islamic minaret. Climb up the narrow stairways for Teruel's best views.

🛏 p237

The Drive » It's 120km southeast to Sagunto, though just a 70-minute drive on the A23. From Teruel, take Avenida de Sagunto south. Just beyond the centre, you'll pass by Dinópolis, a dinosaur theme park that's a hit with families. From here, continue onto the N234 and the A23.

- - - - - - - - - - - - - - - - -

10 Sagunto

The port town of Sagunto offers spectacular panoramas of the coast, Balearics and sea of orange groves

from its hilltop castle complex. Sagunto was once a thriving Iberian community (called – infelicitously, with hindsight – Arse) that traded with Greeks and Phoenicians. A highlight here is the restored Roman theatre. Above it, the stone walls of the castle complex girdle the hilltop for almost 1km.

The Drive » It's about a 30-minute drive to Valencia. From Sagunto, take the N340 south, and merge onto the V23. Around Puçol, merge onto the V21, and enjoy the view along the coast as you near the city.

- - - - - - - - - - - - - - - - -

TRIP HIGHLIGHT

11 Valencia

The vibrant city of Valencia has much going for it, from stunning architecture and scenic

parks to an embarrassing wealth of restaurants.

Bright and spacious, the **Museo de Bellas Artes** (San Pío V; ☎963 87 03 00; www. museobellasartesvalencia. gva.es; Calle de San Pío V 9; ⏰10am-8pm Tue-Sun) ranks among Spain's best. Highlights include the grandiose Roman Mosaic of the Nine Muses, a collection of magnificent late-medieval altarpieces, and works by El Greco, Goya and Velázquez.

For a dose of greenery, stroll the **Jardines del Turia** (🚻). Stretching the length of the Río Turia's former course, this 9km-long park is a fabulous mix of playing fields, walking paths, lawns and playgrounds.

✕ 🛏 p237, p259

235

Eating & Sleeping

Barcelona ❶

✖ La Vinateria del Call — Spanish €€

(☎93 302 60 92; www.lavinateriadelcall.
com; Carrer Salomó Ben Adret 9; raciones
€7-18; ◷7.30pm-1am; 🛜; Ⓜ Jaume I) In a
magical, rambling setting in the former Jewish
quarter, this tiny candlelit jewel-box of a wine
bar serves up divine Iberian sharing plates
dancing from Galician-style octopus and cider-
cooked chorizo to perfect *truites* (omelettes)
and Catalan *escalivada* (roasted peppers,
aubergine and onions). Spot-on service,
super-fresh local ingredients and a wonderful
selection of wines and artisan cheeses from
across Spain.

🛏 Praktik Rambla — Boutique Hotel €€

(☎93 343 66 90; www.hotelpraktikrambla.
com; Rambla de Catalunya 27; s/d/tr from
€122/135/169; ✼ 🛜; Ⓜ Passeig de Gràcia)
On a leafy boulevard, this early-19th-century
gem of a mansion hides a gorgeous little
boutique number designed by beloved local
interior designer Lázaro Rosa-Violán. While
high ceilings, patterned walls and original tiles
have been maintained, the 43 rooms have
bold ceramics, spot lighting and
contemporary art.

The relaxed library and back terrace are
perfect for enjoying the complimentary coffee
and croissants.

Lleida ❷

✖ Bar Bodega Blasi — Tapas €

(☎973 22 88 17; Carrer Sant Martí 2; tapas
€4-12; ◷10am-11.30pm Mon-Sat, noon-5pm
Sun; 🛜) With tables on a small plaza, the
lively, long-running Bar Bodega Blasi is one of
the best places to be on a warm evening. Join
locals over vermouth and an extensive tapas
selection including codfish tortilla, regional
cheese platters, squid croquettes or fried
artichokes in season.

Alquézar ❸

🛏 Hotel Villa de Alquézar — Hotel €€

(☎974 31 84 16; www.villadealquezar.com;
Calle Pedro Arnal Cavero 12; incl breakfast s
€68-86, d €76-125; ◷ closed late Dec-late Jan;
🅿 ✼ 🛜 ⊕) This lovely larger hotel has plenty
of style and period touches in its 34 airy rooms.
The most expensive (top-floor) rooms are large
with wonderful covered balconies – perfect for
watching the sun set over town with a glass of
Somontano wine. The 12m swimming pool is a
notable plus.

Huesca ❹

✖ Tatau Bistro — Tapas €€

(☎974 04 20 78; www.tatau.es; Calle Azara; dishes
€6-24; ◷1-3.30pm & 8.30-10.30pm Tue-Sat; 🛜)
This hugely popular gastro-bar has besuited staff,
1950s-inspired decor and seating at a few tables
or along the bar. The changing menu of artistically
presented offerings ranges from the relatively
simple (meat croquettes) to the likes of trout
tartare or succulent pressed duck. Servings are
mostly small to medium-size, so be ready to order
a few – and arrive early, or book ahead.

Zaragoza ❺

✖ Casa Lac — Tapas €€

(☎976 39 61 96; www.restaurantecasalac.es;
Calle de los Mártires 12; mains €16-27, tapas
€3.50-6, raciones €14-19, set menus €40-43;
◷1-4pm & 8pm-midnight Mon-Sat, 1-4pm Sun)
The grande dame of Zaragoza dining, Casa Lac
opened in 1825 and is reputedly Spain's oldest
licensed restaurant. The cuisine today is tastily
contemporary whether you go for 'gastro-
tapas', a set menu (there's a vegetarian option)
or à la carte. The ground-floor bar is smart but
relatively casual; an elegant staircase leads to
the slightly more formal upstairs dining room
(reservations advised).

🛏 Hotel Sauce   Hotel €

(📞976 20 50 50; www.hotelsauce.com; Calle de Espoz y Mina 33; s €42-70, d €45-80; ❄🛜) This stylish family-run hotel with a great central location provides fresh, cheerful, contemporary rooms with walk-in showers, tasteful watercolours, outstandingly friendly and helpful staff, and a pleasant 24-hour cafe serving excellent breakfasts, cakes and cocktails. Prices are very reasonable given everything the hotel provides.

Daroca ⑥

🛏 La Posada del Almudí   Heritage Hotel €€

(📞976 80 06 06; www.posadadelalmudi.es; Calle Grajera 7; incl breakfast s €45, d €68-80; ❄🛜) This lovely old place exudes charm. The rooms in the main building, a 16th-century palace, have been lovingly restored, while a separate building across the street houses more contemporary rooms with stylish black-and-white decor – all are ample-sized. The restaurant (set menu €12.50) offers good local cuisine.

Albarracín ⑧

🍴 Tiempo de Ensueño   Contemporary Spanish €€

(📞978 70 60 70; www.tiempodeensuenyo.com; Calle Palacios 1B; mains €19-20, menú €42; 🕑1.30-3.30pm Mon & Wed, 1.30-3.30pm & 8.30-10.30pm Thu-Sun) This sleek, light-filled dining room comes with attentive but discreet service and changing menus of innovative food that you'll remember. The venison was the tenderest we've ever had, the *jamón* starter an enormous platter, and the dessert of caramelised *torrija* (French toast) with passion-fruit sorbet divine.

🛏 La Casa del Tío Americano   Boutique Hotel €€

(📞978 71 01 25; www.lacasadeltioamericano. com; Calle Los Palacios 9; s/d incl breakfast €80/100; 🛜) A wonderful small hotel, 'The House of the American Uncle' proffers brightly painted rooms and friendly, impeccable service. The village views from the breakfast terrace (and from galleried rooms 2 and 3) are magnificent. A welcoming bottle of champagne is a lovely touch, and the generous breakfast features local cheeses, honey and ham.

Teruel ⑨

🛏 Hotel El Mudayyan   Boutique Hotel €€

(📞978 62 30 42; www.elmudayyan.com; Calle Nueva 18; s €40-95, d €45-120; ❄🛜) The modern, clean, comfortable rooms and friendly, efficient staff are reason enough to stay here, but pushing the boat out further are fantastic buffet breakfasts, including bacon and eggs and homemade pastries (per person €5.90), and a secret 16th-century tunnel to the priest's house of the church next door (staff give free tours at 10am).

Valencia ⑪

🍴 El Tap   Valencian €€

(📞963 91 26 27; www.facebook.com/ restauranteeltapvalencia; Calle de Roteros 9; mains €10-18; 🕑7.30-11.30pm Mon-Fri, 1.30-3.30pm & 7.30-11.30pm Sat; 🛜) The Tap is one of Barrio del Carmen's rich selection of small, characterful restaurants and is genuinely welcoming. The food is market-based and originally and delightfully prepared. Dishes with local tomatoes are a standout, and there's a carefully chosen list of both wines and boutique beers. Excellent value.

🛏 Hostal Antigua Morellana   Hostal €€

(📞963 91 57 73; www.hostalam.com; Calle En Bou 2; s/d €55/70; ❄@🛜) This friendly, family-run, 18-room spot occupies a renovated 18th-century *posada* (where wealthier merchants bringing produce to market would spend the night) and has cosy, good-sized rooms, many with balconies. It's kept shipshape by the house-proud owners and there are lots of great features, including memory-foam mattresses, handsome fabrics and a lounge with coffee. Higher floors have more natural light. Great value.

STRETCH YOUR LEGS
BARCELONA

Start Parc de la Ciutadella

Finish Casa Batlló

Distance 3.5km

Duration Three hours

Packed with historic treasures and jaw-dropping architecture, Barcelona is a wanderer's delight. This stroll takes you through atmospheric medieval lanes and along elegant boulevards, leading you past Gothic cathedrals, lively tapas bars and palm-fringed plazas.

Take this walk on Trips

Parc de la Ciutadella

The handsomely landscaped Parc de la Ciutadella is a local favourite for a leisurely promenade. Start in the northeast corner, and descend past the monumental **Cascada** (waterfall), then stroll south across the park, passing a small pond and Catalonia's regional parliament.

The Walk » With your back to the park, cross Passeig de Picasso and walk along restaurant-lined Passeig del Born. According to legend, jousting matches were once held here.

Basílica de Santa Maria del Mar

Nothing prepares you for the singular beauty of **Basílica de Santa Maria del Mar** (☏93 310 23 90; www.santamariadelmarbarcelona.org; Plaça de Santa Maria del Mar; guided tour €8.50-10; ⊙9am-8.30pm Mon-Sat, 10am-8pm Sun, tours 1-5pm Sat, from 2pm Sun; Ⓜ Jaume I). Barcelona's most stirring Gothic structure, the 14th-century church was built in just 59 years.

The Walk » Take Carrer de l'Argenteria up to Via Laietana. Cross this busy road, continuing along Carrer de la Llibreteria. Turn right onto Carrer de la Freneria. After a few blocks, you'll see the massive cathedral on your left.

La Catedral

For centuries the spiritual heart of Barcelona, **La Catedral** (☏93 342 82 62; www.catedralbcn.org; Plaça de la Seu; €7, roof or choir €3, chapter house €2; ⊙worship 8.30am-12.30pm & 5.45-7.30pm Mon-Fri, 8.30am-12.30pm & 5.15-8pm Sat, 8.30am-1.45pm & 5.15-8pm Sun, tourist visits 12.30-7.45pm Mon-Fri, 12.30-5.30pm Sat, 2-5.30pm Sun; Ⓜ Jaume I) is at once lavish and sombre, anchoring the city in its past. Begun in the late 13th century and not completed until six centuries later, the cathedral is Barcelona's history rendered in stone.

The Walk » Turn left down Carrer del Bispe, and take a right onto Plaça Sant Jaume. A few blocks further, turn left onto narrow Carrer del Vidre, which leads to the plaza.

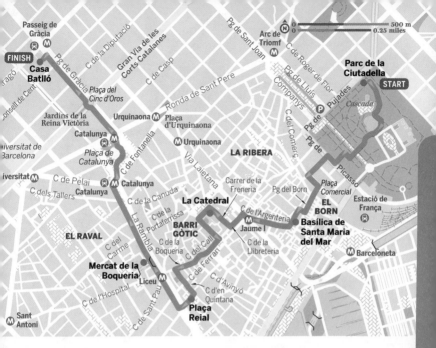

Plaça Reial

One of the most photogenic squares in Barcelona, the Plaça Reial is not to be missed. Numerous eateries, bars and nightspots lie beneath the arcades of 19th-century neoclassical buildings, with a buzz of activity at all hours. The lamp posts by the central fountain are Antoni Gaudí's first known works in the city.

The Walk >> Exit the square onto famous La Rambla, a bustling boulevard with a wide pedestrian-filled strip in the middle. Walk north a few blocks until you see the large cast-iron market off to your left.

Mercat de la Boqueria

This temple of temptation is one of Europe's greatest **food markets** (☎93 318 20 17; www.boqueria.barcelona; La Rambla 91; ⏰8am-8.30pm Mon-Sat; Ⓜ Liceu). Step inside for a seemingly endless bounty of glistening fruits and vegetables, smoked meats, pungent cheeses and chocolate truffles.

The Walk >> Continue north on La Rambla, cross diagonally the Plaça de Catalunya and turn left onto the grand boutique-lined Passeig de Gràcia. A few blocks up, you'll reach Gaudí's architectural masterpiece.

Casa Batlló

Even Gaudí outdid himself with this fantastical **apartment block** (☎93 216 03 06; www.casabatllo.es; Passeig de Gràcia 43; adult/child over 6 yr €29/26; ⏰9am-8pm, last admission 7pm; Ⓜ Passeig de Gràcia): an astonishing confection of rippling balconies, optical illusions and twisted chimney pots along Barcelona's grandest boulevard. The facade, sprinkled with bits of blue, mauve and green tiles and studded with wave-shaped window frames and balconies, rises to an uneven blue-tiled roof with a solitary tower.

The Walk >> Since it's a long walk back to the start, hop on the metro and head to Arc de Trionf station, a short stroll from Parc de la Ciutadella.

Andalucía & Southern Spain

WITH ITS EXHILARATING LANDSCAPES, HISTORIC CITIES AND FIERY FLAMENCO TRADITIONS, Andalucía encapsulates much of the beauty and drama of Spain's sun-baked south.

The region boasts some of the country's greatest monuments and busiest coastal stretches, as well as snow-capped mountains, remote *pueblos blancos* and endless swathes of silver-green olive groves.

A network of well-maintained roads snakes across the ever-changing landscape, leading from the wild peaks of the Sierra Nevada to the Moorish masterpieces of Córdoba and Granada, from seductive Seville to the pearly white villages of Cádiz province and the brassy beach resorts of Málaga's Costa del Sol.

Córdoba Mezquita (p274)
EMPERORCOSAR/SHUTTERSTOCK ©

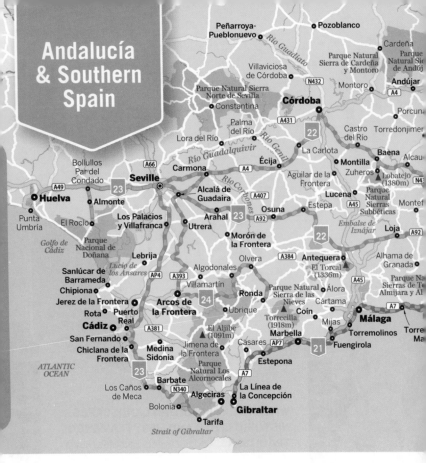

Andalucía & Southern Spain

20 **Mediterranean Meander 7 Days**
More than 1000km of coastal splendour provide an ever-changing window onto the Mediterranean.

21 **Costa del Sol Beyond the Beaches 3–4 Days**
There's far more than tacky resorts on Spain's much-maligned southern Costa.

22 **Golden Triangle 5–7 Days**
Discover the potent legacy of the Moors on this Seville–Córdoba–Granada link-up.

23 **The Great Outdoors 7 Days**
Experience mainland Spain's highest mountains and one of Europe's most unique wetlands.

24 **Andalucía's White Villages 4 Days**
Tour Andalucía's mythical hilltop villages in the region's green, craggy hinterland.

25 **Olive Oil & the Renaissance in Jaén 3–4 Days**
Olive oil and Renaissance architecture go hand in hand on this romp through Andalucía's remote northeast.

DON'T MISS

Zuheros

A spectacular white village in Córdoba province that's off the main *pueblo blanco* circuit. Visit it on trip 22

Cabo de Gata

A slice of unspoiled coastline boasting dramatic cliffs, gorgeous beaches and an arid, semi-desert hinterland. Explore it on trip 20

Paraje Natural Torcal de Antequera

A bizarre, rocky moonscape in the uplands overlooking Antequera; weird and wonderful even by Andalucian standards. Stop by on trip 23

Orchidarium

Europe's largest collection of orchids blooms in a large glass dome in the Costa del Sol beach town of Estepona. Meander through it on trip 21

Sendero del Acantilado

A clifftop path starting in the hip, beach town of Los Canos de Meca on the Costa de la Luz. Hike it on trip 23

Estepona Orchid, Orchidarium (p267)

243

Classic Trip

Mediterranean Meander

20

From Málaga to Barcelona, discover the treasures of Spain's Mediterranean seaboard – Roman ruins, dramatic castles, artistic masterpieces and fabulous festivals.

TRIP HIGHLIGHTS

1107 km

Barcelona's La Rambla
Stretch your legs on Barcelona's celebrated boulevard

Tarragona

FINISH

756 km

Ciudad de las Artes y las Ciencias
See the future at Valencia's cutting edge City of Arts and Sciences

Xàtiva

Cartagena

START

Mojácar

Museo Picasso Málaga
Admire works by the great 20th-century artist in his hometown

1 km

Cabo de Gata
Precious enclave of pure unblemished Mediterranean coastline

249km

**7 DAYS
1107KM / 688 MILES**

GREAT FOR...

BEST TIME TO GO

March to June is sunny, but not too hot, and there are plenty of festivals, including Las Fallas.

ESSENTIAL PHOTO

The chameleonic Sagrada Familia, which which changes every time you visit.

BEST FOR OUTDOORS

Parque Natural de Cabo de Gata-Nijar.

Classic Trip

20 Mediterranean Meander

From the Costa Daurada to the Costa del Sol, from Catalan pride to Andalucian passion, from Roman ruins in Tarragona to Barcelona's flamboyant Modernisme buildings: this drive provides technicolour proof that not all southern Spain is a beach bucket of cheesy tourist clichés. The full 1107km trajectory passes through four regions, two languages, Spain's second-, third- and sixth-largest cities, and beaches too numerous to count.

TRIP HIGHLIGHT

❶ Málaga

The Costa del Sol can seem a pretty soulless place until you hit Málaga, the Andalucian city everyone is talking about. For decades the city was overlooked by the millions of tourists who crowded the Costa's seaside resorts but in recent years it has transformed itself into a hip, stylish metropolis brimming with youthful vigour. It boasts 30-odd museums and an edgy urban art scene as well as contemporary restaurants, boutique hotels and stylish shopping.

Art-lovers are spoiled for choice at museums such as the **Museo Ruso de Málaga** (📞951 92 61 50; www.coleccionmuseoruso. es; Avenida de Sor Teresa Prat 15; €6, incl temporary exhibitions €8, free 4-8pm Sun; ⏰9.30am-8pm Tue-Sun; 🅿) and **Centre Pompidou Málaga** (📞951 92 62 00; www.centrepompidou. es; Pasaje Doctor Carrillo Casaux, Muelle Uno; €7, incl temporary exhibition €9; ⏰9.30am-8pm Wed-Mon), while the **Museo de Málaga** (📞951 91 19 04; www.museosdeandalucia. es/museodemalaga; Plaza de la Aduana; EU member/ non-member free/€1.50; ⏰9am-9pm Tue-Sat, to 3pm Sun) houses an extensive archaeology collection. The city's premier museum is the unmissable **Museo Picasso Málaga** (📞952 12 76 00; www. museopicassomalaga.org; Calle San Agustín 8; €9, incl temporary exhibition €12, free

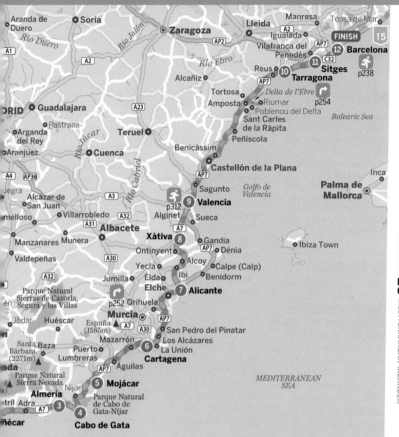

last 2hr before closing Sun;
🕙10am-8pm Jul & Aug, to 7pm
Mar-Jun, Sep & Oct, to 6pm
Nov-Feb), dedicated to the
Málaga-born artist.

For an edgier, urban
scene head to the **Soho**
neighbourhood near the
port where you'll find
giant murals, arty cafes,
ethnic restaurants and
street markets.

 LINK YOUR TRIP

21 Costa del Sol Beyond the Beaches

Can't get enough of the
Mediterranean? Jump
on this trip in Málaga
and hug the coast all
the way to Gibraltar.

15 Artistic Inspiration on the Costa Brava

You can also extend
this trip at its Catalan
nexus, heading north
out of Barcelona along
the Costa Brava.

Classic Trip

✕ 🛏 p258, p269

The Drive » Head east out of Málaga on the A7. This is southern Spain's main coastal road (also known as the E15) and will be your companion for much of this trip. The coast gets ever more precipitous as you move east into Granada province. After 68km turn south on the N340 and follow for 8km into Almuñécar.

----

② Almuñécar

There's a hint of Italy's Amalfi Coast about the Costa Tropical, Granada province's 80km coastline. Named for its subtropical microclimate, it's often dramatically beautiful, with dun-brown mountains and whitewashed villages huddled into coves and bays. The area's main

resort is the popular summer destination of Almuñécar.

Summer action is focused on Almuñécar's long seafront whose two beaches are divided by a rocky outcrop, the **Peñón del Santo** (⊙7am-midnight May-Sep, 8am-10pm Oct-Apr). To the west of this stretches the pebbly **Playa de San Cristóbal**, while to the east the grey-sanded **Playa Puerta del Mar** fronts the old town.

Up in the *casco antiguo*, the small **Museo Arqueológico Cueva de Siete Palacios** (📞958 83 86 23; Calle San Joaquín; combined ticket Castillo de San Miguel adult/child €2.35/1.60; ⊙10am-1.30pm & 6.30-9pm Tue-Sat, 10am-1pm Sun Jul–mid-Sep, shorter hours mid-Sep–Jun) displays ancient finds in a series of underground stone cellars. Tickets also include entry to the hilltop **Castillo**

de San Miguel (📞650 027584; Explanada del Castillo; combined ticket Museo Arqueológico adult/child €2.35/1.60, free 10am-1pm Fri; ⊙10am-1.30pm & 6.30-9pm Tue-Sat, 10am-1pm Sun Jul–mid-Sep, shorter hours mid-Sep–Jun).

The Drive » Continue eastwards on the A7, skirting around Motril and passing increasing numbers of unsightly plastic greenhouses as the landscape becomes ever more arid. Almería beckons. All told, it's about 130km to Almería.

----

③ Almería

Don't overlook Almería, an energetic waterfront city with an illustrious past. Once the main port for the 10th-century Córdoba caliphate, the sun-baked city has a handsome centre, punctuated by palm-fringed plazas and old churches, as well as several museums and

THE PICASSO TRAIL

Málaga and Barcelona are linked by more than Mediterranean beaches – both cities have a strong connection with Pablo Ruiz Picasso (1881–1973). The great painter was born in Málaga and spent the first 10 years of his life there. In 1891 he and his family moved to A Coruña and then, in 1895, he transferred to Barcelona where he lived on and off during the early 1900s.

In Málaga you can get an intimate insight into the painter's childhood at the **Casa Natal de Picasso** (www.fundacionpicasso.malaga.eu; Plaza de la Merced 15; €3, incl Sala de Exposiciones €4; ⊙9.30am-8pm, closed Tue Nov-Mar), the house where he was born in 1881. Nearby, the Museo Picasso Málaga (p246) displays more than 200 of his works. The collection at the Museu Picasso (p257) in Barcelona is even larger, comprising around 3500 works, many from his formative early years.

On a more modest scale, Alicante's Museo de Arte Contemporáneo (p253) displays his *Portrait d'Arthur Rimbaud* (1960), while the Museu Cau Ferrat (p256) is housed in the Sitges home of his friend, the late artist Santiago Rusiñol.

plenty of fantastic tapas bars. Its main draw is its spectacular **Alcazaba** (📞950 80 10 08; Calle Almanzor; 🕙9am-3pm & 7-10pm Tue-Sat mid-Jun–mid-Sep, 9am-8pm Tue-Sat Apr–mid-Jun, 9am-6pm Tue-Sat mid-Sep–Mar, 9am-3pm Sun year-round), once one of the most powerful Moorish fortresses in Spain.

At the foot of the hilltop fort sprawls the maze-like **Almedina**, the old Moorish quarter. Continue through this to the city's six-towered **catedral** (📞605 396483; www.catedralalmeria. com; Plaza de la Catedral 8, entrance Calle Velázquez; €5; 🕙10am-7pm Mon-Fri, 10am-2.30pm & 3.30-7pm Sat, 1.30-7pm Sun Apr-Sep, to 6:30pm Oct-Mar), another formidable structure with an impressive Gothic interior. Nearby, the **Museo de la Guitarra** (📞950 27 43 58; Ronda del Beato Diego Ventaja; adult/reduced €3/2; 🕙10.30am-1.30pm Tue-Sun year-round, plus 6-9pm Tue-Sat Jun-Sep, 5-8pm Tue-Sat Oct-May) charts Almeria's role in the development of the iconic instrument.

Round off your sightseeing with a soak at the **Hammam Aire de Almería** (📞950 28 20 95; www.beaire.com; Plaza de la Constitución 5; 1½hr session Mon-Thu €29, Fri-Sun €35; 🕙9am-10.30pm), a modern-day version of an Arabic bathhouse.

 p258

TOP TIP: TOLL ROADS

The AP7 (also known as E15), is a toll-charging *autopista* (motorway) that parallels much of Spain's southern and eastern coastlines. You will have to stop periodically to pay a toll at manned booths. However, as of 1 January 2020, tolls were scrapped on the AP7 between Tarragona and Alicante.

The confusingly named A7 follows a similar route to the AP7, but is entirely toll-free. The N340 is a third road paralleling Spain's southern coast, although much of it has merged with the A7. Some of the N340 follows the route of the Roman Vía Augustus.

The Drive » Head east out of Almeria on the N340a to join up with the AL12 airport road and its continuation the N344. Continue on this, following signs to San José through a series of small roundabouts near Retamar. Eventually you should emerge onto the AL3108 which runs through low hills to Cabo de Gata (total distance 40km).

- - - - - - - - - - - - - - - - - - -

TRIP HIGHLIGHT

4 Cabo de Gata

Covering Spain's southeastern tip, the **Parque Natural de Cabo de Gata-Níjar** boasts some of Andalucía's most flawless and least crowded beaches. These glorious *playas* lie strung along the area's dramatic cliff-bound coastline while inland remote white villages dot the stark, semi-desert hinterland.

On the park's east coast, the low-key resort of **San José** makes an ideal base. It's well set up with hotels and restaurants and the surrounding coastline hides several sublime beaches. The most beautiful, including **Playa de los Genoveses** (P) and **Playa de Mónsul** (P) are accessible by a dirt road signposted 'Playas' and/or 'Genoveses/Mónsul'.

For more active pursuits, you can walk the park's coastal paths or organise diving, kayaking, bike hire and guided tours at agencies across town – try **MedialunAventura** (📞667 224861; www.medialun aventura.com; Calle del Puerto 7; rental per hour/day kayak €12/40, double kayak €18/60, SUP €12/45, bike hire per half-day/day €15/20; 🕙9am-2pm & 5-8pm, to 10pm summer).

The Drive » Follow the AL3108 inland from San José until you hit the A7 just shy of Nijar. Head northeast towards Valencia for 43km to exit 520. Come off here and follow signs to Mojácar along the A370 and AL6111.

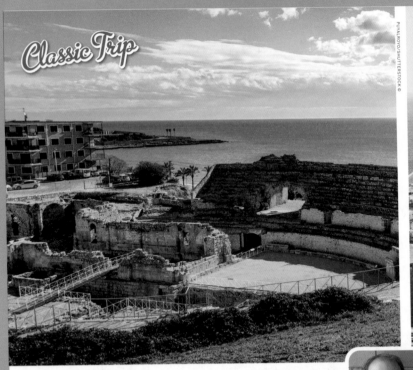

PUYALROYO/SHUTTERSTOCK ©

TONO BALAGUER/SHUTTERSTOCK ©

Classic Trip

WHY THIS IS A CLASSIC TRIP
DUNCAN GARWOOD, AUTHOR

What makes this epic coastal drive so special is the sheer variety it provides. There's history and culture galore with Roman ruins in Tarragona, Picasso paintings in Málaga and modern architecture in Barcelona and Valencia. Boisterous beach resorts offer hedonism and hard partying while peace-lovers will enjoy the unsullied coastal beauty of Cabo de Gata, one of Andalucía's great natural highlights.

Above: **Tarragona** Roman amphitheatre (p255)
Left: **Cabo de Gata** Playa de Mónsul (p249)
Right: **Málaga** Waterfront (p246)

ANDRES GARCIA MARTIN/SHUTTERSTOCK ©

⑤ Mojácar

Tucked away in an isolated corner of Almería province, Mojácar is both a seaside resort and a charming hill town. Mojácar Pueblo, a picturesque jumble of white-cube houses, sits atop a hillside 3km inland from Mojácar Playa, a modern low-rise resort fronting 7km of sandy beach.

Exploring Mojácar Pueblo is mainly a matter of wandering its maze-like streets, stopping off at craft shops, galleries and boutiques. You can see how life in the town once was at the **Casa La Canana** (🕿950 16 44 20; Calle Esteve 6, Mojácar Pueblo; adult/child €2.50/1; ☺10.30am-2.30pm daily, plus 5-8pm Tue, Wed, Fri & Sat), and admire sweeping views from the lofty **Mirador del Castillo** (Plaza Mirador del Castillo, Mojácar Pueblo).

Down at Mojácar Playa, you'll find the best sands at the southern end of town, which also has a pleasant seafront promenade.

🛏 p258

The Drive » Retrace your steps from Mojácar back onto the northbound A7. After 10km merge onto the toll-charging AP7 near Vera and continue to the exit for Cartagena Oeste. Take this and follow the signposted route along the N332 into the city. Mojácar to Cartagena is 134km.

6 Cartagena

Cartagena's fabulous natural harbour has been used for thousands of years. Stand on the battlements of the castle that overlooks the city and you can literally see layer upon layer of history spread below you, from the wharf where Phoenician traders docked their ships to the streets where Roman legionaries once marched, from the factories of the industrial age to the contemporary warships of what is still an important naval base.

As archaeologists continue to unearth the city's ancient roots, it is finally starting to get the recognition it deserves. Highlights include the **Museo Nacional de Arqueología Subacuática** (ARQUA; 968 12 11 66; http://museoarqua.mcu.es; Paseo de Alfonso XII 22; adult/child €3/free, Sat afternoon & Sun free; 10am-8pm or 9pm Tue-Sat, to 3pm Sun), an excellent museum dedicated to underwater archaeology and maritime history, and the **Museo del Teatro Romano** (www.teatroromanocartagena.org; Plaza del Ayuntamiento 9; adult/child €6/5; 10am-8pm Tue-Sat, to 2pm Sun May-Sep, to 6pm Tue-Sat, to 2pm Sun Oct-Apr), centred on a 1st-century-BCE Roman theatre.

✕ 🛏 p191, p258

The Drive ≫ Double back to the AP7 and head north towards Alicante. After 75km the *autopista* rejoins the A7. Follow this for 32km before taking exit 17A signposted for Alicante.

7 Alicante

Of all mainland Spain's provincial capitals, Alicante is the most tourist-driven. Nevertheless, it's a dynamic, attractive city with a castle, old quarter and long waterfront. The eating scene is exciting and the nightlife is legendary.

There are sweeping views over the city from the large 16th-century **Castillo de Santa Bárbara** (965 15 29 69; www.castillodesantabarbara. com; Calle Vázquez de Mella;

DETOUR:
ORIHUELA

Start: 6 Cartagena

Beside the Río Segura and flush with the base of a barren mountain of rock, Orihuela harbours some superb Gothic, Renaissance and baroque buildings. Its old town, once the second city of the kingdom of Valencia, is strung out between the river and the castle-capped mountain.

Standout sights include the 14th-century Catalan Gothic **Catedral de San Salvador** (965 30 48 28; Calle Doctor Sarget; adult/child €2/free; 10.30am-2pm & 4-6.30pm Mon-Fri, 10.30am-2pm Sat), which features three finely carved portals and an exquisite two-level cloister. Nearby, the **Museo Diocesano de Arte Sacro** (673 425681; Calle Mayor de Ramón y Cajal; adult/child €4/free; 10am-2pm & 4-7pm Mon-Sat, 10am-2pm Sun) has a fine display of religious art, culminating in Velázquez' *Temptation of St Thomas*. Also worth searching out is the **Colegio de Santo Domingo** (965 30 02 40; http://colegio.cdsantodomingo.com; Calle Adolfo Clavarana; adult/child €2/1; 9.30am-1.30pm or 2pm & 4-7pm or 5-8pm Tue-Fri, from 10am Sat, 10am-2pm Sun), a 16th-century convent with two fine Renaissance cloisters.

To reach Orihuela, branch west off the AP7 around 60km north of Cartagena and continue on the CV945 and CV95.

⏲10am-10pm Apr-Sep, to 8pm Oct-Mar), which also houses a museum recounting the history of Alicante. Further historical artefacts await in the **Museo Arqueológico de Alicante** (MARQ; ☎965 14 90 00; www.marqalicante. com; Plaza Dr Gómez Ulla; adult/child €3/1.50; ⏲10am-7pm Tue-Fri, 10am-8.30pm Sat, 10am-2pm Sun mid-Sep–mid-Jun, 10am-2pm & 6-10pm Tue-Sat, 10am-2pm Sun mid-Jun–mid-Sep), which has a strong collection of ceramics and Iberian art. For a more contemporary outlook, the free **Museo de Arte Contemporáneo de Alicante** (MACA; ☎965 21 31 56; www.maca-alicante. es; Plaza Santa María 3; ⏲10am-8pm Tue-Sat, from 11am summer, 10am-2pm Sun) impresses with its displays of works by the likes of Dalí, Miró, Picasso and others.

✖ p258

 The Drive » Leave Alicante on the A77 signposted Valencia and continue on to the A7. The *autovía* proceeds north, passing through a couple of tunnels and heading progressively downhill as it forges inland towards Valencia. After almost 90km, exit on the CV645 signposted Xàtiva. From here it's about 5km to the town.

- - - - - - - - - - - - - - - - - -

8 Xàtiva

Xàtiva (Spanish: Játiva) is often visited on a day trip from Valencia or, as in this case, as a

stop on the way north from Alicante. It has an intriguing historic quarter and a mighty castle strung along the crest of the Serra Vernissa, with the town snuggled at its base.

The Muslims established Europe's first paper-manufacturing plant in Xàtiva, which is also famous as the birthplace of the Borgia Popes Calixtus III and Alexander VI. The town's glory days ended in 1707 when Felipe V's troops torched most of the town.

Xàtiva's **castle** (☎962 274 274; www.xativaturismo. com; adult/child €2.40/1.20; ⏲10am-6pm Tue-Sun Nov-Mar, to 7pm Apr-Oct), which clasps the summit of a double-peaked hill overlooking the old town, is one of the most evocative in the Valencia region. Behind its crumbling battlements you'll find flower gardens (bring a picnic), tumbledown turrets, towers and other buildings. The walk up to the castle is a long one (2km), but the views are sensational.

Classic Trip

The Drive » Use the N340 to rejoin the A7 and head north to Valencia. Just outside the city, where the A7 merges with the AP7, take the V31, Valencia's main southern access road for the final push into the city centre. All told, the 63km journey should take around 50 minutes.

TRIP HIGHLIGHT

9 Valencia

Valencia, Spain's third-largest city, exudes confidence. Content for Madrid and Barcelona to grab the headlines, it quietly gets on with being a wonderfully liveable spot, hosting thriving cultural, eating and nightlife scenes. Its star attraction is the strikingly futuristic

Ciudad de las Artes y las Ciencias (City of Arts & Sciences; ☎961 97 46 86; www.cac.es; Avenida del Professor López Piñero; 🚻) on the old Turia riverbed. Counting an opera house, science museum, 3D cinema and aquarium, the complex was largely the work of local-born starchitect Santiago Calatrava.

Other brilliant contemporary buildings grace the city, which also has a fistful of fabulous Modernista buildings, great museums, a long stretch of beach and a large, characterful old quarter. Look out for **La Lonja** (☎962 08 41 53; www.valencia.es; Calle de la Lonja; adult/child €2/1, Sun free; ⊙10am-7pm Mon-Sat, to 2pm Sun), Valencia's late 15th-century silk and commodity exchange, and the **Mercado Central** (☎963 82 91 00; www.

mercadocentralvalencia.es; Plaza del Mercado; ⊙7.30am-3pm Mon-Sat), the vast Modernista market.

The city also enjoys prime foodie credentials as the home of *paella* but its buzzing dining scene offers plenty more besides.

✕ 🛏 p237, p259

The Drive » Leave Valencia on the V21 signposted Puçol. After 23km or so you'll rejoin your old friend, the AP7, which will whisk you 200km up the coast into Catalonia. Come off at exit 38 and continue on the A7 for the final 35km into Tarragona. Reckon on 257km for the entire leg.

10 Tarragona

In the effervescent port city of Tarragona, Roman history collides with beaches, bars and a food scene that perfumes the air with

DETOUR: DELTA DE L'EBRE

Start: 9 Valencia

Near Catalonia's southern border, the Delta de l'Ebre is a remote, exposed place of reed-fringed lagoons, dune-backed beaches and mirror-smooth marshes. Some 78 sq km are protected in the **Parc Natural del Delta de l'Ebre**, northern Spain's most important waterbird habitat. Migration season (October and November) sees bird populations peak, but birds are also numerous in winter and spring.

Even if you're not a twitcher, the park is worth a visit. The landscape, with its whitewashed farmhouses and electric-green rice paddies, is hauntingly beautiful and the flat waterside trails are ideal for cyclists and ramblers.

Scruffy **Deltebre** sits at the centre of the delta but smaller villages like **Riumar** or **Poblenou del Delta** are more appealing.

To reach Deltebre, branch off the AP7 at exit 41, 180km north of Valencia. Take the N340 to connect with the TV3454 which leads to the town some 13km to the east.

Valencia Mercado Central

freshly grilled seafood. The main drawcard is the city's collection of ancient ruins, including a mosaic-packed museum and a seaside amphitheatre where gladiators once faced each other (or wild animals) in mortal combat. The Unesco-listed Roman sites are scattered around town but you can get a combined ticket at the **Museu d'Historia de Tarragona** (MHT; www.tarragona.cat/patrimoni/museu-historia; adult per site/4 sites/all sites €3.30/7.40/11.05, children free).

A roll-call of fantastic places to eat and drink is a good reason to linger in the attractive medieval centre. This maze of cobbled lanes is encircled by steep walls and crowned by a towering **catedral** (www.catedraldetarragona.com; Plaça de la Seu; adult/child €5/3; ⏱10am-8pm Mon-Sat mid-Jun–mid-Sep, to 7pm Mon-Sat mid-Mar–mid-Jun & mid-Sep–Oct, to 5pm Mon-Fri, to 7pm Sat Nov–mid-Mar) with Romanesque and Gothic flourishes.

✕ 🛏 p259

The Drive » From Tarragona use the N240 to get back on the AP7 and head east towards Barcelona. After about 11km take exit 31 onto the C32. Follow this for just over 30km, crossing one viaduct and burrowing through two tunnels, to Sitges.

⑪ Sitges

Just 40km shy of Barcelona, Sitges has been a favourite beach resort since the 19th century. The former fishing village, which was a key location for the Modernisme art movement and is now one of Spain's premier gay destinations, is renowned for its party beach life, riotous carnival celebrations and hedonistic nightlife – at its most bacchanalian in July and August. Despite this, it remains a classy destination with a good array of galleries and museums and plenty of restaurants in its boutique-laden historic centre.

Sunseekers will enjoy its long sandy beach which is flanked by the seafront **Passeig Marítim**. The cultural highlight is the **Museu del Cau Ferrat** (www.museusdesitges.cat; Carrer de Fonollar; incl Museu de Maricel adult/child €10/free; ⏱10am-8pm Tue-Sun Jul-Sep, to 7pm Mar-Jun & Oct, to 5pm Nov-Feb), built in the 1890s as a house-studio by artist Santiago Rusiñol – a pioneer of the Modernisme movement. The whitewashed mansion is full of his own art and that of his contemporaries, including his friend Picasso.

The Drive » It's only 40km to Barcelona. Get back onto the toll-charging C32 and fly through a multitude of tunnels. After about 30km, exit at junction 16B and follow signs for Barcelona, Gran Via and Centre Ciutat.

TRIP HIGHLIGHT

⑫ Barcelona

Barcelona is a guidebook in itself and a cultural colossus to rival Paris or Rome. The city's ever-evolving symbol is Gaudí's **Sagrada Família** (📞93 208 04 14; www.sagradafamilia.org; Carrer de la Marina; adult/child €20/free; ⏱9am-8pm Apr-Sep, to 7pm Mar & Oct, to 6pm Nov-Feb; Ⓜ Sagrada Família), which rises like an unfinished

---

LEGACY OF THE ROMANS

What did the Romans ever do for us? Well, quite a lot actually, as you'll discover as you drive up Spain's Mediterranean coast.

The Roman colonies in Hispania (their name for the Iberian peninsula) lasted from around 400 BCE to 200 BCE, and reminders of their existence lie dotted along the coast, from Andalucía to Catalonia.

In **Málaga** you can admire an **amphitheatre** (Roman Theatre; 📞951 50 11 15; Calle Alcazabilla 8; ⏱10am-6pm Tue-Sat, to 4pm Sun), dating from the 1st century CE when the settlement was called Malaca. An adjacent interpretive centre outlines its history and displays a few artefacts unearthed on the site.

Cartagena (Carthago Nova to the Romans) boasts several Roman sites, including the **Museo del Teatro Romano** (p252), centred on a 1st-century-BCE Roman theatre.

Further north, **Tarragona** (Tarraco) was once capital of Rome's Spanish provinces and has ruins to prove it, including an **amphitheatre** (Parc de l'Amfiteatre; adult/child €3.30/free; ⏱9am-9pm Tue-Sat Easter-Sep, to 7pm Tue-Sat Oct-Easter, to 3pm Sun year round), a forum, street foundations and the two-tiered **Aqüeducte de les Ferreres** (Pont del Diable; ⏱24hr; Ⓟ). Ocean-themed mosaics can be seen in the nearby **Museu Nacional Arqueològic de Tarragona** (www.mnat.cat; Plaça del Rei 5).

Barcelona La Rambla

symphony over L'Eixample district. The surrounding neighbourhood is renowned for its Modernisme architecture, which appears in buildings such as **La Pedrera** (Casa Milà; ☎93 214 25 76; www.lapedrera.com; Passeig de Gràcia 92; adult/child 7-12yr from €25/14; ⊗9am-8.30pm & 9-11pm Mar-Oct, 9am-6.30pm & 7-9pm Nov-Feb; Ⓜ Diagonal), a madcap Unesco-listed masterpiece with a rippling grey-stone facade and chimney pots resembling medieval knights. For more conventional, historical sights head to the Barri Gótic, home to the city's vast Gothic **La Catedral** (☎93 342 82 62; www. catedralbcn.org; Plaça de la Seu; €7, roof or choir €3, chapter house €2; ⊗worship 8.30am-12.30pm & 5.45-7.30pm Mon-Fri, 8.30am-12.30pm & 5.15-8pm Sat, 8.30am-1.45pm & 5.15-8pm Sun, tourist visits 12.30-7.45pm Mon-Fri, 12.30-5.30pm Sat, 2-5.30pm Sun; Ⓜ Jaume I), and the medieval La Ribera quarter where you'll find the excellent **Museu Picasso** (☎93 256 30 00; www.museupicasso. bcn.cat; Carrer de Montcada 15-23; adult/concession/under 18yr permanent collection & temporary exhibit €14/7.50/ free, 6-9.30pm Thu & 1st Sun of month free; ⊗10am-5pm Mon, 9am-8.30pm Tue, Wed & Fri-Sun, to 9.30pm Thu; Ⓜ Jaume I).

A good orientation point in this complex city is **La Rambla** (Ⓜ Catalunya, Liceu, Drassanes) – its tree-lined pedestrian promenade was made with the evening *paseo* (stroll) in mind. La Rambla divides the Barri Gòtic and La Ribera from the bohemian, multicultural El Raval neighbourhood. To the northeast lies the Modernisme-inspired L'Eixample quarter; to the south are the steep parks and gardens of Montjuic, site of the 1992 Olympics.

🍴 🛏 p236, p259

Eating & Sleeping

Málaga ❶

✗ El Mesón de Cervantes   Tapas €€

(☎952 21 62 74; www.elmesondecervantes.
com; Calle Álamos 11; medias raciones €4-10,
raciones €8-18; ⏱7pm-midnight Wed-Mon)
Cervantes started as a humble tapas bar run
by expat Argentine Gabriel Spatz, but has now
expanded into four bar-restaurants (each with
a slightly different bent), all within a block of
each other. This one is the HQ, where pretty
much everything on the menu is a showstopper – lamb stew with couscous; pumpkin
and mushroom risotto; and, boy, the grilled
octopus!

🛏 Molina Lario   Hotel €€€

(☎952 06 20 02; www.hotelmolinalario.com;
Calle Molina Lario 20; d €198-325; ❄🛜🏊)
Situated within confessional distance of the
cathedral, this four-star hotel has gracious
service and a sophisticated, contemporary
feel. The spacious, remodelled rooms are
decorated in subdued tones of beige and
white, with natural wood, crisp white linens and
marshmallow-soft pillows. Topping it all off is a
fabulous rooftop terrace and pool with views to
the sea and the cathedral.

Almería ❸

✗ Casa Puga   Tapas €€

(☎950 23 15 30; www.barcasapuga.es; Calle
Jovellanos 7; tapas from €1.70, raciones €7-18;
⏱noon-4pm & 8pm-midnight Mon-Sat) For an
authentic tapas experience, make a beeline for
this long-standing favourite, on the go since
1870. Shelves of ancient wine bottles and walls
plastered with lottery tickets and old maps set
the scene while well-practised waiters work
the bar, dishing out classical tapas prepared at
the tiny cooking station. Arrive early or expect
crowds.

Mojácar ❺

🛏 Hostal El Olivar   Hostal €

(☎950 47 20 02; www.hostalelolivar.es; Calle
Estación Nueva 11, Mojácar Pueblo; d incl
breakfast €53-70; ❄🛜) Friendly owners
Alberto and Michaela have completely
revamped this stylish boutiquey hostal, with
new paint, curtains, bedspreads, mini-fridges,
handmade furniture and a massage room.
Three rooms have balconies, and there's a
delightful sun terrace for lounging or lingering
over breakfast. An olive theme runs throughout,
with olive oil soaps and a tree whose 'leaves' are
handwritten notes from past guests.

Cartagena ❻

✗ La Marquesita   Spanish €€

(☎968 50 77 47; www.lamarquesita.net; Plaza
Alcolea 6; mains €13-24; ⏱1-4.30pm Tue, Wed
& Sun, 1-4.30pm & 8-11.30pm Thu-Sat; 🛜) On a
tucked-away plaza just off the pedestrian main
drag, this place is easily spotted by its riot of pot
plants. Sit in or out to enjoy quality fish dishes in
particular, with other traditional plates on offer.
The €22.50 weekday set lunch is excellent – you
might get a whole sea bass as a main.

Alicante ❼

✗ Cervecería Sento   Tapas €

(www.somossento.es; Calle Teniente Coronel
Chápuli 1; tapas €2-10; ⏱9am-midnight Sun-
Thu, to 1am Fri & Sat) Top-notch *montaditos*
(little rolls) and inventive grilled tapas (try the
turrón and pork 'Chupa Chups') are the reason
to squeeze into this brilliant little bar. Watching
the cheeky, nonstop staff in action is quite an
experience too: they make every visit intriguing.
It has bigger branches nearby, but this one has
the atmosphere.

Valencia 9

✗ Delicat — Tapas €€

(📞963 92 33 57; Calle Conde Almodóvar 4; dishes €8-18; 🕐1.45-3.30pm & 8.45-11.30pm Tue-Sat, 1.45-3.30pm Sun; 🛜) At this particularly friendly, intimate option, the open kitchen offers an unbeatable-value set menu of samplers for lunch (€14.50) and delicious tapas choices for dinner. The decor isn't lavish but the food is memorable. Book ahead as the small space fills fast.

🛏 Caro Hotel — Hotel €€€

(📞963 05 90 00; www.carohotel.com; Calle Almirante 14; d €170-350; 🅿 ❄ 🛜) Housed in a sumptuous 19th-century mansion, this hotel sits atop two millennia of Valencian history, with restoration revealing a hefty hunk of the Arab wall, Roman column bases and Gothic arches. Each room is furnished in soothing dark shades, with a great king-size bed and varnished concrete floors. Bathrooms are tops. For special occasions, reserve the Marqués suite, once the ballroom.

Tarragona 10

✗ Mercat Central — Market €

(Plaza Corsini; 🕐8.30am-9pm Mon-Sat) In a striking Modernista building, this historic 1915 market is looking better than ever thanks to a €47-million renovation completed in 2017. Temptations abound, from delectable fruits to cheeses and bakery items, plus food counters doling out seafood, charcuterie, sushi and Catalan wines. There's also a supermarket hidden downstairs.

🛏 Hotel Plaça de la Font — Hotel €€

(📞977 24 61 34; www.hotelpdelafont.com; Plaça de la Font 26; s/d/tr €63/80/100; ❄ 🛜) Comfortable modern rooms, individually decorated with photos of local monuments, make this cheerful, convenient hotel one of Tarragona's most attractive options. Rooms at the front have tiny balconies and are well soundproofed from the sociable murmur on bustling Plaça de la Font below. With tables right on the square, the hotel cafe is perfect for light breakfasts (€6).

Barcelona 12

✗ Tapas 24 — Tapas €

(📞93 488 09 77; www.carlesabellan.com; Carrer de la Diputació 269; tapas €4-12; 🕐9am-midnight; 🛜; Ⓜ Passeig de Gràcia) Hotshot chef Carles Abellán runs this basement tapas haven known for its gourmet renditions of old faves, including the *bikini* (toasted ham-and-cheese sandwich, here with truffle and cured ham), freshly cooked tortilla and zesty lemon-infused *boquerones* (anchovies). For dessert, try the creamy *payoyo* cheese. Before 1pm, pop in for superb *entrepans* (filled rolls) and omelettes. You can't book, but it's worth the wait.

🛏 Praktik Rambla — Boutique Hotel €€

(📞93 343 66 90; www.hotelpraktikrambla. com; Rambla de Catalunya 27; s/d/tr from €122/135/169; ❄ 🛜; Ⓜ Passeig de Gràcia) On a leafy boulevard, this early-19th-century gem of a mansion hides a gorgeous little boutique number designed by beloved local interior designer Lázaro Rosa-Violán. While high ceilings, patterned walls and original tiles have been maintained, the 43 rooms have bold ceramics, spot lighting and contemporary art. The relaxed library and back terrace are perfect for enjoying the complimentary coffee and croissants.

Classic Trip

Costa del Sol Beyond the Beaches

Discover the Costa's most celebrated resorts, as well as some little known gems and the culturally vibrant city of Málaga on this sunny coastal jaunt.

21

TRIP HIGHLIGHTS

76 km

Torremolinos
Dine on fresh seafood in a former fishing barrio

58 km

Málaga
Get high on culture at Málaga's superb museums

START
● Nerja

2

3

Mijas ●

Fuengirola

6

● Estepona

● Gibraltar
FINISH

Marbella
Explore Marbella's picturesque historic centre

135km

**3–4 DAYS
208 KM / 129 MILES**

GREAT FOR...

BEST TIME TO GO

March to June or September to November when temperatures are cooler and traffic less.

 ESSENTIAL PHOTO

The old town in Marbella when the bougainvillea is in bloom.

 BEST FOR FAMILIES

Beaches, theme parks, and the Andalucian love for kids.

Classic Trip

Costa del Sol Beyond the Beaches

21

This drive from Nerja in the east to Gibraltar in the west leads through a constantly shifting landscape, taking you from orchards of subtropical fruit trees to shimmering white resorts, from a culture-loving metropolis to the cobbled backstreets of a former fishing village. Be prepared for a trip that challenges any preconceived ideas you may have about this, Spain's most famous, tourist-driven coastline.

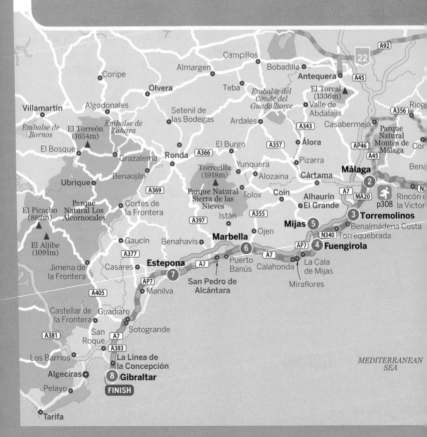

1 Nerja

Sitting in a charmed spot at the base of the Sierra Almijara mountains, this former fishing village has retained its low-rise village charm, despite the proliferation of souvenir shops and the large number of visitors it sees. At its heart is the **Balcón de Europa**, a seafront balcony built over the site of a Moorish castle. Grab a coffee at one of the terraced cafes before heading north of town to the extraordinary **Cueva de Nerja** (www.cuevadenerja.

es; adult/child €14/12; ⏰10am-4.30pm Sep-Jun, to 7pm Jul & Aug). This 4km-long cave complex, which dates back a cool five million years, is a wonderland of extraordinary rock formations, subtle shifting colours, stalactites and stalagmites

The Drive » The quickest route to Málaga is via the main A7 (E15). More scenic, if slower, is the N340 which meanders along the coast, traversing pretty agricultural land and bypassing centuries-old watchtowers. At Rincón de la Victoria join the A7 for the last few kilometres into Málaga. It's a total drive of 58km (1¼ hours).

- - - - - - - - - - - - - - - - - - -

TRIP HIGHLIGHT

2 Málaga

Book a night or two to get the best out of Málaga. The city positively crackles with energy, hosting a buzzing bar life and vibrant restaurant scene. It also boasts genuine cultural credentials and its art museums are seriously impressive – check out the **Museo Carmen Thyssen**

(www.carmenthyssenmalaga.org; Calle Compañía 10; €10, afternoons 2.30-4pm €6; ⏰10am-8pm Tue-Sun), the **Museo Ruso** (p246) and the unmissable **Museo Picasso** (p246), dedicated to the city's most famous son. A short walk away, the 16th-century **Catedral de Málaga** (📞952 22 03 45; www.malagacatedral.com; Calle Molina Lario; cathedral & Ars Málaga €6, incl roof €10; ⏰10am-6pm Sat, 2-6pm Sun year-round, 10am-8pm Mon-Fri Apr-Jun & Oct, to 9pm Jun-Sep, to 6.30pm Nov-Mar) offers fabulous rooftop views and an interior bedecked with gorgeous retables and 18th-century religious art. Travel further back in time at the Roman Amphitheatre (p256) and adjacent **Alcazaba** (📞952 22 72 30; http://alcazabaygibralfaro.malaga.eu; Calle Alcazabilla 2; €3.50, incl Castillo de Gibralfaro €5.50; ⏰9am-8pm Apr-Oct, to 6pm Nov-Mar), a fascinating 11th-century Moorish palace-fortress. For more on Málaga's sights see our walking tour on p308.

 LINK YOUR TRIP

20 Mediterranean Meander

Málaga is the start of this east-coast adventure that takes in several of Spain's most stunning cities, including its final destination: Barcelona.

22 Golden Triangle

Nerja is a speedy hour's drive from Granada, home of the monumental Alhambra; this winning drive also takes in Seville and Córdoba, two of Andalucía's most celebrated cities.

0 ━━━ 20 km
0 ━━━ 10 miles

ANDALUCÍA & SOUTHERN SPAIN **21** COSTA DEL SOL BEYOND THE BEACHES

Classic Trip

🗶 🛏 p258, p269

The Drive » Leaving Málaga, take the A7 in the direction of Algecíras, Torremolinos and Cádiz, then follow the MA20 signposted to Torremolinos. This is a busy stretch of *autovía* that passes the airport. It's a drive of about 18km or 25 minutes.

TRIP HIGHLIGHT

❸ Torremolinos

Torremolinos, once the poster child of industrial-scale package tourism, now attracts a wide cross-section of people, including trendy clubbers, beach-loving families, gay visitors and, yes, even some Spanish tourists. The centre of town revolves around the pedestrian shopping street **Calle San Miguel**, from where steps lead down to the main beach at **Playamar**. To the southwest, round a small rocky outcrop (La Punta), **La Carihuela** is a former fishing *barrio* which is now, fittingly, home to some hugely popular seafood restaurants such as **Casa Juan** (📞952 37 35 12; www. losmellizos.net; Calle San Ginés 20, La Carihuela; mains €14-22; ⏰1-4.30pm & 8pm-midnight Tue-Sat, 1-4.30pm Sun). The beachfront *paseo* continues to Benalmádena, Torre's western twin, where you'll find a large marina designed as a kind of homage to Gaudí and a giant **Buddhist stupa** (www.stupabenalmadena. org; Benalmádena Pueblo; ⏰10am-2pm & 4-6.30pm Tue-Sun; 🅿).

DETOUR: FRIGILIANA

Start: ❶ Nerja

After the cavernous gloom of the Cueva de Nerja, consider heading inland to Frigiliana, a *pueblo blanco* (white village) once voted Andalucía's prettiest by the Spanish tourism authority. It's an enchanting place with a tangible Moroccan feel and a steeply banked old town of pretty, whitewashed houses. Wander its quaint streets and pick up some of its famous sweet wine and honey in the small village shops.

It's a straightforward 7km drive from Nerja: take the M5105 inland, passing groves of mango and avocado trees, and follow signs to the *casco historico* and car park.

🗶 p269

The Drive » It's a straightforward 17km drive to Fuengirola on the N340, which hugs the coast and passes through the busy coastal resort of Benalmádena Costa. Note that there's a 50km speed limit on this scenic stretch.

----

❹ Fuengirola

Fuengirola's appeal, apart from its 7km of beaches, lies in the fact that it is a genuine Spanish working town, as well as a popular resort. It has a large population of foreign residents, many of whom arrived in the '60s and stayed long after their ponytails had gone grey. Stop by **Plaza de la Constitucíon**, a pretty square overlooked by the baroque-style facade of Fuengirola's main church, then explore the surrounding streets lined with idiosyncratic shops and tapas bars. A five-minute walk away, the **Bioparc** (📞952 66 63 01; www. bioparcfuengirola.es; Avenida Camilo José Cela; adult/child €22/17; ⏰10am-sunset; 🅿) is the Costa's best zoo with spacious enclosures and conservation and breeding programmes.

The Drive » From Fuengirola, take Avenida Alcalde Clemente Díaz Ruiz then the Carretera de Mijas to join the A387. This crosses the A7 and continues up to Mijas about 9km (20 minutes) away. In Mijas follow signs to the underground car park (€1 for 24 hours).

⑤ Mijas

The *pueblo blanco* (white village) of Mijas has retained its sugar-cube cuteness despite being on the coach-tour circuit. Art buffs should check out the **Centro de Arte Contemporáneo de Mijas** (CAC; www.cacmijas.info; Calle Málaga 28; adult/child €3/ free; ◷10am-6pm Mon-Sat), a contemporary art museum that houses the world's second-largest collection of Picasso ceramics. Otherwise the village is all about strolling the narrow cobbled streets, dipping into tapas bars and shopping for souvenirs. Be sure to walk up to the **Plaza de Toros**, an unusual square-shaped bullring at the top of the village, surrounded by lush ornamental gardens with spectacular coastal views. For more exercise, there are numerous trails leading out from the village, including a tough, well-marked route up to **Pico Mijas** (1151m) – allow about five hours to get there and back.

The Drive » Return to the A7 *autovia*. This dual carriageway traverses the most densely built-up stretch of the Costa, passing through resorts like Calahonda and Miraflores that were developed during the Costa's 1980s boom period. Continue west along the A7 until you reach the exit for Marbella; a total drive of 33km or 25 minutes.

DETOUR: COMARES

Start: ② **Málaga**

Heading northeast from Málaga brings you to La Axarquía, an area of rugged hiking country stippled with pretty, unspoiled *pueblos* (villages). A highlight, quite literally, is Comares, which sits like a snowdrift on a lofty mountain (739m), commanding spectacular views over the surrounding mountains. Stroll its steep winding lanes and don't miss the remarkable summit cemetery. There are also several walking trails that start here, as well as a 436m-long zip line, the **Tirolina de Comares** (1/2 rides €15/20), which provides a 50-second ride over to the opposite slopes. This is generally open on an appointment-only basis so it's best to book a ride through an activity company like **Vive Aventura** (☎697 218289; www.viveaventura.es). To get to Comares from Málaga, take the A45 towards Granada, Córdoba and Seville, then exit for Casabermeja and continue onto Comares via the A356 (through Riogordo) and MA3107. The journey is about 60km and should take about 70 minutes.

TRIP HIGHLIGHT

⑥ Marbella

Marbella is the Costa del Sol's most high-profile resort town and a good choice for an overnight stop. Well known for its star-studded clubs, shiny restaurants and expensive hotels, it also has other, less ostentatious charms: a magnificent natural setting, sheltered by the beautiful Sierra Blanca mountains, and a gorgeous old town replete with pristine white houses, narrow traffic-free lanes and well-tended flower boxes. At its heart is picturesque **Plaza de los Naranjos**, dating back to 1485 with tropical plants, palms and orange trees. From here you can walk down to the seafront via the lush **Parque de la Alameda** gardens. Follow along the so-called **Golden Mile** (actually, it's about 6km) and you'll eventually reach the luxurious marina of **Puerto Banús**. En route, take time to check out the **Museo Ralli** (www.museoralli.es; Urbanización Coral Beach; ◷10am-3pm Tue-Sat), a wonderful private museum displaying works by primarily Latin American and European artists in bright, well-lit galleries.

Classic Trip

WHY THIS IS A CLASSIC TRIP
DUNCAN GARWOOD, AUTHOR

Loud, brash and always fun, Spain's most famous *costa* makes for a wonderfully entertaining trip. Our route reveals the sunshine coast in all its gaudy glory, taking in Malaga's cultural hits, a giant Buddhist stupa in party-loving Torremolinos, and Marbella's star-studded seafront. Providing the grand finale is Gibraltar, the legendary Rock that guards the gateway to the Mediterranean.

Above: **Málaga** Catedral de Málaga (p263)
Right: **Torremolinos** Buddhist stupa (p264)

...D/SHUTTERSTOCK ©

JUPITERSOUNDS/SHUTTERSTOCK ©

✕ 🛏 p269

The Drive ›› Continue west on the A7 *autovia*, following signs for Algeciras and Cádiz. This stretch of highway is less built up and passes by San Pedro de Alcántara, as well as five golf courses (they don't nickname this the Costa del Golf for nothing!). It's a snappy 20 minutes or just 24km to your next stop: Estepona.

----

❼ Estepona

Estepona was one of the first resorts to attract tourists almost 50 years ago and, despite the surrounding development, it retains a charming historic centre of narrow cobbled streets, simple *pueblo* houses and well-tended pots of geraniums. Make a beeline for Plaza de las Flores with its fountain centrepoint, orange trees and handy **tourist office** (📞952 80 80 81; www.estepona. es; Plaza de las Flores; ⏱9am-3pm Mon-Fri, 10am-2pm Sat). A 10-minute walk from here, Estepona's fabulous **Orchidarium** (📞951 51 70 74; www.orchidariumestepona. com; Calle Terraza 86; adult/child €3/1; ⏱9am-2pm & 3-6pm Tue-Fri, 10am-2pm & 3-6pm

TOP TIP:
TOLL ROAD AP SEVEN

If you're travelling in July and August, consider taking the AP7 toll road, at least between Fuengirola and Marbella, as the A7 can become horribly congested. This particular A7 stretch (formerly part of the N340) used to be notorious for accidents; however, the situation has improved since the introduction of a 80km/h speed limit in former trouble spots.

Sat, 10am-2pm Sun) houses 1500 species of orchid – the largest collection in Europe – as well as 5000 subtropical plants, flowers and trees, and a 17m-high artificial waterfall. To the southwest of the town centre, Puerto Deportivo is the focal point of the town's nightlife, especially at weekends, and is also excellent for water sports.

 p269

The Drive >> For the final leg consider taking the AP7 toll road for the first 20km (€3.35 in peak summer months) as the N340 here is very slow, with numerous roundabouts. At Guadiaro the AP7 merges with the A7 for the rest of the 49km journey. Consider a refreshment stop at swanky Sotogrande harbour, home to Spain's leading golf course, the Real Club Valderrama.

- - - - - - - - - - - - - - - - -

8 Gibraltar

Red pillar boxes, fish-and-chip shops and creaky 1970s seaside hotels – there's no getting away from Gibraltar's Britishness. Poised strategically at the jaws of Europe and Africa, Gibraltar, with its Palladian architecture and camera-hogging

Barbary apes, makes an interesting finale to your trip. The Rock is one of the most dramatic landforms in southern Europe and most of its upper sections (but not the main lookouts) fall within the **Upper Rock Nature Reserve** (incl attractions adult/child £13/8, excl attractions pedestrian £5, combined ticket incl cable car adult/child £22/14; ☺9.30am-6.45pm Apr-Sep, 9am-5.45pm Oct-Mar). Entry to this includes admission to **St Michael's Cave** (St Michael's Rd; incl Upper Rock Nature Reserve & attractions adult/child £13/8; ☺9.30am-6.45pm Apr-Sep, 9am-5.45pm Oct-Mar), the **Apes' Den**, the **Great Siege Tunnels** (incl Upper Rock Nature Reserve & attractions adult/child £13/8; ☺9.30am-6.45pm Apr-Sep, 9am-5.45pm Oct-Mar), the **Military Heritage Centre** (cnr Willis' & Queen's Rds; incl Upper Rock Nature Reserve adult/child £13/8; ☺9.30am-6.45pm Apr-Sep, 9am-5.45pm

Oct-Mar) and **Nelson's Anchorage** (100-Tonne Gun; Rosia Rd; incl Upper Rock Nature Reserve adult/child £13/8; ☺9.30am-6.15pm Apr-Sep, 9am-5.45pm Oct-Mar).

The Rock's most famous residents are the 160 or so tailless Barbary macaques that hang around the top cable-car station and Apes' Den. Most Gibraltar visits start in Grand Casemates Sq, once the sight of public executions but now a jolly square surrounded by bars and restaurants. Learn more about the Rock's history at the fine **Gibraltar Museum** (☎20074289; www.gibmuseum.gi; 18-20 Bomb House Lane; adult/child £5/2.50; ☺10am-6pm Mon-Fri, to 2pm Sat), which displays exhibits ranging from prehistoric and Phoenician Gibraltar to the infamous Great Siege (1779–83).

Eating & Sleeping

Málaga ❷

🍴 Uvedoble Taberna Tapas €

(www.uvedobletaberna.com; Calle Císter 15; tapas €2.40-3.90; ⏰12.30-4pm & 8pm-midnight Mon-Sat; 🛜) A newish tapas bar that draws on old traditions, this boisterous, crowded place evokes the tiled taverns of yore – though you'll likelier see modern art than dog-eared bullfighting posters on its walls. Similarly, the tapas put a modern spin on classic Málaga ingredients: try the smoked sardines on rosemary-tomato focaccia, or tuna tataki with *porra antequerana* (Antequera's lusciously garlicky soup).

🛏 Dulces Dreams Guesthouse €

(📞951 35 78 69; www.dulcesdreamshostel.com; Plaza de los Mártires 6; d with shared/private bathroom from €60/74; ❄🛜) Managed by an enthusiastic young team and delightfully situated in a pedestrianised plaza overlooking a red-brick church, Dulces (sweet) Dreams is a great budget option. The bright, high-ceilinged and whimsically decorated rooms are, appropriately, named after desserts: Cupcake is one of the best. Note that there's no lift, and street noise can be an issue for light sleepers.

Torremolinos ❸

🍴 El Gato Lounge Fusion €€

(📞676 452504; www.elgatolounge.com; Paseo Marítimo 1K; mains €5-10, tapas box menus €16-22; ⏰noon-late Feb-Oct) Don't expect the default sardines at this trendsetting fusion favourite across from Playamar beach's western end. Asian flavours abound in offerings like Sri Lankan curry, chicken satay, tuna tataki and Thai shrimp cakes – but the real showstopper is El Gato's 'tapas experience', featuring a flamboyant assortment of 12 Mediterranean-Asian tapas finished off with apple pie and cinnamon ice cream.

Marbella ❻

🍴 Garum International €€

(📞952 85 88 58; www.garummarbella.com; Paseo Marítimo; mains €12-23; ⏰noon-11.30pm; 🛜) Finnish-owned and set in a dreamy location right on the 'Golden Mile' across from the beach, Garum has a menu that will please those seeking a little gourmet variety. Expect dishes ranging from smoked-cheese soup to Moroccan chicken samosas and red-lentil falafel.

🛏 Hotel San Cristóbal Hotel €€

(📞952 77 12 50; www.hotelsancristobal.com; Avenida Ramón y Cajal 3; s €67-79, d €82-96 incl breakfast; 🛜) Not the most 'Marbella' (ie flashy) of Marbella's hotels, the well-located San Cristóbal dates back to the 1960s. However, regular revamps have kept the place looking solidly contemporary: rooms sport tasteful pale-grey and cream decor and smart navy fabrics. Most rooms have balconies.

Estepona ❼

🍴 La Escollera Seafood €

(📞952 80 63 54; Puerto Pesquero; mains €8-14; ⏰1-4.30pm & 8-11.30pm Tue-Sat, 1-4.30pm Sun) Locals in the know – from dock workers swigging beers to families celebrating a first communion – flock to this port-side eatery to dine on arguably the freshest and best seafood in town. The atmosphere is agreeably bustling and no-frills basic, with plastic tables and paper cloths. But when the fish tastes this good and the beer is this cold, who cares?

Golden Triangle

From Seville's charismatic streets to the Moorish treasures of Granada and Córdoba, this route takes in Andalucía's most celebrated sights, as well as several lesser known gems.

22

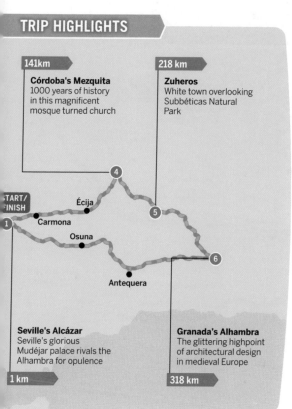

141km

Córdoba's Mezquita
1000 years of history in this magnificent mosque turned church

218 km

Zuheros
White town overlooking Subbéticas Natural Park

4

Écija

5

Carmona

Osuna

6

Antequera

START/ FINISH
1

Seville's Alcázar
Seville's glorious Mudéjar palace rivals the Alhambra for opulence

1 km

Granada's Alhambra
The glittering highpoint of architectural design in medieval Europe

318 km

5–7 DAYS
576KM / 358 MILES

GREAT FOR...

BEST TIME TO GO

April to June is good for multiple spring festivals; September and October to avoid the ferocious summer heat.

ESSENTIAL PHOTO

The Alhambra with the Sierra Nevada in the background.

BEST FOR TAPAS

Seville is renowned for both its traditional and modern tapas.

da Alhambra (p276)

22 | Golden Triangle

The three cities of Seville, Córdoba and Granada have taken it in turns to dominate cultural and political life in Andalucía for the past 1000 years, and between them they guard a truly golden legacy. This triangular drive links all three cities while also revealing snippets of small-town beauty and quiet rural life.

TRIP HIGHLIGHT

1 Seville

Shaped by half a dozen civilisations and reborn in numerous incarnations during its 2000-year history, Seville is a city of flamboyant beauty and contrasting seasonal moods. Historic monuments and romantic plazas adorn its energetic streets which are drenched in spirit-enriching sunshine for much of the year.

Follow our walking tour (p310) to navigate through the former

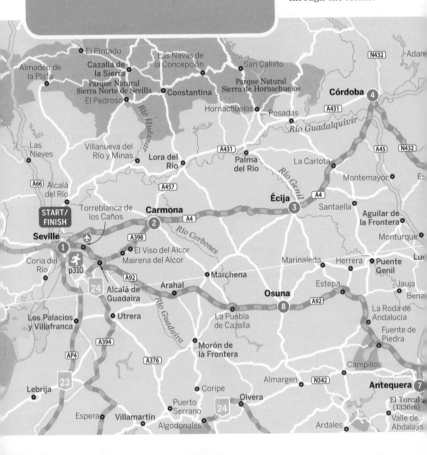

Jewish quarter of **Santa Cruz** and see the city's main sights, including obligatory visits to the Real Alcázar and Catedral. Try to take in a flamenco show and experience enjoying a tapas meal in one of the centre's many teeming bars.

With more time, check out **Plaza de España** in the **Parque de María Luisa** and the **Metropol Parasol** (📞606 635214; www.setasdesevilla.com; Plaza de la Encarnación; €3; ⏰9.30am-10.30pm Sun-Thu, to 11pm Fri & Sat).

Overnighters can get a taste of the city's kicking nightlife on the **Alameda de Hércules**.

✕ 🛏 p278

The Drive » Leave Seville on the eastbound A4 (also known as the E5). Pass Seville airport on your right and follow signs towards Carmona on the fast-moving four-lane carriageway. Take the first exit for Carmona after 33km.

---

2 Carmona

Set atop a ridge overlooking golden, sun-baked plains, Carmona is like a mini-Seville that never grew up. Its centre is packed with stately palaces, Mudéjar churches and two Moorish forts while, nearby, a haunting **Necrópolis Romana** (Roman cemetery; 📞600 143632; www.museosdeandalucia.es; Avenida de Jorge Bonsor 9; EU/non-EU citizens free/€1.50; ⏰9am-9pm Tue-Sat, to 3pm Sun Apr–mid-Jun, 9am-3pm Tue-Sun mid-Jun–mid-Sep, 9am-6pm Tue-Sat, to 3pm Sun mid-Sep–Mar) tells of the town's ancient origins.

The town's signature sight is the **Alcázar de la Puerta de Sevilla** (📞954 19 09 55; Plaza de Blas Infante; adult/child €2/1, Mon free; ⏰10am-6pm Mon-Sat, to 3pm Sun Sep-Jun, 9am-3pm Mon-Fri, 10am-3pm Sat & Sun Jul & Aug), a golden fort built by the Muslim

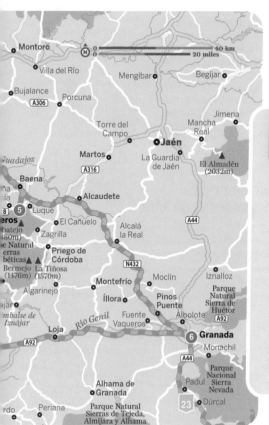

🔗 LINK YOUR TRIP

23 The Great Outdoors

This vastly different take on Andalucía intersects with the Golden Triangle at both Antequera and Osuna.

24 Andalucía's White Villages

After finishing this trip in Seville, retrace 35km to Carmona and join this spectacular mountain drive through Cádiz and Málaga provinces.

Almohads over an earlier Roman structure.

At the other end of the historic centre, the ruined **Alcázar de Arriba** (Alcázar del Rey Don Pedro; Calle Extramuros de Santiago; adult/student/child €2/1/ free; ⏰11am-3pm Mon, Tue, Thu & Fri, to 3pm Sat & Sun) provides a stirring backdrop to Carmona's panoramic **parador** (☎954 14 10 10; www. parador.es/en/paradores/ parador-de-carmona; Alcázar del Rey Don Pedro, Calle Extramuros de Santiago; r €105-200;).

 p259, p278

The Drive >> Double back to the A4 and follow it 53km east to Écija. The agricultural landscapes around the Genil and Guadalquivir river valleys act as a heat-trap in summer earning Écija its nickname, 'El sartén de Andalucía' (the frying pan of Andalucía).

---

❸ Écija

A city of baroque church towers, suffocating summer heat, and an unpronounceable name, Écija (eth-ee-ha) is a hardworking provincial town where tourism is an afterthought and history reverberates around its compact centre.

Of the town's famous spires, most of which date to an 18th-century building boom, the belfry of the **Iglesia de San Juan** (Plaza de San Juan; tower €2; ⏰10am-1pm Tue-Sun) is the only one you can actually climb.

A short walk away, the 18th-century Palacio de Benamejí houses the **Museo Histórico Municipal** (☎954 83 04 31; http://museo.ecija.es; Plaza de la Constitución 1; €3; ⏰10am-1.30pm & 4.30-6.30pm Tue-Fri, 10am-2pm & 5.30-8pm Sat, 10am-3pm Sun mid-Sep–May, 10am-2.30pm Tue-Fri, 10am-

2pm & 8-10pm Sat, 10am-3pm Sun Jun–mid-Sep) and its prize collection of local Roman finds, including a series of stunning mosaics.

The Drive >> Return to the A4 and follow it for 55km to Córdoba. Once in the city, it's best to park on the south side of the Guadalquivir River and walk across the Roman bridge into the historic centre.

TRIP HIGHLIGHT

❹ Córdoba

Córdoba has easier road access than other Andalucian cities, although its labyrinthine centre is best explored on foot.

Its centrepiece is the multi-arched **Mezquita** (Mosque; ☎957 47 05 12; www.mezquita-catedralde cordoba.es; Calle Cardenal Herrero 1; adult/child €10/5, 8.30-9.30am Mon-Sat free; ⏰10am-7pm Mon-Sat, 8.30-11.30am & 3-7pm Sun

---

🗨 LOCAL KNOWLEDGE: SEVILLE'S FLAMENCO CLUBS

Casa de la Memoria (☎954 56 06 70; www.casadelamemoria.es; Calle Cuna 6; adult/ student/child €18/15/10; ⏰11am-6pm, shows 7.30pm & 9pm) Cultural centre that stages passionate shows often touted as the best in Seville.

Museo del Baile Flamenco (☎954 34 03 11; www.museoflamenco.com; Calle Manuel Rojas Marcos 3; adult/child €10/6, incl show €26/15; ⏰10am-7pm) Better known as a museum, this place holds nightly flamenco performances with aficionados yelling encouragement.

Tablao Los Gallos (☎954 21 69 81; www.tablaolosgallos.com; Plaza de Santa Cruz 11; adult/ child €35/20; ⏰shows 8pm & 10pm) Seville's oldest *tablao* (venue for choreographed flamenco) puts on two nightly shows featuring top-notch dancers, singers and guitarists.

LEOKS/SHUTTERSTOCK ©

Seville Plaza de España (p273)

Mar-Oct, 10am-6pm Mon-Sat, 8.30-11.30am & 3-6pm Sun Nov-Feb), a masterpiece of Islamic architecture and one of the only places in the world where you can celebrate Christian mass in a mosque.

The narrow streets of the old **Judería** (Jewish quarter) and Muslim quarter stretch out from the great mosque like capillaries, some clogged with bars, restaurants and tourist bric-a-brac, others delightfully peaceful.

Flower boxes and cool, geranium-clad patios provide bursts of colour, particularly in May during the **Fiesta de los Patios de Córdoba** (http://patios.cordoba.es; 🕐May).

Another prime patio site is the **Palacio de Viana** (📞957 49 67 41; www.palaciodeviana.com; Plaza de Don Gome 2; whole house/patios €8/5, 2-5pm Wed free; 🕐10am-7pm Tue-Sat, to 3pm Sun Sep-Jun, 9am-3pm Tue-Sun Jul & Aug).

Before leaving Córdoba, it's worth making a detour to the archaeological site of **Medina Azahara** (Madinat al-Zahra; 📞957 10 49 33; www.museosdeandalucia.es; Carretera Palma del Río Km 5.5; EU/non-EU citizen free/€1.50, shuttle bus adult/child €2.50/1.50; 🕐9am-9pm Tue-Sat Apr–mid-Jun, to 3pm mid-Jun–mid-Sep, to 6pm mid-Sep–Mar, 9am-3pm Sun year-round; 🅿), 8km west of town.

The ruins of this remarkable 10th-century palace-city testify to Córdoba's past as one of medieval Europe's greatest cities.

🍴 🛏 p278

275

The Drive » Head south from Córdoba on the N432. Soon after bypassing Baena, branch west onto the A318 (Autovía del Olivar). Zuheros will soon appear as a white splash amid the green crags to the south. To reach it, turn onto the CO6209 and wind your way up to the town. Total distance from Córdoba: 77km.

TRIP HIGHLIGHT

⑤ Zuheros

Rising above undulating emerald-green countryside, the charming white village of Zuheros sits in a dramatic location, crouched in the lee of a craggy mountain. It's approached via a steep road through a series of hairpin bends and provides a beautiful base for exploring the northern reaches of the Parque Natural Sierras Subbéticas.

The main sight in the village itself is its small **castle** (📞957 69 45 45; Plaza de la Paz; adult/child incl Museo Arqueológico €2/1.25; ☻10am-2pm & 5-7pm Tue-Fri, tours 11am, 12.30pm, 2pm, 5pm & 6.30pm Sat & Sun Apr-Sep, 10am-2pm & 4-6pm Tue-Fri, tours 11am, 12.30pm, 2pm, 4pm & 5.30pm Sat & Sun Oct-Mar), dramatically grafted onto a rocky pinnacle. Admission tickets are sold at the small **Museo Arqueológico** (Archaeological Museum; 📞957 69 45 45; Plaza de la Paz 1; adult/child incl Castillo €2/1.25; ☻10am-2pm & 5-7pm Tue-Fri, tours 11am, 12.30pm, 2pm, 5pm & 6.30pm Sat & Sun Apr-Sep, 10am-2pm & 4-6pm Tue-Fri, tours 11am, 12.30pm, 2pm, 4pm & 5.30pm Sat & Sun Oct-Mar), just across the square.

🛏 p278

The Drive » Retrace your tracks via the CO6209 and A318 back to the arterial N432 and head 100km southeast towards the Sierra Nevada mountains and Granada nestled beneath them.

TRIP HIGHLIGHT

⑥ Granada

The last bastion of the Moors in Europe, Granada is a gritty, tempestuous city where Andalucía's complex history is laid out in ornate detail. Its great headline act is the **Alhambra** (📞958 02 79 71, tickets 858 95 36 16; www.alhambra-patronato.es; adult/12-15yr/under 12yr €14/8/free, Generalife & Alcazaba only adult/under 12yr €7/free; ☻8.30am-8pm Apr-mid-Oct, to 6pm mid-Oct–Mar, night visits 10-11.30pm Tue & Sat Apr–mid-Oct, 8-9.30pm Fri & Sat mid-Oct–Mar), the Nasrid emir's opulent palace

---

VÍA VERDE DE LA SUBBÉTICA

One of Andalucía's least visited parks, the **Parque Natural Sierras Subbéticas** is criss-crossed by numerous walking and cycling trails, many of which start near Zuheros. The park's easiest and best-marked path is the Vía Verde de la Subbética which runs along a disused railway for 58km across southern Córdoba province from Camporreal near Puente Genil to the Río Guadajoz on the Jaén border.

There are no fierce gradients as it passes through tunnels and over old bridges and viaducts, and with plenty of informative map-boards, it's impossible to get lost. You can fuel up at cafes and hire bikes at outlets in old station buildings along the route.

The **Centro Cicloturista Subbética** (📞672 605088, 691 843532; www.subbetica bikesfriends.com; per half-/full day bikes €12/18, electric bikes €12/25; ☻10am-12.30pm Sat & Sun mid-Jun–mid-Sep, 10am-2pm Mon-Fri, to 7pm Sat & Sun mid-Sep–mid-Jun; 🚻) at Doña Mencía station, 4km downhill from Zuheros, rents a range of different bikes, and can provide local tourist information as well as showers and other services for cyclists.

complex. Below it sprawls the city where bohemian bars and shadowy *teterías* (teahouses) go hand in hand with monumental churches, whitewashed *cármenes* (mansions with walled gardens), and counterculture graffiti art.

If this is your first time in Granada, prioritise the Alhambra, for if ever a monument lived up to the hype, this is it. However, to enjoy the experience, make sure to pre-purchase tickets – you can buy them from two hours to three months in advance, either online or by phone.

When you've visited the Alhambra, take time to explore the steeply stacked **Albayzin** (old Moorish quarter) and admire the street art in the **Realejo** district. More traditional artistic offerings await in the **catedral** (🖋958 22 29 59; www.catedraldegranada.com; Plaza de las Pasiegas; adult/child €5/free; ⏰10am-6.30pm Mon-Sat, 3-5.45pm Sun) and **Capilla Real** (🖋958 22 78 48; www.capillarealgranada.com; Calle Oficios; adult/child €5/free; ⏰10.15am-6.30pm Mon-Sat, 11am-6pm Sun), the last resting place of Spain's *Reyes Católicos* (Catholic Monarchs).

✗ 🛏 p279

The Drive » Head west out of Granada on the main Seville road, the A92. After 95km you'll cross the A45,

the main north–south *autovía* between Málaga and Córdoba. A couple of kilometres further on, turn south on the A7281 to Antequera, which sits nestled beneath the rocky moonscapes of the nearby Torcal uplands.

- - - - - - - - - - - - - - - - - - -

7 Antequera

Antequera is a fascinating town, both architecturally and historically, yet few visitors linger long.

The town has a rich tapestry of architectural and archaeological gems, ranging from two Bronze Age burial sites to a grand Moorish **Alcazaba** (adult/child €4/2, incl Colegiata de Santa María la Mayor €6/3; ⏰10am-6pm), whose substantial remains are within easy (if uphill) walking distance of the town centre. However, the undoubted highlight here is the lavish Spanish baroque architecture that gives the town its character.

✗ p279, p290

The Drive » Get back on the A92 and strike northwest towards Seville. The *autopista* bypasses the towns of La Roda de Andalucía and Estepa before the small but grandiose baroque town of Osuna comes into sight after about 76km.

- - - - - - - - - - - - - - - - - - -

8 Osuna

Osuna is a small provincial town with a legacy that far outweighs its size. Many of its artistic and

architectural treasures were commissioned by the rich dukes of Osuna between the 16th and 18th centuries. Striking heirlooms include a series of baroque mansions and the **Colegiata de Santa María de la Asunción** (🖋954 81 04 44; Plaza de la Encarnación; guided tours €5; ⏰tours 9.30am & hourly 10.15am-1.15pm Tue-Sun, plus 7pm & 8pm Thu mid-Jun–mid-Sep, hourly 10.15am-1.15pm plus 4pm & 5pm Tue-Sun mid-Sep–mid-Jun), a landmark Renaissance monastery filled with baroque art. This formidable ensemble provided a suitably fantastical location for the *Game of Thrones* whose fifth season was partly filmed here – check out the **Museo de Osuna** (🖋954 81 57 32; Calle Sevilla 37; €2.50, Wed free; ⏰9.30am-2.30pm Tue-Sun & 7-9pm Thu mid-Jun–mid-Sep, 10am-2pm & 5-8pm Tue-Sun mid-Sep–mid-Jun) for more on the town's GoT role.

Among the most ornate of Osuna's 18th-century mansions is the Palacio del Marqués de La Gomera (p290), now a princely four-star hotel.

✗ 🛏 p279, p290

The Drive » It's a straightforward 87km drive along the A92 back to Seville. The road heads west and then northwest through increasingly populated outlying towns.

Eating & Sleeping

Seville ①

✗ Bar-Restaurante Eslava   Tapas €€

(☎954 90 65 68; www.espacioeslava.com; Calle Eslava 3; tapas €2.90-4.50, restaurant mains €13.50-26; ⏱bar 12.30pm-midnight Tue-Sat, restaurant 1.30-4pm & 8.30pm-midnight Tue-Sat) You'll almost certainly have to wait for a table at the bar, but it's so worth it, especially if you use the time to start on the excellent wine list. The tapas are superb: contemporary, creative, brilliantly executed and incredible value for money. Standouts include slow-cooked egg served on mushroom puree, and a filo pastry cigar stuffed with cuttlefish and algae.

✗ La Brunilda   Tapas €€

(☎954 22 04 81; Calle Galera 5; tapas €4-7.50, mains €6.50-15; ⏱1-4pm & 8.30-11.30pm Tue-Sat, 1-4pm Sun) Hidden away in an anonymous Arenal backstreet, this tapas hotspot is a guarantee of good times. The look is modern casual with big blue doors, brick arches and plain wooden tables, and the food is imaginative and brilliantly executed. Arrive promptly or expect long queues.

🛏 Hotel Amadeus   Boutique Hotel €€

(☎954 50 14 43; www.hotelamadeussevilla.com; Calle Farnesio 6; d €92-195, tr €121-335, q €180-365; P ❄ 🛜) A soothing oasis of calm in the heart of the old *judería* (Jewish quarter), this delightful hotel charms with its ceramic-tiled lobby, period furniture and collection of musical instruments (which guests are free to play). Rooms, named after composers, are equally stylish, and there's a small rooftop terrace offering views over the Giralda.

🛏 Hotel Casa 1800   Luxury Hotel €€€

(☎954 56 18 00; www.hotelcasa1800sevilla.com; Calle Rodrigo Caro 6; d €170-750, ste €360-1050; ❄ @ 🛜 🏊) A short hop from the cathedral and Alcázar, this stately *casa* (house) is positively regal. Setting the tone is the elegant, period decor – wooden ceilings, chandeliers, parquet floors and plenty of gilt – but everything about the place charms, from the helpful staff to the panoramic rooftop pool and complimentary afternoon tea.

Carmona ②

✗ Molino de la Romera   Andalucian €€

(☎954 14 20 00; www.molinodelaromera.es; Calle Sor Ángela de la Cruz 8; tapas €3.50-6, mains €12-19; ⏱1-4pm & 8.30-11.30pm Mon-Sat) Housed in a cosy, 15th-century olive-oil mill complete with panoramic terrace, a lovely courtyard and coolly rustic interior, this popular restaurant serves hearty, well-prepped meals with a splash of contemporary flair. Particularly good are its chargrilled meat dishes, including juicy cuts of tender Galician beef.

Córdoba ④

✗ Garum 2.1   Tapas €€

(☎957 48 76 73; Calle de San Fernando 122; tapas €3.90-7.90, mains €9.90-16.90; ⏱1-4pm & 8-11pm) Blending a bistro-style approach with gourmet tapas, Garum 2.1 touts itself as a bistronomic tapas bar. This sounds faintly ridiculous but there's nothing off-putting about its tapas which are creatively presented and often quite inspired. A case in point are its churros, here filled with oxtail and chocolate, and the award-wining octopus served with smoked pig's ears. Excellent wine too.

Zuheros ⑤

🛏 Hotel Zuhayra   Hotel €

(☎957 69 46 93; www.zercahoteles.com; Calle Mirador 10; incl breakfast s €43-55, d €53-70; ❄ 🛜 🏊) An arrow's shot from Zuheros' castle, this sunny hotel has breathtaking views of the countryside from each of its white, tile-floored rooms. You can hire bikes here (€10 for four hours, €15 for longer) and the welcoming proprietors, the Ábalos brothers (who speak English), are a mine of local information. There is also a first-class **restaurant** (mains & raciones €7-18.50; ⏱1-3.30pm & 8-10.30pm) on the first floor.

Granada ⑥

✖ Picoteca 3Maneras — Andalucian €€

(☎958 22 68 18; www.facebook.com/picoteca
3maneras; Calle Santa Escolástica 19; mains
€12-17; ⏱1-4.30pm & 8pm-midnight Tue-Sat,
1-4.30pm Sun; 🔊 🍴) Glorious fresh produce,
spot-on service, chic whitewashed decor,
excellent Spanish wines and a deliciously
creative approach to local cuisine make
Picoteca a Realejo gem. South American and
various Asian flavours infuse ambitiously
reimagined dishes such as pork-and-wild-
mushroom risotto, pear-and-pancetta gnocchi,
and tuna in orange sauce; every Sunday there's
a special *arroz* (rice).

✖ El Bar de Fede — Andalucian €€

(☎958 28 88 14; www.facebook.com/
ElbardeFede1; Calle Marqués de Falces 1; raciones
€9-15; ⏱9am-2am Mon-Thu, to 3am Fri & Sat,
11am-2am Sun) 'Fede' refers to hometown poet
Federico García Lorca, whose free, creative
spirit seems to hang over this chicly styled,
gay-friendly bar. Patterned wallpaper, stone
arches and high tables set around a ceramic-
tiled island create a casual feel, and the food
is a joy. Standouts include aubergines drizzled
with honey, chicken in orange sauce and perfect
garlic-parsley squid.

🛏 Casa Morisca — Heritage Hotel €€€

(☎958 22 11 00; www.hotelcasamorisca.com;
Cuesta de la Victoria 9; d €131-231; 🅿 🔊) Live
like a Nasrid emir at Granada's original boutique
hotel, an exquisite late 15th-century mansion in
the lower Albayzín lovingly restored by architect
owners. Atmosphere and history are laid on
thick in the form of timber-beamed ceilings,
brick columns, original stuccowork and an
enchanting turquoise-tiled courtyard. Of the 14
intimate, attractive and individually decorated
rooms, the best have Alhambra views.

🛏 Párragasiete — Boutique Hotel €€

(☎958 26 42 27; www.hotelparragasiete.com;
Calle Párraga 7; s €45-65, d €70-115; 🅿 🔊)
With its blond-wood floors, smart furniture and
clean modern lines, this warmly styled hotel
feels more Scandinavia than southern Spain.
But Granada pops up in wall sketches of local
monuments, a glassed-in interior patio, and
a sleek downstairs bar-restaurant, Vitola –
popular with *granadinos* and ideal for breakfast
or tapas.

Antequera ⑦

✖ Arte de Cozina — Andalucian €€

(☎952 84 00 14; www.artedecozina.com;
Calle Calzada 27; tapas €2.80-3.50, mains
€15-24; ⏱1-11pm; 🔊) It's hard not to notice the
surrounding agricultural lands as you approach
Antequera, and this fascinating little hotel-
restaurant combo is where you get to taste
what they produce. Slavishly true to traditional
dishes, it plugs little-known Antequeran
specialities such as gazpacho made with green
asparagus or *porra* (a cold, thick tomato soup)
with oranges, plus meat dishes that include
lomo de orza (preserved pork loin).

Osuna ⑧

✖ Taberna Jicales — Tapas €

(☎954 81 04 23; www.tabernajicales.es; Calle
Esparteros 11; tapas €2-3.50, raciones €7.50-16;
⏱8am-5.30pm Thu-Tue) Grilled chunks of
tuna served on a bed of thick *salmorejo* (a cold
tomato-based soup) seasoned with roasted red
pepper; pork tenderloin slow cooked in sweet
Pedro Ximénez wine – classic tapas don't get
much better than these. Taberna Jicales is well
known locally and it pays to take your cue from
the townsfolk who pile in at lunchtime for a taste
of superb regional cuisine.

Classic Trip

The Great Outdoors

23

From scaling mainland Spain's highest peak to wildlife-watching in ethereal wetlands, this epic trip highlights the outdoor opportunities offered by Andalucía's diverse environments.

TRIP HIGHLIGHTS

62 km

Parque Nacional de Doñana
Raw, natural world brimming with wildlife

1 km

Capileira
Quiet mountain hikes and the Sierra Nevada's highest peaks

Seville

Osuna

Antequera **2**

Granada

1 START

Los Caños de Meca

9 FINISH

Tarifa
A Moroccan-flavoured, white-sand haven of outdoor fun

783 km

Paraje Natural Torcal de Antequera
Eerily beautiful limestone rock formations

190 km

7 DAYS
783KM / 486 MILES

GREAT FOR...

BEST TIME TO GO
From April to June and September to October for ideal weather.

 ESSENTIAL PHOTO

Tarifa, beaches and kitesurfers backed by Morocco, from Punta Paloma dune.

 BEST FOR WILDLIFE

Huelva's majestic World Heritage-listed Parque Nacional de Doñana.

itesurfing, Playa de Valdevaqueros (p289)

281

Classic Trip

23 The Great Outdoors

Starting high in the Sierra Nevada, this outdoors itinerary swings west and south through a mesmerising patchwork of contrasting landscapes. The long, winding road leads from the dramatic mountain gorges of Las Alpujarras through the dry, billowing plains of the Sevillan Campiña to Doñana national park and on to Tarifa's white-sand surfer beaches. En route, you'll come across historical monuments, archaeological treasures and culinary delights as richly varied as the ever-changing natural backdrop.

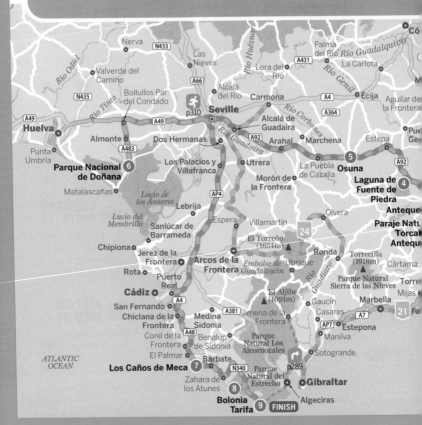

➊ Capileira

Kick things off in pretty Capileira in Las Alpujarras, the 70km stretch of valleys that runs along the southern flank of the Sierra Nevada. At 1436m, the whitewashed village is the highest, largest and prettiest of the three in the Barranco de Poqueira (Poqueira Gorge), sitting high above Pampaneira and Bubión. Despite its dramatic location it's just an hour's drive from the A44 via the A348, A4132 and A4129.

Two nights here allow you to enjoy a full day of walking, mountain cooking and shopping for leather work at **J Brown** (📞958 76 30 92; tallerbrown@gmail.com; Calle Doctor Castilla 7; ⏰10am-2pm & 5-8pm).

There's superb walking in the surrounding mountains, with many trails doable in a day. The area's most dramatic hike is to the summit of Mulhacén (3479m), mainland Spain's highest peak. To tackle this, catch the summer shuttle bus (one way/return €13/9) to the Mirador de Trevélez (2710m), from where it's a three-hour walk to the summit (5.1km, 800m ascent).

The best hiking months are April to mid-June and then mid-September to October; July to early September is best for the high peaks.

✕ 🛏 p290

The Drive » From Capileira, wind 36km downhill past Bubión, Pampaneira, Órgiva and Lanjarón (A4129, A4132 and A348). Take the northbound A44 for 50km, bypassing Granada to join the A92. Continue west for 92km, exiting at turn-off 149 to reach Antequera. Skirt around town to pick up the A343 and then the A7075 to the Paraje Natural Torcal de Antequera. As you climb, the Mediterranean sparkles just south

🔗 LINK YOUR TRIP

24 Andalucía's White Villages

From Osuna, head 61km northwest to Carmona to pick up this trip through Andalucía's classic white villages.

21 Costa del Sol Beyond the Beaches

Pick up the N340 at Tarifa and push northeast on the A7 for the 44km drive to Gibraltar, the endpoint of this whistle-stop tour of the Costa del Sol.

TRIP HIGHLIGHT

❷ Paraje Natural Torcal de Antequera

The bizarre and beautiful rock formations of the Paraje Natural Torcal de Antequera are a magnificent sight. The 12-sq-km park, declared a Unesco World Heritage site in 2016, is a rugged, almost other-worldly area of gnarled, serrated and pillared limestone that formed as a seabed 150 million years ago but now rises to a height of 1336m (El Torcal).

Leave your car at the park's excellent **Centro de Visitantes** (📞952 24 33 24; www.torcaldeantequera. com; ◷10am-7pm Apr-Oct, to 5pm Nov-Mar) and continue on foot along one of three walking trails: the 1.5km Ruta Verde (Green Route), the 3km Ruta Amarilla (Yellow Route), or the 3.6km Ruta Naranja (Orange Route).

The Drive » Drive back into Antequera, where there's convenient underground parking on Calle Diego Ponce north of Plaza de San Sebastián.

❸ Antequera

Despite its impressive collection of archaeological riches and Spanish-baroque sights, Antequera gets refreshingly little tourist traffic.

Looming over the historic centre are the imposing hilltop remains of a 14th-century Moorish Alcazaba (p277). Down in the heart of town, the **Museo de la Ciudad** (Museo Municipal; Plaza del Coso Viejo; ◷10am-2pm & 4.30-6.30pm Tue-Fri, from 9.30am Sat, 9.30am-2pm Sun) has an impressive array of Roman artefacts, including a 1.4m bronze statue, *Efebe*, that's considered one of the finest examples of Roman sculpture ever unearthed in Spain.

Travel further back in time at Antequera's **dolmens** (◷9am-3pm & 8-10pm Tue-Sat, 9am-3pm Sun Jul–mid-Sep, hours vary rest of year), some 1km out of the centre. Built by Bronze Age people in around 2500 BCE, the **Dolmen de Veira** and **Dolmen de Menga** are two of Europe's oldest burial chambers. The **Dolmen del Romeral** (Cerro Romeral; ◷9am-3.30pm Tue-Sun mid-Jun–mid-Sep, hours vary rest of year), another 3km to the northeast, dates to 1800 BCE.

🍴 🛏 p279, 290

The Drive » Continue 16km northwest on the A92 to the signposted Laguna de Fuente de Piedra turn-off. 'Laguna' signs lead you through Fuente de Piedra village to the lagoon's visitor centre (2km).

❹ Laguna de Fuente de Piedra

When it's not dried up, Laguna de Fuente de Piedra is Andalucía's largest natural lake and one of Europe's two main breeding grounds for the greater flamingo (the other is in the Camargue region of southwestern France). After a wet winter as many as 20,000 pairs of flamingos will breed here.

The birds arrive in January or February, and

TOP TIP:
SIERRA NEVADA HIKING MAPS

Get maps and hiking advice at **Nevadensis** (📞659 109662, 958 76 31 27; www.nevadensis.com; Plaza de la Libertad; ◷10am-2pm Mar, Jul, Aug & Nov, 10am-2pm & 4-6pm Apr-Jun, Sep & Oct, 10am-2pm Fri-Sun Dec-Feb) in Pampaneira. Many local hotels also provide their own maps with walk descriptions. The best maps for Las Alpujarras are Editorial Alpina's *Sierra Nevada, La Alpujarra* (1:40,000) and Editorial Penibética's *Sierra Nevada* (1:40,000).

THE IBERIAN LYNX

For wildlife-watchers, the Iberian lynx is Doñana's most sought-after prize. Along with the Sierra Morena, Parque Nacional de Doñana and Parque Natural de Doñana are the main habitats for this elusive feline, one of the world's most endangered cats.

Over the years, the park's lynxes have had to battle a disastrous slump in Doñana's population of rabbits (the lynx's main prey), as well as threats from hunters, developers, habitat loss, and even tourism. Some resident lynxes have also been run over around Doñana – in 2019, 29 lynxes were killed in road accidents in the park and elsewhere in Spain.

However, recent years have seen an increase in numbers and there are now reckoned to be between 70 to 100 individuals in the Doñana area – the official figure in 2018 was 94, up significantly from the 41 recorded in 2002. Factors contributing to this include the recent release of 10,000 rabbits into the area and an increasingly successful captive breeding program – in 2020, 26 breeding pairs were expected to produce between 37 and 45 kittens.

Catch live videos of lynxes at Doñana's breeding centre at the **Centro de Visitantes El Acebuche** (☑959 43 96 29; ⊙8am-3pm & 4-9pm May–mid-Sep, to 7pm mid-Sep–Mar, to 8pm Apr).

the chicks hatch in April and May. The flamingos stay until about August, when the lake, which they share with about 170 other bird species, no longer contains enough water to support them.

For maps, binoculars and bird-spotting tips, swing by the lakeside **visitor centre** (☑952 71 25 54; www.visitasfuentepiedra.es; ⊙10am-3pm mid-Dec–Feb & mid-Jun–mid-Sep, to 4pm mid-Sep–mid-Dec, to 5pm Mar–mid-Jun).

The Drive » From Fuente de Piedra, it's a 54km spin west on the A92 to Osuna. As you go you'll pass low-lying hills, endless olive groves and the hillside town of Estepa.

---

5 Osuna

Unassuming Osuna harbours a cache of architectural and artistic treasures courtesy of the fabulously wealthy dukes of Osuna.

A steep climb from Plaza Mayor leads to the magnificent Renaissance Colegiata de Santa María de la Asunción (p277) – actually two superposed churches set above the 16th-century crypt of the Duques de Osuna. Its impressive art collection includes paintings by José de Ribera (El Españoleto) and a fine sculpture by Juan de Mesa.

Stroll the streets northwest of Plaza Mayor to uncover Osuna's other stars: a string of ornately decorated baroque mansions, including the late-18th-century **Palacio de los Cepeda** (Calle de la Huerta 10; ⊙closed to the public).

✕ 🛏 p279, p290

The Drive » Head west on the A92 across the flat, dry Campiña region (82km). Follow 'Huelva' signs to bypass Seville and link up with the A49 to Portugal. Drive 49km west, then exit onto the A483 for the last 27km south to El Rocío. Please heed lynx warning signs as you enter the Doñana area.

TRIP HIGHLIGHT

6 Parque Nacional de Doñana

Welcome to Spain's most celebrated national park, a hauntingly beautiful 601-sq-km expanse of wetlands, beaches, dunes and woodlands. Its protected habitats provide refuge for a huge variety of flora and fauna, including 360 bird species and the endangered Iberian lynx, one of 37 types of mammal. Much of the park's perimeter is bordered by the separate

Parque Natural de Doñana.

The obvious base for the park is **El Rocío**, a dusky, sand-blown town which bursts into life every Penetecost weekend for the the **Romería del Rocío**, Spain's largest religious pilgrimage. Two nights here gives you a full day for Doñana.

El Rocío's gleaming wetlands offer some of Doñana's finest bird- and wildlife-watching. Look out for spoonbills, pink flamingos, horses and deer from the waterfront promenade and the **Francisco Bernis Birdwatching Centre** (☎959 44 23 72; www.facebook.com/centroFranciscoBernis; Paseo Marismeño; ⏱9am-2pm & 4-6pm Tue-Sun).

You can't enter the national park in your own car, though you can drive to the four visitor centres, including the Centro de Visitantes El Acebuche (p285), 12km south of El Rocío. To access the park, you'll need to go on a guided trip with a licensed operator such as **Doñana Nature** (☎630 978216, 959 44 21 60; www.donana-nature.com; Calle Moguer 10; per person €30), **Cooperativa Marismas del Rocío** (☎959 43 04 32; www.donanavisitas.es; Centro de Visitantes El Acebuche; tours €30) or **Doñana Reservas** (☎959 44 24 74, 629 060545; www.donanareservas.com; Avenida de la Canaliega; tours per person €30). These offer four-hour trips in all-terrain vehicles. Book as far ahead as possible, especially in spring and summer.

✗ ⇢ p291

The Drive ⟫ Rev up for a 245km drive. Backtrack to the A49 from El Rocío and head east. Follow signs for 'A4 Cádiz' to circumnavigate Seville onto the AP4 and whizz 85km south. Continue south on the A4 and A48 for 48km, then turn onto the A2232 to Conil. From here it's 15km on the A2233 to Los Caños de Meca.

❼ Los Caños de Meca

Los Caños de Meca sprawls along a series of stunning white-sand beaches on the wind-battered Costa de la Luz. Once a hippie hangout, it still attracts beach-lovers of all stripes with its bohemian summer scene, nudist beaches and excellent water sports – kitesurfing, windsurfing and board-surfing are all big here.

WHY THIS IS A CLASSIC TRIP
DUNCAN GARWOOD, AUTHOR

This trip is the perfect showcase for Andalucía's diverse landscapes, leading from mainland Spain's highest mountains to wild, windswept beaches and eerie wetlands. One day you'll be be inching up steep valley roads in the Sierra Nevada, the next you'll be spying on flocks of pink flamingos in the other-worldly Parque Nacional de Doñana. It's a thrilling ride.

CHIKONAVAS/SHUTTERSTOCK ©

Left: **Paraje Natural Torcal de Antequera** El Torcal (p284)
Right: **Parque Nacional de Doñana** Flamingo (p285)

Classic Trip

Follow a tiny side road (often covered in sand) at the western end of town to a lighthouse, the **Cabo de Trafalgar**, off which the Spanish navy was defeated by Nelson's British fleet in 1805. Nearby, stop off at the ultimate relaxation spot, **Las Dunas** (☎956 43 72 03; www.barlasdunas.es; Carretera del Cabo de Trafalgar; dishes €4-12; ⊗9am-midnight Sep-Jun, to 3am Jul & Aug; ⚲) for Bob Marley tunes, great *bocadillos* (filled rolls), and a chilled, beach-shack vibe.

For a good walk, head to the eastern end of Caños. Here you can pick up the 7.2km **Sendero del Acantilado**, a spectacular clifftop path that runs to Barbate through the protected pine forests and marshlands of the 50-sq-km **Parque**

Natural de la Breña y Marismas del Barbate (www.juntadeandalucia.es). Then retrace your steps or jump on a bus back to Caños (Monday to Friday).

🛏 p291

The Drive » This is classic Costa de la Luz driving. From Caños, head 10km east to Barbate, then take the A2231 for 10km to Zahara de los Atunes. Turn inland here and continue past towering wind turbines to the N340. Join this and push southeast for 15km to the signposted CA8202 Bolonia turn-off, from where it's a lovely, hilly 7km drive to Bolonia.

----

8 Bolonia

With its gorgeous white-sand dune, broad beach and wind-bashed *chiringuitos* (beach bars) nestled beneath rolling green hills, sleepy Bolonia makes a wonderfully low-key stop on your trip down the Costa de la Luz.

Sands aside, the main draw here is the ruined

Roman settlement of **Baelo Claudia** (☎956 10 67 97; www.museosdeandalucia. es; EU/non-EU citizens free/€1.50; ⊗9am-9pm Tue-Sat Apr–mid-Jun, 9am-3pm & 6-9pm Tue-Sat mid-Jun–Jul, 9am-3pm Tue-Sat Aug–mid Sep, 9am-6pm Tue-Sat Sep-Mar, 9am-3pm Sun year-round), one of Andalucía's most important archaeological sites. The town, which flourished during the reign of Claudius (41–54 CE), was known across the Roman world for its garum (a spicy seasoning made from leftover fish parts). Nowadays, its magnificent seaside ruins – with views across to Morocco – include the substantial remains of thermal baths, workshops, a theatre, a paved forum and basilica. There's also a good museum.

The Drive » Backtrack to the N340 for the 15km drive southeast to Tarifa. Parking in Tarifa can be tricky, but there's metered space on Avenida de la Constitución beside the Alameda.

----

9 Tarifa

Wrap up this epic drive in Tarifa, on Spain's southernmost tip where the Mediterranean meets the Atlantic. The town, which gives off a tangible North African feel, is a haven

---

✓ **TOP TIP:**
SURFING EL PALMAR

Cádiz' Costa de la Luz boasts brilliant windsurfing and kitesurfing. El Palmar beach, about 7km northwest of Los Caños, has Andalucía's best board-surfing waves from October to May. For classes and boards, contact **Escuela de Surf 9 Pies** (☎620 104241; www.escueladesurf9pies.com; Paseo Marítimo; board & wetsuit rental per 2/4hr €12/18, 2hr group class €28).

DETOUR:
PARQUE NATURAL LOS ALCORNOCALES

Start: 🟢 Tarifa

The Parque Natural Los Alcornocales, a gorgeous 1736-sq-km reserve of crinkled, medium-height hills and extensive *alcornocales* (cork-oak woodlands), sits about 75km inland from the Strait of Gibraltar. Rich in archaeological, historical and natural interest, it's particularly rewarding to explore with your own wheels.

The best base is bucolic sun-bleached **Jimena de la Frontera**, about an hour's drive (64km) northeast of Tarifa. The town's 13th-century Nasrid **castle** (⊙9am-10pm Apr-Sep, to 8pm Oct-Mar) commands mesmerising views of Gibraltar and Africa, while trails offer excellent hiking.

One of the park's best trails is the 3.3km **Sendero Subida al Picacho** which leads up through cork-oak forest to the park's second-highest peak, **El Picacho** (882m). To do this walk, and a number of other local hikes, you'll need a (free) permit – you must request this at least three days in advance from the **Oficina del Parque Natural Los Alcornocales** (📞856 58 75 08; www.juntadeandalucia.es; Carretera Alcalá-Benalup, Km 1, Alcalá de los Gazules; ⊙8.30am-3.30pm Mon-Fri).

of sporting fun with a laid-back, surf-inspired buzz, long history and international-focused culinary scene.

Duck under the Mudéjar **Puerta de Jerez** to enter the old town, whose narrow, whitewashed streets are mostly of Islamic origin. The main sight here is the 10th-century **Castillo de Guzmán El Bueno** (Calle Guzmán el Bueno; adult/child €4/free; ⊙10am-4pm), where Reconquista hero Guzmán El Bueno legendarily sacrificed his own son in 1294 to save Tarifa from Moroccan attackers. A short hop away, the **Miramar** (📞607 984871; Calle Amargura; ⊙10am-4pm)

commands spectacular views across to Africa just 14km away.

For a change of scene, check out the surf-style boutiques on Calle Batalla del Salado. Then hit the bleach-blond sands that stretch 10km northwest to **Playa de Valdevaqueros** and **Punta Paloma**, one of Andalucía's most fabulous beaches.

Tarifa's waters provide some of Europe's finest kitesurfing and windsurfing, particularly in May, June and September. Link up with operators like **ION Club Hurricane** (📞956 68 90 98; www.ion-club.net; Carretera N340, Km 78, Hurricane Hotel;

6hr group kitesurfing or windsurfing beginner course €250; ⊙10.30am-8.30pm Jul & Aug, to 7pm Jun & Sep, to 6.30pm Mar-May & Oct-Dec) for equipment rental and classes.

Aventura Ecuestre (📞626 480019, 956 23 66 32; www.aventuraecuestre.com; Carretera N340, Km 79.5, Hotel Dos Mares) runs fabulous horse rides.

The **tourist office** (📞956 68 09 93; www.turismodetarifa.com; Paseo de la Alameda; ⊙10am-1.30pm & 4-6pm Mon-Fri, 10am-1.30pm Sat & Sun) can provide details of other activities including hiking, diving, biking and whale-watching.

✕ 🛏 p291

Eating & Sleeping

Capileira ①

✖ El Corral del Castaño   Andalucian €€

(📞958 763 414; Plaza del Calvario 16; mains
€8-23; 🕐1-4pm & 8-10pm Thu-Tue; 🍴) Enjoy
a lovely plaza setting and excellent Andalucian
cooking with creative, international influences
at this welcoming village restaurant. The menu
roams from traditional Alpujarras classics
like the meaty *plato alpujarreño* to inventive
numbers such as Moroccan-style veg-stuffed
pastela (pastry) or pork cheeks in red wine, plus
home-baked pizzas and desserts.

🛏 Hotel Real de Poqueira   Hotel €€

(📞958 76 39 02; www.hotelespoqueira.es; Plaza
Panteón Viejo; s €50, d €55-95; 🕐mid-Feb–
mid-Jan; ❄🛜🏊) Occupying a typical old
house opposite Capileira's church, this terrific
three-star hotel is the pick of several village
accommodations run by the same welcoming
family. Rooms are elegantly minimalist and
modern, with smart bathrooms and shimmery
bedding, and there's a small pool, garden bar
and a restaurant.

Antequera ③

✖ Baraka   Tapas €

(📞664 390778; Plaza de las Descalzas; tapas €2-
4; 🕐10am-2am Mon & Wed-Fri, from 11am Sat &
Sun) Sombreros off to the brave staff at Baraka,
who cross a busy road, trays loaded, risking life
and limb to serve punters sitting in a little park
opposite. Like all good Antequera restaurants,
Baraka doesn't stray far from excellent local
nosh (*porra antequerana* calls loudly), although
it does a nice sideline in *pintxos* (Basque tapas)
and serves heavenly bread.

🛏 Hotel Coso Viejo   Hotel €

(📞952 70 50 45; www.hotelcosoviejo.es;
Calle Encarnación 9; d incl breakfast €43-
56; 🅿❄🛜) This converted 17th-century
neoclassical palace is right in the heart of
Antequera, opposite Plaza Coso Viejo and the
town museum (p284). The simply furnished
rooms are set around a handsome patio with a
fountain, and the excellent Mesón Las Hazuelas
tapas bar and restaurant is just next door.

Osuna ⑤

✖ Casa Curro   Tapas €€

(📞955 82 07 58; www.facebook.com/
restaurantecasacurro; Plaza Salitre 5; tapas
€2.50-3, mains €9-15; 🕐noon-midnight Tue-
Sun) A favourite with the *Game of Thrones* cast
when they were filming in town, this is one of
Osuna's best-known tapas bars, frequented by
locals and visitors alike. It certainly looks the
part with its long polished bar, cluttered walls
and blackboard menus, and the traditional food
is reliably good.

🛏 Hotel Palacio
Marqués de la Gomera   Historic Hotel €€

(📞954 81 26 32; www.hotelpalaciodelmarques.
es; Calle San Pedro 20; s €51-70, d €56-89;
❄🛜) Live like nobility at this palatial four-star
hotel, elegantly housed in one of Osuna's finest
baroque mansions. Tiled floors and sandstone
arches remain from the original building,
decorating the sumptuous arched courtyard
and spacious, individually styled rooms. There's
even an ornate private chapel, as well as a smart
restaurant and peaceful back patio. Rates are
available with or without breakfast.

Parque Nacional de Doñana 6

✕ Restaurante Toruño   Andalucian €€

(📞959 44 24 22; www.toruno.es; Plaza
Acebuchal; mains €13-25; ⏱1-4pm & 8-11pm; ✈)
With its traditional Andalucian atmosphere, good
food and huge portions, Toruño is a perennial
El Rocío favourite. Menu highlights include the
free-range *mostrenca* calf, unique to Doñana; for
noncarnivores, the *parrillada* (grilled assortment)
of vegetables is fantastic. Dine in front of the
restaurant by the 1000-year-old *acebuche* (olive)
tree or out back overlooking the wetlands.

⊨ Hotel Toruño   Hotel €€

(📞959 44 23 23; www.toruno.es; Plaza
Acebuchal 22; s €35-59, d €50-80, all incl
breakfast; P✱🛜📶) This brilliantly white
villa 350m east of the Ermita directly abuts
the *marismas* (wetlands), where you can
spot flamingos going through their morning
beauty routine. Inside, tile murals continue the
wildlife theme. Interior rooms are uninspiring,
especially on the ground floor; request one
overlooking the marshes if available. Across the
plaza, the hotel's Restaurante Toruño is among
El Rocío's best.

⊨ Parador de Mazagón   Hotel €€€

(📞959 53 63 00; www.paradores.es; Carretera
San Juan del Puerto-Matalascañas, Km 31; d
€150-334; ✱@🛜🏊) Perched above the
sea in a pine forest at Doñana's western edge,
Mazagón stands out among Spain's nationwide
parador (luxury state-owned hotels) network
as a true haven for nature lovers. From the
hotel's front door, it's a five-minute walk to
the seemingly endless expanse of cliff-fringed
sandy beach below. Alternatively, stay up top
to enjoy the gardens, pool, spa and on-site
bar-restaurant.

Los Caños de Meca 7

⊨ Hotel Madreselva   Hotel €€

(📞956 43 72 55; www.califavejer.com; Avenida
de Trafalgar 102; d €75-135; ⏱Apr–mid-Oct;
P🛜🏊) Strung around a leafy courtyard, this
mellow, peachy-orange hacienda-style hideaway
has 18 charmingly rustic rooms with surfy vibes,
vintage furniture and private terraces. There's
a summer-only Spanish restaurant, all just a
minute's walk from Caños' beach.

Tarifa 9

✕ Café Azul   Cafe €

(www.cafeazul-tarifa.com; Calle Batalla del
Salado 8; dishes €2-9; ⏱9am-3pm; 🛜✈)
This long-established Italian-run cafe with
eye-catching blue-and-white Morocco-inspired
decor whips up some of the best breakfasts in
Andalucía. You'll want to eat everything. The
fruit salad with muesli, yoghurt and coconut,
and the fruit-and-yoghurt-stuffed crêpe are
works of art. It also serves Italian coffee, honey-
sweetened teas, fresh smoothies and juices,
bocadillos and cooked breakfasts, with delicious
gluten-free and vegan options.

✕ Surla   Cafe €

(📞956 68 51 75; www.facebook.com/surlatarifa;
Calle Pintor Pérez Villalta 64; dishes €4-8; ⏱9am-
5pm Mon-Fri, to 7pm Sat & Sun; ✈) Decorative
surfboards, wall-mounted chairs and Balinese
umbrellas fill the leafy, tropical-feel interior of
this wonderful laid-back cafe, where the focus
is on organic local, seasonal ingredients: *jamón*
from Huelva's mountains, Granada olive oil,
Cádiz' own free-range eggs, salt and *payoyo*
cheese.

⊨ Hostal África   Hostal €

(📞956 68 02 20; www.hostalafrica.com; Calle
María Antonia Toledo 12; s €40-75, d €60-95,
tr €90-120; ⏱Mar-Nov; 🛜) This mellow,
revamped 19th-century house within Tarifa's
old town is one of Cádiz province's best *hostales*
(budget hotels). Full of potted plants and sky-
blue-and-white arches, it's run by hospitable, on-
the-ball owners, and the 13 unfussy, all-different
rooms (including one triple) sparkle with bright
colours. Enjoy the lovely roof terrace, with its
loungey cabana and Africa views.

⊨ Riad   Boutique Hotel €€€

(📞856 92 98 80; www.theriadtarifa.com; Calle
Comendador 10; d €99-210) A seductively
converted 17th-century town house, the Riad
opens through a polished-concrete lobby adorned
by an ornamental fountain/pool, fresh lilies
and flickering candles. It's dressed with original
architecture: exposed-stone walls, antique doors,
red-brick arches, a frescoed facade. Off the
patio are a *hammam*, a rooftop lounge and nine
intimate rooms styled with *tadelakt* (waterproof
plaster) walls, Morocco-made tiles and soothing
Andalucía-meets-Morocco design.

Andalucía's White Villages

Discover a world of blanched beauty, hilltop history, bucolic walks and remote mountain passes as you weave your way through Andalucía's classic white towns.

24

TRIP HIGHLIGHTS

START
● Carmona

161 km

Grazalema
Rugged mountain beauty and gorgeous natural park walks

● Olvera

Algodonales ●

El Bosque ●

2

3

7 **FINISH**

Arcos de la Frontera
The white town of your dreams

111 km

Ronda
A spectacular clifftop mountain town steeped in historical drama

239 km

4 DAYS
239KM / 148 MILES

GREAT FOR...

BEST TIME TO GO
May, June, September and October for perfect temperatures.

 ESSENTIAL PHOTO

Arcos de la Frontera's clifftop panoramas.

 BEST FOR OUTDOORS

Beautiful Sierra de Grazalema mountain walks.

de la Frontera Dramatically positioned white village (p295)

24 Andalucía's White Villages

Crumbling, eons-old fortifications soar over whitewashed terracotta-tiled homes huddled together in a rocky, green landscape: a visual spectacle that threads through this tour of Andalucía's prettiest *pueblos blancos*. This trip showcases the historical allure of the region's quintessential white towns while also paving the way for some fantastic hiking and exhilarating driving over spine-tingling mountain roads. Kick off with Roman tombs in Carmona; end with mountain magic in Ronda.

1 Carmona

Crowning a low-rise hill 35km east of Seville, Carmona provides a living snapshot of Andalucian history. The town's tumultuous past is writ large on its maze-like old town whose narrow streets are crammed with Mudéjar and Christian churches, aristocratic mansions, centuries-old monuments, and buzzy tapas bars.

Dig back to Paleolithic times at the **Museo de la Ciudad** (📞954 14

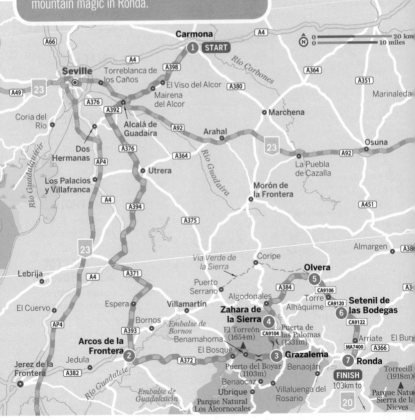

01 28; www.museociudad.
carmona.org; Calle San
Ildefonso 1; adult/student/
child €2.50/1.20/free, Tue
free; ⊙11am-2pm Mon, to
7pm Tue-Sun Sep–mid-Jun,
10am-2pm mid-Jun–Aug)
before stopping off at
the splendidly over-the-
top **Prioral de Santa
María de la Asunción**
(📞954 19 14 82; www.
santamariacarmona.org; Plaza
Marqués de las Torres; adult/
child €3/1.80; ⊙9.30am-2pm
& 5-7pm Tue-Fri, 9.30am-2pm
Sat) with its gorgeous
Patio de los Naranjos.
A short walk away, the
Puerta de Córdoba (Calle
de Dolores Quintanilla; adult/
child €2/1; ⊙11am-3pm Mon,
Tue, Thu & Fri, 10am-3pm Sat &
Sun) provides great photo
opportunities.

On Carmona's
southwestern fringe
stands the eerily
fascinating 1st- and
2nd-century **Necrópolis
Romana** (Roman cemetery;

LINK YOUR TRIP

 20 Mediterranean Meander

Make for Málaga, 103km
southeast of Ronda, to
hook up with this coastal
cruise to Barcelona.

 23 The Great Outdoors

From Carmona head
61km southeast to
Osuna to join this epic
outdoors adventure.

📞600 143632; www.
museosdeandalucia.es;
Avenida de Jorge Bonsor 9; EU/
non-EU citizens free/€1.50;
⊙9am-9pm Tue-Sat, to 3pm
Sun Apr–mid-Jun, 9am-3pm
Tue-Sun mid-Jun–mid-Sep,
9am-6pm Tue-Sat, to 3pm Sun
mid-Sep–Mar).

🛏 p299

The Drive » Take the A398
southwest, then continue on
the A392 and A376 to Utrera
(50km). Here pick up the A394
and continue down this and the
NIV towards Jerez de la Frontera.
Turn off the NIV onto the A371,
signposted to Villamartín, and
after 4km or so, turn right
towards Espera. Arcos is about
14km beyond Espera on the
A393.

- - - - - - - - - - - - - - - - - -

TRIP HIGHLIGHT

❷ Arcos de la Frontera

If there's one white town
in Cádiz province that
outshines them all, it's
Arcos de la Frontera.
Thrillingly sited atop
a dramatic sheer-sided
crag, it charms with its
whitewashed arches,
twisting alleyways and
air of historical mystery.

The main attraction
is **Plaza del Cabildo**
which commands
spectacular vistas over
the Río Guadalete from
its vertiginous **mirador**.
The real knockout view,
though, is the dramatic
clifftop panorama from
the adjacent **parador**
(📞956 70 05 00; www.
parador.es; Plaza del Cabildo;
r €120-150; ❋ @ 🛜).

Bordering the plaza's
northern edge is the
Gothic-baroque **Basílica
Menor de Santa María
de la Asunción** (Plaza del
Cabildo; €2; ⊙10am-12.45pm
& 4-6.30pm Mon-Fri, 10am-
1.30pm Sat Mar–mid-Dec), an
intriguing church whose
gold-leaf altarpiece is a
miniature of the one in
Seville's cathedral.

 🛏 p299

The Drive » It's a tame
30km eastbound drive on
the A372 to El Bosque, then
suddenly you find yourself
on a thrilling, winding 20km
climb to Grazalema. Stop at
the signposted Puerto del
Boyar (1103m) for glorious
mountainscapes.

- - - - - - - - - - - - - - - - - -

TRIP HIGHLIGHT

❸ Grazalema

Craving some physical
activity? Clinging to
verdant rocky slopes,
rust-roofed Grazalema is
an idyllic white mountain
town as well as an ideal
base for exploring the
rugged, 534-sq-km
Parque Natural Sierra
de Grazalema. It's also
reputed to be the rainiest
spot in Spain (yes, really).

Stretch your legs on
the **El Calvario-Corazón
de Jesús** trail to a ruined
chapel, or choose from
numerous paths starting
near Grazalema. **Horizon**
(📞956 13 23 63, 655 934565;
www.horizonaventura.com;
Calle Las Piedras 1; ⊙10am-
2pm & 5-8pm, reduced
hours Oct-Apr) organises
all kinds of adventure
activities: hiking,

kayaking, canyoning and paragliding.

In town, you can hang out on **Plaza de España** and learn about Grazalema's traditional wool production at the **Museo de Artesanía Textil** (www.mantasdegrazalema.com; Carretera deRonda; ☺8am-2pm & 3-6.30pm Mon-Thu, 8am-2pm Fri).

🛏 p299

The Drive » What a fantastic 17km. Full of sharp switchbacks, the steep CA9104 snakes north from Grazalema over the 1331m Puerto de las Palomas to Zahara de la Sierra. The views are fabulous: Zahara's reservoir twinkles turquoise as jagged mountains melt into the distance.

④ Zahara de la Sierra

Laced around a vertiginous castle-topped crag at the foot of the Grazalema mountains, Zahara de la Sierra is a vision of classic white-town beauty. A Moorish stronghold in the 14th and 15th centuries, it's now a popular base for hiking the Garganta Verde (p298).

To reach the 12th-century **castillo** (☺24hr), it's a steep-ish 10- to 15-minute climb up a path starting opposite Hotel Arco de la Villa.

The castle's recapture from the Christians by Abu al-Hasan of Granada in 1481 triggered the last phase of the Reconquista, culminating in the 1492 fall of Granada.

The Drive » Exit Zahara northbound and work your way down to the A2300 which skirts Zahara's reservoir for around 6km to the A384. Whizz along this for about 22km to Olvera, which you'll spot from miles away across the sun-drenched, olive-cloaked countryside. The road passes the Peñón de Zaframagón, an important griffon vulture refuge.

Ronda White town that straddles the Tajo gorge (p298)

⑤ Olvera

Gutsier than its
neighbours, Olvera is
as known for its olive
oil as for the wonderful
36km **Vía Verde de la
Sierra** (www.viasverdes.
com), considered the
finest of Andalucía's 23
vías verdes (disused
railway lines transformed
into hiking/cycling
greenways). Rent bikes
(€12 per day) at **Sesca**
(☎657 987432, 687 676462;
www.sesca.es; Calle Pasadera
4; regular/electric bike hire per
day €10/20; ◷9am-2pm &
4-6pm Oct-May, reduced hours
Jun-Sep; 🚲) and spin west
to Puerto Serrano along

four viaducts and 30
tunnels.

The town, which
probably dates to Roman
times and was used as a
bandit refuge until the
mid-19th century, is also
well worth exploring.
Main sights include the
630m-high, late-12th-
century **Castillo Árabe**
(Plaza de la Iglesia; incl La
Cilla €2; ◷10.30am-2pm &
4-8pm Tue-Sun Jun–mid-Sep,
10.30am-2pm & 4-6pm Tue-Sun
mid-Sep–May), neoclassical
**Iglesia Parroquial
Nuestra Señora de la
Encarnación** (Plaza de la
Iglesia; €2; ◷11am-1pm &
4-6pm Tue-Sun) and the
town's history museum

inside **La Cilla** (Plaza de
la Iglesia; incl Castillo Árabe
€2; ◷10.30am-2pm &
4-8pm Tue-Sun Jun–mid-Sep,
10.30am-2pm & 4-6pm Tue-
Sun mid-Sep–May).

The Drive ⟫ Follow the CA9106
and CA9120 southwards from
Olvera past rolling hills, through
Torre Alháquime, to Setenil de
las Bodegas, 15km away.

⑥ Setenil
de las Bodegas

Setenil de las Bodegas is
something of a historic
anomaly. While most
white towns sought
protection atop lofty
crags, the folk of Setenil
burrowed into the caves

LOCAL KNOWLEDGE:
SIERRA DE GRAZALEMA WALKS

Lovely marked walking trails fan out across the Sierra de Grazalema. Pick up maps and info at the **Centro de Visitantes El Bosque** (📞956 70 97 33; www. juntadeandalucia.es; Calle Federico García Lorca 1, El Bosque; ⏱10am-2pm, closed Mon Jun-Sep), **Punto de Información Zahara de la Sierra** (📞956 12 31 14; Plaza del Rey 3; ⏱10am-2pm Tue-Sun) or Grazalema's **Oficina de Turismo** (📞956 13 20 52; www. grazalema.es; Plaza de los Asomaderos; ⏱9am-3pm Tue-Sun Jun-Sep, 10am-2pm & 3-5.30pm Tue-Sun Oct-May).

The following walks all require free pre-booked permits from the Centro de Visitantes El Bosque.

Garganta Verde Starting 3.5km south of Zahara de la Sierra (off the CA9104), this 2.5km (one hour) path meanders into the precipitous Garganta Verde (Green Throat), a lushly vegetated gorge over 100m deep. It's one of the Sierra's most spectacular walks.

El Torreón (⏱16 Oct-May) El Torreón (1648m) is Cádiz province's highest peak and, on clear days, you can see Gibraltar, the Sierra Nevada and Morocco's Rif mountains from the summit. The challenging 3km trail (2½ hours) begins 8km west of Grazalema on the A372.

El Pinsapar This 12km (six-hour) walk winds past rare dark-green *pinsapos* (Spanish firs) to Benamahoma. It starts 2km uphill from Grazalema off the CA9104.

beneath the steep cliffs of the Río Trejo. The strategy clearly worked as it took the Christian armies 15 days to dislodge the Moors from Setenil in 1484. Swing by to explore original cave-houses, the 12th-century **castle** (Calle Villa; €1; ⏱11am-6pm) and the rustic bar-restaurants on and around Plaza de Andalucía.

The Drive ⟩⟩ Zip 17km south into Málaga province to Ronda via the CA9122, MA7403, and from Arriate, the MA7400.

- - - - - - - - - - - - - - - - - - -

TRIP HIGHLIGHT

7 Ronda

End your trip on a high at rugged Ronda.

Spectacularly straddling the 100m-wide Tajo gorge, Ronda is the largest and busiest of Andalucía's white towns and the (alleged) birthplace of modern bullfighting.

The town's most recognisable sight is the 18th-century **Puente Nuevo** (New Bridge; interpretive centre adult/concession €2.50/2; ⏱interpretive centre 10am-6pm Mon-Fri, to 3pm Sat & Sun) which spans the dramatic gorge separating the old and new towns. The old town (aka La Ciudad) is a walled tangle of streets, peppered with Renaissance mansions

and intriguing museums such as the **Museo de Ronda** (Palacio Mondragón, Plaza Mondragón; €3.50; ⏱10am-7pm Mon-Fri, to 3pm Sat & Sun Apr-Sep, shorter hours Oct-Mar).

In the new town, **Plaza de España** was the scene of events in the Civil War that inspired a grisly episode in Hemingway's *For Whom the Bell Tolls*. Nearby, the 200-year-old **Plaza de Toros** (Calle Virgen de la Paz; €8, incl audio guide €9.50; ⏱10am-8pm Apr-Sep, to 7pm Mar & Oct, to 6pm Nov-Feb) is one of Spain's oldest and most celebrated bullrings.

✕ ⌂ p299

Eating & Sleeping

Carmona ➊

🛏 El Rincón de las Descalzas
Boutique Hotel €€

(☎954 19 11 72; www.elrincondelasdescalzas. com; Calle de las Descalzas 1; s €46-66, d €50-116, ste €121-178; ❋ 🛜) Discreetly sited in a revamped 18th-century townhouse, this delightfully sprawling hotel offers 13 colourful rooms and a picturesque, orange-hued patio. Each room is different, and some are better than others, but all sport a refined heritage look with carved-wood beds, exposed brick and sandstone, timber arches and the occasional fireplace.

Arcos de la Frontera ➋

🍴 Taberna Jóvenes Flamencos
Tapas €

(☎657 133552; www.facebook.com/pg/ taberna.jovenesflamencos; Calle Deán Espinosa 11; tapas €2-4; ⏱ noon-midnight Thu-Tue; 🖐) Along with oh-so-Andalucía flamenco/ bullfighting decor, tiled floors and hand-painted tables, cheerful and popular Jóvenes Flamencos has an enticing menu of meat, seafood and vegetarian tapas and *raciones* (large/full plate servings), including chunky tortilla, goat's cheese drizzled with local honey and soul-warming onion soup topped with *payoyo* cheese. All ingredients and wines are from Cádiz province; service is impeccable; and music and dance break out regularly.

🛏 La Casa Grande
Heritage Hotel €€

(☎956 70 39 30; www.lacasagrande.net; Calle Maldonado 10; r €74-105, ste €110-125; ⏱ closed 6-31 Jan; ❋ @ 🛜) This gorgeous, rambling, cliff-side mansion dating to 1729 once belonged to the great flamenco dancer Antonio Ruiz Soler, and still feels more arty home than hotel, with original tiling and arches. The seven rooms are individually styled with modern-rustic design and most have divine valley views. Great breakfasts (€10), a well-stocked library, a rooftop terrace, and on-demand massage and yoga complete a tempting package.

Grazalema ➌

🛏 La Mejorana
Guesthouse €

(☎956 13 25 27; www.lamejorana.net; Calle Santa Clara 6; d incl breakfast €62; ❋ 🛜 ✦) An exceptionally welcoming house towards the upper end of Grazalema, La Mejorana has nine comfy rooms in colourful, updated rustic style. Some have private lounges and sky-blue Moroccan-style arches; others balconies, terraces, huge mirrors or wrought-iron bedsteads. A lounge, library and breakfast terrace, with gorgeous village views, overlook the leafy hammock-strung garden and twinkling pool.

Ronda ➐

🍴 Almocábar
Andalucian €€

(☎952 87 59 77; Calle Ruedo Alameda 5; tapas €2, mains €15-25; ⏱12.30-4.30pm & 8-11pm Wed-Mon) Tapas here include *montaditos* (small pieces of bread) topped with delicacies like duck breast and chorizo. Mains are available in the elegant dining room, where meat dominates – rabbit, partridge, lamb and beef cooked on a hot stone at your table. There's a bodega upstairs, and wine tastings and dinner can be arranged for a minimum of eight people (approximately €50 per person).

🛏 Hotel Soho Boutique Palacio San Gabriel
Hotel €€

(☎952 19 03 92; www.sohohoteles.com; Calle Marqués de Moctezuma 19; d incl breakfast from €90; ❋ 🛜) Despite new chain-hotel management, this heavyweight historic edifice retains its age-old charm, filled with antiques and faded photographs that offer an insight into Ronda's history – bullfighting, celebrities and all. Ferns hang down the huge mahogany staircase, and there's a billiard room, a cosy living room stacked with books, and a DVD-screening room with 10 velvet-covered seats rescued from Ronda's theatre.

Olive Oil & the Renaissance in Jaén

Take to the quiet roads of this little-visited corner of Andalucía and you'll find charming country towns, exquisite Renaissance architecture and oceans of olive trees.

25

TRIP HIGHLIGHTS

84 km

Úbeda's Old Town
An architectural and culinary feast

115 km

Baeza
Winding streets lined by gorgeous stone mansions and churches

Jódar

Mancha Real

Torres

Albánchez de Mágina

1 START

4

6

FINISH

Jaen's Castillo de Santa Catalina
Magnificent views over Jaén and countryside

1 km

3–4 DAYS
115KM / 71 MILES

GREAT FOR...

BEST TIME TO GO
From April to June, and September and October for perfect weather.

 ESSENTIAL PHOTO
The panorama of mountains and olive groves from the Castillo de Albánchez.

 BEST FOR AESTHETES
The architectural composition of Úbeda's Plaza Vázquez de Molina.

Olive groves (p302)

301

25

Olive Oil & the Renaissance in Jaén

The 16th-century grandees of this rural region beautified their towns just as classically inspired Renaissance architecture was sweeping into Spain from Italy. The resulting buildings dazzle to this day, particularly in World Heritage–listed Úbeda and Baeza. Beyond these towns, the landscape is a never-ending carpet of silvery-green olive trees, an almost hypnotic spectacle that will whet the appetite of olive oil aficionados.

TRIP HIGHLIGHT

❶ Jaén

Everything in the charming, if mildly dilapidated, historic centre of this provincial capital is dwarfed by the **Catedral de la Asunción** (www.catedraldejaen.org; Plaza de Santa María; adult incl audio guide €5, child/senior €1.50/2; ⊙10am-2pm & 4-7pm Mon-Fri, to 5.30pm Sat, 10-11.30am & 4-5.30pm Sun), designed by Andrés de Vandelvira, the master Renaissance architect whose work

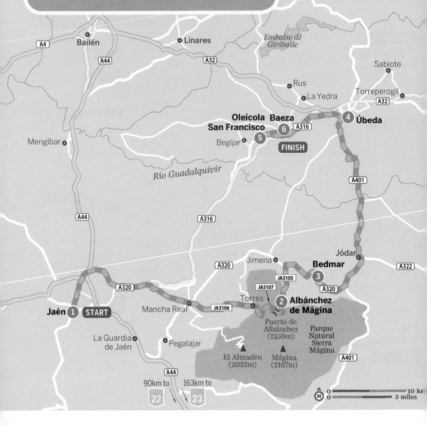

you'll see more of in Úbeda and Baeza. The cathedral's huge, round arches, clustered Corinthian columns, beautifully carved stone ceilings and great circular dome are all part and parcel of its Renaissance aesthetic.

Avoid the aggravation of Jaén's traffic system by taking a taxi (€7) or walking (about 40 minutes) up to the **Cerro de Santa Catalina**, the wooded hill towering above the city. The views from the large cross at the end of the castle ridge are magnificent. The castle itself, the **Castillo de Santa Catalina** (Cerro de Santa Catalina; adult/reduced €3.50/1.50, 3-6pm Wed free; ☻10am-6pm Mon-Sat, to 3pm Sun; **P**), was built by the conquering Christians to replace the Muslim fortress they captured in 1246. What exists today is only about one-third of the original castle – the rest was demolished to make way for a luxury hotel, the Parador Castillo de Santa Catalina (p307), in the 1960s. If you're not staying at the *parador*, drop in for a drink to see the extraordinary vaulted ceilings in the main salon and restaurant.

Back down in the centre, get a taste of Jaén's atmosphere with an evening tour of the ancient and atmospheric tapas bars clustered in the wafer-thin streets north of the cathedral.

📖 p307

The Drive » The quickest route to Albánchez de Mágina is along the A316, then the A320 via Mancha Real and Jimena, and finally the JA3105. For a more scenic drive, head to the pretty village of Torres from Mancha Real. Then, from Torres take the dramatic JA3107 which winds over the 1250m-high Puerto de Albánchez pass and down to Albánchez de Mágina. Either way, it's about 46km.

- - - - - - - - - - - - - - - -

➋ Albánchez de Mágina

This classic white village nestled beneath a towering cliff is home to one of Jaén province's most dramatic apparitions: the **Castillo de Albánchez** (☻24hr). The castle's 14th-century leaning tower is spectacularly perched atop a sheer cliff rising directly above the village. You can, amazingly enough, walk up to it in about 20 steep minutes – ask for directions in the central Plaza de la Constitución. Make the effort and you're rewarded with stunning bird's-eye views over the whitewashed village and surrounding mountains. Back in the village, there are several cafes and bars if you'd like refreshments.

The Drive » From Albánchez, head north down the JA3105 and turn right along the A320 as you enter Jimena. It's 8km to Bedmar.

- - - - - - - - - - - - - - - -

➌ Bedmar

Stop at this sizeable white village, with a backdrop of rugged crags, to wander its winding streets up to the picturesque remains of a 15th-century castle set on a panoramic rocky outcrop at the top of the village.

The Drive » Continue along the A320 to the A401 where you should turn left towards Jódar and Úbeda. Parking in Úbeda's old town is free but often difficult to find – the best bet is the 24-hour free car park on Redonda de Miradores.

LINK YOUR TRIP

22 Golden Triangle

From Jaén zip 90km down the A44 to Granada to link with this tour of Andalucía's most splendid cities.

23 The Great Outdoors

Continue past Granada to the Sierra Nevada to start this adventurous exploration of Andalucía's wild, unspoiled spaces.

FRANCK BOSTON/SHUTTERSTOCK ©

4 Úbeda

Beautiful Renaissance buildings grace almost every street and plaza in Úbeda's charming *casco antiguo* (old quarter). The World Heritage–listed town also offers top-class restaurants and tapas bars, making a stopover a real delight.

Start your exploring in **Plaza Vázquez de Molina**, Úbeda's elegant showpiece square bedecked with orange and cypress trees and framed by grand Renaissance buildings. At its east end stands the **Sacra Capilla de El Salvador** (Sacred Chapel of the Saviour; www. fundacionmedinaceli.org; Plaza Vázquez de Molina; adult/child incl audio guide €5/2.50; ⊙9.30am-2.30pm & 4.30-7.30pm Mon-Sat, 11.30am-3pm & 4.30-7.30pm Sun Apr-Sep, to 6pm Mon-Sat, to 7pm Sun Oct-Mar), **built between 1536 and 1559** by Andrés de Vandelvira for local aristocrat Francisco de los Cobos y Molina. Its ornately sculpted facade is a superb example of the early Renaissance style known as plateresque.

On the plaza's northern flank, the **Palacio de Vázquez de Molina** (Plaza Vázquez de Molina; ⊙8am-8pm Mon-Fri, 10am-2pm & 5-7.30pm Sat & Sun) is Úbeda's strikingly beautiful *ayuntamiento* (town hall). This perfectly proportioned Italianate mansion was built by Vandelvira in about 1562 for Juan Vázquez de Molina, whose coat of arms surmounts the doorway.

Other standout sights include the medieval **Sinagoga del Agua** (📞953 75 81 50; www. sinagogadelagua.com; Calle Roque Rojas 2; tours adult/child

Úbeda Sacra Capilla de El Salvador

€4.50/3.50; ⊘ tours every 45min 10.30am-1.30pm & 4.45-7pm Sep-Jun, 10.30am-1.30pm & 5.45-8pm Jul & Aug), a sensitive re-creation of a centuries-old synagogue and rabbi's house, and the **Casa Museo Andalusí** (☑659 508766; www.vandelviraturismo.com; Calle Narváez 11; €4; ⊘ tours 11.30am or by arrangement), a private museum in a 16th-century house with a huge collection of antiques. Informal guided tours led by the owner's art-historian daughter make it all come alive.

✗ p307

The Drive ≫ Head west out of Úbeda onto the A316. Then exit onto the A6109 at the Baeza Oeste turn-off and continue on to Begíjar via the JA4107. On the edge of Begíjar, turn right after a petrol station and you'll reach Oleícola San Francisco after about 200m.

- - - - - - - - - - - - - - - - - - - -

5 Oleícola San Francisco

As you'll have guessed from all those olive trees out there, Jaén province produces a *lot* of olive oil – up to a fifth of the world's total, in fact. For a first-hand lowdown on the business, the **Oleícola San Francisco**

(☑953 76 34 15; www. oleoturismojaen.com; Calle Pedro Pérez, Begíjar; tours in Spanish €7.50, in English or French €8.50; ⊘ tours in Spanish 11am & 5pm, in English or French 12.30 & 4.30pm) runs fascinating tours of its modern mill. You'll learn all you could ever want to know about the process of turning olives into oil, how the best oil is made and what distinguishes extra virgin from the rest. At the end you'll get the chance to taste a few varieties and buy a bottle or two. Reserve ahead and specify your preferred language.

JAEN'S RENAISSANCE MASTERMIND

Most of the finest buildings you'll see in Úbeda, Baeza and Jaén are the creations of one man: Andrés de Vandelvira, born in Alcaraz, Castilla-La Mancha, in 1509. Under the patronage of Úbeda's powerful Cobos and Molina families, Vandelvira almost single-handedly brought the Renaissance to Jaén province. Little is known about his life but his oeuvre is a jewel of Spanish culture, spanning all the main phases of Spanish Renaissance architecture, as shown by three exemplary buildings in Úbeda – the ornamental early phase called plateresque, on the **Sacra Capilla de El Salvador**; the purer lines and classical proportions of the later **Palacio de Vázquez de Molina**; and the sober late-Renaissance style of the **Hospital de Santiago** (Avenida Cristo Rey; ☺exhibition halls 11am-2pm & 5.30-9pm Tue-Sat), completed the year he died in 1575.

The Drive » Return to the A6109 and head east, following signs into Baeza. Street parking is fairly limited in town so your best bet is to leave your car at the underground car park on Calle Compañía.

- - - - - - - - - - - - - - - - - -

TRIP HIGHLIGHT

6 Baeza

With its beautiful historic centre, Baeza will ensure you finish your trip on a high. Most of the town's sights are clustered in the narrow streets south of the central Plaza de España and broad Paseo de la Constitución (once Baeza's marketplace and bullring). The principal monument is the **Catedral de Baeza** (Plaza de Santa María; adult/child €4/1.50, free 9.30-11am Mon; ☺9.30am-2pm & 4-7pm Mon, 10am-2pm & 4-7pm Tue-Fri, 10am-7pm Sat, 10am-6pm Sun). Dating to the 13th century, the church is something of an architectural hybrid, though the predominant style is 16th-century Renaissance, visible in the facade on Plaza de Santa María and the basic design of the three-nave interior (by Andrés de Vandelvira). Climb the tower for great views over the town and countryside.

Other architectural gems include **Plaza del Pópulo** (Plaza de los Leones), a handsome square surrounded by elegant 16th-century buildings, and **Palacio de Jabalquinto** (Plaza de Santa Cruz; ☺10.30am-1pm & 4-6pm), with a flamboyant Gothic facade featuring a bizarre array of naked humans clambering along the moulding over the doorway.

For a post-sightseeing breather, stroll along the **Paseo de las Murallas** for superb views over to the distant mountains of the Sierra Mágina (south) and Sierra de Cazorla (east). For more energetic entertainment, catch a gig at the **Café Teatro Central** (☎953 74 43 55; www.facebook. com/cafeteatrocentral; Calle Barreras 19; ☺4pm-3am Sun-Thu, to 4am Fri & Sat; 🛜).

✗ 🛏 p307

Eating & Sleeping

Jaén ❶

🛏 Parador Castillo de Santa Catalina　　Luxury Hotel €€

(🤙953 23 00 00; www.parador.es/parador-de-jaen; Castillo de Santa Catalina; d €120-183; P ❄ @ 🛜 ♨) Next to the castle high on the Cerro de Santa Catalina, Jaén's *parador* reopened in spring 2020 after an exhaustive renovation. Beyond the allure of its incomparable setting, it dazzles with theatrically vaulted halls and luxuriously dignified rooms with plush furnishings, some with four-poster beds. There is also an excellent restaurant and a bar with panoramic terrace seating.

Úbeda ❹

🍴 Misa de 12　　Andalucian €€

(🤙953 82 81 97; www.facebook.com/MisaDe12Ubeda; Plaza 1º de Mayo 7; raciones €10-24; ⏱ noon-4pm & 8.30pm-midnight Wed-Sun) Grab a table overlooking the plaza or hunker down in the cosy interior to sample a succession of truly succulent platters – from perfectly grilled slices of *presa ibérica* (a tender cut of Iberian pork) to *revuelto de pulpo y gambas* (eggs scrambled with octopus and shrimp). Despite the place's wild popularity, staff are unfailingly attentive and efficient.

🍴 Cantina La Estación　　Andalucian €€

(🤙687 777230; www.cantinalaestacion.com; Cuesta Rodadera 1; mains €15-24; ⏱1-3pm & 8pm-midnight Thu-Mon, 1-3pm Tue; 🛜) The charming originality here starts with the design – three rooms with railway themes (the main dining room being the deluxe carriage). Seasonally inspired fusion dishes, such as wild boar in red-wine sauce, or octopus with garlic chips and paprika, share the menu with traditional Úbeda recipes like *andrajos* (a stew of meat and/or fish with tomatoes, peppers and spices).

Baeza ❻

🍴 El Arcediano　　Tapas €

(Calle Barbacana 4; montaditos €3-7, raciones €7-15; ⏱8.30pm-midnight Thu, 1-4pm & 8.30pm-midnight Fri-Sun) Always buzzing with locals, this welcoming spot with dangling chandeliers, grapevines painted on the ceiling and tables on the narrow pedestrian lane out front serves up excellent large *montaditos* (slices of toasted bread with toppings). Scrumptious standouts such as thin-sliced Barbate tuna and smoked cod complement more standard offerings like pork, anchovies, assorted cheeses, or mashed tomato and olive oil.

🛏 Hotel Puerta de la Luna　　Heritage Hotel €€

(🤙953 74 70 19; www.hotelpuertadelaluna.com; Calle Canónigo Melgares Raya 7; d €87-175; P ❄ @ 🛜 ♨) If they were to return today, Baeza's Renaissance-era nobility would doubtless stay at this luxurious hotel in a 17th-century mansion. Orange trees and a pool grace its elegant patio, complemented by beautifully furnished salons with welcoming fireplaces. The spacious rooms are enhanced by classical furnishings, artwork and large bathrooms. Buffet breakfast costs €15, and **Bar Pacos** (Calle de Santa Catalina; tapas & medias raciones €5-10; ⏱1.30-4pm & 8.30pm-midnight) downstairs serves good tapas.

STRETCH YOUR LEGS
MÁLAGA

Start/Finish
Centre Pompidou Málaga

Distance 3.2km

Duration Three to four hours

This walk touches on the very best of Málaga, taking in a sophisticated shopping street, a bustling market, two iconic museums and a historic tapas bar with views of both a Roman amphitheatre and a Moorish fortress.

Take this walk on Trips

Centre Pompidou Málaga

Down by the port, the Centre Pompidou Málaga (p246) is housed in a low-slung modern building crowned by Daniel Buren's multicoloured cube. Thought-provoking, well-curated main exhibits rotate through on an annual or biannual basis, drawing on the museum's vast collection of contemporary art.

The Walk >> Walk eastwards along the port until you reach Plaza de la Marina. Follow on to the major thoroughfare Alameda Principal and continue until the corner of Calle Tómas Heredia.

Soho

The formerly rundown district between the Alameda and the port, known as Soho, has been transformed into an open-air gallery. Murals, sometimes several stories high, brighten the *barrio*'s walls, including an eye-catching painting of birds by renowned Chinese muralist DaLeast. Amidst the artworks you also find many hip cafes, idiosyncratic shops and ethnic restaurants.

The Walk >> Cross the Alameda Principal and continue straight down Calle Torregordo, past a beautiful frescoed building and across Calle Atarazanas to the market.

Mercado Atarazanas

The striking 19th-century **Mercado Atarazanas** (Calle Atarazanas; ⊙ market 8am-3pm Mon-Sat; Ⓟ) incorporates the Moorish gate that once connected the city with the port, as well as a magnificent stained-glass window depicting historical episodes. Browse the stalls laden with swaying hams and sausages, glistening seafood, cheese, olives and ripe seasonal fruit and veg.

The Walk >> Exit eastwards and continue past Casa Aranda (which sells the best churros in town) to Plaza de Félix Sáenz. Head north on pedestrianised Calle Nueva and, at the end, turn right onto Plaza de la Constitución.

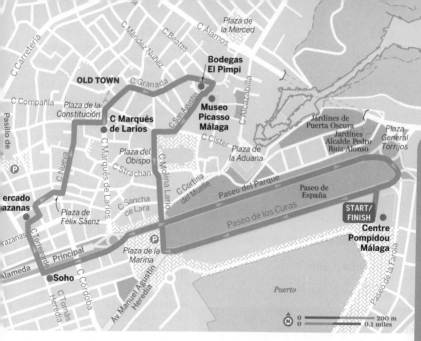

Calle Marqués de Larios

Running off Plaza de la Constitución, Calle Marqués de Larios is Malaga's most famous shopping street. It's an elegant strip with glossy marble-clad paving, handsome balconied buildings and a mix of designer boutiques, chain stores, cafes and *farmacias*.

The Walk » From Plaza de la Constitucíon follow pedestrianised Calle Granada until the street narrows and you come to number 62 and your next stop.

Bodegas El Pimpi

Relax with a tapa and drink at the **Bodegas El Pimpi** (www.elpimpi.com; Calle Granada 62; noon-2am;), a rambling Málaga institution. The interior, decorated with historic *feria* (fair) posters and barrels signed by famous customers, encompasses a warren of rooms, and there's a terrace overlooking the Roman amphitheatre.

The Walk » Exit onto Calle Granada and take the street just to your east, Calle San Agustín; the Picasso Museum is on your left.

Museo Picasso Málaga

Housed in a 16th-century palace, the superb Museo Picasso Málaga (p246) has an enviable collection of 200-plus works donated and loaned by Christine Ruiz-Picasso (wife of Paul, Picasso's eldest son) and Bernard Ruiz-Picasso (Picasso's grandson). These catalogue the artist's sparkling career with a few notable gaps (the 'blue' and 'rose' periods are largely missing).

The Walk » Carry on Calle San Agustín, turn right past the cathedral and then left onto Calle Molina Lario to the port. End your walk with an amble through the Paseo de España park, crossing Paseo de los Curas to return to your start point.

STRETCH
YOUR LEGS
SEVILLE

Start/Finish Jardines de Murillo

Distance 3.5km

Duration Three hours

Seville's tightly packed historic centre is no place for cars. Park in the underground car park near the Jardines de Murillo, then continue on foot into the atmospheric Santa Cruz district and onto headline sights such as the city's Gothic cathedral and breathtaking royal palace complex.

Take this walk on Trip

Santa Cruz

Formerly Seville's Jewish quarter, picturesque Santa Cruz is a white warren of cobbled streets, orange-scented plazas, tapas bars and flamenco clubs. In the heart of the district, the **Hospital de los Venerables Sacerdotes** (☏954 56 26 96; www.hospitaldelosvenerables. es; Plaza de los Venerables 8; adult/student/ child €10/8/free; ☺10am-8pm Mar-Jun & Sep-Nov, 10am-2pm & 5.30-9pm Jul & Aug, 10am-6pm Dec-Feb) houses masterpieces by Diego Velázquez and Bartolomé Murillo.

The Walk » Weave your way through Santa Cruz via Calle Agua and Plaza de los Venerables – you'll probably get lost at some point but that's half the fun.

Real Alcázar

If you're short on time, visit the **Real Alcázar** (☏954 50 23 24; www.alcazarsevilla. org; Plaza del Triunfo; adult/student/child €11.50/3/free, 6-7pm Mon Apr-Sep free, 4-5pm Mon Oct-Mar free; ☺9.30am-7pm Apr-Sep, to 5pm Oct-Mar) opposite the cathedral. While the latter can be enjoyed from the outside, 95% of the Alcázar's beauty lies within, behind its crenellated 12th-century walls. The centrepiece is the Palacio de Don Pedro, one of the highpoints of Mudéjar architecture in Spain. Also glorious are the Eden-like gardens.

The Walk » Exit the Alcázar and you'll see Seville's cathedral on the other side of Plaza del Triunfo.

Catedral

The world's largest Gothic church, Seville's mighty **catedral** (☏902 09 96 92; www.catedraldesevilla.es; Plaza del Triunfo; adult/child incl Iglesia Colegial del Divino Salvador €10/free, incl rooftop guided tours €16, 4.30-6pm Mon free; ☺11am-3.30pm Mon, to 5pm Tue-Sat, 2.30-6pm Sun Sep-Jun, 10.30am-4pm Mon, to 6pm Tue-Sat, 2-7pm Sun Jul & Aug) is a staggering sight with its soaring exterior, signature bell tower (Giralda) and astonishing gold altarpiece.

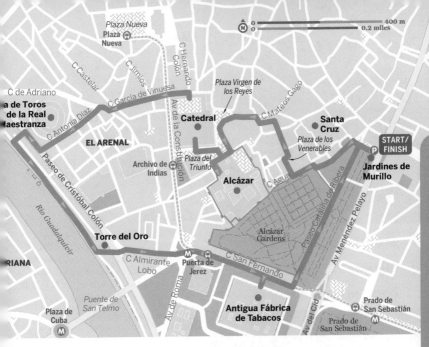

Christopher Columbus' tomb stands in the immense interior, while orange trees blossom in the cathedral's charming Moorish courtyard.

The Walk » Exit the Cathedral, turn left, cross Avenue de la Constitución and follow Calle García de Vinuesa into the Arenal quarter. At a complicated five-point junction, take Calle Antonia Díaz towards the river.

Plaza de Toros de la Real Maestranza

Seville's **bullring** (📞954 21 03 15; www.realmaestranza.com; Paseo de Cristóbal Colón 12; tours adult/child €8/3, 3-7pm Mon free; ⏱9.30am-9pm Apr-Oct, to 7pm Nov-Mar, to 3pm bullfight days) is one of the largest and most important in Spain as well as the oldest. Visits, by guided tour only, take in the arena, a small art museum, the stables and the altar where matadors pray before a fight.

The Walk » Cross Paseo de Cristóbal Colón and follow the footpath as it flanks the Guadalquivir River to the Torre del Oro.

Torre del Oro

One of Seville's landmark sights, this distinctive riverside **tower** (📞954 22 24 19; Paseo de Cristóbal Colón; adult/6-14yr €3/1.50, Mon free; ⏱9.30am-6.45pm Mon-Fri, 10.30am-6.45pm Sat & Sun) dates to around 1220. Over the centuries, it has served as a chapel, prison, and naval office; nowadays it houses a maritime museum and viewing platform.

The Walk » Cross the Paseo and cut along Calle Almirante Lobo to Puerta de Jerez. Follow Calle San Fernando past the neo-Mudéjar Hotel Alfonso XIII to the Antigua Fábrica de Tabacos on your right.

Antigua Fábrica de Tabacos

Seville's colossal **university building** (📞954 55 10 00; Calle San Fernando; ⏱8am-9pm Mon-Fri, to 2.30pm Sat), the fictional setting of Bizet's opera *Carmen,* was a tobacco factory from the 18th century until the 1950s.

The Walk » Take the path through the lush Jardines del Murillo back to your start point.

STRETCH YOUR LEGS
VALENCIA

Start/Finish Mercado Central

Distance 2.25km

Duration Two hours

A historic port and industrial city (as well as the spiritual home of paella), Valencia has successfully transformed itself into a cosmopolitan cultural hub. The contemporary Ciudad de las Artes y las Ciencias is its star attraction, but here we highlight the sights of its historic centre, including the city's medieval cathedral and a striking Gothic trading hall.

Take this walk on Trips

Mercado Central

Situated less than 200m from an underground car park on the corner of Avenida Barón de Cárcer and Calle del Hospital, Valencia's Modernista market (p254), constructed in 1928, is a swirl of smells, movement and colour. A classy tapas bar lets you sip wine and enjoy the atmosphere.

The Walk » Exit the market and walk around the back into Plaza del Mercado, where you'll see the distinctive crenellated walls and tower of La Lonja.

La Lonja

La Lonja (p254) was Valencia's 15th-century silk and commodity exchange. Check out the Sala de Contratación, a colonnaded hall with twisted Gothic pillars, and the Consulado del Mar with its stunning coffered ceiling.

The Walk » Take Calle de les Mantes off the Plaza del Mercado. Turn right into Calle de los Derechos (also known as Carrer del Drets). Plaza Redonda is on the left through a covered arcade.

Plaza Redonda

Trim, smart, and touristy, the circular 19th-century **Plaza Redonda** (⊙ hours vary) – once the abattoir of Valencia's Mercado Central – is ringed by stalls.

The Walk » Exit the plaza via the opposite arch and turn left into Calle de Jofrens. At the end of the street turn right into busy Plaza de la Reina. The cathedral is at the far end of the plaza.

Catedral

Valencia's **catedral** (📞 963 91 81 27; http://museocatedralvalencia.com; Plaza de la Reina; adult/child/family €8/5.50/18; ⊙10.30am-6.30pm Mon-Fri, 10.30am-5.30pm Sat, 2-5.30pm Sun Mar–mid-Jul & mid-Sep–Oct, 10.30am-6.30pm Mon-Sat, 2-6.30pm Sun mid-Jul–mid-Sep, 10.30am-5.30pm Mon-Sat, 2-5.30pm Sun Nov, 10.30am-5.30pm Mon-Sat Dec-Feb) **was** built over a mosque after the 1238 reconquest. Its brick-vaulted triple nave is mostly Gothic, with neoclassical side chapels. Highlights include Italianate frescoes above the altarpiece, a pair

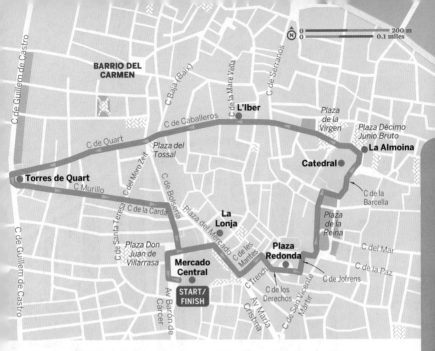

of Goyas, and a Roman-era cup that's claimed to be the Holy Grail.

The Walk » Take Calle de la Barcella on the east side of the cathedral and follow it around until it opens out into another plaza.

La Almoina

Beneath the square east of the cathedral is **La Almoina** (962 08 41 73; www.valencia.es; Plaza Décimo Junio Bruto; adult/child €2/1, Sun free; 10am-7pm Mon-Sat, to 2pm Sun), an archaeological site showcasing ruins from the Roman, Visigoth and Islamic city through a water-covered glass canopy.

The Walk » Continue around the back of the cathedral, cross Plaza de la Virgen and head along Calle de Caballeros until you come to L'Iber on the right.

L'Iber

With more than 95,000 pieces on display, **L'Iber** (Museo de Soldaditos de Plomo; 963 91 86 75; www.museoliber. org; Calle de Caballeros 22; adult/under 27yr

€8/5; 11am-2pm & 4-7pm Sat, 11am-2pm Sun Sep-Jun, 11am-2pm & 4-7pm Wed-Sun Jul & Aug) claims to be the world's largest collection of toy soldiers. The huge model of the Battle of Almansa (1707) has 9000 combatants, while glass cases teem with yet more troops.

The Walk » Continue along Calle de Caballeros as it becomes Calle de Quart. Follow this until the Torres de Quart gateway appears before you.

Torres de Quart

Spain's most magnificent city **gate** (618 803907; www.valencia.es; Calle de Guillem de Castro; adult/child €2/1, Sun free; 10am-7pm Tue-Sat, to 2pm Sun) is quite a sight. You can clamber to the top of the 15th-century structure, which faces towards Madrid and the setting sun. Notice the pockmarks caused by French cannonballs during the Napoleonic invasion.

The Walk » From the gate's southern tower double back along Calle Murillo and Calle de la Carda to Plaza del Mercado.

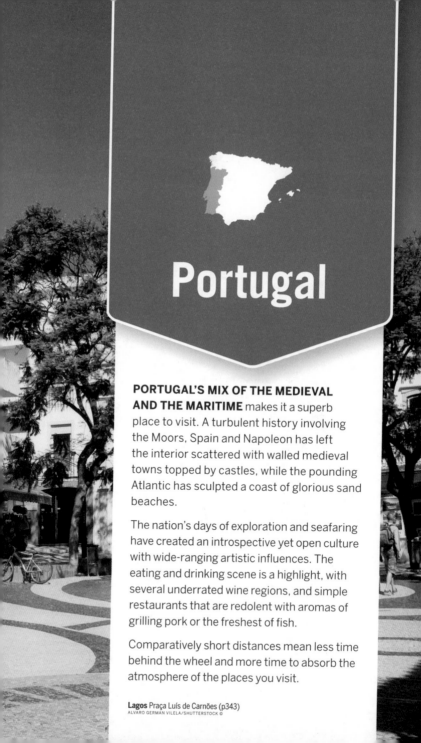

Portugal

PORTUGAL'S MIX OF THE MEDIEVAL AND THE MARITIME makes it a superb place to visit. A turbulent history involving the Moors, Spain and Napoleon has left the interior scattered with walled medieval towns topped by castles, while the pounding Atlantic has sculpted a coast of glorious sand beaches.

The nation's days of exploration and seafaring have created an introspective yet open culture with wide-ranging artistic influences. The eating and drinking scene is a highlight, with several underrated wine regions, and simple restaurants that are redolent with aromas of grilling pork or the freshest of fish.

Comparatively short distances mean less time behind the wheel and more time to absorb the atmosphere of the places you visit.

Lagos Praça Luís de Carnões (p343)
ALVARO GERMAN VILELA/SHUTTERSTOCK ©

Lisbon Fado performers (p352)

26 **Atlantic Coast Surf Trip 5–7 Days**
Lively towns, great seafood, and top beaches with monster waves.

Classic Trip
27 **Douro Valley Vineyard Trails 5–7 Days**
Heartbreakingly beautiful river valley laced with vines producing sensational ports and reds.

Classic Trip
28 **Alentejo & Algarve Beaches 4–6 Days**
Some of the world's great beaches and towns with Moorish heritage.

29 **Medieval Jewels in the Southern Interior 6–9 Days**
Understand Portugal's turbulent history through castles, monasteries and standing stones.

30 **The Minho's Lyrical Landscapes 2–4 Days**
Green Portugal, green wine and handsome historic cities.

31 **Tasting the Dão 2–4 Days**
Explore the wineries that produce the nation's silkiest reds.

32 **Highlands & History in the Central Interior 5–7 Days**
Student life, evocative villages and spectacular mountain scenery in Portugal's heartland.

 DON'T MISS

Wine Tasting
Often underrated, Portugal's wines are one of the region's great pleasures. Visit wineries and taste wines and ports on Trips **27** **31**

Castles
Love thy neighbour? Not in Iberia: Portugal is studded with castles staring defiantly towards Spain. See the best of them on Trips **27** **29** **32**

Surfing
Portugal is one of Europe's surfing hotspots: despite the Mediterranean vibe, this is the Atlantic, and those are serious waves on Trips **26** **28**

Music
Fado can encapsulate the stirrings of Portugal's sometimes melancholy soul. The two centres to hear it are Lisbon and Coimbra, on Trips **29** **32**

Hiking
Jump out of the car for some picturesque hill walking on Trips **27** **28** **30** **32**

Atlantic Coast Surf Trip

Get ready to ride the big ones on Portugal's wild, wave-lashed west coast – an alluring mix of sunshine, terrific surf, dune-backed beaches and nicely chilled towns.

26

TRIP HIGHLIGHTS

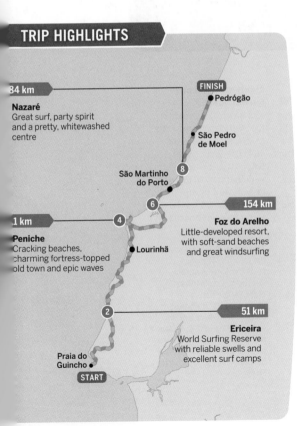

184 km

Nazaré
Great surf, party spirit and a pretty, whitewashed centre

FINISH
● Pedrógão

● São Pedro de Moel

São Martinho
do Porto

154 km

Foz do Arelho
Little-developed resort, with soft-sand beaches and great windsurfing

91 km

Peniche
Cracking beaches, charming fortress-topped old town and epic waves

● Lourinhã

51 km

Ericeira
World Surfing Reserve with reliable swells and excellent surf camps

Praia do
Guincho ●

START

5–7 DAYS
225KM / 140 MILES

GREAT FOR...

BEST TIME TO GO

From spring to early autumn for the best surf and sunshine.

📷 ESSENTIAL PHOTO

Snap the surf rolling in at sunset anywhere on the Atlantic Coast.

✓ BEST TWO DAYS

The 129km between Peniche and Nazaré pack the biggest surfing punch.

26 Atlantic Coast Surf Trip

If endless crashing surf sounds like your idea of heaven, you've come to the right country. Surfers and kitesurfers of all levels are in their element on Portugal's sparkling Atlantic coast, which is thrashed by some of Europe's biggest rollers. First-rate (and inexpensive) surf camps, gleaming white towns with authentic seafood restaurants, golden beaches fringed by dunes and pines, and memorable sunsets wrap up this little road trip nicely.

1 Praia do Guincho

Just half an hour's drive west of Lisbon, Praia do Guincho is hammered by some terrific Atlantic waves. The site of previous World Surfing Championships, this long, wild, dune-backed beach holds plenty of pulling power for surfers, windsurfers and kitesurfers with its massive crashing rollers. Beware of the strong undertow which can be dangerous for swimmers and novice surfers. If you're keen to ride the waves, check out the surfing course available at the highly rated **Moana Surf School** (☎964 449 436; www.moanasurfschool.com; Estrada do Abano, Praia do Guincho; private lesson per hr €50, group lesson €30, 5-lesson course €120), which arranges private lessons and group courses for all levels. It also rents out boards and wetsuits.

The Drive » From Guincho, the scenic N247 swings north through the rippling, forest-cloaked mountains of the Parque Natural de Sintra-Cascais, at its most atmospheric when veiled in early-morning mist. Roll down the window and breathe in that fresh air as you cruise north on the hour-long (51km) drive to Ericeira.

ATLANTIC OCEAN

Berlenga Grande

Ba

p323

4 Peniche

Lourinh

N2

Ericeira 2

N247

M

Parque Natural de Sintra-Cascais

N247

Sintra

A16

START 1 Cascais

Praia do Guincho

Estoril

A5

N

FINISH

Praia do Pedrogão

Praia do Pedrógão **11**

Praia da Vieira **10**

Monte Real

Pinhal de Leiria

A17

50km to **32**

92km to **31**

São Pedro de Moel **9**

Marinha Grande

Leiria

A8

N242

A1

Nazaré **8**

São Jorge Cruz

Batalha

Porto de Mós

A8

N8

nto Martinho do Porto **7**

Alcobaça

Minde

; do lho **6**

N360

Caldas da Rainha

Parque Natural das Serrasde Aire e Candeeiros

N1

N114

Óbidos

Rio Maior

A15

A1

A8

Alcoentre

Santarém

N1

rres dras

Cartaxo

Almeirim

N9

N3

A1

A13

Rio Tejo

N118

A10

Vila Franca de Xira

N10

A9

Alverca do Ribatejo

N119

A1

LISBON

Montijo

A13

Almada

Barreiro

0 —— 20 km
0 —— 10 miles

TRIP HIGHLIGHT

2 Ericeira

Picturesquely draped across sandstone cliffs with grandstand Atlantic views, sunny, whitewashed Ericeira has a string of golden beaches that have surfers itching to grab their boards and jump in. This is one of just four World Surfing Reserves, starring alongside Malibu and Santa Cruz in California and Manly Beach in Australia. The swells are reliable and the mightiest waves roll in to cliff-backed Praia da Ribeira d'Ilhas. A World Qualifying Series (WQS) site and frequent host to Portuguese national

LINK YOUR TRIP

31 Tasting the Dão

Wine after the waves? Detour inland 120km from Praia do Pedrógão to Santa Comba Dão for tastings and cellar tours in a deliciously rural setting.

32 Highlands & History in the Central Interior

Why not tag on a road trip of Portugal's culture-loaded interior? The soulful university town of Coimbra is just a 77km drive northeast of Praia do Pedrógão.

surfing championships, the beach is famous for having one of the best reef breaks in Europe. The other biggie is Coxos, a right-hand point break producing incredible barrels. Most amateurs will find the waves at the nearby Praia de São Sebastião challenging enough. Standing out among the surf camps in Ericeira, **Rapture** (☏919 586 722; www.rapturecamps. com; Rua do Lizandro 6; surf lessons €30, board & wetsuit rental per day €20, dm/d with shared bathroom incl half-board €45/100) offers nicely chilled digs right on the beach and lessons with proficient instructors. For a post-surf beer or cocktail, stop by **Sunset Bamboo** (☏261 864 827; Travessa Jogo da Bola 3; ☺10am-10pm Thu-Tue summer, noon-8pm Thu-Tue rest of year; ☏).

✕ ⊨ p327

The Drive » From Ericeira, the N247 veers north close to the contours of the coast, taking you through gently rolling farmland and past sun-bleached *aldeas* (hamlets), orchards and pinewoods. After a pleasant hour (40km) behind the wheel, you emerge in Lourinhã.

- - - - - - - - - - - - - - -

❸ Lourinhã

Lourinhã is less known than other west-coast surfing hotspots, yet it deserves more than just a cursory glance. In the peaceful shoulder seasons, you'll practically have its waves all to yourself on dune-fringed Praia Areal and Praia da Areia Branca. The former hosts national surfing events, while the latter is perfect for beginners and bodyboarders.

The Drive » It's an easy 20km drive north on the countrified N247 and N114 to Peniche. The road takes you through softly undulating farmland, past bone-white hamlets and the odd ruin and windmill. To the west, you can often glimpse the hazy blue outline of the Atlantic.

- - - - - - - - - - - - - - -

TRIP HIGHLIGHT

❹ Peniche

Ask a local to rattle off Portugal's top surfing spots and Peniche invariably makes the grade. Straddling a headland with the sea on all sides, it is popular for its long, fabulous town beach and nearby surf strands, with the added charm of a pretty walled historic centre and a 16th-century fortress. But it's the waves you are here for – and what epic waves they are! Long a favourite of clued-up

---

CULTURE FIX

If you can tear yourself away from the surf for a minute, factor in a detour to some of the hinterland's cultural treasures. Here are three worth the drive.

Óbidos

A 25km drive east of Peniche, this fortified wonder conceals a historic centre that is a maze of cobbled streets and flower-bedecked, whitewashed houses livened up with dashes of vivid yellow and blue paint. A hill lifts a medieval castle high above town.

Batalha

A detour off the road between Nazaré and São Pedro de Moel, Batalha's crowning glory is its Manueline monastery, a riot of flying buttresses and pinnacles, with gold stone carved into forms as delicate as snowflakes and as pliable as twisted rope.

Alcobaça

A 17km drive east of Nazaré, Alcobaça conceals a charming centre that is dwarfed by the magnificence of the 12th-century Mosteiro de Santa Maria de Alcobaça, one of Portugal's most memorable Unesco World Heritage sites.

DETOUR:
BERLENGA GRANDE

Start: ❹ **Peniche**

Sitting about 10km offshore from Peniche, Berlenga Grande is a spectacular, rocky and remote island, with twisting, shocked-rock formations and gaping caverns. It's the only island of the Berlenga archipelago you can visit – the group consists of three tiny islands surrounded by clear, calm, dark-blue waters full of shipwrecks that are great for snorkelling and diving; try **AcuaSubOeste** (📞918 393 444; www. acuasuboeste.com; Armazém 3, Avenida do Porto de Pesca; 2 dives €70-80; ⏱9-10am & 5-7pm). From June to September, **Viamar** (📞262 785 646; www.viamar-berlenga.com; Largo da Ribeira Velha 2, Marina de Peniche; day round-trip adult/child €20/13; ⏱8.30am-1pm & 3-6pm Jun & Sep, 8.15am-1pm & 3-7pm Jul & Aug) makes the 45-minute boat trip twice daily. In the 16th century Berlenga Grande was home to a monastery, but now the most famous inhabitants are thousands of nesting seabirds, especially guillemots. The birds take priority over visitors and development has been confined to housing for a small fishing community and a lighthouse.

surfers, Peniche shot to celebrity status when Supertubos beach, south of town, was selected as a stop on the ASP World Tour. Supertubos has some of Europe's best beach and reef breaks. Conditions are great year-round. Kitesurfing is also big. On the far side of high dunes about 500m east of the old town, **Peniche Kite & Surf Center** (📞919 424 951; www.penichesurfcenter. com; Avenida Monsenhor Bastos, Praia de Peniche de Cima; ⏱9.30am-7.30pm Mar-Oct) offers surfing and kitesurfing lessons.

✕ 🛏 p327

The Drive >> About 5km to the northeast of Peniche is the scenic island-village of Baleal, connected to the mainland village of Casais do Baleal by a causeway.

- - - - - - - - - - - - - - - - -

❺ **Baleal**

A fine swoop of pale golden sand protected by dunes, Baleal is a paradise of challenging but, above all, consistent waves that make it an ideal learners' beach. Depending on the season, surf camps here charge between €250 and €650 for a week of classes, including equipment and lodging (with both dorms and private apartments available).

Well-established picks include **Baleal Surfcamp** (📞961 316 204; www.balealsurfcamp.com; Rua Amigos do Baleal 2; 2-day course with 3 nights lodging in hostel/villa/apt €255/315/355) and **Peniche Surfcamp** (📞962 336 295; www. penichesurfcamp.com; Avenida do Mar 162, Casais do

Baleal; ⏱1/2/10 surf classes €35/60/250). You can also rent boards and wetsuits (around €30/175 per day/week).

The Drive >> From Baleal, connect up with the N114, taking you onto the A8 north, before veering west onto the N360. The road makes a sweeping arc, leading through pine forest and past farmland and low-rise hills. It skirts the impressive fortified city of Óbidos, where you might want to factor in a pitstop. It's around a 38km drive.

- - - - - - - - - - - - - - - - -

TRIP HIGHLIGHT

❻ **Foz do Arelho**

With a vast, gorgeous tract of sandy beach backed by a river-mouth estuary ideal for windsurfing, Foz do Arelho remains remarkably undeveloped. It makes a fine place to laze in the sun, and

LOCAL KNOWLEDGE:
THE INSIDE SCOOP ON SURFING

Read on for the lowdown on when to surf, what to take, surf tuition and rentals.

When to Surf

Spring and autumn tend to be the best for surfing action. Waves at this time range from 2m to 4.5m high. This is also the low season, meaning you'll pay less for accommodation, and the beaches will be far less crowded.

Even during the summer, however, the coast gets good waves (1m to 1.5m on average) and, despite the crowds, it's fairly easy to head off and find your own spots (you can often be on your own stretch of beach just by driving a few minutes up the road).

What to Take

The water temperature here is colder than it is in most other southern European countries, and even in the summer you'll probably want a wetsuit.

Board and wetsuit hire are widely available at surf shops and surf camps: you can usually score a discount if you rent long-term, otherwise, you'll be paying around €20 to €35 per day for a board and wetsuit, or €15 to €25 per day for the board alone.

Tuition

There are dozens of schools that run lessons and courses for surfers of all levels. Surf camps mostly offer weekly packages including simple accommodation (dorms, bungalows or camping), meals and transport to the beach.

Surf Sites

www.magicseaweed.com International site with English-language surf reports for many Portuguese beaches.

www.wannasurf.com Global site with the lowdown on surfing hotspots along Portugal's coast. Navigate by interactive map.

www.surfingportugal.com Official site of the Portuguese Surfing Federation.

www.surftotal.com Portuguese-language site with news about the national surf scene and webcams showing conditions at a dozen popular beaches around Portugal.

Nazaré View from Promontório do Sítio (p326)

outside July and August it'll often be just you and the local fishermen. The beach has a row of relaxed bars and restaurants.

Escola de Vela da Lagoa (☎262 978 592, 962 568 005; www. escoladeveladalagoa.com; Rua Engenheiro Luís Paiva e Sousa 105; ☺10am-sunset Jun-Sep, Fri-Mon Oct-Mar, Thu-Mon Apr, Wed-Mon May) hires out sailboats (€16 per hour), SUP (€12), kayaks (€15), windsurf boards (from €15) and catamarans (from €25).

The school also provides windsurfing and sailing lessons (two hours, €60 for one, €90 for two) and kayak lessons (one hour, €25 for one, €40 for two). From Foz do Arelho village, it's a 3.5km drive: turn left on the road that follows the lagoon's inland edge past the curious rock called Penedo Furado and continue.

The Drive ≫ A minor road, the Estrada Atlântica, hugs the coastline as it threads north to Santo Martinho do Porto, a drive of around 15km.

----

❼ Santo Martinho do Porto

Fancy some time to hang out on the beach? Unlike nearby Nazaré, Santo Martinho do Porto is no party town, but it's a cheery place with a broad arc of a half-moon bay, perfect for swimming and just slowing the pace a notch or two.

The Drive ≫ Back behind the wheel, you'll be edging your way north on the N242 through pine woods and farmland before crossing the Río Alcobaça and arriving in Nazaré, 14.5km away.

⑧ Nazaré

With a warren of narrow, cobbled lanes running down to a wide, cliff-backed beach, Nazaré is Estremadura's most scenic coastal resort. The sands are packed with multicoloured umbrellas in July and August and the town centre is jammed with seafood restaurants and bars with a party vibe.

Nazaré generates some of the world's biggest waves. Rodrigo Koxa set a world record when he surfed a 23.77m giant in 2017. Smaller and less intimidating are the waves on the main beach in town, which is less exposed.

To get an entirely different perspective of Nazaré, take the funicular up to **Promontório do Sítio**, where picture-postcard coastal views unfold from the 110m-high cliffs, gazing down to the thrashing waves on one side and the village on the other. It's nice to walk back down, escaping the crowds of trinket sellers.

✕ 🛏 p327

The Drive ⟫ From Nazaré, the small, coast-hugging Estrada Atlântica heads 21km north through pockets of pine forest and past high sand dunes, affording the occasional tantalising glimpse of ocean. Wind down those windows for delicious breezes.

⑨ São Pedro de Moel

For a more offbeat experience than Nazaré, turn your gaze north to São Pedro de Moel, which sees some pretty good waves (both lefts and rights) but receives just a trickle of surfers by comparison.

The surf here is fairly consistent year-round, though bear the rocks in mind. The village itself is a pretty whitewashed number, with a low-key vibe and some knockout sunsets.

Spreading immediately north of São Pedro de Moel is the **Pinhal de Leiria**. First planted by a forward-looking monarch some 700 years ago, this vast forest of towering pines backs one of the loveliest stretches of Portugal's Atlantic coast. Monarch Dom Dinis (1261–1325) expanded it significantly as a barrier against encroaching dunes and also as a source of timber for the maritime industry – a great boon during the Age of Discovery.

The Drive ⟫ Continue north on the pretty Estrada Atlântica for the 15km drive to Praia da Vieira. The narrow road cuts through the sun-dappled pinewoods of Pinhal de Leiria and scrubby dunes, with the occasional glimpse of ocean.

⑩ Praia da Vieira

Backed by the sun-dappled Pinhal de Leiria, Praia da Vieira entices with broad golden sands and consistent surf with beach breaks.

Come during the week rather than at the weekend to experience it at its tranquil best.

The Drive ⟫ From Praia da Vieira, it's a cruisy 5km drive north to Praia do Pedrógão, taking you once again through lush green coastal pinewoods.

⑪ Praia do Pedrógão

Your final stop on this road trip is Pedrógão, which has lovely broad, dune-backed sands, few surfers and some pretty impressive beach breaks (both to the left and right). After all those big waves, you might want to take the chance just to kick back and watch in wonder as the Atlantic rolls in before you.

Eating & Sleeping

Ericeira ❷

✗ Mar à Vista   Seafood €€

(☎261 862 928; Largo das Ribas 16; seafood per kg €20-90; ⏱noon-10pm Thu-Tue) Crustaceans of every kind are on display at this hearty frill-free local *marisqueira* (seafood restaurant) known for its shellfish (no fish, no meat). Phenomenal crabs (both *santola* and *sapateira*) are eaten from the shell, while lobsters (both *lavagante* and *lagosta*) can be whipped up into memorable seafood rices.

Excellent starters include *doses* of oysters, clams or garlic shrimp, all accompanied by beer on tap or a fresh white wine. Cash only. Reserve ahead!

🛏 Blue Buddha Beachhouse   Guesthouse €€

(☎910 658 849; www.bluebuddhahostel.com; Rua Florêncio Granate 19; r €75-140; 🛜) The nearest thing to your own modern beach house, this delightful spot has seven bright, white and very smart rooms, plus an ocean vista to die for. A spacious communal living room with couches, cable TV and mod cons adds to the appeal, plus there's a guest kitchen. Multilingual proprietor Luzia knows the lot, from surfing spots to the latest bars.

Peniche ❹

✗ Taberna do Ganhão   Portuguese €€

(☎988 451 600; Largo dos Amigos do Baleal, Baleal; mains €6-18; ⏱10am-10pm Thu-Tue; 🛜) This 'new-school tavern' is a reconstituted 'old-school tavern' where fishermen bought wine and groceries (plus it was the first in the area to have a telephone). The current owners have reinvigorated its spirit by maintaining its red-and-white-checked tables and elevated traditional daily plates (sweet-and-sour fried chicken, cuttlefish with garlic and so on). In the evenings, grab a beer and a *petisco* (tapas) or three (€6 to €14 per plate). It's in a stunning location at the end of the causeway.

🛏 Surfers Lodge   Design Hotel €€€

(☎262 700 030; www.surferslodgepeniche. com; Avenida do Mar 132, Ferrel; d/tw/f €225/180/330; ❄🛜) This hip spot is all about the design. And experience. Given its apparent target market (surfers who are riding a money wave, and are happy to spend it), it redefines the image of the hippie dude living out of a combi van. The funky decor incorporates polished concrete and recycled woods, and comprises clean lines, whites and natural hues.

The restaurant/guest-common-area downstairs is lovely, as is the rooftop terrace for post-surf fun. But glurfing (you heard it here first: glamorous surfing) comes at a price.

Nazaré ❽

✗ A Tasquinha   Seafood €€

(☎262 551 945; Rua Adrião Batalha 54; mains €10-19; ⏱noon-3pm & 7-10.30pm Tue-Sun Mar-Dec) This exceptionally friendly family affair has been running for 50-plus years, serving high-quality seafood in a pair of snug but prettily tiled dining rooms. Solo travellers delight: *arroz de marisco* (shellfish rice) for one person (€18)! Expect queues on summer nights. However many people there are, the delightful owners always try and squeeze you in, even if it's at someone else's table. Good value.

🛏 Lab Hostel   Hostel €

(☎262 382 339; www.labhostel.pt; Rua de Rio Maior 14; dm/d/q €22/65/120; 🛜) One of Portugal's band of growing 'glostels' (glamorous hostels) – stylish, minimal design, attention to detail and some of the brightest and cleanest rooms around make this worth a look. There's a female dorm and a family room – and breakfast is included. It was a former laboratory (the owner's father-in-law was a pharmacist), and old chemist jars and bottles make for fun objets d'art.

Cute loft rooms are the only ones with air-conditioning, but are not for tall people.

Classic Trip

Douro Valley Vineyard Trails

27

The Douro is a little drop of heaven. Uncork this region on Porto's doorstep and you'll soon fall head over heels in love with its terraced vineyards, wine estates and soul-stirring vistas.

TRIP HIGHLIGHTS

193 km

Pinhão
Wine tastings and Douro cruises on a gorgeous bend in the river

171 km

Quinta do Crasto
Eyrie-like winery in the Unesco-listed Alto Douro region

FINISH
Miranda do Douro

START
1

Peso da Régua
4 **7**
8

Vila Nova de Foz Côa

Porto
Medieval core, historic port lodges galore and a whole lotta soul

1 km

Casal de Loivos
Gasp-eliciting views of Douro vines cascading down the hillsides

197 km

5–7 DAYS
381KM / 237 MILES

GREAT FOR...

BEST TIME TO GO

Spring for wildflowers, early autumn for the grape harvest.

ESSENTIAL PHOTO

The staggering view of the Douro vineyards from Casal de Loivos *miradouro*.

BEST FOR FOODIES

Chef Rui Paula keeps it seasonal and regional at DOC, with sublime vineyard and river views from its terrace.

Valley Vineyard terraces

27 | Douro Valley Vineyard Trails

You're in for a treat. This Unesco World Heritage region is hands-down one of Portugal's most evocative landscapes, with mile after swoon-worthy mile of vineyards spooling along the contours of its namesake river and marching up terraced hillsides. Go for the food, the fabulous wines, the palatial *quintas* (estates), the medieval stone villages and the postcard views around almost every bend.

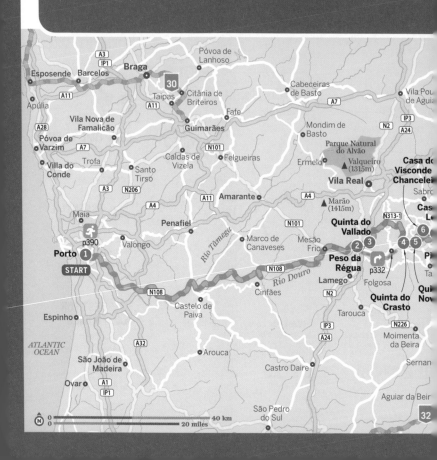

TRIP HIGHLIGHT

❶ Porto

Before kick-starting your road trip, devote a day or two to Porto, snuggled on banks of the Río Douro, where life is played out in the mazy lanes of the medieval Ribeira district. From here, the double-decker bridge **Ponte de Dom Luís I**, built by an apprentice of Gustav Eiffel in 1877, takes the river in its stride. Cross it to reach Vila Nova de Gaia, where grand 17th-century port lodges march up the hillside. Many open their barrel-lined cellars for guided tours and tastings – usually of three different ports – that will soon help you tell your tawny from your late-bottled vintage. Top billing goes to British-run **Taylor's** (☎223 772 973; www.taylor.pt; Rua do Choupelo 250; tours incl tasting adult/child €15/6; ☺10am-6pm) and its the immense 100,000L barrel, **Graham's** (☎223 776 492, 223 776 490;

LINK YOUR TRIP

30 **The Minho's Lyrical Landscapes**

Porto is a 55km drive from castle-crowned Guimarães, birthplace of Portugal and a fine starting point for this Minho meander.

32 **Highlands & History in the Central Interior**

Dip south of Porto 120km to Coimbra for a foray into Portugal's history-crammed interior and the inspiring Serra da Estrela mountains.

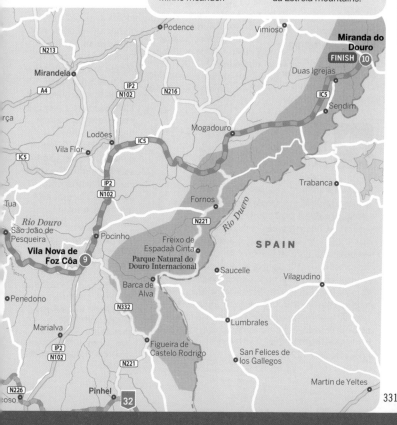

www.grahams-port.com; Rua do Agro 141; tours incl tasting from €18.50; ⊙9.30am-6.30pm Apr-Oct, to 6pm Nov-Mar) and **Calém** (☎916 113 451; www.calem.pt; Avenida Diogo Leite 344; tours incl tasting from €13; ⊙10am-7pm).

The Drive » There are quicker ways of getting from A to B, but for immersion in Douro wine country, you can't beat the three-hour (137km) drive east on the N108. The serpentine road shadows the Río Douro, with views of hillsides combed with vines, little chapels and woodlands.

------

❷ Peso da Régua

Terraced hills scaled with vines like a dragon's backbone rise around riverside Peso da Régua.

The sun-bleached town is the region's largest, abutting the Río Douro at the western end of the demarcated port-wine area. It grew into a major port-wine entrepôt in the 18th century. While not as charming as its setting, the town is worth visiting for its **Museu do Douro** (www.museudodouro.pt; Rua Marquês de Pombal; adult/concession €6/3; ⊙10am-6pm Mar-Oct, to 5.30pm Nov-Feb). Housed in a beautifully converted riverside warehouse, the museum whisks you through the entire wine spectrum, from impressionist landscapes to the remains of an old flat-bottomed port hauler. Down at the pier, you'll find frequent 50-minute boat trips to Pinhão, offered by **Tomaz do Douro** (☎222 082 286; www.tomazdodouro.pt; Praça da Ribeira 5; cruises from €10), for instance.

> ### ↱ DETOUR: DOC
>
> **Start:** ❷ **Peso da Régua**
>
> Architect Miguel Saraiva's ode to clean-lined, glass-walled minimalism, **DOC** (☎254 858 123; www.docrestaurante.pt; Estrada Nacional 222, Folgosa; mains €31-35, menu €90-100; ⊙12.30-3.30pm & 7.30-11pm; ◢) is headed by Portuguese star chef Rui Paula. Its terrace peering out across the river is a stunning backdrop. Dishes give a pinch of imagination to seasonal, regional flavours, from fish *açordas* (stews) to game and wild mushrooms – all of which are paired with carefully selected wines from the cellar. It's in Folgosa, midway between Peso da Régua and Pinhão, on the south side of the river. Take the N2 south of Peso da Régua, then hook onto the N222 heading east.

✕ ≋ p337

The Drive » Take the first exit onto the N2 at the roundabout at the end of Rua Dr Manuel de Arriaga, then the third exit at the next roundabout to join the N313. Turn right onto the N313-1 when you see the yellow sign to Quinta do Vallado. It's around a 5km drive.

------

❸ Quinta do Vallado

Ah, what views! The vineyards spread picturesquely before you from **Quinta do Vallado** (☎254 318 081; www.quintadovallado.com; Vilarinho dos Freires; r €200-280; ℗❄️🛜🏊), a glorious 70-hectare winery. It brings together five rooms in an old stone manor and eight swank rooms in an ultra-modern slate building, decked out with chestnut and teak wood, each complete with a balcony. They all share a gorgeous pool. Guests get a free tour of the winery, with a tasting. Have a fine wine-paired meal and stay the night. The staff can also help arrange activities like cycling, hiking, fishing or canoeing.

The Drive » From Quinta do Vallado, the N313-2, CM1258 and N322-2 take you on a 29km drive east through the curvaceous wine terraces of the Alto Douro, past immaculate rows of vines and chalk-white hamlets, with tantalising glimpses of the river below. After Gouvinhas, the wiggling road takes you south to Quinta do Crasto.

④ Quinta do Crasto

Perched like an eyrie on a promontory above the Río Douro and a spectacular ripple of terraced vineyards, **Quinta do Crasto** (☎254 920 020; www.quintado crasto.pt; Gouvinhas, Sabrosa; tours incl tasting €25; ⊙ by appointment) quite literally takes your breath away. The winery is set amid the lyrical landscapes of the Alto Douro, a Unesco World Heritage site. Stop by for a tour and tasting or lunch. It produces some of the country's best wines. Designed by Portuguese starchitect Eduardo Souto Moura, the plunge pool here appears to nosedive directly into the valley below.

The Drive » From Quinta do Crasto it's an easy 4km drive east along the mellow banks of the Río Douro to Quinta Nova via the N322-2 and CM1268.

⑤ Quinta Nova

Set on a ridge, surrounded by 120 hectares of ancient vineyards, overlooking the Douro river with mountains layered in the distance, **Quinta Nova** (☎254 730 420; www. quintanova.com; Covas do Douro; r €200-310; 🛜🛏) is simply stunning. Besides plush lodgings in a beautifully restored 19th-century manor, it offers romantic grounds, a pool gazing out across rolling vineyards, a restaurant,

wine tours, tastings and some of the region's top walking trails (the longest of which is three hours).

The Drive » It's a 10km drive east from Quinta Nova to Casa do Visconde de Chanceleiros on the CM1268, tracing the contours of the emerald-green vines unfurling around you.

⑥ Casa do Visconde de Chanceleiros

Fancy staying the night up in the hills of the sublime Alto Douro? **Casa do Visconde de Chanceleiros** (☎254 730 190; www.chanceleiros. com; r €140-190; P🛜🛏) is a gorgeous 250-year-old manor house, with spacious rooms featuring classic decor and patios. The expansive views of the valley and lush terraced gardens steal the show, but so does the outdoor pool, tennis court, Jacuzzi, and sauna in a wine barrel. Delicious dinners (€38) are served on request.

The Drive » A gentle 7.5km drive east along the M590, with spirit-lifting views across the terraced vineyards, the deep-green Douro and family-run *quintas*, brings you to Pinhão.

⑦ Pinhão

Encircled by terraced hillsides that yield some of the world's best port – and some damn good table wines too – little Pinhão sits on a particularly

lovely bend of the Río Douro. Wineries and their competing signs dominate the scene and even the delightful train station has *azulejos* (hand-painted tiles) depicting the grape harvest. The town, though cute, holds little of interest, but makes a fine base for exploring the surrounding vineyards. From here, you can also cruise upriver into the heart of the Alto Douro aboard a traditional flat-bottomed port boat with **Douro-a-Vela** (☎918 793 792; www. douroavela.pt; Estrada Nacional 222, Folgosa; 2hr cruise €60). Catch the boat from the Folgosa do Douro pier. Or enjoy sublime views over two rivers while wine tasting at **Quinta do Tedo** (☎254 789 165; www.quintadotedo.com; N222, Folgosa; tours incl 3-wine tasting €12, other tastings €22-60; ⊙10am-7pm Apr-Oct, 9am-6pm Nov-Mar).

✕ 🛏 p337

The Drive » Veer slightly west of Pinhão on the N323 and turn right onto the M585, following the sign for Casal de Loivos, 4.5km away. The country road weaving up through the vines, with the river below, later becomes the cobbled Rua da Calçada, passing *socalcos* (stone-walled terraced vineyards).

⑧ Casal de Loivos

It's a tough call, but Casal de Loivos has hands-down one of the most staggeringly beautiful

WHY THIS IS A
CLASSIC TRIP
REGIS ST LOUIS,
AUTHOR

The meandering journey along
the Río Douro takes in some of
Portugal's most breathtaking
scenery. Hilltop vineyards and
sleepy riverside villages encourage
you to take your time, sample the
great wine (and food) on offer,
overnight at guesthouses among
the vines and get off the beaten
path. The region also has plenty of
surprises, including an astonishing
collection of Paleolithic rock
art and a forest- and cliff-filled
wilderness reserve.

Above: **Pinhão** Train station (p333)
Left: **Pinhão** Winery (p333)
Right: **Porto** Ponte de Dom Luís I (p331)

views in the region. From the *miradouro* (viewpoint), the uplifting vista reduces the Douro to postcard format, taking in the full sweep of its stone-walled terraced vineyards, stitched into the hillsides and fringing the sweeping contours of the valley, and the river scything through them. To maximise these dreamy views, stay the night at **Casa de Casal de Loivros** (📞254 732 149, 927 283 122; www.casadecasal deloivos.com; Cabo da Rua, Casal de Loivos; r €170-190; @ 🏊). The elegant house has been in this winemaking family for nearly 350 years. The halls are enlivened by museum-level displays of folkloric dresses, and the perch is spectacular. Swim laps in the pool while peering down across the vines spreading in all directions.

The Drive » Backtrack on the N323, then pick up the N222 south of the river for the 64km drive southeast to Vila Nova de Foz Côa. The winding road takes you through some picture-book scenery, with whitewashed hamlets and *quintas* punctuating vines, orchards and olive groves.

----

❾ Vila Nova de Foz Côa

Welcome to the heart of the Douro's *terra quente* (hot land). This once-remote, whitewashed town has been on the map since the 1990s, when researchers, during a proposed project for

a dam, stumbled across an astounding stash of Paleolithic art. Thousands of these mysterious rock engravings speckle the Río Côa valley. Come to see its world-famous gallery of rock art at the **Parque Arqueológico do Vale do Côa** (📞279 768 260; www.arte-coa.pt; Rua do Museu; each park site adult/ child €15/7.50, museum €6/3; 🕐museum & park 9.30am-6pm Tue-Sun Mar-May, to 7pm Jun-Sep, 9am-5.30pm Oct-Feb). The three sites open to the public include Canada do Inferno, with departures at around 9.30am from the park museum in Vila Nova de Foz Côa, which is the ideal place to understand just how close these aeons-old drawings came to disappearing.

The Drive » Wrap up your road trip by driving 120km northeast to Miranda do Douro via the N102, IP2 and IC5. Closer to the Spanish border you'll notice the shift in scenery, with lushness giving way to more arid, rugged terrain, speckled with vineyards and olive groves.

----

⑩ Miranda do Douro

A fortified frontier town hunkering down on the precipice of the Río Douro canyon, Miranda do Douro was long a bulwark of Portugal's 'wild east'. While its crumbling castle and handsomely severe 16th-century cathedral still lend an air of medieval charm, modern-day Miranda now receives weekend Spanish tourists. For an insight on the region's border culture, including ancient rites such as the 'stick dancing' of the *pauliteiros*, visit the **Museu da Terra de Miranda** (Praça de Dom João

III 2; €2, Sun morning free; 🕐10am-1pm & 2-6pm Wed-Sun, 2-6pm Tue Apr-Oct, 9.30am-1pm & 2-5.30pm Wed-Sun, 2-5.30pm Tue Nov-Mar). If you'd rather get a taste of the rugged nature on Miranda's doorstep, **Europarques** (Crucero Ambiental Arribes del Duero; 📞273 432 396; www. europarques.com; tour €18-22; 🕐 trips 4pm daily, plus 11am Sat & Sun) runs one- and two-hour river boat trips along a dramatic gorge.

Boats leave from beside the dam on the Portuguese side. Stop by the **Parque Natural do Douro Internacional Office** (📞273 431 457; www. natural.pt; Largo do Castelo; 🕐8.30am-1pm & 2-4.30pm Mon-Fri) for the inside scoop on hiking among the woods and towering granite cliffs of the 832-sq-km park. It's home to bird species including black storks, peregrine falcons and golden eagles.

🍴 🛏 p337

LOCAL KNOWLEDGE: WINES OF THE DOURO

The Douro has been world-famous for port-wines for centuries, but only recently has the region carved out a reputation for its equally outstanding table wines. The region's steep, terraced slopes, schist soils (with good drainage), blisteringly hot summers and cold winters, and old, established vines are a winning combination.

Dozens of grape varieties – nearly all of which are red and uniquely Portuguese – are grown in the region. Alone or as a blend, these grapes produce well-structured, tannic and powerful wines, with finesse, length and ripe-fruit flavours. The more expensive ones kept for ageing are usually labelled 'Reserva' or 'Grande Reserva' and these are big, gutsy wines – complex, oaky and full of jammy dark-fruit flavours.

White grapes account for a tiny proportion of wine production, but they have also come on in leaps and bounds. Grapes such as malvasia, viosinho, gouveio and rabigato produce pale whites that are crisp-edged, minerally, fresh and fruity. Those kept for ageing are gold-hued and more complex, with oaky, nutty flavours.

Eating & Sleeping

Peso da Régua ②

✕ Castas e Pratos Portuguese €€€

(📞254 323 290; www.castasepratos.com; Avenida José Vasques Osório; mains €22-35; ⏰12.30-3.30pm & 7.30-11pm) The coolest dining room in town is set in a restored wood-and-stone railyard warehouse with exposed original timbers. You can order grilled *alheira* sausage or octopus salad from the tapas bar downstairs, or opt for green asparagus risotto or roasted kid goat and potatoes with turnip sprouts in the mezzanine.

🛏 Casa do Romezal B&B €€

(📞919 866 186; www.casadoromezal.com; Calçada do Barreiro, Vilarinho dos Freires; d €110; ⏰Mar-Oct; ❄🛜🏊) Young brother-sister team Luís and Margarida run this charming B&B encircled by a small winery, set on a hillside that's been in their family since the 12th century. Three colourful, sunlit upstairs rooms share access to a swimming pool, a shaded front terrace with dreamy vineyard views, and a stone-walled library-lounge with wood stove, foosball table and vinyl record collection. Guests enjoy free tours of the attached winery, along with tastings of the wine, olive oil and jams produced on site.

Pinhão ⑦

✕ Veladouro Portuguese €€€

(📞254 738 166; Rua da Praia 3; mains €16-27; ⏰10am-midnight) Wood-grilled meats and fish are the speciality at this schist-walled restaurant by the riverfront. On sunny days, the vine-shaded front terrace is the place to be, with views of local fishermen under their umbrellas on the adjacent dock. From the train station, follow the main road left for 150m, then turn left again under a railway bridge to the river.

🛏 Casa Cimeira Inn €€

(📞254 732 320, 914 550 477; www.casacimeira-douro.com; Rua do Cimo do Povo, Valença do Sul; s/d €75/80; P❄🛜🏊) Set in a

200-year-old home at the top of the hilltop town of Valença – its cobbled streets wrapped with vineyards and olive tree groves and alive with old country warmth – this is the domain of the charming Nogueira family. Rooms are quaint and spotless, and there's a small pool, a sun deck and family-style dinners featuring their own house wine.

🛏 Morgadio da Calçada Heritage Hotel €€€

(📞915 347 555, 254 732 218; www.morgadiodacalcada.com; Rua Cabo de Vila 18, Provesende; r €130-150; P❄🛜🏊) Housed in a 17th-century manor in the gorgeous hillside village of Provesende, a 20-minute drive from Pinhão, this welcoming guesthouse has eight minimalist rooms inside old stables, with skylights, pinewood floors and original details. Run by the 19th-generation owner, who also produces wine and soaps based on an old family recipe, this special hideaway serves up heritage and stories aplenty.

Miranda do Douro ⑩

✕ São Pedro Portuguese €€

(📞273 431 321; Rua Mouzinho de Albuquerque 20; mains €9-15; ⏰noon-3pm Sun, noon-3pm & 7-10pm Tue-Sat) Just in from the main old-town gate, this restaurant serves up a fine *posta á São Pedro* (grilled veal steak dressed with garlic and olive oil). The good-value *menu do dia* (from €13) includes soup or salad, main course, dessert, wine and water.

🛏 Hotel Parador Santa Catarina Hotel €€

(📞273 431 005; www.hotelparadorsantacatarina.pt; Largo da Pousada; s/d/ste €60/80/90; P❄🛜) Every guest gets a private veranda with spectacular views of the gorge at this luxurious hotel perched on the canyon's edge. The 12 rooms and suites are a handsome mix of traditional and contemporary, with hardwood floors, TVs and large marble bathrooms. The attached restaurant is the most upmarket in town.

Classic Trip

Alentejo & Algarve Beaches

In this sunny coastal drive you'll experience some of Europe's finest beaches and explore the picturesque, formerly Moorish towns of Portugal's south.

28

TRIP HIGHLIGHTS

70 km
Aljezur
Pretty castle-topped town, gateway to glorious beaches

310 km
Faro
Evocative old town, estuary trips and a bone chapel

Nova de Milfontes
START

nbujeira do Mar

4

Silves

9

FINISH
Cacela Velha

15

Sagres
End-of-the-world cliffs and an impressive fortress

145 km

Lagos
Handsome, hedonistic town with great beaches, restaurants and nightlife

180 km

4–6 DAYS
360KM / 224 MILES

GREAT FOR...

BEST TIME TO GO
Good all year, but crowded in July and August.

ESSENTIAL PHOTO
The rock formations at Praia da Marinha.

BEST FOR WILDLIFE
The Sagres area offers great birdwatching and boat trips to view dolphins and perhaps whales.

eiro Praia da Marinha rock formations (p346)

Classic Trip

28 Alentejo & Algarve Beaches

Portugal's southern coasts offer a Mediterranean ideal, with fragrances of pine, rosemary, wine and grilling fish drifting over some absolutely stunning beaches. Only this isn't the Med, it's the Atlantic, so add serious surfable waves, important maritime history and great wildlife-watching opportunities to the mix. This drive takes in some of the finest beaches in the region, and explores the intriguing towns, which conserve their tight-knit Moorish street plans.

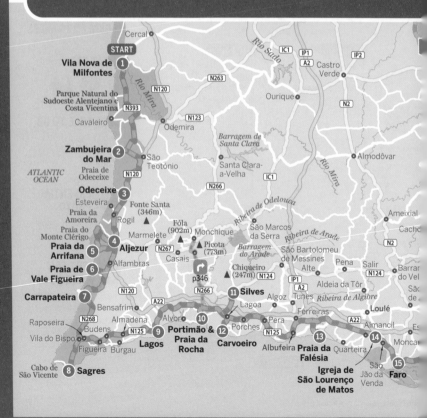

1 Vila Nova de Milfontes

One of the loveliest towns along this stretch of the coast, Vila Nova de Milfontes has an attractive, whitewashed centre, sparkling beaches nearby and a laid-back population who couldn't imagine living anywhere else. Milfontes remains much more low-key than most resort towns, except in August when it's packed to the hilt with surfers and sun-seekers. It's located in the middle of the beautiful Parque Natural do Sudoeste Alentejano e Costa Vicentina and is still a port (Hannibal is said to have sheltered here) alongside a lovely, sand-edged limb of estuary.

Milfonte's narrow lanes, tiny plazas and beach harbour offer varied eating and drinking options. The town beach is sheltered but can get busy; the best strand in the vicinity is fantastic **Praia do Malhão**, backed by rocky dunes and covered in fragrant scrub, around 7km to the north.

The Drive » It's a 26km drive through protected parkland on the N393 south to Zambujeira do Mar.

----

2 Zambujeira do Mar

Enchantingly wild beaches backed by rugged cliffs form the setting of this sleepy seaside village. The main street terminates at the cliff; paths lead to the attractive sands below. Quieter than Vila Nova, Zambujeira attracts a backpacker, surfy crowd, though in August the town is a party place and hosts the massive music fest, **Festa do Sudoeste**. The high-season crowds obscure Zambujeira's out-of-season charms: fresh fish in family-run restaurants, blustering cliff-top walks and a dramatic, empty coast.

📖 p349

The Drive » Cutting back to the main road, you then head south on the N120. It's about 25km to Odeceixe through beautiful coastal woodland.

----

3 Odeceixe

Located just as you cross into the Algarve from the Alentejo, Odeceixe is an endearing whitewashed village cascading down a hill below a picture-perfect windmill on the southern side of the Riberia de Seixe valley. It's a sleepy town, except in summer,

LINK YOUR TRIP

24 **Andalucía's White Villages**

From the end of this trip, it's an easy 192km on the A22 and A49 motorways, skirting Seville, to Carmona, the starting point of this route.

29 **Medieval Jewels in the Southern Interior**

From the end of this trip, head 75km north to Mértola, the finishing point of this route, and do it in reverse.

when it fills with people keen on its nearby beach. This tongue of sand is winningly set at a rivermouth and flanked by imposing schist cliffs (try saying that with a mouthful of porridge...). It's a particularly good option for families, as smaller children can paddle on the peaceful river side of the strand while older kids tackle the waves on the ocean side. The beach is 3.5km from Odeceixe itself along a charming country road. At the beach, a small village has eating and surfing options. The **Rota Vicentina**, a long-distance walking path that leads right to the southwestern tip of Portugal, passes through Odeceixe, and there are great day walks in the vicinity.

The Drive » It's an easy 15km down the N120 to Aljezur, through woodland and open shrubland patched with heather and gorse.

- - - - - - - - - - - - - - - - - -

TRIP HIGHLIGHT

❹ Aljezur

The old part of Aljezur is an attractive village with a Moorish feel. A collection of cottages winds down the hill below a ruined 10th-

century hilltop **castle** (Rua dom Paio Pires Correia; ⏱24hr). Aljezur is close to some fantastic beaches, edged by black rocks that reach into the white-tipped, bracing sea – surfing hot spots. The handsomest beach in the Aljezur area, on the north side of the picturesque rivermouth and backed by wild dunes, is **Praia da Amoreira**. It's 9km by road from Aljezur, signposted off the main road north of town.

The Drive » A couple of kilometres south of Aljezur, the beaches of Monte Clérigo and Arrifana are signposted off to the right. At the top of the hill, head right (towards Monte Clérigo) for the full coastal panorama before winding your way south to Arrifana.

- - - - - - - - - - - - - - - - - -

❺ Praia da Arrifana

Arrifana is a seductive fingernail-shaped cove embraced by cliffs. Just to add to the picturesqueness, it also sports an offshore pinnacle and a petite traditional fishing harbour. The beach is wildly popular with surfers of all abilities and there are several surf schools in the area. The beach break is reliable, but there's also a right-hand reef break that can offer some of the Algarve's best surfing when there's a big swell. There's a small, very popular beachside

restaurant, and clifftop eateries near the ruined fortress up above, which offer breathtaking vistas. Good diving is also possible here.

The Drive » Praia de Vale Figueira is reached by a rough, partly-paved road that runs some 5km from the main road at a point 10km south of Aljezur. Before reaching the turnoff, you must turn right off the N120 on to the N268.

- - - - - - - - - - - - - - - - - -

❻ Praia de Vale Figueira

One of the remoter west coast beaches, this is a long, wide and magnificent stretch of whitish sand with an ethereal beauty, backed by stratified cliffs hazy in the ocean spray. It's reached by a rough, partly paved road and there are no facilities. The beach faces due west and has pretty reliable surf, especially when a southeaster is blowing. It's one of those lonely, romantic beaches that's great to stroll, even when the weather's nasty.

The Drive » Head back to the main road (N268) and turn right onto it. It's about 10km from here to Carrapateira.

- - - - - - - - - - - - - - - - - -

❼ Carrapateira

Surf-central Carrapateira is a tranquil, pretty, spread-out village offering two fabulous beaches with spectacular settings and turquoise seas. Bordeira is a mammoth swath of sand merging into dunes 2km from the north side of town. Amado, with even better surf, is at the southern end. The circuit of both from Carrapateira (9km) is a visually stunning hike (or drive), with lookouts over the beaches and rocky coves and cliffs between them. In town, the **Museu do Mar e da Terra da Carrapateira** (☑282 970 000; www.cm-aljezur.pt; Rua do Pescador; adult/child €2.70/1.10; ⏰10am-4.30pm Mon-Fri) is an intriguing place to visit, with great views.

The Drive » The N268 barrels on right down to Portugal's tip at Sagres (22km), via the regional centre of Vila do Bispo.

TRIP HIGHLIGHT

8 Sagres

The small, elongated village of Sagres, with a rich nautical history, has an appealingly out-of-the-way feel. It sits on a remote peninsula amid picturesque seaside scenery with a sculpted coastline and stern **fortress** (☑282 620 142; www.monumentosdoalgarve.pt; adult/child €3/1.50; ⏰9.30am-8pm May-Sep, to 5.30pm Oct-Apr) leading to a stunning clifftop walk. It also appeals for its access to fine beaches and water-based activities; it's especially popular with a surfing crowd.

Outside town, the striking cliffs of **Cabo de São Vicente** (N258), the southwesternmost point of Europe, make for an enchanting visit, especially at sunset. Make sure you pop into the small **museum** (☑282 624 606; www.faros.pt; N268; adult/child €1.50/1; ⏰10am-6pm Apr-Oct, to 5pm Nov-Mar) here, which has interesting background information on the Algarve's starring role in the Age of Discovery.

From Sagres' harbour, worthwhile excursions head out to observe dolphins and seabirds. **Mar Ilimitado** (☑916 832 625; www.marilimitado.com; Porto da Baleeira; tour from €25) is a recommended operator.

 p349

The Drive » Head back to Vila do Bispo and turn right onto the N125 that will take you to Lagos, a total drive of 34km. Promising beach detours include Zavial and Salema.

TRIP HIGHLIGHT

9 Lagos

Touristy, likeable Lagos lies on a riverbank, with 16th-century walls enclosing the old town's pretty, cobbled streets and picturesque plazas. A huge range of restaurants and pumping nightlife add to the allure provided by fabulous beaches and numerous watery activities.

Aside from the hedonism, there's plenty of history here: start by visiting the lovably higgledy-piggledy **Museu Municipal** (☑282 762 301; www.cm-lagos.com; Rua General Alberto da Silveira; adult/child €3/1.50; ⏰9.30am-12.30pm & 2-5pm Tue-Sun), which incorporates the fabulous baroque church **Igreja de Santo António** (Rua General Alberto da Silveira; adult/child incl museum €3/1.50; ⏰9.30am-12.30pm & 2-5pm Tue-Sun). Heading out on to the water is a must, perhaps cetacean-spotting with **Algarve**

✓ **TOP TIP:**
THE SAGRES EAT SCENE

A closely packed string of surfer-oriented places on Rua Comandante Matoso offer a bit of everything, whether it's a coffee or a caipirinha you're after. They are cafes by day, restaurants serving international favourites by night, whatever time hunger drags you away from the beach and lively bars. Further down the same street, near the port, is a cluster of more traditional Portuguese restaurants.

Water World (📞969 988 027; www.algarvewaterworld. com; Marina de Lagos; 90min tour adult/child €40/25, 75min grotto tour €20/10; ☻Mar-Oct), paddling with **Kayak Adventures** (📞918 888 831; www.kayaktrip. pt; Cais da Solara, Avenida dos Descobrimentos; 2½hr kayaking trip €35; ☻Mar-Oct) or learning to surf with **Lagos Surf Center** (📞282 764 734; www.lagossurfcenter. com; Rua da Silva Lopes 31; 1-/3-/5-day courses €60/165/250). East of town stretch the long, golden sands of **Meia Praia**, backed by worthwhile beach restaurants.

✖ p349

The Drive » Portimão is really just along the coast from Lagos, but it's a 24km detour inland via the N125 in a car.

🔟 Portimão & Praia da Rocha

The Algarve's second-largest town, Portimão's history dates back to the Phoenicians before it became the region's fishing and canning hub in the 19th century. Though that industry has since declined, it's still an intriguing port with plenty of maritime atmosphere. Learn all about the town's fishing heritage in the excellent **Museu de Portimão** (📞282 405 230; www. museudeportimao.pt; Rua Dom Carlos I; adult/child €3/free; ☻2.30-6pm Tue, 10am-6pm Wed-Sun Sep-Jul, 7.30-11pm Tue, 3-11pm Wed-Sun Aug), before strolling through the no-frills sardine restaurants of the fishers'

quarter of Largo da Barca near the road bridge. At the southern end of Portimão stretches the impressive resort beach of **Praia da Rocha**, backed by numerous restaurants and nightlife options.

The Drive » The N125 leads you east to the junction with the N124-1 that takes you north to Silves. It's a drive of only 20km.

🔟 Silves

Silves is one of the Algarve's prettiest towns and replete with history: it was an important trading city in Moorish times and preserves a tightly woven medieval centre. At the top of the town, its sizeable **castle** (📞282 440 837; www.cm-silves.pt; Rua da Cruz de Portugal; adult/

WHY THIS IS A CLASSIC TRIP
REGIS ST LOUIS, AUTHOR

There's a reason why so many people think of coastline when they imagine southern Portugal: the beaches here are simply spectacular. Among the bounty, you'll find dramatic cliff-backed shorelines, hidden coves nestled beside white-washed villages, and sun-drenched strands perfect for surfing, kayaking and other aquatic adventures. There are also alluring island sands that can only be reached by boat — in short, a paradise for beach lovers.

GKUNA/SHUTTERSTOCK ©

Left: **Lagos** Kayaking (p343)
Right: **Sagres** Fortress (p343)

child €2.80/1.40, incl Museu Municipal de Arqueologia €3.90; ⏰9am-7pm Jun, to 10pm Jul & Aug, to 8pm Sep–mid-Oct, to 5.30pm mid-Oct–May) offers great views from the ramparts. Originally occupied in the Visigothic period, what you see today dates mostly from the Moorish era, though the castle was heavily restored in the 20th century.

Below this, the atmospheric **catedral** (Rua da Sé; by donation; ⏰9am-12.30pm & 2-5.30pm Mon-Fri year-round, plus 9am-1pm Sat Jun-Aug) is the region's best-preserved Gothic church. The **Museu Municipal** (☎282 444 838; www.cm-silves.pt;

Rua das Portas de Loulé 14; adult/child €2.10/1.05, incl Castelo €3.90; ⏰10am-6pm) gives good background on the city's history and is built around a fascinating Moorish-era well, complete with spiral staircase. The old-town streets are great for strolling.

The Drive » Cruise 14km straight down the N124-1 to the beach at Carvoeiro.

⓬ Carvoeiro

Carvoeiro is a cluster of whitewashed buildings rising up from tawny, gold and green cliffs and backed by hills. This diminutive seaside resort is prettier and more laid-back than many of the bigger resorts. The town beach is pretty but small and crowded – there are lots of other excellent options in the area. The

most picturesque of all, with stunning rock formations, is **Praia da Marinha**, 8km east of Carvoeira. On foot, it's best reached by the **Percurso dos Sete Vales Suspensos** clifftop walk, beginning at Praia Vale Centianes, 2.3km east of town.

🛏 p349

The Drive » Head back to Lagoa to join the N125 eastwards. After 25km, turn right and head towards the coast, emerging atop the long beach. It's a 37km total drive.

⓭ Praia da Falésia

This long, straight strip of sand offers one of the region's most impressive first glimpses of coast as you arrive from above. It's backed by stunning cliffs in white and several shades of ochre, gouged by weather into intriguing shapes and topped by typical pines.

The areas near the car parks get packed in summer (especially as high tides cover much of the beach), but as the strip is over 3km long, it's easy enough to walk and find plenty of breathing room. It's a good beach for strolling, as the cliffscape constantly changes colours and shapes, and there's a surprising range of hardy seaside plants in the cracks and crevices.

↱ DETOUR: MONCHIQUE

Start: ⓾ Portimão & Praia da Rocha

High above the coast, in cooler mountainous woodlands, the picturesque little town of Monchique makes a lovely detour, with some excellent options for day hikes, including climbing the Algarve's highest hills, Picota and Fóia, for super views over the coast. Monchique and the surrounding area have some excellent eating choices and nearby Caldas de Monchique is a sweet little spa hamlet in a narrow wooded valley.

The N266 heads north from the N124 north of Portimão; it's a 27km drive from Lagos to Monchique, then another 30km on to Silves.

SAIKO3PV/SHUTTERSTOCK ©

Faro Igreja de Nossa Senhora do Carmo (p348)

The Drive ⟫ Head back to the N125 and continue eastwards. Just after bypassing the town of Almancil, there's an exit to 'Almancil, São Lourenço, praias'. The church is signposted from here.

---

⑭ Igreja de São Lourenço de Matos

It's worth stopping here to visit the marvellous interior of this small **church** (Church of St Lawrence of Rome; www.diocese-algarve. pt; Rua da Igreja, Almancil; €2; ⊘3-6pm Mon, 10am-1pm & 3-6pm Tue-Sat), built over a ruined chapel after local people, while digging a well, had implored the saint for help and

then struck water. The resulting baroque masterpiece, built by fraternal master-team Antão and Manuel Borges, is wall-to-wall *azulejos* (painted tiles) inside, with beautiful panels depicting the life of the Roman-era saint, and his death by barbecue. In the 1755 earthquake, only five tiles fell from the roof.

The Drive ⟫ Back on the N125, head south-eastwards and after 12km you're in Faro.

TRIP HIGHLIGHT

⑮ Faro

The capital of the Algarve has a distinctly Portuguese feel and

plenty to see. Its evocative waterside old town is very scenic and has several interesting sights, including the excellent **Museu Municipal** (☏289 870 827; www.cm-faro.pt; Praça Dom Afonso III 14; adult/child €2/free; ⊘10am-6pm Tue-Fri, 10.30am-5pm Sat & Sun), set in a former convent.

The area is centred around Faro's **catedral** (www.paroquiasedefaro. org; Largo da Sé; adult/child €3.50/free; ⊘10am-5.30pm Mon-Fri, to 1pm Sat), built in the 13th century but heavily damaged in the 1755 earthquake. What you see now is a variety of Renaissance, Gothic and Baroque features. Climb

347

the tower for lovely views across the walled town and estuary islands. Part of the Parque Natural da Ria Formosa, these islands can be explored on excellent boat trips run by **Formosamar** (☎918 720 002; www.facebook.com/formosamar; Avenida da República, Faro Marina, Stand 1). The cathedral has a small bone chapel, but much spookier is the one at the **Igreja de Nossa Senhora do Carmo** (http://diocese-algarve.pt; Largo do Carmo; €2; ☉church 9am-5pm Mon-Fri, 9am-1pm Sat, chapel 10am-1pm & 3-5.30pm Mon-Fri, 10am-1pm Sat), built from the mortal remains of over a thousand monks.

Faro's impressive modern **market building** (www.mercadomunicipal defaro.pt; Largo Dr Francisco Sá Carneiro; ☉stalls 7am-3pm Mon-Sat; 🛜) makes a great place to wander, people-watch, buy fresh produce, sit down on a terrace with a coffee, or lunch at one of the several worthwhile eateries.

❌ p349

The Drive » It's 35km east along the N125 to Tavira. Despite the road's proximity to the coast, you won't see much unless you turn off: Fuzeta is a pleasant waterside village to investigate, with boat connections to island beaches.

TOP TIP: FAMILY ATTRACTIONS

This central section of the Algarve coast is great for families, with numerous water parks and other attractions in the area. Two of the most popular are **Slide & Splash** (☎282 340 800; www.slidesplash.com; Vale de Deus 125, Estômbar; adult/child €29/21; ☉10am-6pm Jul–mid-Sep, to 5pm Apr, May & mid-Sep–Oct) and **Aqualand** (☎282 320 230; www.aqualand.pt; N125, Sítio das Areias, Alcantarilha; adult/child €29/21; ☉10am-6pm Jul-Sep, to 5pm Jun).

---

16 Tavira

Set on either side of the meandering Rio Gilão, Tavira is a charming town. The ruins of a hilltop **castle** (Largo Abu-Otmane; ☉8am-5pm Mon-Fri, 9am-7pm Sat & Sun Apr-Oct, 8am-5pm Mon-Fri, 9am-5pm Sat & Sun Nov-Mar), now housing a pleasant little botanic garden; the Renaissance **Igreja da Misericórdia** (https://diocese-algarve.pt; Largo da Misericórdia; church incl museum €2.50; ☉10am-12.30pm & 3-6.30pm Tue-Sat Jul & Aug, 9.30am-12.30pm & 2-5.30pm Tue-Sat Sep-Jun); and the **Núcleo Islâmico** (☎281 320 570; www.cm-tavira.pt; Praça da República 5; adult/child €2/1, incl Palácio da Galeria €3/1.50; ☉9.15am-12.30pm & 1.30-4.30pm Tue-Sat) museum of Moorish history are among the attractions. It's ideal for wandering; the warren of cobblestone streets hides pretty, historic gardens and shady plazas. Tavira is the launching point for the stunning, unspoilt beaches of the Ilha de Tavira, a sandy island that's another part of the Parque Natural da Ria Formosa.

🛏 p349

The Drive » Cacela Velha is 14km east of Tavira: head along the N125 and you'll see it signposted; it's 1km south of the N125.

---

17 Cacela Velha

Enchanting, small and cobbled, Cacela Velha is a huddle of whitewashed cottages edged with bright borders, and has a pocket-sized fort, orange and olive groves, and gardens blazing with colour. It sits above a gorgeous stretch of sea, with a bar, plus other restaurants, a church and heart-lifting views. From nearby Fábrica, you can get a boat across to the splendid Cacela Velha beach, which has a low-key LGBTIQ+ scene in summer.

Eating & Sleeping

Zambujeira do Mar ②

⌷ Herdade do Touril   Inn €€€

(☏283 950 080; www.herdadedotouril.pt; off CM 1158; r €180-260; @ 🛜 🏊) Four kilometres north of Zambujeira do Mar is this upmarket *quinta* (estate) building with rooms and apartments – some are within the original building (built in 1826), others are converted farm cottages. The design of this tranquil place has an African safari-lodge feel – without the lions, of course. Instead, storks nest in nearby cliffs (note, this area is not safe for children). There's a seawater pool, a buffet breakfast and free bikes.

Sagres ⑧

✕ A Tasca   Seafood €€

(☏282 624 177; Porto da Baleeira; mains €14-30, tapas €4-16, seafood platters €60-120; ⊘12.30-3pm & 6.30-10pm Thu-Tue) Seafood doesn't come fresher than at this converted fish warehouse, with a timber-decked terrace overlooking the marina and Ilhotes do Martinhal offshore. A live tank sits alongside the bar strung with strands of dried garlic and chillies. Daily-changing platters and *cataplanas* (seafood stews) are specialities.

⌷ Pousada do Infante   Boutique Hotel €€€

(☏282 620 240; www.pousadas.pt; Rua Patrão António Faustino; d/ste from €170/250; P ❄ @ 🛜 🏊) On the promontory's clifftop, this modern *pousada* occupies a never-to-be-outbuilt position. All rooms and suites (with king-size beds and whirlpool baths) have balconies, but those at the front face the car park, so it's definitely worth paying extra for one overlooking the fortress and ocean to take in the dazzling sunsets.

Lagos ⑨

✕ A Forja   Portuguese €€

(☏282 768 588; Rua dos Ferreiros 17; mains €9-24; ⊘noon-3pm & 6.30-10pm Mon-Sat) Hearty, top-quality traditional food served in a bustling environment at great prices sees this buzzing *adega típica* (wine bar) pull in the crowds. Daily specials are always reliable, as are simply prepared fish dishes such as grilled sole, turbot and mackerel on stainless steel plates, and two-person *cataplanas*.

Carvoeiro ⑫

⌷ O Castelo   Guesthouse €€

(☏919 729 259; www.ocastelo.net; Rua do Casino 59; d €75-180; ❄ 🛜) Right on the beach, this guesthouse is gleamingly maintained. Most of the 12 rooms with colourful, contemporary striped bed linens have a terrace or balcony with sea (and sunrise) views, and can accommodate an extra bed. The family room, with a double bed and two singles, also has a kitchenette. Breakfast (€12.50) is served on a sea-facing terrace.

Faro ⑮

✕ Vila Adentro   Portuguese €€

(☏933 052 173; www.vilaadentro.pt; Praça Dom Afonso III 17; mains €14-20, cataplanas for two €39-49; ⊘9am-midnight; 🖉 🚹) With tables on the square in Faro's old town and a dining room decorated with floor-to-ceiling *azulejos*, this Moorish 15th-century building is a romantic spot for elevated Portuguese cuisine: lobster and mixed seafood *cataplanas* (stew) for two, goat's milk cheese puff pastry with figs, and tangerine-stuffed pork tenderloin. Wines hail from around the country.

Tavira ⑯

⌷ Vila Galé Albacora   Hotel €€€

(☏281 380 800; www.vilagale.com; Quatro Águas; s/d €135/150; ⊘Mar-Oct; P ❄ 🛜 🏊) Overlooking Ilha de Tavira 4km east of town, this four-star, 161-room property has been converted from, and ingeniously incorporates, an entire former tuna village, complete with the original school and chapel. Along with sleek modern rooms (the former tuna workers' living premises), there are indoor and outdoor pools, a spa, two restaurants and two bars. Kids under 12 stay (and eat) free.

Medieval Jewels in the Southern Interior

29

This drive is a goldmine of medieval architecture, with a stunning assemblage of walled towns and sturdy castles taking their place alongside some of the peninsula's most arresting monasteries.

TRIP HIGHLIGHTS

150 km

Batalha
Monastery built commemorating a military victory

240 km

Tomar
Peaceful town overlooked by the stern Templar headquarters

Portalegre

★ LISBON
START

Elvas

11

550 km

Évora
Architectural beauty packed with historical treasures

Beja

Óbidos
Beautifully preserved walled historic centre, ideal for strolling

Mertola
FINISH

4 km

6–9 DAYS
720KM / 448 MILES

GREAT FOR...

BEST TIME TO GO

From March to June and September to October for pleasant weather without extreme heat.

ESSENTIAL PHOTO

Any of the medieval town walls at sunset.

BEST TWO DAYS

From Alcobaça to Tomar, with a dash to Évora if you have time.

Fortified walls (p354)

Medieval Jewels in the Southern Interior

29

War defined medieval Portugal. Towns were fortified with sturdy walls, castles defended them, and when you won a victory, you built a monastery in thanks to the powers that be. That turbulent history has left a region studded in architectural jewels. This drive takes you from Portugal's romantic capital around a stunning selection of them, through typical hill landscapes softened by cork-oaks and pine. Hearty inland cuisine adds to the authentically Portuguese experience.

① Lisbon

Spread across steep hillsides overlooking the Rio Tejo (Tagus), Portugal's capital offers real enchantment in its narrow cobbled streets, centenarian cafes and local *bairro* (neighbourhood) life.

On either side of the low central district, Baixo, rise hills. Bairro Alto is a bohemian district of restaurants and bars, while facing it, Alfama is Lisbon's Moorish time capsule: a medina-like district of tangled alleys, hidden palm-shaded squares and narrow terracotta-roofed houses that tumble down to the glittering Tejo. It is the birthplace of fado, the melancholic Portuguese singing that you can investigate at the excellent **Museu do Fado** (www.museudofado.pt; Largo do Chafariz de Dentro; adult/child €5/3; ☺10am-6pm Tue-Sun). Atop the district is the dramatic **Castelo de São Jorge** (www.castelodesaojorge.pt; adult/student/child €10/5/free; ☺9am-9pm Mar-Oct, to 6pm Nov-Feb), which still has a residential district within its outer walls.

Farther afield, in the district of Belém, the spectacular Manueline **Mosteiro dos Jerónimos** (www.patrimoniocultural.gov.pt; Praça do Império; adult/child €10/5; ☺10am-6pm Tue-Sat, 2-6pm Sun Jun-Sep, 10am-5pm Tue-Sat, 2-5pm Sun Oct-May) and **Torre de Belém**

(www.patrimoniocultural.gov.
pt; Av de Brasília; adult/child
€6/3; ⊙10am-6.30pm Tue-
Sun Apr-Sep, to 5.30pm Oct-
Mar) fortress jutting out
onto the river, are World
Heritage–listed sights.

✗ p359

The Drive » It's a fairly dull
84km run north up the A8
motorway to Óbidos.

TRIP HIGHLIGHT

❷ Óbidos

Surrounded by a classic
crenellated wall, Óbidos'
gorgeous historic
centre is a labyrinth of
cobblestoned streets
and flower-bedecked,
whitewashed houses
livened up with dashes
of vivid yellow and blue
paint. The main gate,
Porta da Vila, leads
directly into the main

LINK YOUR TRIP

6 **Ancient Extremadura**

From Évora, it's a direct
160km northeast on
motorways A6 and A5 to
Mérida in Spain, starting
point for this trip.

28 **Alentejo & Algarve Beaches**

After all the inland scenery,
time to hit the coast! You
can do this route in reverse
by hitting Cacela Velha,
75km south of Mértola.

street, Rua Direita, lined with chocolate and cherry-liqueur shops. It's quite touristy, so wind your way away from it and you'll soon capture some of the town's atmosphere in more peace. There are pretty bits outside the walls too.

You can walk around the wall for uplifting views over the town and surrounding countryside. The walls date from Moorish times (later restored), but the *castelo* (castle) itself is one of monarch Dom Dinis' 13th-century creations. It's a stern edifice, with lots of towers, battlements and big gates. Converted into a palace in the 16th century (some Manueline touches add levity), it's now a deluxe hotel.

The town's elegant main church, **Igreja de Santa Maria** (Praça de Santa Maria; ☺9.30am-12.30pm & 2.30-7pm Apr-Sep, to 5pm Oct-Mar), stands out for its interior, with a wonderful painted ceiling and tiled walls.

The aqueduct, southeast of the main gate, dates from the 16th century and is 3km long.

🛏 p359

The Drive » It's a quick but unexciting 42km drive north up the IC1/A8. Take exit 22, signposted to Alcobaça among other places.

- - - - - - - - - - - - - - - - - - -

③ Alcobaça

The little town of Alcobaça has a charming if touristed centre with a little river and bijou bridges. All, however, yields centre stage to the magnificent 12th-century **Mosteiro de Santa Maria de Alcobaça** (☎262 505 120; www.mosteiroalcobaca.gov.pt; Praça 25 de Abril; €6, incl Tomar & Batalha €15; ☺9am-7pm Apr-Sep, to 6pm Oct-Mar).

One of Iberia's great monasteries, it utterly dominates the town. Hiding behind the imposing baroque facade lies a high, austere, monkish church (free entry) with a forest of unadorned 12th-century arches. But make sure you visit the rest too:

the beautiful cloisters, atmospheric refectory, vast dormitory and other spaces bring back the Cistercian life, which, according to sources, wasn't quite as austere here as it should have been.

The monastery was founded in 1153 by Afonso Henriques, first king of Portugal. The monastery estate became one of the richest and most powerful in the country, apparently housing 999 monks, who held Mass nonstop in shifts. In the 18th century, however, it was the monks' growing decadence that became famous. The party ended in 1834 with the dissolution of the religious orders.

🛏 p359

The Drive » It's a short drive eastwards on the IC9, then northwards on the IC2 to Batalha, 24km away.

- - - - - - - - - - - - - - - - - -

TRIP HIGHLIGHT

④ Batalha

The 1385 Battle of Aljubarrota fought here put the Castilians from Spain in their place and set the foundations for Portugal's golden age. An extraordinary abbey, the **Mosteiro de Santa Maria da Vitória** (☎244 765 497; www.mosteiro batalha.gov.pt; Largo Infante Dom Henrique; €6, incl Alcobaça & Tomar €15, church free; ☺9am-

TOP TIP:
COMBINED
MONASTERY TICKET

If you're planning to visit the monasteries at Alcobaça and Batalha, as well as the Convento de Cristo in Tomar, you can get (from any one of them) a combined ticket for €15 (a saving of €3) that will let you in to all three and is valid for a week.

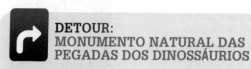

DETOUR:
MONUMENTO NATURAL DAS PEGADAS DOS DINOSSÁURIOS

Start: ④ Batalha

On your way between stops 4 and 5, turn off onto the N360 at Minde, head north for 7km, then another 5km east. On the N357, 10km south of Fátima in a village called Bairro, the **Monumento Natural das Pegadas dos Dinossáurios** (☎249 530 160; www.pegadasdedinossaurios.org; Estrada de Fátima, Bairro; adult/child €3/2; ☺10am-12.30pm & 2-6pm Tue-Fri, to 8pm Sat & Sun Apr-Sep, 10am-12.30pm & 2-6pm Tue-Sun Oct-Mar; 🖕) is one of the most important locations for sauropod prints in the world.

The visit starts with a 20-minute video in Portuguese, then you take a 1.5km walk around the quarry, first seeing the prints from above then walking among them (ask at the admissions counter for info in English).

These, the oldest and longest sauropod tracks in the world, record walks in the mud 175 million years ago. As you walk across the slope, you can clearly see the large elliptical prints made by the hind feet and the smaller, half-moon prints made by the forefeet.

6.30pm Apr-Sep, to 6pm Oct-Mar), was built to commemorate it. Most of the monument was completed by 1434 in Flamboyant Gothic, but Manueline exuberance steals the show, thanks to additions made in the 15th and 16th centuries. The sublime Claustro Real is a masterpiece, as are the unfinished Capelas Imperfeitas.

The battlefield itself is on the southern edge of town. Here, the **Batalha de Aljubarrota Centro de Interpretação** (www.fundacao-aljubarrota. pt; Avenida Nuno Álvares Pereira 120; adult/student/child/family €7/5/3.50/20; ☺10am-5.30pm Tue-Sun) is a museum whose crowning glory is a blood-and-thunder 30-minute film depicting the battle.

🛏 p359

The Drive » This picturesque one-hour drive takes you south on the N362 to castle-topped Porto de Mós. The N243 then takes you across the lonely landscapes of the Serra de Aire before the A23 brings you to Constância, near the next stop.

---

⑤ Castelo de Almourol

Like the stuff of legend, 10-towered **Castelo de Almourol** (Praia do Ribatejo; ☺10am-12.30pm & 2.30-7pm Tue-Sun Apr-Sep, to 5.30pm Oct-Mar) stands tantalisingly close to shore but just out of reach in the Rio Tejo. The castle is 5km from Constância. Boats (€4, five minutes) leave regularly from a riverside landing directly opposite the castle. Once on the island, a short walk leads up to the

ramparts, where you're free to linger as long as you like.

The island, almost jumping distance from land, was once the site of a Roman fort; the castle was built by Gualdim Pais, Grand Master of the Order of the Knights Templar, in 1171. It's no surprise that Almourol has long caught the imagination of excitable poets longing for the Age of Chivalry.

The Drive » The next stop lies around 30km north, easily accomplished by following the N358 through typical central Portuguese farmland.

TRIP HIGHLIGHT

⑥ Tomar

Tomar is one of central Portugal's most appealing small towns, with a pedestrian-friendly historic centre and pretty riverside park in a charming natural setting adjacent to the lush Mata Nacional dos Sete Montes (Seven Hills National Forest).

But to understand what makes Tomar truly extraordinary, cast your gaze skywards. Wrapped in splendour and mystery, the Knights Templar held enormous power in Portugal from the 12th to 16th centuries, and largely bankrolled the Age of Discovery. The **Convento de Cristo** (www. conventocristo.pt; Rua Castelo dos Templários; adult/under 12yr €6/free, incl Alcobaça & Batalha €15; ⏱9am-6.30pm Jun-Sep, to 5.30pm Oct-May), their headquarters, sits on wooded slopes above the town and is enclosed within 12th-century walls. It's a stony expression of magnificence, with chapels, cloisters and choirs in diverging styles, added over the centuries by successive kings and Grand Masters.

The **Charola**, an extraordinary 16-sided church, dominates the complex. Its eastern influences give it a very different feel to most Portuguese churches; the interior is otherworldly in its vast heights – an awesome combination of simple forms and rich embellishment. It's said that the circular design enabled knights

to attend Mass on horseback.

The Drive ›› It's time to head into deep Portugal, first south on the A13, then eastwards along the A23. Take exit 15 onto the IP2 towards Portalegre, then slip onto the N246 heading east. It's a total drive of 125km through increasingly wild inland landscapes.

- - - - - - - - - - - - - - - -

⑦ Castelo de Vide

High above lush, rolling countryside, Castelo de Vide is one of Portugal's most attractive and underrated villages. Its fine hilltop vantage point, dazzlingly white houses, flower-lined lanes and proud locals are reason alone to visit. Originally inhabitants lived within the walls of the **castle** (Rua Bartolomeu Álvares de Sant; ⏱9.30am-5pm Sep-May, to 6pm Jun-Aug), which preserves a small inner village. Nearby is a Jewish quarter with a **synagogue** and **museum** (Rua da Judiaria; ⏱9am-1pm & 2-5pm Tue-Sun Sep-May, to 6pm Jun-Aug). Castelo de Vide is famous for its crystal-clear mineral water, which spouts out of numerous pretty public fountains.

The Drive ›› Marvão is just 10km east of Castelo de Vide, signposted off the N246.

- - - - - - - - - - - - - - - -

⑧ Marvão

On a jutting crag high above the surrounding countryside, the narrow lanes of Marvão feel like

JACQUES VAN DINTEREN/GETTY IMAGES ©

a retreat far removed from the settlements below. The whitewashed village of picturesque tiled roofs and bright flowers has marvellous views, a splendid **castle** (Rua do Castelo; adult/student €2/1; ⏱10am-7pm) built into the rock at the western end of the village, and a handful of low-key guesthouses and restaurants.

🛏 p359

The Drive ›› Take the N359 to Portalegre, then continue south on the N246 through a typical Alentejan landscape of shrubs and cork-oaks to Elvas, 78km from your starting point.

Évora Templo Romano (p358)

9 Elvas

The impressive Unesco-listed fortifications zigzagging around this pleasant little town reflect an extraordinarily sophisticated military technology. Its moats, fort and heavy walls would indicate a certain paranoia if it weren't for Elvas' position, near the Spanish border. Inside the stout, buttressed fortifications, you'll find a lovely town plaza, some quaint museums, narrow medina-like streets and a few excellent eateries. Outside, a magnificently ambitious **aqueduct** brings water from a point 7km west of town.

The Drive » Head west and a little south from Elvas to reach Vila Viçosa, some 40km away via the N4.

---

10 Vila Viçosa

Once home to the Bragança dynasty, this is the most rewarding of several 'marble towns' hereabouts. One of Portugal's largest palaces dominates the centre of town. The **Paço Ducal** ([☎]268 980 659; www.fcbraganca.pt; Terreiro do Paço; adult/child €7/free; ⊘2-5pm Tue, 10am-1pm & 2-5pm Wed-Sun, to 6pm Jun-Sep), built in the 16th century, is imposingly enormous. The palace's best furniture went to Lisbon after Dom João IV ascended the throne, and some went to Brazil after the royal family fled there in 1807, but there are still some stunning pieces on display. Lots of royal portraits put into context the interesting background on the royal family.

The Drive » The more scenic of the routes to Évora is the N254 running southwest. It's around 60km between stops via the handsome little town of Redondo.

TRIP HIGHLIGHT

⑪ Évora

One of Portugal's most beautifully preserved medieval towns, Évora is an enchanting place to delve into the past. Inside the 14th-century walls, Évora's narrow, winding lanes lead to striking architectural works. Guarded by a pair of rose granite towers, the fortress-like medieval **catedral** (www.evoracathedral.com; Largo do Marquês de Marialva; cathedral & cloister €2.50, incl towers €3.50, incl museum & towers €4.50; ☺9am-5pm) has fabulous cloisters and a museum jam-packed with ecclesiastical treasures.

Once part of the Roman Forum, the cinematic columns of the **Templo Romano** (Temple of Diana; Largo do Conde de Vila Flor), dating from the 2nd or early 3rd century, are a heady slice of drama right in town. The city's main square, **Praça do Giraldo**, has seen some potent moments in Portuguese history, including the 1483 execution of Fernando, Duke of Bragança; the public burning of victims of the Inquisition in the 16th century; and fiery debates on agrarian reform in the 1970s. The narrow lanes to the southwest were once the *judiaria* (Jewish quarter).

Aside from its historic and aesthetic virtues, Évora is also a lively university town, and its many attractive restaurants serve up hearty Alentejan cuisine.

✖ ⌂ p359

The Drive » Head west of Évora on the N114, then after 11km take a left turn signposted to Guadalupe and the Cromeleque dos Almendres. Follow signs to reach the monument, some 17km in total from Évora.

---

⑫ Cromeleque dos Almendres

Set within a beautiful landscape of olive and cork trees stands the Cromeleque dos Almendres. This huge, spectacular oval of standing stones is the Iberian Peninsula's most important megalithic group and an extraordinary place to visit.

Some 95 rounded granite monoliths – some of which are engraved with symbolic markings – spread down a rough slope. They were erected over different periods, it seems, with basic astronomic orientations, and were probably used for social gatherings or sacred rituals back in the dawn of the Neolithic period.

Two and a half kilometres before Cromeleque dos

Almendres stands **Menir dos Almendres**, a single stone about 4m high, with some very faint carvings near the top. Look for the sign; to reach the menhir you must walk a few hundred metres from the road.

The Drive » Backtrack through the Évora ringroad and onto the N256 southeast. When you hit the IP2, head south across the Alentejan hills and plains, skirting the city of Beja before continuing on the IC27/N122 to Mértola, a total drive of 150km.

---

⑬ Mértola

Spectacularly set on a rocky spur, high above the peaceful Rio Guadiana, the cobbled streets of medieval Mértola are a delightful place to roam. A small but imposing castle stands high, overlooking the jumble of dazzlingly white houses and a picturesque church that was once a mosque.

A long bout of economic stagnation at this remote town has left many traces of Islamic occupation intact, so much so that Mértola is considered a *vila museu* (open-air museum).

There's a lot to see here, from the parish church, formerly a mosque, to the castle and a group of museums covering various aspects of the town's history.

Eating & Sleeping

Lisbon ❶

✗ Bairro de Avillez   Portuguese €€

(☏210 998 320; www.bairrodoavillez.pt; Rua Nova da Trindade 18; small plates €3-17, mains €8-20; ⏱noon-midnight; ☎) Step into the latest culinary dream by Portugal's most famous chef – Michelin-starred maestro José Avillez – who has set up his gastronomic dream destination: a 'neighbourhood' featuring several dining environments, including everything from a traditional tavern to an avant-garde cabaret.

Óbidos ❷

🛏 Casa d'Óbidos   Hotel €€

(☏262 950 924; www.casadobidos.com; Quinta de São José; d €100, 2-/4-/6-person apt €105/150/190; Ⓟ🛜☎) In a whitewashed 1887 villa below town, this delightful option features breezy rooms with modern bathrooms and period furnishings, plus a swimming pool and lovely grounds with sweeping views of Óbidos' bristling walls and towers. Breakfast is served at a common dining table (fresh bread and breakfast fixings are delivered every morning to the apartments).

Alcobaça ❸

🛏 Challet Fonte Nova   Boutique Hotel €€€

(☏262 598 300; www.challetfontenova.pt; Rua da Fonte Nova 8; s/d/ste €85/120/130; Ⓟ❄☎) Set amid pretty gardens, this elegant, 19th-century chalet has grand common areas with gleaming wood floors and period furnishings. The main house is especially attractive: decorated rooms with big plush beds, tall French windows and a downstairs self-serve bar with billiard table. There's also a whitewashed modern annexe with suites and a small spa complex.

Batalha ❹

🛏 Hotel Casa do Outeiro   Hotel €€

(☏244 765 806; www.hotelcasadoouteiro. com; Largo Carvalho do Outeiro 4; s/d/tr/f from €67/77/97/146; Ⓟ❄🛜🚗) This modern 23-room hotel with a guesthouse feel is awash with the whimsical and colourful artwork of the owner, who also makes some of the arts and crafts in the lobby shop. The rooms are all modern, commodious and attractive – set in bright colour schemes, many have balconies framing astonishing monastery views across the orange rooftops.

Marvão ❽

🛏 Train Spot   Guesthouse €€

(☏963 340 221; www.trainspot.pt; Largo da Alfândega, Beirã; r with shared/private bathroom €45/65, apt €90; Ⓟ☎) Some 11km north of Marvão in the tiny village of Beirã, this extraordinary place offers lodging in a beautifully converted building that was once part of the now inactive train station. It's a designer's dream, with lovely tile-work, a spacious lounge with fireplace and intriguing details (including a bicycle dangling from the ceiling).

Évora ⓫

✗ Bistro Barão   Portuguese €€

(☏266 706 180; Rua da Zanguela 8; mains €15-26; ⏱6.30-10pm Mon, 12.30-3pm & 6.30-10pm Tue-Sat; ☏) This tiny family-run restaurant serves exquisitely prepared Portuguese dishes using high-quality products. Start with sautéed shrimp with garlic or stuffed mushrooms, before moving on to black-pork tenderloin, lightly breaded octopus, grilled ribs and other hearty main courses.

🛏 Albergaria do Calvario   Boutique Hotel €€€

(☏266 745 930; www.adcevora.com; Travessa dos Lagares 3; r €120-175; Ⓟ❄🛜) Unpretentiously elegant and comfortable, this beautifully designed guesthouse has an ambience that travellers adore. The kind-hearted staff are discreetly attentive and provide the best service in Évora, and breakfasts are outstanding, with locally sourced seasonal fruits, homemade cakes and egg dishes.

The Minho's Lyrical Landscapes

Portugal's northwestern corner is made for road-tripping, with its trilogy of medieval cities, pilgrimage sites and dune-flanked Atlantic beaches. Brace yourself for lyrical landscapes and cultural highs.

30

TRIP HIGHLIGHTS

208 km

Peneda
Mountain gateway to Parque Nacional da Peneda-Gerês

9 FINISH

Ponte da Barca

Ponte de Lima

6

32 km

Braga
Church bells chime in the country's most devout city

Esposende
Barcelos

3

Citânia de Briteiros

1

1 km

Viana do Castelo
A double hit of medieval charm and gorgeous, dune-flanked beaches

START

Guimarães
Alluring medieval centre topped by a 1000-year-old castle

99 km

2–4 DAYS
208KM / 129 MILES

GREAT FOR...

BEST TIME TO GO
Year-round in the cities; spring to autumn on the coast.

ESSENTIAL PHOTO
Escadaria do Bom Jesus – a real baroque stunner of a staircase.

 BEST FOR OUTDOORS
Hit the trail in the granite wilds of Parque Nacional da Peneda-Gerês.

Escadaria do Bom Jesus (p364)

30

The Minho's Lyrical Landscapes

Sidling up to Spain on Portugal's northwestern tip, the Minho is the birthplace of the Portuguese kingdom and the home of its emblematic cockerel – and you feel it. The region has a pinch of everything that makes this country special – fortified villages and vineyards, gorgeous dune-backed beaches and lush river valleys, high meadows patrolled by shepherds, granite peaks, and cities with both medieval looks and personality.

TRIP HIGHLIGHT

❶ Guimarães

The cradle of the Portuguese nation, Guimarães is the birthplace of Alfonso Henriques, who became Portugal's first king in 1139. Guimarães hides one of the most exquisitely preserved medieval centres in the country – a warren of cafe-filled plazas and labyrinthine lanes. Unesco duly noted this and made its alley-woven heart a World Heritage

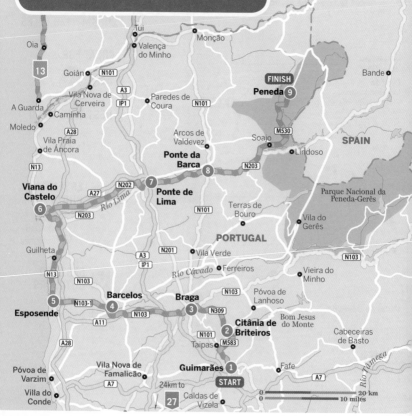

site. It is crowned by a 1000-year-old bird's nest of a **castle** (📞253 412 273; https://pacodosduques. gov.pt; adult/child €2/ free; ⏱10am-6pm), which commands sweeping views over town to a ripple of hills beyond.

Looming over the city on Guimarães' hilltop, with its crenulated towers and cylindrical brick chimneys, **Paço dos Duques de Bragança** (Ducal Palace; 📞253 412 273; https://pacodosduques. gov.pt; Rua Conde D Henrique; adult/child €5/ free; ⏱10am-6pm) was first built in 1401 and later pompously restored as a presidential residence for Salazar. Its rooms now house Flemish

LINK YOUR TRIP

27 Douro Valley Vineyard Trails

From Guimarães, it's just a 55km drive to Porto, from where you can easily dip into the terraced vineyards and outstanding wineries of the Unesco World Heritage Douro.

13 Coast of Galicia
Head just across the border to A Guarda, for a drive along Galicia's wild, storm-buffeted coast, past quaint fishing villages and coves steeped in legend.

tapestries, medieval weapons and a chapel with glittering stained-glass windows.

Some 7km southeast of Guimarães up a twisting, cobbled road is Penha (617m), whose cool woods make it a wonderful escape from the summer heat. If you'd rather leave the car in town, hitch a ride on the Teleférico da Penha, 600m east of Guimarães' old centre.

✖ 🛏 p367

The Drive » Head on the N101 northwest of Guimarães, then the M583 (direction Prazins), which leads through gentle countryside and takes you onto the N309 to Citânia de Briteiros. It's a 16km drive.

- - - - - - - - - - - - - - - -

➋ Citânia de Briteiros

Factor in at least an hour or so for a ramble around one of Portugal's most evocative archaeological sites, **Citânia de Briteiros** (adult/child incl museum €3/1.50; ⏱9am-6pm Apr-Sep, to 5pm Oct-Mar). This is the largest of a liberal scattering of northern Celtic hill settlements, or *citânias* (fortified villages), which date back at least 2500 years. It's likely that this sprawling 3.8-hectare site, inhabited from 300 BCE to 300 CE, was the last stronghold against the invading Romans.

The Drive » It's a 16km drive from Citânia de Briteiros to Braga. The N309 northwest heads through undulating countryside sprinkled with orchards, woods and church-topped villages. Before reaching Braga, allow time to visit Bom Jesus do Monte.

- - - - - - - - - - - - - - - -

➌ Braga

Stay the night in Braga and your wake-up call will be the alarm of some three dozen church bells. *Bemvindo* (welcome) to Portugal's most devout city. Highest on your list should be the Romanesque **Sé** (www. se-braga.pt; Rua Dom Paio Mendes; adult/child €2/free; ⏱9.30am-12.30pm & 2.30-6.30pm Apr-Oct, to 5.30pm Nov-Mar), Portugal's oldest cathedral dating to 1070. Don't miss the intricate west portal, carved with scenes from *Reynard the Fox*, the filigree Manueline towers and the cloister lined with Gothic chapels. But Braga is more than the sum of its prayers – students and a vibrant cafe scene inject it with youthful spirit. Start or finish your evening in one of the cafes lining the **Praça da República**.

Lying around 5km east of central Braga, Bon Jesus do Monte is the goal of legions of penitent pilgrims every year. One of Portugal's most recognisable icons, the sober neoclassical church

JORISVO/GETTY IMAGES ©

PORTUGAL **30** THE MINHO'S LYRICAL LANDSCAPES

stands atop a forested hill that affords grand sunset views across the city. But most come for the extraordinary tiered baroque staircase, **Escadaria do Bom Jesus** (Monte do Bom Jesus). The lowest staircase is lined with chapels representing the Stations of the Cross. The area is chocked with tourists on summer weekends – best avoided if you want to experience the place at its peaceful best.

✘ ⊨ p367

The Drive » On the A11 it's a 23km drive west to Barcelos. A slightly slower alternative is to take the prettier, more relaxed N103 through pinewoods, cultivated fields and low-rise hills.

- - - - - - - - - - - - - - - - -

④ Barcelos

Sitting on the Rio Cávado and hiding a pretty medieval core, dinky Barcelos is worth more than a cursory glance. This town is famous for its roosters (adorning every souvenir stall), pottery and, above all, its massive **Feira de Barcelos** (Barcelos Market; Campo da República; ☉ sunrise-sunset Thu) market, still a largely rural affair, with villagers hawking everything from scrawny chickens to hand-embroidered linen and carved ox yokes.

The Drive » The N103-1 takes you straight west through countryside and small settlements for the 16km drive to Esposende.

- - - - - - - - - - - - - - - - -

⑤ Esposende

After immersing yourself in the rural delights of the hinterland, it's time to hit the coast for a restorative blast of Atlantic air. Consistent swells and breezes attract surfers and kite-surfers to Esposende's broad golden beaches flanked by low dunes.

Parque Nacional da Peneda-Gerês (p366)

The Drive » Trace the contours of the coast north on the N13 past fields, little farms and villages on the 28km drive to Viana do Castelo. Or hop on the A28 instead to carve 15 minutes off your journey.

- - - - - - - - - - - - - - - -

TRIP HIGHLIGHT

⑥ Viana do Castelo

The Costa Verde's biggest stunner, Viana do Castelo is a double shot of medieval centre and gorgeous beaches. Narrow lanes lined with Manueline manors and rococo palaces unfurl to **Praça da República**, with its Renaissance fountain and fortress-like town hall.

For wondrous views down the coast and up the Lima Valley, hop on the funicular up to the eucalyptus-cloaked **Monte de Santa Luzia** and linger to glimpse the fabulously over-the-top, neo-Byzantine **Templo do Sagrado Coração de Jesus** (Templo Monumento Santa Luzia, Temple of the Sacred Heart of Jesus; www.templo santaluzia.org; dome €2; ⊗8am-6pm Jun & Oct, to 7pm Jul-Sep, 8am-5pm Nov-May). A five-minute **ferry** (☎962 305 595; adult/child one-way €1.60/0.90; ⊗9am-6pm May-Sep) trip across the river brings you

to **Praia do Cabedelo**, one of the Minho's best beaches, where powder-soft sands fold into grassy dunes and wind-blown pines.

✖ ⊨ p367

The Drive » The 30km drive east along the N202 to Ponte de Lima weaves past orchards, fields and a succession of low-key, whitewashed villages.

- - - - - - - - - - - - - - - -

⑦ Ponte de Lima

The name is a giveaway – Ponte de Lima's showstopper is its 31-arched **Ponte Medieval** (Ponte Romana)

365

LOCAL KNOWLEDGE:
PARQUE NACIONAL DA PENEDA-GERES

Spread across four impressive granite massifs in Portugal's northernmost reach, this 703-sq-km park encompasses boulder-strewn peaks, precipitous valleys, and lush forests of oak and fragrant pine. It shelters more than 100 granite villages and hamlets that have changed little over the centuries. Many of the oldest villages are found in the Serra da Peneda and remain in a time warp, with oxen being trundled along cobbled streets by black-clad widows; distinctive *espigueiros* (stone granaries); and shepherds herding livestock up to high pastures for five months each year.

This is a wild landscape and in its remotest parts, a few wolves roam, as do wild boar, badgers and otters. With luck, you may catch a glimpse of roe deer and wild ponies. Hiking trails ranging from 1km to 30km abound in all sections of the park and mountain-bike rental is easy to source. For the lowdown on the park, including marked trail descriptions and an accommodation booking service, visit www.adere-pg.pt.

---

loping across the Rio Lima – the finest medieval bridge in all Portugal. Most of it dates from the 14th century, though the segment on the north bank is bona fide Roman.

The town itself is mellow and photogenic, with **Ecovia cycling trails** (www.ciclovia.pt) along the river, two crenulated 14th-century towers and a cute old town for a mosey. The town cranks to life at weekends and every other Monday, when a vast market spreads along the river bank.

🛏 p367

The Drive » It's a 19km drive east of Ponte de Lima on the quaint and countrified N203 to Ponte da Barca.

---

⑧ Ponte da Barca

Serene Ponte da Barca takes its name from the *barca* (barge) that once ferried pilgrims and others across the Rio Lima. Slow the pace here with a stroll along the willow-shaded riverfront or a bike ride into a wooded valley. **ADERE Peneda-Gerês** (📞258 452 250; www.adere-pg.pt; Rua Dom Manuel I; ⏰9am-12.30pm & 2.30-6pm Mon-Fri) is a great source of information on the national park.

The Drive » From Ponte da Barca, the N203 swings northeast, with snapshot views initially of the Rio Lima, then twists and turns through the verdant, mountainous heart of the Parque National de Peneda-Gerês, affording fabulous views on almost every corner. It's around an hour and a half's drive (60km) to Peneda.

TRIP HIGHLIGHT

⑨ Peneda

There are many bases for striking out into the Parque Nacional da Peneda-Gerês, but few rival Peneda for sheer beauty. This is one of the park's most stunning mountain villages and the *serra*'s namesake. It straddles both sides of a deep ravine and is backed by a domed mountain and gushing waterfall. Come for a quiet slice of village life and terrific hiking opportunities. A 1km trail takes you to a lake high in the hills where wild horses graze.

🛏 p367

Eating & Sleeping

Guimarães ❶

✖ Résvés   Tapas €€

(📞253 067 491; www.facebook.com/
resvesrestaurante; Rua de Santa Maria 39;
tapas €8-10, mains €12-20; ⏱12.30-3pm &
7.30-10pm Tue-Sat, 12.30-3pm Sun) The upstairs
restaurant and the downstairs bar are equally
inviting at this spot opposite one of Guimarães'
prettiest squares. Feast on tapas or grilled
meat on the 1st-floor terrace or sip drinks in the
grassy back garden below. The wide-ranging
menu features everything from garlic shrimp,
mussels and clams to *picanha* (rump steak),
mushrooms with asparagus and pork belly
gyoza.

🛏 1720 Quinta da Cancela   Guesthouse €€

(📞919 199 299; www.quintadacancela.com; Rua
da Liberdade, S Lourenço de Sande; r/cottage
€130/180; 🅿 🛜 ♿) Halfway between Braga
and Guimarães, this lovingly run 18th-century
country wine estate has four guest rooms filled
with family antiques and heirlooms, a cosy
four-person cottage and a natural pool on site.
Guests who book directly receive breakfast and
a bottle of the estate's own *vinho verde* (young,
slightly sparkling wine). Three-course dinners
are available on request, prepared by the
gracious, English-speaking owners.

Braga ❸

✖ Casa de Pasto das Carvalheiras   Fusion €€

(📞253 046 244; www.facebook.com/
casadepastodascarvalheiras; Rua Dom Afonso
Henriques 8; small plates €6-18; ⏱noon-3pm &
7pm-midnight Mon-Fri, noon-midnight Sat & Sun)
This colourful eatery with a long bar serves up
delectable, weekly changing *pratinhos* (small
plates), from codfish confit with bok choy and
noodles, to mushrooms with creamy polenta,
to tasty concoctions of *alheira* (a light garlicky
sausage of poultry or game) and turnip greens.
Weekday lunch menus go for €10 or €13,
depending on the number of dishes you order.

Viana do Castelo ❻

✖ O Marquês   Portuguese €

(Rua do Marquês 72; mains from €7-14;
⏱noon-3pm & 7-10pm Mon-Fri, noon-3pm
Sat) A tremendous backstreet find, this place
is absolutely jammed with locals for the *platos
do dia*. Think baked cod with white beans or
roasted turkey leg with potatoes and salad. It's
a friendly, satisfying, family-run affair.

🛏 Dona Emília   Guesthouse €€

(📞917 811 392; www.dona-emilia.com; Rua Manuel
Espregueira 6; d with shared/private bathroom
from €60/80; 🛜) This phenomenal B&B in a
19th-century townhouse commands front-row
perspectives of Viana's historical centre from
its luminous, high-ceilinged common areas and
six guest rooms. Second-floor units have shared
facilities, while suites under the eaves have
beautifully tiled private bathrooms. All abound in
period details; two have terraces with views over
Viana's main square or the leafy backyard.

Ponte de Lima ❼

🛏 Mercearia da Vila   Guesthouse €€

(📞258 753 562; www.merceariadavila.pt; Rua
Cardeal Saraiva 34-36; d €70-85; ❄ 🛜) Six
rooms hide above a charming old grocery store
in a perfect town-centre location. Each comes
with a theme (from green tea to chocolate), as
well as hardwood floors and original furniture.
Some have balconies, while others have
windows with picture-postcard views over the
historic centre and the river.

Peneda ❾

🛏 Miradouro do Castelo   Guesthouse €

(📞251 465 469; www.facebook.com/
miradourodocastelo; Castro Laboreiro; s/d
€36/50; 🅿 🛜) The sweeping views from the
simple rooms with hardwood floors steal the show
at this guesthouse in Castro Laboreiro, located
some 17km northeast of Peneda. Of the seven
rooms, three have the 'wow' view. The downstairs
restaurant serves good local staples (€8 to €16).

Tasting the Dão

Dip into one of Portugal's little-frequented regions and you'll have its vineyards, woods, authentic villages and mountain trails pretty much to yourself.

31

TRIP HIGHLIGHTS

56 km

Santar
One of the Dão's prettiest villages and outstanding wineries

72 km

Viseu
Enticing medieval city topped by a splendid Romanesque cathedral

Penalva do Castelo

5

Mangualde

4

Tondela

3

Santa Comba Dão
START

9

FINISH

Carregal do Sal
Taste noble regional wines and food in an 18th-century manor

30 km

Seia
Base for mountain hikes in Parque Natural da Serra da Estrela

151 km

**2–4 DAYS
151KM / 94 MILES**

GREAT FOR...

BEST TIME TO GO

Spring through autumn for mild weather and seasonal colour.

 ESSENTIAL PHOTO

The countryside rippling far and wide from the top of Caramulinho.

 BEST FOR FOODIES

Head to Tres Pipos for regional food cooked to a tee and paired with superb Dão wines.

31 Tasting the Dão

The Dão is off-the-beaten track Portugal in a nutshell. Get ready to slow-tour the country's rural heartland, an enticing ensemble of vineyards, pine and eucalyptus woods, family-run wineries and whitewashed villages full of sleepy charisma. Cellar tours, manor-house sleeps, hearty meals with beefy red wines and hikes in the wilds of the country's highest peaks in Serra da Estrela all await. Wind down the window. Hear that? Silence.

❶ Santa Comba Dão

With its cluster of whitewashed, red-roofed houses tucked among low-rise hills, *miradouros* (lookouts) gazing across the Rio Dão, and a fine, twin-towered baroque church, this market town makes an appealing stop for an hour or so. Santa Comba Dão is the start of the wine region proper and used to be the terminus of the narrow-gauge Dão railway line to and from Viseu. Most Portuguese recognise the name as

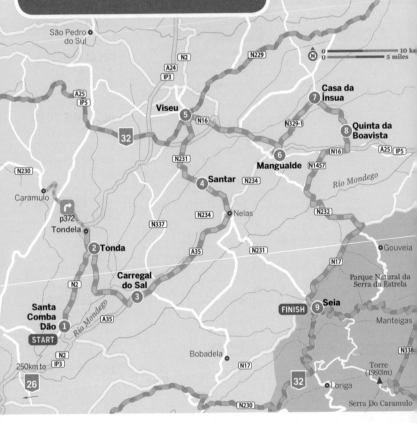

the birthplace of the notorious dictator and former prime minister António de Oliveira Salazar, who was born and buried in the nearby village of Vimieiro.

The Drive ›› From Santa Comba Dão, the N2 blazes 15km north past arable countryside, woodlands of pine and eucalyptus, and small settlements, with Serra do Caramulo rippling northwest in the distance. Before reaching Tondela, exit right following the signs to Tonda, Couço and Mouraz.

---

② Tonda

For a hearty meal while on the wine trail, head straight to **Tres Pipos** (📞232 816 851; www.3pipos. pt; Rua de Santo Amaro 966, Tonda; mains €12-26;

LINK YOUR TRIP

26 Atlantic Coast Surf Trip

Swing over to the Atlantic Coast for a sun and surf fix. Praia de Pedrogão is 120km southwest from Santa Comba Dão.

32 Highlands & History in the Central Interior

Detour 52km southwest of Santa Comba Dão to Coimbra, the start of a drive with historic cities and evocative fortress towns on every turn.

⏱noon-3pm & 7-10pm Tue-Sat, noon-3pm Sun) in the small village of Tonda. It's a convivial, family-run affair, dishing up spot-on regional dishes like *cabrito* (roast kid) and *polvo à lagareiro* (octopus cooked with potatoes, garlic and olive oil) in atmospheric dining rooms with old wooden ceilings and thick stone walls. There's a good selection of Dão wines on the list and also a shop where you can stock up on local *vinho* as well as regional honeys, preserves, sausages, oils and black earthenware from nearby Molelos.

The Drive ›› From Tonda, a minor road threads 14.5km south through pine and eucalyptus woodlands and past tiny orchards and vineyards and unassuming villages like Nagozela, before crossing the Rio Dão. As you approach Carregal do Sal, turn right at the roundabout to reach Quinta de Cabriz.

TRIP HIGHLIGHT

③ Carregal do Sal

The main attraction in Carregal do Sal is **Quinta de Cabriz** (📞232 961 222; www.globalwines.pt; Carregal do Sal, off EN234; tour €10; ⏱shop 10am-1pm & 2-7pm Mon-Sat, 10am-4pm Sun, restaurant noon-3pm & 7-10pm Mon-Sat), the headquarters of Global Wines Portugal, one of the region's major producers. Here you can stock up at the

wine boutique, savour regional dishes expertly paired with wines in the restaurant, enjoy a tasting or hook onto a guided tour of the vineyards (no booking required, just turn up). Fine wines produced here include the Cabriz Touriga Nacional, a spicy, dark-fruit number, and Cabriz Encruzado, a crisp, lemony white.

The Drive ›› The A35, N234 and N231 take you northeast from Quinta de Cabriz to Santar, 26km away. The second half of the route is more attractive, leading past pockets of pine woodland, neat rows of vines and cultivated fields.

TRIP HIGHLIGHT

④ Santar

Santar is a dinky little village and one of the Dão's prettiest, with narrow lanes twisting past baroque villas. The biggest draw, however, is its standout wineries. Top billing goes to the centrally located **Paço dos Cunos de Santar** (📞232 945 452; www. facebook.com/pacodoscunhas; Largo do Paço, Santar; fixed-price menu lunch €14, 3-/4-/5-course €25/35/45; ⏱10am-6pm Tue-Thu, to 10pm Fri & Sat, to 4.30pm Sun), a 17th-century estate, where you can tour the vineyard before a tasting of its noble wines and olive oils, which go nicely with the seasonal, creative takes on regional cuisine in the

DETOUR:
SERRA DO CARAMULO

Start: ② Tonda

From Tonda, the N230 wiggles up through little hamlets and spruce and eucalyptus woods to Caramulo, a good base for striking out into the surrounding Serra do Caramulo. Here fields flanked by woods of oak, pine and chestnut rise to granite, boulder-speckled heights, where small waterfalls and brooks run swift and clear. The mountains are loveliest when wildflowers like heather, oleander and broom bloom in spring and early summer. The range tops off at the 1076m peak of Caramulinho, worth climbing if it is a clear day for far-reaching views stretching all the way to the Serra da Estrela in the south and Aveiro and the Atlantic to the west. The trail begins close to Hotel Caramulo – ask locals to point you in the right direction.

contemporary restaurant. Close by is the **Casa de Santar** (☎232 942 937; www.casadesantar.com; Av Viscondessa Taveiro, Santar; tours adult/child from €15/ free; ☺guided tours by appointment 11am-3pm Tue-Sun, shop 10am-noon & 2-6pm Tue-Sat), a family-owned winery with attractive grounds and baroque architecture. A guided visit takes you deep into its granite cellars, where robust reds are aged in oak barrels. There is also a gourmet shop where you can pick up some bottles and regional specialities.

The Drive » The N231 swings north from Santar to Viseu, a 16km drive away. It's a relaxed country road, taking you past small vineyards and stands of olive and pine.

TRIP HIGHLIGHT

⑤ Viseu

Viseu merits at least half a day of your time, or stay overnight to really absorb the atmosphere of the alley-woven medieval city.

Start off the day by paying a visit to the **Catedral de Viseu** (Sé; Adro da Sé; ☺9am-noon & 2-6pm), a striking hybrid of architectural styles. Originally built in the 13th century, it now has a 17th-century mannerist facade and a soaring 16th-century columned interior. Particularly impressive is the vaulted Manueline ceiling with ribs carved to resemble knotted strands of rope and the

double-tier cloister, an early example of Italian-inspired Renaissance architecture.

Nearby, the **Museu Grão Vasco** (☎232 422 049; Adro da Sé; adult/ child €4/free; ☺2-6pm Tue, 10am-1pm & 2-6pm Wed-Sun) showcases an important collection of works by local-born Vasco Fernandes, aka Grão Vasco (the Great Vasco; c 1475–1543), one of Portugal's seminal Renaissance artists.

✗ ⊨ p375, p387

The Drive » Take the meandering N16 east of town through pinewoods, with views of low-rise mountains and past stone-walled vineyards before crossing a bridge over the Rio Dão. Then follow the A25, taking exit 22 onto the N329-1 to Mangualde. It's a 17km drive.

---

⑥ Mangualde

Mangualde is an elegant town, crowned by a hilltop neoclassical church, **Igreja de Nossa Senhora do Castelo**, which is reached by a long flight of steps. Climb up here for sweeping views over the surrounding countryside.

The Drive » From Mangualde, the N329-1 swings 12km north past hamlets and hills thickly cloaked in pines and eucalyptus. As you enter Penalva do Castelo, head straight at the second roundabout for Casa da Ínsua.

Viseu Museu Grão Vasco

7 Casa da Ínsua

Just outside the sleepy village of Penalva do Castelo, you can rejuvenate at the sublime **Casa da Ínsua** (📞232 640 110; www.montebelohotels. com; Penalva do Castelo; r €120-240; P ❄ 🛜). This 18th-century manor and winery has been lovingly converted into a five-star hotel, complete with manicured landscape gardens, chandelier-lit salons, high-ceilinged rooms brimming with historic charm, a wine-tasting room and highly regarded restaurant. Staff arrange activities including afternoons in the vineyards and cheese- and preserve-making workshops.

The Drive » Veer southeast from Casa da Ínsua, head straight at the roundabout onto a minor road that takes you east through undulating countryside. Continue on this road southeast to Quinta da Boavista, roughly 7km away.

LOCAL KNOWLEDGE: WINES OF THE DÃO

The Dão rivals the Douro and Alentejo when it comes to the quality of its wines, some of Portugal's best. The conditions are ideal for wine-growing, with granitic soils, a temperate climate and shelter provided by the Serra da Estrela, Serra do Caramulo and Serra da Nave.

If the region has sidestepped the global spotlight until recently, it is because viticulture here still tends to be small scale, with vineyards still often little bigger than your average backyard, tucked between cultivated fields, orchards and mountains wreathed with pine and eucalyptus woods. These little wineries work hand in hand with large cooperatives.

Most wine lovers rave about the region's smooth reds, made from grapes like the touriga nacional, tinta roriz, jaen and alfrocheiro. These are ruby-hued, velvety and full-bodied, with aromas of spices, black cherry and other dark fruits.

The region also produces some very decent whites – keep an eye out, particularly, for those made from the tangy encruzado grape, which are fresh and citrusy, with flavours of apple, lemon and melon.

---

8 Quinta da Boavista

A shining example of ecotourism, **Quinta da Boavista** (Tavares de Pina; 📱919 858 340; www.quintadaboavista.eu; Penalva do Castelo; ⊘visits by appointment) in Penalva do Castelo is a winery run with a passion by João Tavares de Pina and his family. The eco-aware farmhouse sits in a secluded spot and offers well-equipped apartments, wine tastings of its full-bodied reds and delicious home-cooked meals. There's also a swimming pool. It's a chilled spot to wind out your road trip of the Dão wine region.

The Drive ≫ It's a 43km drive south to Seia on the N1457, N232 and N17. The drive takes you through tranquil countryside streaked with olive trees and vines and backed by low-rise, forested hills.

TRIP HIGHLIGHT

9 Seia

Besides sweeping views over the surrounding lowlands, Seia's big draw is its cluster of museums, including the **Centro de Interpretação da Serra da Estrela** (CISE; 📱238 320 300; www.cise.pt; Rua Visconde Molelos; adult/child €4/2.50; ⊘10am-6pm Tue-Sun), providing an excellent introduction to the mountainous region. This is the best place for information

on hiking routes, maps and arranging guided hikes.

From here you can easily strike out into the **Parque Natural da Serra da Estrela**, the country's largest protected area at 1.11 hectares. It's a wilderness of rugged boulder-strewn meadows and icy lakes, crowned by mainland Portugal's greatest peak, 1993m-high Torre. Crisp air and immense vistas make this a trekking paradise. As surprisingly few people get off the main roads, you'll often feel as though you have the park all to yourself.

🛏 p375

Eating & Sleeping

Viseu ⑤

✕ O Hilário — Portuguese €€

(📞232 436 587; Rua Augusta Hilário 35; mains €8-12; 🕙10am-3pm & 7.30-10pm Mon-Sat; 🖋) An authentic slice of old Portugal, this homely restaurant is a cheerful, family-run place popular with visitors and locals alike for its mighty *doses* (daily specials) of stews, sausages and grilled steaks. Meat dominates the menu, but you'll also find a few fishy options and they'll even rustle up a vegetarian dish or two if asked. It's named after the 19th-century fado singer who once lived down the street.

🛏 Casa da Sé — Boutique Hotel €€

(📞232 468 032; www.casadase.net; Rua Augusta Cruz 12; d standard €75-120, ste €135-175; ❄🖥) Right in the heart of old Viseu, this handsome boutique hotel is owned by an antique dealer, so the charming 18th-century building is full of period furniture and objets d'art, all for sale should one take your fancy. Its 12 individually decorated rooms are classically attired, and the helpful staff create a warm, hospitable atmosphere.

Expect some street noise at weekends.

🛏 Pousada de Viseu — Pousada €€€

(📞210 407 610; www.pousadas.pt; Rua do Hospital; r €120-210; 🅿❄@🖥🏊) This superbly refashioned *pousada* (upmarket inn) set in a 19th-century hospital is a top luxury option. The original three floors, all with ridiculously high ceilings and spacious modern rooms, have been enhanced with a 4th floor dedicated to superior rooms with panoramic terraces. The enormous central courtyard, with bar, is a neoclassical delight; the elegant former pharmacy is now a cosy lounge.

Indoor and outdoor pools, plus a gym and spa complex, complete the picture. Excellent value.

Seia ⑨

✕ Taberna da Fonte — Portuguese €

(📞238 082 304; Largo da Misericórdia 1; mains €8-12; 🕙9.30am-10pm Tue-Sun) With a prime position looking up to the Igreja de Misericórdia and an attractive slate-floored interior, this central place is a good spot for a taste of *serra* cuisine. That means plenty of ham and cheese, sausages and *morcela* (black pudding), and rich daily specials of *chanfana* (highland goat) and *bacalhau* (dried salt-cod).

Adjacent to the restaurant is a shop selling wines, olive oils and a range of gourmet treats.

🛏 Casas da Ribeira — Cottage €€

(📞238 311 221; www.casasdaribeira.com; Póvoa Velha; cottages 2-person €65-75, 4-person €95-125; 🖥) Close to Seia's services but feeling a million miles away, this cluster of traditional granite cottages sits in a secluded hamlet above town. The six rustic houses are all snug and well set up for the chilly mountain air, with kitchens and stone fireplaces (firewood included). A delicious breakfast with home-baked bread is provided. There's normally a two-night minimum stay.

From Seia, climb the Sabugueiro road for about 5km, then turn left 1km to Póvoa Velha. Call ahead.

🛏 Casa das Tílias — Heritage Hotel €€

(📞964 008 585; www.casadastilias.com; Rua das Tílias, São Romão; d €65-85, tr €90-120, apt for 2/4 people from €95/165; 🅿🖥🏊) In São Romão, 4km from Seia, this is a gorgeous retreat, complete with walled garden and outdoor pool. The central manor house, dating to the 19th century and sporting plenty of polished wood, high ceilings and stucco work, has six rooms. An adjacent modern annex houses three self-catering apartments, sleeping from two to six people.

Highlands & History in the Central Interior

32

This wide-ranging trip takes in many Portuguese historic highlights, from buzzing university town Coimbra to stern borderland fortresses, picturesque villages and the natural majesty of the Serra da Estrela.

TRIP HIGHLIGHTS

620 km

Viseu
Beautiful inland city with strollable historic quarter

200 km

Manteigas
Mountain village at the heart of the Serra da Estrela

● Sernancelhe

● Trancoso

(12)

● Almeida

START/ FINISH

(4)

(1)

● Piódão

(7)

Coimbra
Picturesque and lively university town overlooking a river

1 km

Monsanto
Soaring castle-topped village high above the plains

330 km

5–7 DAYS
770KM / 480 MILES

GREAT FOR...

BEST TIME TO GO

From May to October for best temperatures.

 ESSENTIAL PHOTO

The sweeping mountaintop view from Fragão de Covão above Manteigas.

 BEST FOR OUTDOORS

Hiking the Serra da Estrela around Manteigas.

32 Highlands & History in the Central Interior

History is tangible at every turn in Portugal's interior and this route combines some of the nation's most evocative historic sights, from the venerable university library of Coimbra or Viseu's cathedral, to picture-perfect traditional villages like Piódão or Idanha-a-Velha. Sturdy fortress towns like Almeida and Trancoso shore up the border with Spain, while the Serra da Estrela mountains offer superb vistas and glorious hiking opportunities.

TRIP HIGHLIGHT

❶ Coimbra

While Porto and Lisbon take the headlines, the university town of Coimbra, between the two, is one of Portugal's highlights. Its atmospheric historic centre cascades down a hillside above the Rio Mondego: a multicoloured assemblage of buildings covering a millennium of architectural endeavour.

The spiritual heart of the old town is

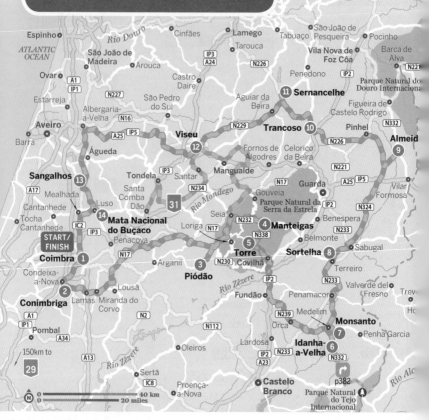

the **Universidade de Coimbra** (📞239 242 744; www.uc.pt/turismo; Pátio das Escolas; adult/child incl Paço das Escolas, Biblioteca Joanina, Capela de São Miguel & Museu da Ciência €12.50/free, without Biblioteca €7/free; 🕙9am-7pm mid-Mar–Oct, 9am-1pm & 2pm-5pm Nov–mid-Mar), whose stunning 16th- to 18th-century buildings surround the Patio des Escolas square. The **Biblioteca Joanina** library is the sumptuous highlight. Within a short stroll are two other Coimbra masterpieces: the **Sé Velha** (Old Cathedral; 📞239 825 273; www. sevelha-coimbra.org; Largo da Sé Velha, Rua do Norte 4; €2.50; 🕙10am-5.30pm Mon-Sat, 11am-5pm Sun) is one of Portugal's finest Romanesque buildings, while the altogether more modern **Museu**

LINK YOUR TRIP

29 Medieval Jewels in the Southern Interior

Head down to Lisbon from Coimbra to explore more of the interior, or connect part-way along in Tomar, 80km south of Coimbra.

31 Tasting the Dão

From Viseu you can access this pleasure-trip around Portugal's silkiest reds.

Nacional de Machado de Castro (📞239 853 070; www.museumachadocastro. pt; Largo Dr José Rodrigues; adult/child €6/3, cryptoportico only €3; 🕙2-6pm Tue, 10am-6pm Wed-Sun) presents an excellent collection of art as well as taking you down to the city's Roman origins.

🍴 🛏 p386

The Drive » It's a short drive southeast along the IC3/N1 some 16km to Condeixa-a-Nova, on whose outskirts sit the Roman ruins of Conímbriga.

---

❷ Conímbriga

Hidden amid humble olive orchards in the rolling country southwest of Coimbra, Conímbriga boasts Portugal's most extensive and best-preserved **Roman ruins** (📞239 941 177; www. conimbriga.pt; Condeixa-a-Velha; ruins & museum adult/child €4.50/free; 🕙10am-7pm Mar-Oct, to 6pm Nov-Feb), and ranks with similarly lauded sites on the entire Iberian Peninsula.

To get your head around the history, begin at the small **museum** near the entrance. Displays present every aspect of Roman life from mosaics to medallions. Then, head out to the **ruins** themselves. A massive defensive wall running right through the site speaks of times of sudden crisis. In contrast, the extraordinary mosaics

of the Casa dos Repuxos speak of times of peaceful domesticity.

The Drive » It's two hours in the car to the next stop. The most interesting route is to take the N342 east, turning north onto the N236, then taking the N17 and IC6 northeast. The last stretch on the N230 is a spectacular if occasionally nerve-racking drive, following valleys with breathtaking views, sheer drops and tight curves.

---

❸ Piódão

Remote Piódão offers a chance to see rural Portugal at its most pristine. This tiny traditional village clings to a terraced valley in a beautiful, surprisingly remote range of vertiginous ridges, deeply cut valleys, rushing rivers and virgin woodland called the Serra de Açor (Goshawk Mountains).

Until the 1970s you could only reach Piódão on horseback or by foot, and it still feels as though you've slipped into a time warp. The village is a serene, picturesque composition in schist and slate; note the many doorways with crosses over them, said to offer protection against curses and thunderstorms.

Houses descend in terraces to the square, where you'll find the fairy-tale parish church, the **Igreja Nossa Senhora Conceição** (🕙10am-1pm & 2-5pm Wed-Sun), and a low-key touristy scene

COIMBRA FADO

If Lisbon represents the heart of Portuguese fado (traditional Portuguese melancholic song), Coimbra is its head. The 19th-century university was male-only, so the town's womenfolk were of great interest to the student body. Coimbra fado developed partly as a way of communicating with these heavily chaperoned females, usually in the form of serenades sung under the bedroom window. For this reason, fado is traditionally sung only by men, who must be students or ex-students.

The Coimbra style ranges from hauntingly beautiful serenades and lullabies to more boisterous students-out-on-the-piss type of songs. The singer is normally accompanied by a 12-string *guitarra* (Portuguese guitar) and perhaps a Spanish (classical) guitar too. Due to the clandestine nature of these bedroom-window concerts, audience appreciation is traditionally indicated by softly coughing rather than clapping.

There are several excellent venues in Coimbra to hear fado, including **À Capella** (☎239 833 985; www.acapella.com.pt; Rua do Corpo de Deus; entry with/without drink €10/5; ⏰7pm-2am, shows 9.30pm).

selling local liqueurs and souvenirs.

🛏 p386

The Drive >> It's only 66km to the next stop, but with the winding roads, spectacular scenery and intriguing villages en route, it may take you some time. Retrace your steps, then head northeast on the N338. The N231 takes you to Seia; from there the N339 then N232 is one of Portugal's great drives, through typical landscapes of the Serra da Estrela and down a vertiginous descent into Manteigas. At Penhas Douradas, at the top of the hill before the long descent into Manteigas, don't miss the stunning view from a stub of rock called Fragão do Corvo; just follow the signs.

TRIP HIGHLIGHT

④ Manteigas

In the heart of the Serra da Estrela, Portugal's loftiest and most spectacular highland region, this is the most atmospheric of

the mountain towns hereabouts. Cradled at the foot of the beautiful Vale do Zêzere, with high peaks and forest-draped slopes dominating the horizon in all directions, Manteigas enjoys a spectacular natural setting.

There are lots of good marked walks in the surrounding area, so you may want to set aside a day to explore the *serra* landscapes on foot. Walk through the glacial valley above town and you'll still encounter terraced meadows, stone shepherds' huts and tinkling goat-bells, while in Manteigas itself cobblestone streets and older homes still hold their own against the high-rise development that has taken root on the Serra da Estrela's fringes.

🛏 p386

The Drive >> The drive from Manteigas to Torre (22km, around 35 minutes) is especially breathtaking, first following the N338 along the Vale do Zêzere. After turning right onto the N339 towards Torre, you pass through the Nave de Santo António – a traditional high-country sheep-grazing meadow – before climbing through a surreal moonscape of crags and gorges. Visible near the turn-off for Torre is Cântaro Magro, a notable rock formation, rising 500m straight from the valley below.

⑤ Torre

In winter, Torre's road signs are so blasted by freezing winds that horizontal icicles barb their edges. Portugal's highest peak, at 1993m, Torre ('Tower') produces a winter freeze so reliable that it has a small ski resort with mainly beginners' slopes.

Outside the snow season (mid-December

to mid-April), Portugal's pinnacle is rather depressing, though a park visitors centre with displays about the region's natural and cultural history is worthwhile.

Even if you give Torre itself a miss, it's worth the drive here to survey the astoundingly dramatic surroundings.

The Drive » Retrace your steps from Torre and continue straight on along the N339 to eventually descend steeply into Covilhã. Take the IP2/A23 motorway south, then the N18 and N239 roughly eastwards, finally reaching the N332 which takes you the last stretch to Idanha-a-Velha. It's a drive of around 90km.

- - - - - - - - - - - - - - - - - -

6 Idanha-a-Velha

Extraordinary Idanha-a-Velha is a very traditional small village with a huge history. Nestled in a remote valley of patchwork farms and olive orchards, it was founded as the Roman city of Igaeditânia (Egitania). Roman ramparts still define the town, though it reached its apogee under Visigothic rule: they built a **catedral** (Sé; Rua da Sé; ⏱10am-12.30pm & 2.30-4.30pm Tue-Sun) and made Idanha their regional capital. It's also believed that their legendary King Wamba was born here.

Moors were next on the scene, and the cathedral was turned into a mosque during their tenure. They, in turn, were driven out by the Knights Templar in the 12th century. It's believed that a 15th-century plague virtually wiped out the town's inhabitants. Today a small population of shepherds and farmers live amid the Roman, Visigothic and medieval ruins.

Wandering this picturesque village is an enchanting trip back in time.

The Drive » Head north up the N332 again, then turn right at the N239. The turnoff to Monsanto is clearly marked. It's only a 15km drive. Passengers who want to stretch their legs could walk the pretty 7km trail from Idanha to Monsanto.

- - - - - - - - - - - - - - - - - -

`TRIP HIGHLIGHT`

7 Monsanto

Like an island in the sky, the stunning village of Monsanto towers high above the surrounding plains. A stroll through its steeply cobbled streets, lined with stone houses that seem to merge with the boulder-strewn landscape, is reason enough to come. But to fully appreciate Monsanto's rugged isolation, climb the shepherds' paths above town to the abandoned and crumbling hilltop **castle**. This formidable stone fortress seems almost to have grown out of the boulder-littered hillside that supports it. It's a beautiful site, windswept and populated by lizards and wildflowers. Immense vistas include Spain to the east and the Barragem da Idanha dam to the southwest. Walkers will also appreciate the network of hiking trails threading through the vast cork-oak-dominated expanses below.

 p387

The Drive » Sortelha is about 60km north of Monsanto across a variety of hilly landscapes.

LOCAL KNOWLEDGE: WALKS FROM MANTEIGAS

The **Trilhos Verdes** (www.manteigastrilhosverdes.com) is an excellent network of marked trails in the Manteigas area. Each route is viewable online and has its own leaflet available at the park information office in town.

The relatively easy ramble (11km one way) through the magnificent, glacier-scoured **Vale do Zêzere**, one of the park's most beautiful and noteworthy natural features, is a highlight. It's quite exposed in summer.

Head due north from Monsanto, eventually linking up with the N233. Turn off in the village of Terreiro, following the brown signs for Sortelha.

---

8 Sortelha

Perched on a rocky promontory, Sortelha is the oldest of a string of fortresses guarding the frontier in this region. Its fortified 12th-century castle teeters on the brink of a steep cliff, while immense walls encircle a village of great charms. Laid out in Moorish times, it remains a winning combination of stout stone cottages, sloping cobblestone streets and diminutive orchards.

'New' Sortelha lines the Santo Amaro–Sabugal road. The medieval hilltop fortress is a short drive, or a 10-minute walk, up one of two lanes signposted '*castelo*'.

The entrance to the fortified old village is a grand, stone Gothic gate. From here, a cobbled lane leads up to the heart of the village, with a *pelourinho* (pillory) in front of the remains of a small castle and the parish church. Higher still is the bell tower – climb it for a view of the entire village. For a more adventurous and scenic climb, tackle the ramparts around the village (beware precarious stairways and big steps).

✖ p387

The Drive ≫ Head east to Sabugal, then turn north, following the N324 north before joining the N340 for the final run northeast to Almeida. It's a drive of around 65km.

9 Almeida

After Portugal regained independence from Spain in the 1640s, the country's border regions were on constant high alert. Almeida's vast, star-shaped fortress is the handsomest of the defensive structures built during this period.

The fortified old village is a place of great charm, with enough history and muscular grandeur to set the imagination humming.

Most visitors arrive at the fortress via the **Portas de São Francisco**, two long tunnel-gates separated by an enormous dry moat.

The long arcaded building just inside is the 18th-century **Quartel das Esquadras**, the former infantry barracks.

Not far away, the interesting **Museu Histórico Militar de Almeida** (🖉271 571 229; adult/child €3.50/1; ⏰9.15am-noon & 2-5pm Tue-Fri, from 10am Sat & Sun) is built into the *casamatas* (casemates or bunkers), a labyrinth of 20 underground rooms used for storage, barracks and shelter for troops in times of siege. Piles of cannonballs fill a central courtyard of the museum, with British and Portuguese cannons strewn about nearby.

DETOUR:
PARQUE NATURAL DO TEJO INTERNACIONAL

Start: 6 Idanha-a-Velha

Still one of Portugal's wildest landscapes, this 230-sq-km park shadows the Rio Tejo (Tagus), the border between Portugal and Spain. It shelters some of the country's rarest bird species, including black storks, Bonelli's eagles, royal eagles, Egyptian vultures, black vultures and griffon vultures.

The best-marked hiking trail, the **Rota dos Abutres** (Route of the Vultures), descends from Salvaterra do Extremo (34km southeast of Idanha-a-Velha) into the dramatic canyon of the Rio Erges. It's an 11km circuit that includes a vulture colony viewing point, and great views of a castle over in Spain.

Monsanto Red-roofed stone houses (p381)

Make sure you also see the attractive **Picadero d'el Rey**, once the artillery headquarters, and what's left of the **castle**, blown to smithereens during a French siege in 1810.

The Drive ≫ Retrace your steps down the N340, then head northwest on the N324. At Pinhel, turn westwards onto the N221/N226, all the way to Trancoso, around 60km in total.

- - - - - - - - - - - - - - -

🔟 Trancoso

A warren of cobbled lanes squeezed within Dom Dinis' mighty 13th-century walls makes peaceful Trancoso a delightful retreat from the modern world. The walls run intact for over 1km around the medieval core, which is centred on the main square, Largo Padre Francisco Ferreira. The square, in turn, is anchored by an octagonal *pelourinho* dating from 1510. The Portas d'El Rei (King's Gate), surmounted by the ancient coat of arms, was always the principal entrance, whose guillotine-like door sealed out unwelcome visitors. On a hill in the northeast corner of town is the tranquil **castle** (🕑10am-12.30pm & 2-5.30pm Mon-Fri, 10am-1pm & 3-6pm Sat & Sun), with its crenellated towers and the distinctively slanted walls of the squat, Moorish Torre de Menagem, which you can climb for views.

The Drive ≫ Head 30km northwest along the N226 to reach the next stop, Sernancelhe.

- - - - - - - - - - - - - - -

🔟 Sernancelhe

Located 30km northwest of Trancoso, Sernancelhe has a wonderfully preserved centre fashioned out of warm, beige-coloured stone. Sights include a 13th-century church that boasts Portugal's only free-standing Romanesque sculpture, an old Jewish quarter with crosses to mark the homes of the converted and several grand 17th- and 18th-century town houses. The finest manor of all is the **Solar dos Carvalhos** (Praça da República), believed to be the birthplace of the famed 18th-century statesman and strong-armed reformer Marquês de Pombal. Just outside of town are hills that bloom with what are considered to be Portugal's best chestnuts.

**The Drive ›› ** The N229 leads you 55km southwest through increasingly fertile countryside to Viseu.

TRIP HIGHLIGHT

⑫ Viseu

One of central Portugal's most appealing cities, Viseu has a well-preserved historical centre that offers numerous enticements to pedestrians: cobbled streets, meandering alleys, leafy public gardens and a central square – Praça da República, aka the 'Rossio' – graced with bright flowers and fountains. Sweeping vistas over the surrounding plains unfold from the town's highest point, the square

fronting the 13th-century granite cathedral (p372), whose gloomy Renaissance facade conceals a splendid 16th-century interior, including an impressive Manueline ceiling.

🗙 🛏 p375, p387

**The Drive ›› ** It's a drive of 90km to the next stop. The quickest way is to take the A25 motorway west, turning south onto the IC2.

- - - - - - - - - - - - - - - - -

⑬ Sangalhos

In the village of Sangalhos, in the Bairrada wine-producing region between Aveiro and Coimbra, the extraordinary **Aliança Underground Museum** (📞234 732 090; www. bacalhoa.pt; Rua do Comércio 444, Sangalhos; guided tour €3; ⊙tours 10am, 11.30am, 2.30pm, 4pm) is part *adega* (winery), part repository of an eclectic, enormous, and top-quality art and artefact collection. Under the winery, vast vaulted chambers hold sparkling wine, barrels of maturing aguardente, and a series of galleries displaying a huge range of objects. The highlight is at the beginning – a superb collection of African sculpture, ancient ceramics and masks – but you'll also be impressed by the spectacular mineral and fossil collection

SAIKOBP/SHUTTERSTOCK ©

and the beauty of some of the spaces. Other pieces include *azulejos* (tiles), a rather hideous collection of ceramic and faience animals, and an upstairs gallery devoted to India. The only complaint is that there's no information on individual pieces, and you don't have time to linger over a particular item. Phone ahead to book your visit, which can be conducted in English and includes a glass of sparkling wine.

**The Drive ›› ** It's an easy 20km drive down the N235 to the town of Luso and on up the hill to the Buçaco forest.

Coimbra Universidade de Coimbra (p379)

⑭ Mata Nacional do Buçaco

This famous, historic national **forest** (☎231 937 000; www.fmb.pt; per car/cyclist/pedestrian €5/free/free; ⏰9am-6pm) is encircled by high stone walls that for centuries have reinforced a sense of mystery. The aromatic forest is criss-crossed with trails, dotted with crumbling chapels and graced with ponds, fountains and exotic trees. In the middle, like in a fairy tale, stands a royal palace. Now a luxury hotel, it was built in 1907 as a royal summer retreat on the site of a 17th-century Carmelite monastery. This wedding cake of a building is over-the-top in every way: outside, its conglomeration of turrets and spires is surrounded by rose gardens and swirling box hedges in geometric patterns; inside (nonguests are more or less prohibited entry) are neo-Manueline carvings, suits of armour on the grand staircases and *azulejos*.

Nearby, **Santa Cruz do Bussaco** (www.fmb.pt; adult/child €2/free, guided tour €3.50; ⏰9am-1pm & 2-6pm) is what remains of a convent where the Duke of Wellington-to-be rested after the Battle of Bussaco in 1810. The atmospheric interior has decaying religious paintings, an unusual passageway right around the chapel, some guns from the battle, and the much-venerated image of *Nossa Senhora do Leite* (Our Lady of Milk), with ex-voto offerings. Outside the forest walls lies the old-fashioned little spa town of Luso.

✕ ⛺ p387

The Drive » Heading back to Coimbra, ignore your GPS and make sure to take the lovely foresty N235, which later joins the IP3. It's a picturesque drive.

Eating & Sleeping

Coimbra ❶

✕ Sete Restaurante
Modern Portuguese €€

(📞239 060 065; www.facebook.com/seterestaurante; Rua Dr Martins de Carvalho 10; mains €12-21; ⏱12.30-3pm & 7-11pm Wed-Mon) Squeezed into a corner behind the Igreja de Santa Cruz, this intimate restaurant is one of the most popular in town. Its casual wine bar vibe, personable service and modern take on Portuguese cuisine ensure it's almost always buzzing. Book ahead to avoid disappointment.

🛏 Casa Pombal
Guesthouse €€

(📞239 835 175; www.casapombal.com; Rua das Flores 18; r €50-70, with shared bathroom €40-60; ❉ 🛜) In a lovely old-town location, this snug guesthouse squeezes tons of charm into a small space. Interiors boast dark wood floors, ceramic tiles and aquamarine blues, while rooms are cosy and individually decorated – two boast magnificent views. Breakfast is good and the friendly staff can provide multilingual advice.

A small terrace peers out across the rooftops. Book ahead from Easter to October.

🛏 Quinta das Lágrimas
Luxury Hotel €€€

(📞239 802 380; www.quintadaslagrimas.pt; Rua António Augusto Gonçalves; r €175-275; 🅿 ❉ 🛜 ⛱) Coimbra's sole five-star hotel is charmingly ensconced in the romantic Jardim Quinta das Lágrimas on the west bank of the Mondego. Choose between classic, richly furnished rooms in the original 18th-century palace, or go for something more minimalist in the modern annex. There's a formal fine-dining restaurant for gourmet dinners, and a fully equipped spa.

Piódão ❸

🛏 Casa da Padaria
B&B €€

(📞235 732 773; www.casadapadaria.com; Rua Cónego Manuel Fernandes Nogueira; s/d €60/65) A picture-perfect rural hideaway, this handsome B&B has an exceptionally friendly host, great breakfasts and attractive, rustic guestrooms. It's in a former bakery on the far side of the village from where you arrive.

Manteigas ❹

🛏 Casa das Obras
Guesthouse €€

(📞275 981 155; www.casadasobras.pt; Rua Teles de Vasconcelos; r €60-85; 🅿 🛜 ⛱) Live like nobility at this glorious 18th-century mansion, the pick of the town-centre accommodation. The manor house has been in the same family for centuries and is a picture of old-world charm with its stone-flagged floors, grand fireplace and original period furniture. It's no shrine, though, and you're made to feel very at home.

The antique-filled rooms are stylish, but the real joy comes from the public areas, including a wonderful breakfast room where you all eat around a lord-of-the-manor-style long table, and a games room with a billiard table. There's also a pool in a grassy courtyard across the street.

🛏 Casa das Penhas Douradas
Design Hotel €€€

(📞275 981 045; www.casadaspenhasdouradas.pt; Penhas Douradas; r €130-190, ste €240-290; 🅿 ❉ @ 🛜 ⛱) Make it up to this fantastic mountain hideaway and you won't want to leave. Everything about the place is just so right, from its panoramic setting to the minimalist Scandinavian-inspired chalet design and impeccable service (evening drinks, afternoon teas). And that's before you've even plunged into the heated pool or grabbed a spa treatment (the massages are amazing).

For meals, it's hard to go past the hotel's gourmet **restaurant** (📞275 981 045; www.casadaspenhasdouradas.pt; Penhas Douradas; fixed-price lunch/dinner menu €30/40; ⏱1-3pm & 8-10pm), also open to the public. Less fancy snacks are available. When you eventually decide to hit the outdoors, there are marked trails and a lake nearby. Rooms vary from the more modestly priced attic rooms in the original building to a stylish, airy suite, but all are immaculate and most offer stirring views.

Monsanto 7

Adega Típica O Cruzeiro — Portuguese €€

(☎936 407 676; Rua Fernando Namora 4; mains €11-15; ⏲12.30-3pm & 7-9pm Thu-Mon) Just below the village proper, this likeable place is a rather surprising find, situated as it is in a modern municipal building. The panoramic dining area boasts spectacular views over the plains below, and the superfriendly staff serve tasty dishes from a seasonal menu.

Monsanto Geo-Hotel Escola — Design Hotel €€

(☎277 314 061; www.monsantoghe.com; Rua da Capela 1; r €65-130; ❄📶) This hip hotel brings a dash of contemporary design to Monsanto's granite-grey centre. Occupying a renovated mansion, it has 10 spacious rooms, each a picture of understated cool. Plain white walls are paired with polished wood floors, colourful accents and memorable views. The friendly and welcoming staff are a further plus.

Sortelha 8

Restaurante Dom Sancho — Portuguese €€

(☎271 388 267; Largo do Corro; mains €14-20; ⏲noon-2.30pm & 7-9.30pm Tue-Sat, noon-3pm Sun) The only restaurant in the old village, Dom Sancho sits just inside the main Gothic gate. It's touristy but the traditional food is spot on – mainly game and hearty stews – and its snug, stone-walled dining room is an attractive place to dine. For lighter snacks and drinks, try the bar downstairs (with cosy fireplace in winter).

Viseu 12

O Cortiço — Portuguese €€

(☎232 416 127; www.facebook.com/cortico.tradicional; Rua Augusto Hilário 45; mains €11-19; ⏲noon-3pm & 7-10pm Tue-Sat, noon-3pm Sun) With its stone walls and low wood-beamed ceilings, this cosy eatery specialises in traditional recipes collected from surrounding villages. Generous portions are served in heavy tureens, and the good house wine comes in medieval-style wooden pitchers. Finish your meal with a glass of the local firewater made from olives.

Palácio dos Melos — Boutique Hotel €€

(☎232 439 290; www.hotelpalaciodosmelos.pt; Rua Chão Mestre 4; s/d €76/100; P❄@📶) This friendly, central hotel enjoys a remarkable location, in a renovated mansion built into the city walls. Its public areas are elegant with high ceilings and period furniture while guest rooms come in a range of looks, from modern business-like to refined classical. All are comfortable and spacious, though. Check for money-saving packages online.

Mata Nacional do Buçaco 14

Pedra de Sal — Portuguese €€

(☎919 701 310; Rua Francisco A Dinis 33, Luso; mains €12-22; ⏲7-10pm Wed, noon-3pm & 7-10pm Thu-Mon) Winningly done out in dark wood, this cosy wine-bar-restaurant is the best in Luso by far. Its menu covers the usual array of meat and fish dishes; however, it's the succulent cuts of Iberian pork and expertly grilled steaks that stand out. The wine list and service are also excellent. Book ahead at weekends.

Palace Hotel do Buçaco — Historic Hotel €€€

(☎231 937 970; www.almeidahotels.pt/pt/hotel-coimbra-portugal; Mata Nacional do Buçaco; r €140-275; P) Originally a royal hunting lodge, this Gothic-Manueline palace in the Buçaco forest is a delightfully ostentatious place to stay. Common areas are stunning – particularly the lobby area and grand staircase – though some of the old-fashioned guest rooms feel a little musty. Don't expect mod cons – there's no air-con, and wi-fi is only available in communal areas – but do expect a dreamy setting and memorable meals.

Significant discounts are often available online.

STRETCH YOUR LEGS
LISBON

Start/Finish Praça do Comércio

Distance 2.5km

Duration Three to four hours

Regal plazas, old-school shops in Baixa, Wonka-like elevators and *miradouros* (viewpoints) with knockout views over the cityscape – it's all packed into this 'greatest hits' walk of downtown Lisbon. Wear flat, comfy shoes to pound these steep, cobbled streets.

Take this walk on Trip

29

Praça do Comércio

With grand 18th-century arcades, lemon facades and mosaic cobbles, riverfront **Praça do Comércio** is a square to out-pomp them all. Everyone arriving by boat used to disembark here; it still feels like the gateway to Lisbon, thronging with activity and rattling trams. At its centre rises the dashing equestrian statue of **Dom José I**.

The Walk » Cross the square heading north to reach the Arco da Vitória and Rua Augusta.

Rua Augusta

As you approach Rua Augusta, you'll pass under the monumental **Arco da Rua Augusta** (Rua Augusta 2-10; €3; ⊘9am-7pm), a triumphal arch built in the wake of the 1755 earthquake. A lift whisks you to the top, where fine views of Praça do Comércio, the river and the castle await. The arch leads through to pedestrianised, mosaic-cobbled Rua Augusta, which buzzes with street entertainers and shoppers.

The Walk » Follow Rua Augusta north and turn right when the narrow pedestrian lane ends.

Praça da Figueira

Praça da Figueira is framed by Pombaline townhouses, old-school stores and alfresco cafes with stellar views of hilltop Castelo de São Jorge. At its centre rises **King João I**, once celebrated for his 15th-century discoveries in Africa, now targeted by pigeons and gravity-defying skateboarders.

The Walk » Bear left onto Rua do Amparo to reach Rossio.

Rossio

Simply **Rossio** to locals, **Praça Dom Pedro IV** throngs around the clock. Shoe-shiners and lottery-ticket sellers, buskers and office workers drift across its wavelike cobbles, gazing up to its ornate fountains and **Dom Pedro IV** (Brazil's first emperor), perched on a marble pedestal. Don't miss **Estação do Rossio**, a frothy neo-Manueline train

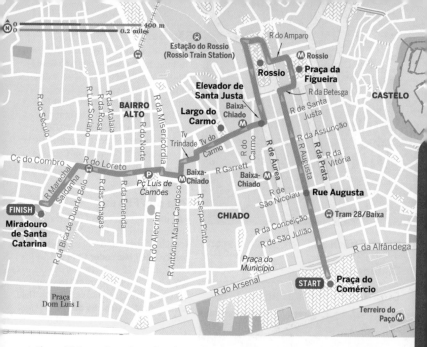

station with horseshoe-shaped arches and swirly turrets.

The Walk » Head south along Rua de Áurea and turn right onto Rua de Santa Justa to reach the Eiffel-esque lift.

Elevador de Santa Justa

If the lanky, wrought-iron **Elevador de Santa Justa** (www.carris.pt/en; cnr Rua de Santa Justa & Largo do Carmo; return trip €5.30; ⏱7.30am-11pm May-Oct, to 9pm Nov-Apr) seems familiar, it's probably because the neo-Gothic marvel is the handiwork of Raul Mésnier, Gustave Eiffel's apprentice. It's Lisbon's only vertical street lift. Zoom to the top for 360-degree views over the city's skyline.

The Walk » At the top, follow the gangplank a few paces west to the Largo do Carmo.

Largo do Carmo

Jacaranda trees shade pavement cafes and the 18th-century **Chafariz do Carmo** fountain on this pretty plaza. Rising above it all are the ethereal arches of **Convento do Carmo** (www.

museuarqueologicodocarmo.pt; adult/child €5/ free; ⏱10am-7pm Mon-Sat Jun-Sep, to 6pm Oct-May), which was all but devoured by the 1755 earthquake, which is what makes it so captivating. Its shattered pillars and wishbone-like arches are completely exposed to the elements.

The Walk » Edge west along Travessa do Carmo and Travessa da Trindade to Praça Luís de Camões, with a statue of its namesake 16th century poet. Head straight onto Rua do Loreto, turning left onto Rua Marechal Saldanha to reach Miradouro de Santa Catarina.

Miradouro de Santa Catarina

Students bashing out rhythms, hippies, stroller-pushing parents and loved-up couples all meet at the precipitous **Miradouro de Santa Catarina**. The views are fantastic, stretching from the river to the Ponte 25 de Abril and Cristo Rei. Pause for a drink at **Noobai** (www. noobaicafe.com; Miradouro de Santa Catarina; ⏱10am-midnight).

The Walk » It's around a 15-minute walk east back to the starting point, Praça do Comércio.

STRETCH YOUR LEGS
PORTO

Start/Finish São Bento train station

Distance 2.3km

Duration Two to three hours

This laid-back walk takes you through Porto's Unesco World Heritage heart, Ribeira. The alley-woven neighbourhood rises in a helter-skelter of chalk-coloured houses, soaring bell towers and Gothic and baroque churches. Every so often the cityscape cracks open to reveal spectacular *miradouros*.

Take this walk on Trip

São Bento

One of the world's most beautiful train stations, Beaux Arts–style **São Bento** (Praça Almeida Garrett; ⏰5am-1am) evokes a more graceful age of rail travel. The *azulejo* (tile) panels in the front hall are the real attraction. Designed by Jorge Colaço in 1930, some 20,000 tiles depict historic battles (including Henry the Navigator's conquest of Ceuta).

The Walk » Cross the street to duck down the Rua das Flores opposite.

Rua das Flores

Rua das Flores is one of Ribeira's most charming streets, lined with boutiques, speciality shops and cafes like elegant, pastry-filled **Mercador Café** (📞223 323 041; snacks €3.50-7; ⏰9am-8pm Mon-Sat; 📶). Check out the vibrant street-art-splashed electricity boxes. Nearby, the **Museu da Misericórdia do Porto** (www.mmipo.pt; adult/student €6/4; ⏰10am-6.30pm Apr-Sep, to 5.30pm Oct-Mar) unites cutting-edge architecture, a prized collection of 15th- to 17th-century sacred art and portraiture, and one of Ribeira's finest churches, Igreja da Misericórdia.

The Walk » Veer right on Rua de Belmonte, then immediately left down Rua Ferreira Borges, to reach Jardim do Infante Dom Henrique. Henry the Navigator sits high on a pedestal in front of the 19th-century Mercado Ferreira Borges.

Palácio da Bolsa

Presiding over Jardim do Infante D Henrique is **Palácio da Bolsa** (www.palaciodabolsa.com; Rua Ferreira Borges; tours adult/student/child €11/7.50/free; ⏰9am-6.30pm Apr-Oct, 9am-1pm & 2-5.30pm Nov-Mar). Built from 1842 to 1910, this splendid neoclassical monument honours Porto's past and present money merchants. No expense was spared on its mosaic- and mural-lined halls, sweeping granite staircase, and kaleidoscopic Salão Árabe, with stucco teased into complex designs, arabesques and stained-glass windows.

The Walk » Swing a right to the Igreja de São Francisco, Porto's most striking church.

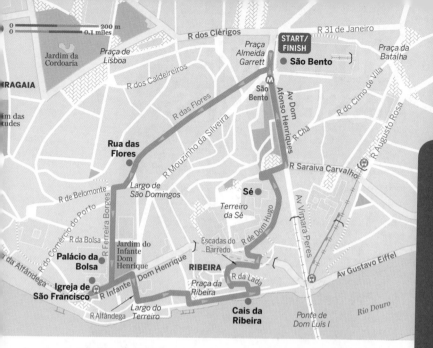

Igreja de São Francisco

Looking austerely Gothic from the outside, **Igreja de São Francisco** (€7.50; ⊙9am-7pm Mar-Oct, to 6pm Nov-Feb) hidesone of Portugal's most dazzling displays of baroque finery inside. Hardly an inch escapes unsmothered, as otherworldly cherubs and sober monks are drowned by nearly 100kg of gold leaf. Note the masterful Tree of Jesse in the nave and wander the eerie catacombs in contemplative silence.

The Walk ›› As you exit, bear left on Rua do Infante D Henrique, then right onto Rua Alfândega, passing Casa do Infante, the medieval town house where Henry the Navigator was born in 1394. Turn left onto Rua da Fonte Taurina, then right to reach Cais da Ribeira.

Cais da Ribeira

Strolling along **Cais da Ribeira** is your golden ticket to the city's soul, with the Ribeira's pastel houses daubing the hillside behind you and the Douro unfurling before you. Colourful *barcos rabelos* (flat-bottomed boats once used to ship port wine along the river) bob in front of pavement cafes and restaurants and the graceful swoop of the double-decker Ponte de Dom Luís I frames the picture neatly.

The Walk ›› Climb up Rua da Lada, turning right then right again onto Escadas do Barredo, a steep, narrow flight of steps, wedged between brightly painted houses. At the top, Rua de Dom Hugo sweeps up to the cathedral.

Sé

Gazing proudly over the city from its hilltop perch, the fortress-like **Sé** (Terreiro da Sé; cloisters adult/student €3/2; ⊙9am-6.30pm Apr-Oct, to 5.30pm Nov-Mar) is where Henry the Navigator was baptised and King John I married. History reverberates in its Romanesque-meets-baroque nave and *azulejo* cloister, and the terrace commands photogenic views over Porto's higgledy-piggledy lanes and rooftops.

The Walk ›› From the Sé, bear left on Avenida Dom Afonso Henriques for a five-minute stroll back to your starting point at São Bento.

ROAD TRIP ESSENTIALS

Spain & Portugal Driving Guide

With picturesque scenery, good-quality roads and an extensive highway network, Spain and Portugal are excellent for road tripping – no matter where you roam.

DRIVING LICENCE & DOCUMENTS

Drivers must carry the following at all times:

→ passport or an EU national ID card
→ valid driving licence
→ car-ownership papers
→ proof of third-party liability insurance

An International Driving Permit (IDP) is not required when renting a car but can be useful in the event of an accident or police stop, as it translates and vouches for the authenticity of your home licence.

INSURANCE

Third-party motor insurance is a minimum requirement in Spain, Portugal and throughout Europe. Ask your insurer for a European Accident Statement form, which can simplify matters in the event of an accident. A European breakdown-assistance policy such as the AA Five Star Service or RAC Eurocover Motoring Assistance is a good investment. Car-hire companies also provide this minimum insurance, but be careful to understand what your liabilities and excess are, and what waivers you are entitled to in case of accident or damage to the hire vehicle.

Road Trip Websites

AUTOMOBILE ASSOCIATIONS

RAC (www.rac.co.uk/drive/travel/country/spain and www.rac.co.uk/drive/travel/country/portugal) Info for British drivers on driving in Spain and Portugal.

ROUTE MAPPING

Mappy (www.mappy.es)
Michelin (www.viamichelin.com)

HIRING A CAR

To hire a car in Spain or Portugal you have to have a licence, be aged 21 or over and, for the major companies at least, have a credit or debit card. Smaller firms in areas where car hire is particularly common (such as the Balearic Islands) can sometimes live without this last requirement. Although those with a non-EU licence should also have an International Driving Permit (IDP), you will find that national licences from countries such as Australia, Canada, New Zealand and the USA are usually accepted without question.

Driving Tips

➡ First thing if you're British: watch your instinct to drive on the left. The golden rule: when leaving a parking lot, petrol station or motorway off-ramp, do it on the right and your instinct to stay right will kick in.

➡ The law says to give way to traffic on the right, even when you're on a main road. So it's wise to ease off on the foot whenever you get to a junction.

➡ Never go below a third of a tank, even if you think there's cheaper petrol further down the road; sometimes the next station's a long way off.

Most car-hire companies do not charge extra if you plan to drive between Spain and Portugal, but you should inform them of your travel plans. Smaller companies may charge an additional fee.

Rental cars with automatic transmission are rare in Spain and Portugal; book well ahead for these.

Car-hire companies:

Autojardim (www.auto-jardim.com) Offers some of the best rates in Portugal.

Auto Europe (www.autoeurope.com) US-based clearing house for deals with major car-rental agencies.

Autos Abroad (www.autosabroad.com) UK-based company offering deals from major car-rental agencies.

Avis (www.avis.es)

Europcar (www.europcar.es)

Hertz (www.hertz.es)

Holiday Autos (www.holidayautos.es) A clearing house for major international companies.

Motorvana (www.motorvana.com) Offers recreational vehicle (RV) and motorhome rental in Spain and Portugal.

Pepecar (www.pepecar.com) Local low-cost company, but beware of 'extras' that aren't quoted in initial prices.

Sixt (www.sixt.es)

BRINGING YOUR OWN VEHICLE

Any foreign motor vehicle entering Spain or Portugal must display a sticker or licence plate identifying its country of registration. Right-hand-drive vehicles brought from the UK or Ireland must have deflectors affixed to the headlights to avoid dazzling oncoming traffic.

MAPS

We recommend that you purchase detailed regional driving maps, as they will help you navigate back roads and explore alternative routes. Michelin publishes a 234-page spiral-bound road atlas of Spain and Portugal. For walking and hiking, maps by IGN/CNIG, Spain's civilian survey organisation, are among the best. You can purchase maps from vendors like Stanfords (www.stanfords.co.uk).

Centro Nacional de Información Geográfica (CNIG; www.cnig.es) Publishes a range of 1:200,000 provincial road maps and 1:25,000-scale hiking maps of national parks as well as some city maps.

Michelin (http://travel.michelin.co.uk) Sells tear-proof yellow-orange 1:400,000-scale regional maps tailor-made for cross-country driving. It also sells detailed city maps to places like Madrid, Barcelona and Granada.

Portugal Road Distances (km)

	Coimbra	Évora	Faro	Lisbon	Porto	Viseu
Coimbra	---					
Évora	251	---				
Faro	468	244	---			
Lisbon	202	138	296	---		
Porto	123	368	585	317	---	
Viseu	86	366	554	288	127	---

Spain Road Distances (km)

	Alicante	Badajoz	Barcelona	Bilbao	Córdoba	Granada	León	Madrid	Málaga	Oviedo	Pamplona	San Sebastián	Seville	Toledo	Valencia	Valladolid
Badajoz	696															
Barcelona	515	1022														
Bilbao	817	649	620													
Córdoba	525	272	908	795												
Granada	353	438	868	829	166											
León	755	496	784	359	733	761										
Madrid	422	401	621	395	400	434	333									
Málaga	482	436	997	939	187	129	877	544								
Oviedo	873	614	902	304	851	885	118	451	995							
Pamplona	673	755	437	159	807	841	404	407	951	463						
San Sebastián	766	768	529	119	869	903	433	469	13	423	92					
Seville	609	217	1046	933	138	256	671	538	219	789	945	1007				
Toledo	411	368	692	466	320	397	392	71	507	510	478	540	458			
Valencia	166	716	349	633	545	519	685	352	648	803	501	594	697	372		
Valladolid	615	414	663	280	578	627	134	193	737	252	325	354	589	258	545	
Zaragoza	498	726	296	324	725	759	488	325	869	604	175	268	863	396	326	367

ROAD CONDITIONS

Spain and Portugal have an extensive network of roads and highways. Here's a breakdown of various types of intercity roads in Spain.

→ *Autovías/auto-estradas* (highway names beginning with A) are multilane divided highways. In Spain, toll roads are further designated AP (*autopistas*). Toll-road signage is usually in blue and indicates tolls (*peajes* in Spanish, *portagens* in Portuguese).

→ National highways (Carreteras Nacionales) are marked with N or CN.

→ Regional highways (Carreteras Autonómicas) are marked with one or two letters indicating the region, ie A in Andalucía, CL in Castilla y León.

→ Provincial highways are marked with two letters indicating the province, ie LU (Lugo), MA (Málaga).

→ Municipal highways are marked with two letters indicating the municipality. Portugal, meanwhile, uses a slightly different nomenclature for its roads. Top of the range are *auto-estradas* (motorways):

→ A prefixes indicate Portugal's toll roads.

→ IP (*itinerário principal*) indicates main highways in the country's network.

→ IC (*itinerário complementar*) indicates subsidiary highways.

Numbers for the main two-lane *estradas nacionais* (national roads) have no prefix letter on some road maps, whereas on other maps they're prefixed by N.

Roads are generally in good shape in Spain and Portugal. A growing number of cars on the road can lead to heavy congestion in developed areas, both in cities and in resort areas along the coast. Keep in mind that Spain, owing to the siesta, has four rush hours: typically 8am to 9.30am, 1pm to 2.30pm, 3.30pm to 5pm and 6.30pm to 8.30pm.

ROAD RULES

Despite the sometimes chaotic relations between drivers, there are rules. To begin with, driving is on the right, overtaking is on the left and most signs use international symbols. An important rule to remember is that traffic from the right usually has priority.

By law, car safety belts must be worn in the front and back seats, and children under 12 years may not ride in the front. The police can impose steep on-the-spot fines for speeding and parking offences, so save yourself a big hassle and remember to toe the line.

Key points to keep in mind:

→ **Blood-alcohol limit** The limit is 0.05%. Breath tests are common, and if found to be over the limit, you can be judged, condemned, fined and deprived of your licence within 24 hours. Fines can be up to around €600 for serious offences. Nonresident foreigners may be required to pay up on the spot (at 30% off the full fine). Pleading linguistic ignorance will not help – the police officer will produce a list of infringements and fines in as many languages as you like. If you don't pay, or don't have a Spanish resident to act as guarantor for you,

Driving Problem Buster

I can't speak the language; will that be a problem? While it's preferable to learn some Spanish or Portuguese before travelling, road signs are mostly of the 'international symbol' variety, and English is increasingly spoken among the younger generation. In a worst-case scenario, a good attitude and sign language can go a long way.

What should I do if my car breaks down? Safety first: turn on your flashers, put on a safety vest (compulsory in rental cars, usually in glove compartments) and place a reflective triangle (also compulsory) 30m to 100m behind your car to warn approaching motorists. Call for emergency assistance (112) or walk to the nearest roadside call box (stationed at 2km intervals on motorways). If renting a vehicle, your car-hire company's service number may help expedite matters. If travelling in your own car, verify before leaving home whether your local auto club has reciprocal roadside-assistance arrangements in Spain and Portugal.

What if I have an accident? For minor accidents you'll need to fill out a Parte Europeo de Accidente (European Accident Statement, sometimes provided in rental-car glove compartments) and report the accident to your insurance and/or rental-car company. If necessary, contact the police (112).

What should I do if I get stopped by the police? Show your passport (or EU national ID card), licence and proof of insurance.

What's the speed limit and how is it enforced? Speed limits (indicated by a black-on-white number inside a red circle) range from 30km/h in small towns to 130km/h on the fastest autoroutes. If the police pull you over, they'll fine you on the spot or direct you to the nearest police station to pay. If you're caught by a speed camera (placed at random intervals along highways), the ticket will be sent to your rental-car agency, which will bill your credit card, or to your home address if you're driving your own vehicle. Fines depend on how much you're over the limit.

How do Iberian tolls work? Some Spanish and Portuguese autoroutes charge tolls. Take a ticket from the machine upon entering the highway and pay as you exit. Some exit booths are staffed by people; others are automated and will accept only chip-and-PIN credit cards or coins.

What if I can't find anywhere to stay? During summer and holiday periods, book accommodation in advance whenever possible. Local tourist offices can sometimes help find you a bed during normal business hours. Otherwise, try your luck at chain hotels, which are typically clustered at autoroute exits outside urban areas.

your vehicle could be impounded, although this is rare.

⇒ **Motorcyclists** Headlights must be used at all times and a helmet must be worn if riding a bike of 125cc or more.

⇒ **Overtaking** Spanish truck drivers often have the courtesy to turn on their right indicator to show that the way ahead of them is clear for overtaking (and the left one if it is not and you are attempting this manoeuvre).

⇒ **Roundabouts (traffic circles)** Vehicles already in the circle have the right of way.

⇒ **Speed limits** Unless otherwise marked, in built-up areas the speed limit is 50km/h (and in some cases, such as inner-city Barcelona, 30km/h), which increases to 90km/h on major roads and up to 120km/h on *autovías* and *autopistas* (toll-free and tolled dual-lane highways, respectively). Cars towing caravans are restricted to a maximum speed of 80km/h.

SAFETY

Rental cars are especially at risk of break-ins or petty theft in larger towns, so don't leave anything of value visible in the car. Ultracautious drivers unscrew the radio antenna and leave it inside the car at night; they might also put the wheel covers (hubcaps) in the boot (trunk) for the duration of the trip.

PARKING

In city centres, most on-the-street parking places are metered from 9am to 2pm and 4pm to 8pm Monday to Friday, and from 9am to 2pm on Saturday. Buy a ticket at the nearest coin-fed ticket machine and place it on your dashboard with the time stamp clearly visible. Bigger cities also have public parking garages. Metered zones (indicated by blue lines on the street) are known as *zona azul* (blue zone). Plain white lines typically indicate free parking.

In Spain, if you've parked in a street parking spot and return to find that a parking inspector has left you a parking ticket, don't despair. If you arrive back within a reasonable time after the ticket was issued (what constitutes a reasonable time varies from place to place, but it is

rarely more than a couple of hours), don't go looking for the inspector, but instead head for the nearest parking machine. Most machines in most cities allow you to pay a small penalty (usually around €5) to cancel the fine (keep both pieces of paper just in case). If you're unable to work out what to do, ask a local for help.

FUEL

Gasolina (petrol) in Spain is pricey, but generally slightly cheaper than in its major EU neighbours (including France, Germany, Italy and the UK). It's even more expensive in Portugal (by about 20%).

Petrol is about 10% cheaper in Gibraltar than in Spain and 15% cheaper in Andorra.

There are plenty of service stations, and credit cards are accepted at most.

RADIO

Radio Nacional de España (RNE) has Radio 1, with general-interest and current-affairs programmes; Radio 5, with sport and entertainment; and Radio 3 (Radio d'Espop). Stations covering current affairs include the left-leaning Cadena SER, or the right-wing COPE. The most popular commercial pop and rock stations are LOS40, Kiss FM, Cadena 100 and Onda Cero.

Portugal's national radio stations consist of state-owned Rádiodifusão Portuguesa (RDP; www.rtp.pt), which runs Antena 1, 2 and 3 and plays Portuguese broadcasts and evening music (Lisbon frequencies 95.7, 94.4 and 100.3). For English-language radio there's the BBC World Service (Lisbon 90.2) and Voice of America (VOA), or a few Algarve-based stations, such as Kiss (95.8 and 101.2).

Iberian Playlist

Malamente Rosalía

Maria Lisboa Mariza

Nueva Vida Ojos de Brujo

O Pastor Madredeus

Pokito a Poko Chambao

Rosas La Oreja de Van Gogh

Spain & Portugal Travel Guide

GETTING THERE & AWAY

Spain is one of Europe's top holiday destinations and is well linked to other European countries by air, rail and road. There are ferry links to the UK, Italy, France, Morocco and the Canary Islands, among other places.

Unless visiting on a cruise, those coming to Portugal usually arrive by air.

AIR

All of Spain's airports share the user-friendly website and flight information telephone number of **Aena** (☑91 321 10 00; www.aena.es), the national airports authority.

Rental cars are available at all of the major airports.

Madrid's Aeropuerto de Barajas is Spain's busiest (and Europe's fourth- or fifth-busiest) airport.

Other major airports on mainland Spain include Barcelona's Aeroport del Prat and the airports of Málaga, Alicante, Girona, Valencia, Seville and Bilbao.

There are also airports at Almería, Asturias, Jerez de la Frontera, Murcia, Reus, Santander and Santiago de Compostela.

In Portugal, Lisbon, Porto and Faro are the main international gateways. For more Portugal-related information, including live flight arrival and departure schedules, see www.ana.pt.

CAR & MOTORCYCLE

Entering Spain or Portugal from other parts of the EU is usually a breeze – no border checkpoints and no customs

– thanks to the Schengen Agreement. Things are a little different in Andorra, where old-fashioned document and customs checks are still the norm when passing through – many border guards, however, will simply wave you through.

SEA

Brittany Ferries (☑in the UK 0330 159 7000; www.brittany-ferries.co.uk) runs the following services:

➡ Plymouth to Santander (20 hours, one weekly, mid-March to October only)

➡ Portsmouth to Bilbao (24 to 32 hours, two to three weekly)

➡ Portsmouth to Santander (24 to 32 hours, three weekly)

➡ Rosslare (Ireland) to Bilbao (28 to 32 hours, two weekly March to October only)

An alternative is to catch a ferry across the Channel (or the Eurotunnel vehicle train beneath it) to France and motor down the coast.

The fastest sea crossings travel between Dover and Calais, and are operated by P&O Ferries (www.poferries.com). For travel through the Channel Tunnel, visit Eurotunnel (www.eurotunnel.com).

TRAIN

Rail services link Spain (and Portugal via Spain) with France and beyond.

Renfe (☑91 232 03 20; www.renfe.com) is the excellent national train system that runs most of the services in Spain. Portugal has a good rail network as well, operated by Comboios de Portugal (www.cp.pt).

DIRECTORY A–Z

ACCESSIBLE TRAVEL

Spain and Portugal are not overly accommodating for travellers with disabilities but some things are slowly changing. For example, disabled access to some museums, official buildings and hotels represents a change in local thinking. In major cities more is slowly being done to facilitate disabled access to public transport and taxis; in some cities, wheelchair-adapted taxis are called 'Eurotaxis'. Newly constructed hotels in most areas of Spain are required to have wheelchair-adapted rooms. With older places, you need to be a little wary of hotels who advertise themselves as being disabled-friendly, as this can mean as little as wide doors to rooms and bathrooms, or other token efforts.

For tips on travel and thoughtful insights on traveling with a disability, download Lonely Planet's free Accessible Travel guide from www.shop.lonelyplanet. com/ categories/accessible-travel.com.

Worthy of a special mention is Barcelona's **Inout Hostel** (☑93 280 09 85; www.inouthostel.com; Major del Rectoret 2; dm €22-33; @🛜🏊; 🚇FGC Baixador de Vallvidrera), which is completely accessible, and nearly all the staff who work there have disabilities of one kind or another. The facilities and service are first class.

ACCOMMODATION

Spain and Portugal have a wide range of accommodation, and it's generally of good value. You'll find everything from backpacker or youth hostels and small, family-run guesthouses to boutique hotels and the old-world opulence of *paradores/ pousadas* (state-owned hotels in heritage buildings).

Categories

At the lower end of the budget category there are dorm beds (from €20 per person) in youth hostels or private rooms with shared bathrooms in the corridor. If you're willing to pay a few euros more, there are many budget places, with good, comfortable rooms and private bathrooms.

Spain and Portugal generally have excellent midrange hotels. You should always have your own private bathroom, and breakfast is sometimes included in the room price. Boutique hotels, including many that occupy artistically converted historical buildings, largely fall into this category and are usually good choices.

At the top end you'll find a raft of cutting-edge, hip design hotels with stylish lounges in the big cities and major resort areas. Wherever you stay, expect to pay more for a room with a view – especially sea views or with a balcony.

Guesthouses

There are various types of guesthouses; prices typically range from €60 to €90 for a double room with private bathroom (and as little as €40 for the simplest lodgings with shared bathrooms).

➡ The *hostal* (Spain) or *residencial* (Portugal) is generally the most comfortable type of guesthouse, with breakfast usually included.

➡ The *pensión/pensão* is a slight step down in comfort and quality. These typically offer some rooms with shared bathrooms or rooms with only a shower or sink.

➡ The *hospedaría* or *casa de huéspedes/casa de hóspedes* is at the bottom of the heap, with low prices and very basic rooms, usually with shared bathrooms; breakfast is rarely served.

Paradores/Pousadas

One of the best places to stay in Spain or Portugal is at a *parador/pousada* (Spain: www.parador.es; Portugal: www. pousadas.pt). These are former castles, monasteries and palaces that have been turned into luxurious hotels, roughly divided into rural and historic options. In Portugal the prices range from €90 to €220. In Spain prices run from €100 to €250. Prices are lower during the week and there are often discounts and deals.

Rural Tourism in Spain

Rural tourism has become quite popular in Spain, with accommodation available in many new and often charming *casas rurales*. These are usually comfortable, renovated village houses or farmhouses with a handful of rooms. Lower-end prices typically hover around €40/60 for a single/double per night, but classy boutique establishments can easily charge €100 or more for a double. Many are rented out by the week.

Agencies include the following:

Associació Agroturisme Balear (www.rusticbooking.com)

Casas Cantabricas (www.casas.co.uk)

Cases Rurals de Catalunya (www.casesrurals.com)

Escapada Rural (www.escapadarural.com)

Fincas 4 You (http://en.fincas4you.com)

James Villa Holidays (www.jamesvillas.co.uk)

Ruralka (www.ruralka.com)

Rustic Rent (www.rusticrent.com)

Rusticae (www.rusticae.es)

Secret Places (www.secretplaces.com)

Traum Ferienwohnungen (www.traum-ferienwohnungen.de)

Vintage (www.vintagetravel.co.uk)

VRBO (ww.vrbo.com)

Turihab Properties in Portugal

These charming properties offer accommodation in a farmhouse, manor house, country estate or rustic cottage. High-season rates for two people, either in a double room or a cottage, range from €75 to €150. Some properties have swimming pools, and most include breakfast (often with fresh local produce).

Sleeping Price Ranges

SPAIN

The following price ranges refer to a double room with private bathroom in high season (prices are higher in Barcelona and Madrid).

€ less than €65

€€ €65–140

€€€ more than €140

PORTUGAL

Price categories refer to a double room with bathroom in high season. Unless otherwise stated, breakfast is included in the price.

€ less than €60

€€ €60–120

€€€ more than €120

There are three types of Turihab lodgings:

Casas no Campo (www.casasnocampo.net) Country houses, cottages and luxury villas.

Solares de Portugal (www.solaresdeportugal.pt) Grand manor houses, some of which date from the 17th or 18th centuries.

Aldeias de Portugal (www.aldeiasdeportugal.pt) Lodging in rural villages in the north, often in beautifully converted stone cottages.

Camping

Camping is popular in Spain and Portugal, though Spain – with around 1000 *campings* (campgrounds) – has a greater selection. Some of these are well located in woodland or near beaches or rivers, but others are on the outskirts of towns or along highways. Few of them are near city centres. Facilities generally range from reasonable to very good, although any campground can be crowded and noisy at busy times (especially July and August). The best sites have swimming pools, supermarkets, restaurants, laundry service, children's playgrounds and tennis courts.

Campgrounds usually charge per person, per tent and per vehicle – typically €5 to €10 for each. Children usually pay a bit less than adults. Many campgrounds close from around October to Easter.

Spain

Campinguía (www.campinguia.com) Comments (mostly in Spanish) and links.

Guía Camping (www.guiacampingfecc.com) Online version of the annual *Guía Camping* (€16), which is available in bookshops around the country.

Vaya Camping (www.vayacamping.net/spain) Info and booking service.

Portugal

➡ Generally, campgrounds run by Orbitur (www.orbitur.pt) offer the best services. Some towns have municipal campgrounds, which vary in quality.

➡ For detailed listings of campgrounds nationwide, pickup the *Roteiro Campista* (www.roteiro-campista.pt; €9), updated annually and sold at *turismos* (tourist offices) and bookshops. It contains details of most Portuguese campgrounds, with maps and directions.

Seasons

➡ On the coast, high season is summer, particularly August. Finding a place to stay without booking ahead in July and August in the Algarve or along the Mediterranean Coast can be difficult and many places require a minimum stay of at least two nights during high season.

➡ In ski resorts, high season is Christmas, New Year and the February to March school holidays.

➡ Hotels in inland cities sometimes charge low-season rates in summer.

➡ Rates often drop outside the high season – in some cases by as much as 50%.

➡ In the Pyrenees hotels sometimes close between seasons, from around May to mid-June and from mid-September to early December.

➡ Weekends are high season for boutique hotels and *casas rurales* (rural homes), but low season for business hotels (which often offer generous specials) in Madrid and Barcelona. Always check out hotel websites for discounts.

➡ Prices skyrocket for major festivals, such as Seville's Semana Santa and Barcelona's La Mercè.

ELECTRICITY

Type C
220V/50Hz

Type F
230V/50Hz

FOOD

Settling down to a meal with friends is one of life's great pleasures in Spain and Portugal. You'll find a great variety of eateries and drinking spots (food and drink go hand in hand in Iberia).

Adega (Portugal) Literally 'wine cellar', usually decorated with wine barrels and having a rustic ambience. Expect heavy, inexpensive meals.

Asador Restaurant specialising in roasted meats.

Bar de copas Gets going around midnight and serves hard drinks.

Casa de comidas Basic restaurant serving well-priced home cooking.

Cervecería/Cervejaria The focus is on *cerveza* (beer) on tap.

Chiringuito Beach bar.

Churrasqueira (Portugal) Restaurant specialising in chargrilled meats.

Horno de asador Restaurant with a wood-burning roasting oven.

Marisquería/marisqueira Bar or restaurant specialising in seafood.

Tasca Tapas bar; in Portugal a *tasca* is an old-fashioned place with daily specials, low prices and a local crowd.

Terraza Open-air bar, for warm-weather tippling and tapas.

Taberna Usually a rustic place serving tapas and *raciones* (large tapas).

Vinoteca Wine bars where you can order by the glass.

Ordering Tapas in Spain

Unless you speak Spanish, the art of ordering can seem one of the dark arts of Spanish etiquette. Fear not – it's not as difficult as it first appears.

In the Basque Country and in many bars in Madrid, Barcelona and elsewhere, it couldn't be easier. With tapas varieties lined up along the bar, you either take a small plate and help yourself or point to the morsel you want. If you do this, it's customary to keep track of what you eat (by holding on to the toothpicks, for example) and then tell the bar staff how many you've had when it's time to pay. Otherwise, many places have a list of tapas, either on a menu or posted up behind the bar. If you can't choose, ask for '*la especialidad de la casa*' (the house speciality) and it's hard to go wrong.

Another way of eating tapas is to order *raciones* (literally 'rations'; large tapas servings) or *medias raciones* (half-rations; smaller tapas servings). Remember, however, that after a couple of *raciones* you'll be full. In some bars you'll also get a small (free) tapa when you buy a drink.

Portuguese Couvert

Throughout Portugal, waiters bring bread, olives and other goodies to your table when you sit down. This unordered appetiser is called '*couvert*' and it is *never* free (*couvert* can cost from €1.50

to upwards of €8 per person at flashier places). If you don't want it, send it away, no offence taken.

Meal Times

➡ Spaniards rarely eat lunch before 2pm (restaurant kitchens usually open from 1pm until 4pm).

➡ It does vary from region to region, but in Spain most restaurants open for dinner from 8.30pm to midnight, later on weekends.

➡ In Portugal, meal times are typically earlier – from noon to 3pm for lunch, and 7pm to 10pm for dinner. The siesta is not common in Portugal.

INTERNET ACCESS

Wi-fi is almost universally available at hotels, as well as in some cafes, restaurants and airports; usually (but not always) it's free. Connection speed often varies from room to room in hotels (and coverage is sometimes restricted to the hotel lobby), so always ask when you check in or make your reservation if you need a good connection. Some tourist offices can provide a list of wi-fi hot spots in their area.

A convenient and more universally reliable alternative to wi-fi – especially if you're travelling outside the cities – is to purchase a Spanish or Portuguese SIM card for your phone. Many local prepaid plans include generous data allowances at surprisingly low rates.

LGBTIQ+ TRAVELLERS

Same-sex marriage is legal in Spain and Portugal, but the LGBTIQ+ community generally keeps a fairly low profile – though people are more out in Madrid, Barcelona, Sitges and Torremolinos. Lisbon, Porto and the Algarve also have a LGBTIQ+ scene, but it's fairly low-key. Sitges is a major destination on the international gay party circuit; including taking a leading role in the wild Carnaval there in February/March. As well, there are parades, marches and events in several cities on and around the last Saturday in June, when Madrid's Pride march takes place (Seville, Porto and Lisbon also have Pride fests).

Eating Price Ranges

The following price ranges refer to a standard main dish:

€ less than €12

€€ €12–20

€€€ more than €20

MONEY

The most convenient way to bring your money is in the form of a debit or credit card, with some extra cash for use in case of an emergency.

ATMs

Many credit and debit cards can be used for withdrawing money from a *cajeros automáticos* (automatic teller machine – labelled 'Multibanco' in Portugal) that displays the relevant symbols such as Visa, MasterCard, Cirrus etc. Remember that there is usually a charge (around 2%) on ATM cash withdrawals abroad.

Cash

Most banks will exchange major foreign currencies and offer better rates than exchange offices at the airport. Ask about commissions – these can vary from bank to bank – and take your passport.

Credit & Debit Cards

These can be used to pay for most purchases. You'll often be asked to show your passport or some other form of identification. Among the most widely accepted are Visa, MasterCard, American Express (Amex), Cirrus, Maestro, Plus and JCB. Diners Club is less widely accepted. If your card is lost, stolen or swallowed by an ATM, you can call the card issuer's free-call telephone number to have an immediate stop put on its use.

Money Changers

You can exchange both cash and traveller's cheques at exchange offices – which are usually indicated by the word *cambio* (exchange). Generally they offer longer opening hours and quicker service than banks, but worse exchange rates and higher commissions.

OPENING HOURS

Following are standard hours for various types of business in Spain and Portugal (note that these can fluctuate by an hour either way in some cases).

Banks 8.30am to 2pm or 3pm Monday to Friday

Bars 6pm to 2am

Cafes 9am to 7pm

Tipping Guide

Menu prices include a service charge. Most people leave some small change if they're satisfied: 5% is normally fine and 10% extremely generous. Porters will generally be happy with €1. Taxi drivers don't have to be tipped but a little rounding up won't go amiss.

Nightclubs 11pm to 6am Thursday to Saturday

Post offices 9am to 5pm Monday to Friday

Restaurants 1pm to 3.30pm and 8pm to 11pm in Spain; noon to 3pm and 7pm to 10pm in Portugal

Shops 10am to 2pm and 5pm to 8pm Monday to Friday, 10am to 2pm Saturday in Spain; 10am to noon and 2pm to 7pm Monday to Friday, 10am to 2pm Saturday in Portugal

Supermarkets 9am to 8pm

PUBLIC HOLIDAYS

Spain

Año Nuevo (New Year's Day) 1 January

Viernes Santo (Good Friday) March/April

Fiesta del Trabajo (Labour Day) 1 May

La Asunción (Feast of the Assumption) 15 August

Fiesta Nacional de España (National Day) 12 October

La Inmaculada Concepción (Feast of the Immaculate Conception) 8 December

Navidad (Christmas) 25 December

Regional governments set five holidays and local councils two more.

Portugal

New Year's Day 1 January

Carnaval Tuesday February/March; the day before Ash Wednesday

Good Friday March/April

Liberty Day (celebrating the 1974 revolution) 25 April

Labour Day 1 May

Practicalities

→ **Time** Portugal is on GMT/UTC time. Spain is one hour ahead (GMT/UTC plus one hour). In both countries there is daylight saving from the last Sunday in March to the last Sunday in October, so during this period Portugal is GMT plus one hour, Spain is GMT plus two hours.

→ **TV and DVD** Like the UK, Portugal and Spain use the PAL system – incompatible with US and French systems.

→ **Weights and measures** Metric.

→ **Smoking** In Spain, smoking is banned in indoor spaces. In Portugal, it's allowed in some restaurants and bars with separate smoking sections.

Corpus Christi May/June; ninth Thursday after Easter

Portugal Day (also known as Camões and Communities Day) 10 June

Feast of the Assumption 15 August

Republic Day (commemorating the 1910 declaration of the Portuguese Republic) 5 October

All Saints' Day 1 November

Independence Day (commemorating the 1640 restoration of independence from Spain) 1 December

Feast of the Immaculate Conception 8 December

Christmas Day 25 December

SAFE TRAVEL

The main thing to be wary of is petty theft (which may, of course, not seem so petty if your passport, cash, travellers cheques, credit card and camera go missing). Be careful but don't be paranoid.

Scams

There must be 50 ways to lose your wallet. As a rule, talented petty thieves work in groups and capitalise on distraction. Tricks usually involve a team of two or more (sometimes one of them an attractive woman to distract male victims). While one attracts your attention, the other empties your pockets. More imaginative strikes include someone dropping a milk mixture on to the victim from a balcony. Immediately a concerned citizen comes up to help you brush off what you assume to be pigeon poo, and thus suitably occupied you don't notice the contents of your pockets slipping away.

Beware: not all thieves look like thieves. Watch out for an old classic: the ladies offering flowers for good luck. We don't know how they do it, but if you get too involved in a friendly chat with these people, your pockets almost always wind up empty.

On some highways, especially the AP7 from the French border to Barcelona, bands of thieves occasionally operate. Beware of men trying to distract you in rest areas, and don't stop along the highway if people driving alongside indicate you have a problem with the car. While one inspects the rear of the car with you, his pals will empty your vehicle. Another gag has them puncturing tyres of cars stopped in rest areas, then following and 'helping' the victim when they stop to change the wheel. Hire cars and those with foreign plates are especially targeted. When you do call in at highway rest stops, try to park close to the buildings and leave nothing of value in view. If you do stop to change a tyre and find yourself getting unsolicited aid, make sure doors are all locked and don't allow yourself to be distracted.

In some towns fairly dodgy self-appointed parking attendants operate in central areas where you may want to park. They will direct you frantically to a spot. If possible, ignore them and find your own. If unavoidable, you may well want to pay them some token not to scratch or otherwise damage your vehicle after you've walked away. You definitely don't want to leave anything visible in the car under these circumstances.

Theft

Theft is mostly a risk in tourist resorts, big cities and when you first arrive in a new city and may be off your guard. You are at your most vulnerable when dragging around luggage to or from your hotel. Barcelona, Madrid and Seville have the worst reputations for theft and, on very rare occasions, muggings.

Anything left lying on the beach can disappear in a flash when your back is turned. At night avoid dingy, empty city alleys and backstreets, or anywhere that just doesn't feel 100% safe.

Report thefts to the national police. You are unlikely to recover your goods but you need to make this formal *denuncia* (complaint) for insurance purposes. To avoid endless queues at the *comisaría* (police station), you can make the report on the web at www.policia.es (click on 'Denuncias por internet' at the bottom of the home page). The following day you go to the station of your choice to pick up and sign the report, without queuing.

TELEPHONE SERVICES

Mobile Phones

➡ Spain and Portugal use GSM 900/1800, which is compatible with the rest of Europe and Australia but not with the North American GSM 1900 or the totally different system in Japan (though some North Americans have tri-band phones that work in Europe).

➡ If you're from the EU, there is EU-wide roaming so that call and data plans for mobile phones from any EU country should be valid in Spain without any extra roaming charges.

➡ If you're from outside the EU, check with your service provider about roaming charges – dialling a mobile phone from a fixed-line phone or another mobile can be incredibly expensive.

➡ It's often cheaper to buy your own Spanish or Portuguese SIM card – and locals you meet are much more likely to ring you if your number doesn't require making an international call.

➡ All the Spanish mobile-phone companies (MoviStar, Orange, Vodafone and Yoigo) offer *prepagado* (prepaid) accounts for mobiles. The SIM card costs from €10, to which you add some prepaid phone time. Phone outlets are

scattered across the country. You can then top up in their shops or by buying cards in outlets, such as *estancos* (tobacconists) and news stands.

➡ In Portugal the process is identical, although the big mobile providers are Vodafone, Nos and MEO.

Phone Codes

➡ Emergency ☎112 (Spain or Portugal)

➡ International access code ☎00

➡ Spain country code ☎34

➡ Portugal country code ☎351

➡ Portuguese mobile phone numbers begin with 9

➡ Spanish mobile numbers begin with 6

Phonecards

Cut-rate prepaid phonecards can be good value for international calls. They can be bought from tobacconists, small grocery stores and news stands in the main cities and tourist resorts. If possible, try to compare rates.

TOURIST INFORMATION

➡ All cities and many smaller towns have an *oficina de turismo* (usually signposted 'turismo' in Portuguese). National and natural parks also often have their own visitor centres offering useful information.

➡ Turespaña (www.spain.info) is Spain's national tourism body, and it operates branches around the world. Check the website for office locations.

➡ Turismo de Portugal (www.visitportugal.com) is Portugal's useful national tourist board.

VISAS

Visas are not required for EU nationals or citizens of Iceland, Norway and Switzerland. They are required only for stays greater than 90 days for citizens of Australia, the USA, the UK, Canada, Israel, Japan, Malaysia, New Zealand, Singapore, South Korea and many Latin American countries.

Language

The pronunciation of most Spanish sounds is very similar to that of their English counterparts. If you read our coloured pronunciation guides as if they were English, you'll be understood. Note that kh is a throaty sound (like the 'ch' in the Scottish *loch*), r is strongly rolled, ly is pronounced as the 'lli' in 'million' and ny as the 'ni' in 'onion'. You may also notice that the 'lisped' th sound is pronounced as s in Andalucia.

Portuguese pronunciation is not difficult because most sounds are also found in English. The exceptions are the nasal vowels (represented in our pronunciation guides by ng after the vowel), which are pronounced as if you're trying to make the sound through your nose; and the strongly rolled r (represented by rr in our pronunciation guides). Also note that the symbol zh sounds like the 's' in 'pleasure'. The stress generally falls on the second-last syllable of a word. In our pronunciation guides stressed syllables are indicated with italics.

SPANISH BASICS

Hello.	*Hola.*	o·la
Goodbye.	*Adiós.*	a·dyos
How are you?	*¿Qué tal?*	ke tal
Fine, thanks.	*Bien, gracias.*	byen *gra*·syas
Excuse me.	*Perdón.*	per·*don*
Sorry.	*Lo siento.*	lo *syen*·to
Yes.	*Sí.*	see
No.	*No.*	no
Please.	*Por favor.*	por fa·*vor*
Thank you.	*Gracias.*	*gra*·syas
You're welcome.	*De nada.*	de *na*·da

My name is ...
Me llamo ...   me *lya*·mo ...

What's your name?
¿Cómo se llama Usted?   ko·mo se *lya*·ma oo·*ste* (pol)
¿Cómo te llamas?   ko·mo te *lya*·mas (inf)

Do you speak English?
¿Habla inglés?   a·bla een·*gles* (pol)
¿Hablas inglés?   a·blas een·*gles* (inf)

I don't understand.
No entiendo.   no en·*tyen*·do

DIRECTIONS

Where's ...?
¿Dónde está ...?   don·de es·*ta* ...

What's the address?
¿Cuál es la dirección?   kwal es la dee·rek·*syon*

Can you please write it down?
¿Puede escribirlo, por favor?   pwe·de es·kree·*beer*·lo por fa·*vor*

Can you show me (on the map)?
¿Me lo puede indicar (en el mapa)?   me lo pwe·de een·dee·*kar* (en el *ma*·pa)

EMERGENCIES

| Help! | *¡Socorro!* | so·ko·ro |

I'm lost.
Estoy perdido/a.   es·*toy* per·dee·do/a (m/f)

ON THE ROAD

I'd like to hire a ...	*Quisiera alquilar ...*	kee·sye·ra al·kee·lar ...
4WD	*un todo-terreno*	oon to·do·te·re·no
bicycle	*una bicicleta*	oo·na bee·see·kle·ta
car	*un coche*	oon ko·che
motorcycle	*una moto*	oo·na mo·to

Want More

For in-depth language information and handy phrases, check out Lonely Planet's *Spanish* and *Portuguese* phrasebooks. You'll find them at **shop.lonelyplanet.com**.

child seat	asiento de seguridad para niños	a·syen·to de se·goo·ree·da pa·ra nee·nyos
diesel	gasóleo	ga·so·le·o
helmet	casco	kas·ko
mechanic	mecánico	me·ka·nee·ko
petrol	gasolina	ga·so·lee·na
service station	gasolinera	ga·so·lee·ne·ra

How much is it per day/hour?
¿Cuánto cuesta por día/hora? kwan·to kwes·ta por dee·a/o·ra

Is this the road to ...?
¿Se va a ... por esta carretera? se va a ... por es·ta ka·re·te·ra

(How long) Can I park here?
¿(Por cuánto tiempo) Puedo aparcar aquí? (por kwan·to tyem·po) pwe·do a·par·kar a·kee

The car has broken down (at ...).
El coche se ha averiado (en ...). el ko·che se a a·ve·rya·do (en ...)

I have a flat tyre.
Tengo un pinchazo. ten·go oon peen·cha·tho

I've run out of petrol.
Me he quedado sin gasolina. me e ke·da·do seen ga·so·lee·na

Are there cycling paths?
¿Hay carril bicicleta? ai ka·reel bee·thee·kle·ta

Is there bicycle parking?
¿Hay aparcamiento de bicicletas? ai a·par·ka·myen·to de bee·thee·kle·tas

---

PORTUGUESE BASICS

Hello.	Olá.	o·laa
Goodbye.	Adeus.	a·de·oosh
How are you?	Como está?	ko·moo shtaa
Fine, and you?	Bem, e você?	beng e vo·se
Excuse me.	Faz favor.	faash fa·vor
Sorry.	Desculpe.	desh·kool·pe
Yes.	Sim.	seeng
No.	Não.	nowng
Please.	Por favor.	poor fa·vor
Thank you. (m)	Obrigado.	o·bree·gaa·doo
	Obrigada.	o·bree·gaa·da (f)
You're welcome.	De nada.	de naa·da

What's your name?
Qual é o seu nome? kwaal e oo se·oo no·me

My name is ...
O meu nome é ... oo me·oo no·me e ...

Do you speak English?
Fala inglês? faa·la eeng·glesh

I don't understand.
Não entendo. nowng eng·teng·doo

DIRECTIONS

Where's (the station)?
Onde é (a estação)? ong·de e (a shta·sowng)

Can you show me (on the map)?
Pode-me mostrar (no mapa)? po·de·me moosh·traar (noo maa·pa)

EMERGENCIES

Help!	Socorro!	soo·ko·rroo
I'm lost.	Estou perdido.	shtoh per·dee·doo (m)
	Estou perdida.	shtoh per·dee·da (f)

ON THE ROAD

I'd like to hire a ...	Queria alugar ...	ke·ree·a a·loo·gaar ...
bicycle	uma bicicleta	oo·ma bee·see·kle·ta
car	um carro	oong kaa·rroo
motorcycle	uma mota	oo·ma mo·ta

child seat	cadeira de criança	ka·day·ra de kree·ang·sa
helmet	capacete	ka·pa·se·te
mechanic	mecânico	me·kaa·nee·koo
petrol/gas	gasolina	ga·zoo·lee·na
service station	posto de gasolina	posh·too de ga·zoo·lee·na

Is this the road to ...?
Esta é a estrada para ...? esh·ta e a shtraa·da pa·ra ...

(How long) Can I park here?
(Quanto tempo) Posso estacionar aqui? (kwang·too teng·poo) po·soo shta·see·oo·naar a·kee

The car/motorbike has broken down (at ...).
O carro/A mota avariou-se (em ...). oo kaa·rroo/a mo·ta a·va·ree·oh·se (eng ...)

I have a flat tyre.
Tenho um furo no pneu. ta·nyoo oong foo·roo noo pe·ne·oo

I've run out of petrol.
Estou sem gasolina. shtoh seng ga·zoo·lee·na

BEHIND THE SCENES

SEND US YOUR FEEDBACK

We love to hear from travellers – your comments help make our books better. We read every word, and we guarantee that your feedback goes straight to the authors. Visit **lonelyplanet. com/contact** to submit your updates and suggestions.

Note: We may edit, reproduce and incorporate your comments in Lonely Planet products such as guidebooks, websites and digital products, so let us know if you are happy to have your name acknowledged. For a copy of our privacy policy visit lonelyplanet.com/legal.

WRITER THANKS

REGIS ST LOUIS

I'm indebted to countless locals, expats and fellow travellers who shared tips and cultural insight along the way – special thanks to John Noble. I'm grateful to Lara Yuste in Toledo, Isabel Fernández in El Toboso, Saray García in Cuenca, Ramon and Amparo in Villanueva de los Infantes and Álvaro Jimenez in Oropesa. *Besos* to Cassandra, Magdalena and Genevieve for the warm homecoming.

GREGOR CLARK

Muchísimas gracias to the many Andalucians and fellow travellers who shared their recommendations, expertise and enthusiasm for Spain's sunny south – especially Ramón, Laura, José Manuel, Michaela, Eva, Daniel, Alfredo, Alberto, John and Isabella. Across the Atlantic, *un gran abrazo* to Gaen, who makes every day a voyage of discovery, and coming home always the best part of the trip.

DUNCAN GARWOOD

At Lonely Planet, thanks to Darren O'Connell and Sandie Kestell whose rapid responses and helpful advice have been much appreciated over the course of the project. As always, a big hug to Lidia, Ben and Nick.

ANTHONY HAM

Madrid is home and it is impossible to thank everyone who has contributed to this guide. Special thanks to Javi and Sandra for so many key suggestions, and to Marina and Alberto for their ongoing kindness and hospitality. Many thanks also to so many skilled and dedicated people with whom I have worked with at Lonely Planet through the years.

JOHN NOBLE

Extra special thanks to Carmen and Luis, Eneida and Nacho, Lucía, Rafa, Bruno and Mari Carmen; to Camino and camping companions Rick, Sue, Katie, Bertie, Ted, María, Kaje (officially Sarkaaj), Jean Marie and Margarete, who contributed much to my pre-research and enthusiasm for the green north; and to Isabella, the ideal colleague.

ACKNOWLEDGEMENTS

Climate map data adapted from Peel MC, Finlayson BL & McMahon TA (2007) 'Updated World Map of the Köppen-Geiger Climate Classification', *Hydrology and Earth System Sciences*, 11, 1633–44.

Cover photograph: Arcos de la Frontera, Andalucía, Spain, Ivan Soto Cobos/Shutterstock ©

THIS BOOK

This 2nd edition of Lonely Planet's *Spain & Portugal's Best Road Trips* guidebook was researched and written by Regis St Louis, Gregor Clark, Duncan Garwood, Anthony Ham and John Noble. The previous edition was also written by Regis, Anthony and John, with Stuart Butler, Kerry Walker, Isabella Noble, Josephine Quintero, Brendan Sainsbury and Andy Symington. This guidebook was produced by the following:

Commissioning Editors Sandie Kestell, Kirsten Rawlings

Product Editors Kirsten Rawlings, Claire Rourke

Cartographers Anthony Phelan, Julie Sheridan

Book Designers Gwen Cotter, Aomi Ito

Assisting Editors Will Allen, Gemma Graham, Carly Hall, Charlotte Orr, Mani Ramaswamy

Cover Researcher Fergal Condon

Thanks to Sonia Kapoor

INDEX

M

N

Duncan Garwood

From facing fast bowlers in Barbados to sidestepping hungry pigs in Goa, Duncan's travels have thrown up many unique experiences. These days he largely dedicates himself to Spain and Italy, his adopted homeland where he's been living since 1997. He's worked on more than 50 Lonely Planet titles, including guidebooks to Spain, Andalucía, Italy, Rome, Sardinia, Sicily and Portugal, and has contributed to books on world food and epic drives. He's also written on Italy for newspapers, websites and magazines.

Follow Duncan on Twitter @DuncanGarwood

Anthony Ham

Anthony is a freelance writer and photographer who specialises in Spain, East and Southern Africa, the Arctic and the Middle East. When he's not writing for Lonely Planet, Anthony writes about and photographs for newspapers and magazines in Australia, the UK and US. In 2001, after years of wandering the world, Anthony finally found his spiritual home when he fell irretrievably in love with Madrid on his first visit to the city. Less than a year later, he arrived there on a one-way ticket, with not a word of Spanish and not knowing a single person in the city. He now divides his time between Spain and Australia.

Follow Anthony at www.anthonyham.com

John Noble

A quarter-century of living in Spain has taught John that it's a great country to drive in (except for city centres, which are best negotiated by other means!) Roads are good, and traffic is mostly light. John has co-authored well over 100 Lonely Planet guides covering more than 20 countries. Above all, he loves mountains, from the Picos de Europa to the Himalaya.

Follow John on Instagram @johnnoble11

OUR WRITERS

OUR STORY

A beat-up old car, a few dollars in the pocket and a sense of adventure. In 1972 that's all Tony and Maureen Wheeler needed for the trip of a lifetime – across Europe and Asia overland to Australia. It took several months, and at the end – broke but inspired – they sat at their kitchen table writing and stapling together their first travel guide, *Across Asia on the Cheap*. Within a week they'd sold 1500 copies. Lonely Planet was born.

Today, Lonely Planet has offices in the US, Ireland and China, with a network of more than 2000 contributors in every corner of the globe. We share Tony's belief that 'a great guidebook should do three things: inform, educate and amuse'.

Regis St Louis

A lifelong fan of fado, flamenco and Catalan cooking, Regis fell hard for the Iberian Peninsula after extensive travels there in the early 2000s. Over the last two decades, he has explored far-flung corners of Spain and Portugal, and he has vivid memories of meeting shepherds in Portugal's Serra da Estrela, roaming the small towns of the Basque Country in search of the world's best *pintxos*, and watching with fear and admiration as human towers rose towards the sky during the Festes de Santa Tecla in Tarragona. Regis speaks Spanish and Portuguese, and has contributed to various editions of *Portugal*, *Spain*, *Barcelona*, *Bilbao & San Sebastián* and more than 100 other Lonely Planet titles. He's currently based in New Orleans.

Follow Regis on Instagram @regisstlouis

Gregor Clark

Gregor Clark is a US-based writer whose love of foreign languages and curiosity about what's around the next bend have taken him to dozens of countries on five continents. Since 2000, Gregor has contributed to Lonely Planet guides regularly, with a focus on Europe and the Americas. Titles include *Italy*, *France*, *Brazil*, *Costa Rica*, *Argentina*, *Portugal*, *Switzerland*, *Mexico* and *Montreal & Quebec City*. Gregor was born in New York City. He has lived in California, France, Spain and Italy prior to settling with his wife and two daughters in his current home state of Vermont.

Follow Gregor on Twitter @thewideopenroad

 ## MORE WRITERS

Published by Lonely Planet Global Limited
CRN 554153
2nd edition – Oct 2022
ISBN 978 1 7865 758 0 7
© Lonely Planet 2022 Photographs © as indicated 2022
10 9 8 7 6 5 4 3 2 1
Printed in China